Global Political Theory

Global Political Theory

Edited by
DAVID HELD AND PIETRO MAFFETTONE

polity

First published in 2016 by Polity Press

Polity Press
65 Bridge Street
Cambridge CB2 1UR, UK

Polity Press
350 Main Street
Malden, MA 02148, USA

ISBN-13: 978-0-7456-8517-5
ISBN-13: 978-0-7456-8518-2(pb)

A catalogue record for this book is available from the British Library.

Library of Congress Cataloging-in-Publication Data

Names: Held, David, editor. | Maffettone, Pietro, editor.
Title: Global political theory / edited by David Held, Pietro Maffettone.
Description: Malden, MA : Polity Press, 2016. | Includes bibliographical references and
    index.
Identifiers: LCCN 2015046789 (print) | LCCN 2016006792 (ebook) | ISBN 9780745685175
    (hardback) | ISBN 9780745685182 (pbk.) | ISBN 9780745685205 (Mobi) |
    ISBN 9780745685212 (Epub)
Subjects: LCSH: International relations–Moral and ethical aspects. | International
    economic relations–Moral and ethical aspects. | International organization–Moral and
    ethical aspects. | International cooperation–Moral and ethical aspects. | Globalization–
    Political aspects.
Classification: LCC JZ1306 .G655 2016 (print) | LCC JZ1306 (ebook) | DDC 172/.4–dc23
LC record available at http://lccn.loc.gov/2015046789

Typeset in 9.5 on 13 pt Swift Light
by Toppan Best-set Premedia Limited
Printed in Great Britain by CPI Group (UK) Ltd, Croydon

For further information on Polity, visit our website: politybooks.com

Contents

Contributors

Michael Blake is Professor of Philosophy and Public Affairs, and Director of the Program on Values in Society, at the University of Washington, Seattle. His recent works include *Justice and Foreign Policy* (2013) and *Debating Brain Drain: May Governments Restrict Emigration?* (with Gillian Brock, 2014). His main research interests are in global distributive justice and the ethics of migration policy.

Peter Dietsch is an Associate Professor in the Philosophy Department at the University of Montreal, and directs the ethics and economics research axis at the Centre de recherche en éthique (CRE). He is the author of *Catching Capital: The Ethics of Tax Competition* (2015), co-editor, with Thomas Rixen, of *Global Tax Governance: What is Wrong with it and How to Fix it* (2016), and author of numerous journal articles. His research interests lie at the intersection of political philosophy and economics, with a particular focus on questions of income distribution as well as on the normative dimensions of economic policies.

Marcello Di Paola teaches Global Justice and Sustainability Theories at LUISS University in Rome, where he is affiliated with the Centre for Ethics and Global Politics. He writes on climate change and the Anthropocene, with a focus on the role of individuals in the face of complex global issues. He has recently co-edited *Canned Heat: the Ethics and Politics of Global Climate Change* (with Gianfranco Pellegrino, 2014).

Rainer Forst is Professor of Political Theory and Philosophy at the Goethe University, Frankfurt. He is co-director of the Cluster of Excellence 'The Formation of Normative Orders', of the Centre for Advanced Studies 'Justitia Amplificata' and Member of the Directorate of the Institute for Advanced Study in the Humanities in Bad Homburg. His work in moral and political philosophy focuses on questions of practical reason, justice and toleration. His major publications are *Contexts of Justice* (2002), *The Right to Justification* (2012), *Toleration in Conflict* (2013), *Justification and Critique* (2013), *The Power of Tolerance* (with Wendy Brown, 2014), *Justice, Democracy and the Right to Justification* (with Replies by Critics; 2014) and *Normativität und Macht* (2015).

Axel Gosseries is Maître de recherches at the Fonds de la Recherche Scientifique (Belgium), Professor at the University of Leuven (UCL, Hoover Chair) and a Franz Weyr Fellow (Czech Academy of Science). He is the author of *Penser la justice entre les générations* (2004), the co-editor of three books, including one on intellectual property issues (2008), and another on issues of intergenerational justice (2009), and of more than 50 articles and chapters in philosophy, law and economics. He works in the field of political philosophy, especially on issues of intergenerational justice and on the respective role of states and firms.

David Held is Master of University College and Professor of Politics and International Relations, at Durham University. Among his most recent publications are *Gridlock: Why Global Cooperation is Failing* (2013), *Cosmopolitanism: Ideals and Realities* (2010), *Globalization/Anti-Globalization* (2007), *Models of Democracy* (2006), *Global Covenant* (2004), *Global Transformations: Politics, Economics and Culture* (1999) and *Democracy and the Global Order: From the Modern State to Cosmopolitan Governance* (1995). His main research interests include globalization, changing forms of democracy, and regional and global governance. He is a Director of Polity Press, which he co-founded in 1984, and General Editor of *Global Policy*.

Aaron James is Professor and Chair of Philosophy at the University of California, Irvine. He is author of *Fairness in Practice: A Social Contract for a Global Economy* (2012) and numerous articles on metaethics, moral theory and political philosophy. He has been an ACLS Burkhardt Fellow, a fellow at the Center for Advanced Study in the Behavioral Sciences, Stanford University, and a visiting professor of philosophy at New York University.

Dale Jamieson is Professor of Environmental Studies and Philosophy, Affiliated Professor of Law, Affiliated Professor of Bioethics, and Chair of the Environmental Studies Department at New York University. He is also Distinguished Visiting Professor at the Dickson Poon School of Law at King's College London, and Adjunct Professor at the University of the Sunshine Coast in Australia. His most recent books are *Reason in a Dark Time: Why the Struggle to Stop Climate Change Failed – and What It Means For Our Future* (2014), and, with the novelist Bonnie Nadzam, *Love in the Anthropocene* (2015), a collection of short stories and essays.

Seth Lazar is a Senior Research Fellow in Philosophy at the Australian National University. He is the author of *Sparing Civilians* (2015) and editor of *The Morality of Defensive War* (2014) and *The Oxford Handbook of Ethics of War* (2016). His work has appeared in journals such as *Ethics*, *Philosophy & Public Affairs*, and the *Australasian Journal of Philosophy*. Besides the morality of war, his research interests include the ethics of risk and the foundations of associative duties.

David Lefkowitz is an Associate Professor of Philosophy and founding coordinator of the programme in Philosophy, Politics, Economics and Law (PPEL) at the University of Richmond, Virginia. His research interests include the morality of obedience and disobedience to law, analytical questions in the philosophy of international law, and topics in international ethics such as secession and the just conduct of war. He has published papers in numerous journals, including *Ethics, Legal Theory, Journal of Political Philosophy* and *The Canadian Journal of Law and Jurisprudence*, as well as chapters in *The Philosophy of International Law, The Oxford Handbook on the Sources of International Law* and several other edited collections.

Terry Macdonald is Senior Lecturer in International Relations at the University of Melbourne, having previously held positions at Merton College, University of Oxford, the Centre for Applied Philosophy and Public Ethics at the Australian National University, and Monash University. She is the author of *Global Stakeholder Democracy: Power and Representation Beyond Liberal States* (2008) and co-editor of *Global Political Justice* (with Miriam Ronzoni, 2013). She has published further on topics of global democracy, legitimacy and political justice in journals including *Ethics & International Affairs, Political Studies, European Journal of International Law* and *European Journal of Political Theory*. She currently serves as an associate editor of the journal *Global Governance*.

Pietro Maffettone is Lecturer in Global Politics and Ethics in the School of Government and International Affairs at Durham University. He received his BA from La Sapienza (Rome) and his PhD from the London School of Economics and Political Science. He works on global justice, ethics and international affairs, and contemporary moral and political philosophy.

David Miller is Professor of Political Theory at the University of Oxford, and an Official Fellow of Nuffield College. Among his published books are *On Nationality* (1995), *Principles of Social Justice* (1999), *Citizenship and National Identity* (2000), *National Responsibility and Global Justice* (2007), *Justice for Earthlings: Essays in Political Philosophy* (2013) and *Strangers in Our Midst: The Political Philosophy of Immigration* (2016). Besides theories of territory, his research interests include social and global justice, human rights and immigration.

Darrel Moellendorf is Cluster Professor of International Political Theory at the Cluster of Excellence 'The Formation of Normative Orders', and Professor of Philosophy at Johann Wolfgang Universität Frankfurt am Main. He is the author of *Cosmopolitan Justice* (2002), *Global Inequality Matters* (2009), and *The Moral Challenge of Dangerous Climate Change: Values, Poverty, and Policy* (2014). He co-edited *Jurisprudence* (with Christopher J. Roederer, 2004), *Current Debates in Global Justice* (with Gillian Brock, 2005), *Global Justice: Seminal Essays* (with Thomas Pogge, 2008) and *The Routledge Handbook of Global Ethics* (with Heather

Widdows, 2014). He has been a member of the School of Social Sciences at the Institute for Advanced Study (Princeton), a Senior Fellow at Justitia Amplificata at Goethe Unviersität-Frankfurt and the Forschungskolleg Humanwissenschaften (Bad Homburg) and the recipient of NEH (USA) and DAAD (German) grants.

Margaret Moore is a Professor in the Political Studies Department at Queen's University, Ontario. She is the author of *A Political Theory of Territory* (2015), *Ethics of Nationalism* (2001) and *Foundations of Liberalism* (1993). Her main current interests are territorial rights, issues of historic injustice, global justice and the relationship between just war, secession and rebellion.

Laura Valentini is an Associate Professor of Political Science at the London School of Economics and Political Science. Her research interests lie in contemporary political theory, with a particular focus on international normative theory, methodology in political theory, and democratic theory. She is the author of *Justice in a Globalized World: A Normative Framework* (2011) and of several articles on international and domestic justice. She is a co-founder of The Global Justice Network and a co-editor of the online journal *Global Justice: Theory Practice Rhetoric*.

Leif Wenar holds the Chair of Philosophy and Law at the School of Law, King's College London. His book is *Blood Oil: Tyrants, Violence and the Rules that Run the World* (2016).

Danielle Zwarthoed is a Postdoctoral Fellow at the University of Montreal. She is the author of *Comprendre la pauvreté. John Rawls, Amartya Sen* (2009) and has contributed to *Theory and Research in Education* and the *Review of Economic Philosophy*. Her main research interests include intergenerational justice, the political philosophy of education, and migrations.

Preface

This book explores the main topics in, and approaches to, global political theory. The acceleration of globalization since the 1980s has fundamentally challenged the thought that normative political ideas can be confined to the internal life of states. Partly as a result of this transformation of the political landscape, global political theory, in the last three decades, has attracted an increasing amount of attention within the broader fields of moral and political philosophy.

This original and comprehensive volume aims to provide a conceptual map of contemporary global political theory. Its authors include many of the most prominent scholars who have worked in the field as well as important emerging voices. The collection offers theoretical contributions to the most significant research topics in global political theory and international ethics more broadly. The themes covered include: global distributive and political justice, human rights, just war theory, trade, capital mobility, territorial rights, natural resources, climate change and intergenerational justice.

Many edited volumes have appeared in recent years on specific aspects of global political theory. However, we think that none of these fully capture the fact that global political theory is increasingly becoming part of the core curriculum for advanced undergraduate and graduate students interested in moral and political philosophy. We have thus attempted to construct a book that can be used for both research and teaching purposes. The number of original essays (15, including the editors' introduction) and the conceptual progression of the chapters make this collection an ideal basic text for a course on global political theory. At the same time, the fact that the contributions are all originally developed for this volume means that scholars and research students alike will find the book relevant to their work.

As for all successful collective endeavours, cooperation and mutual learning have been at the heart of our experience acting as editors of this collection. The responsiveness and positive engagement, not to mention the intellectual acumen, that all the contributors brought to the table for the whole duration of the project has been remarkable. Over the past two years, we have not so much been in charge of a task as part of a global philosophical conversation. For this, we are delighted and grateful.

Last but not least, we would like to thank Polity, and especially Louise Knight, Pascal Porcheron and Sarah Dancy, for their moral and material support and, most of all, for their unflinching patience. Publishers have the daunting task of reconciling academic delays with real world pressures. The graciousness and professionalism shown by Polity, in this and many other respects, has been outstanding. Finally, we would like to acknowledge the research assistance of David Van-Rooyen and thank him for all his hard work.

David Held and Pietro Maffettone
Durham, 2016

Introduction: Globalization, Global Politics and the Cosmopolitan Plateau

David Held and Pietro Maffettone

Introduction

Philosophers have never shied away from interrogating the nature of our obligations beyond borders. From Hobbes to the international lawyers Grotius, Pufendorf and Vattel, and of course Kant, modern philosophy has always attempted to define the nature and shape of a just international order, and the types of mutual obligations members of different political communities might share.

However, it is also fair to say that, in the past four decades, topics related to global politics have occupied a central part of the philosophical debate. Why is this? It is of course impossible to articulate fully the precise contours of an intellectual shift of this magnitude. Yet we believe that at least one part of the story pertains to the globalization of political relations. The argument offered, in the first section of this introduction, is that the globalization of politics should be seen as an important contributing factor to the increased attention that philosophers have paid to the moral aspects of global affairs. The deep forms of social, economic and political interdependence that characterize globalization have pushed the disciplines of moral and political philosophy to find a central place for the normative aspects of world politics.

In the second section, we move to the current debate in global political theory. This debate has reached what we call a cosmopolitan plateau. Moral cosmopolitanism has come to articulate the boundaries of reasonable disagreement in global political theory. We trace what we take to be the most important implication of this cosmopolitan plateau, namely, the commitment to basic human rights. We also note that agreement on basic human rights has not evolved into widespread acceptance of a single approach to global political and distributive justice. We go on to describe what we see as further significant trends in the debate, including its move towards more applied and specialized discussions, and the attempt to cross-fertilize global

1

political theory with more traditional areas of international ethics such as just war theory. Finally, in the third section, we provide a brief overview of the contributions to the volume and how these fit into the conceptual framework developed in sections 1 and 2.

1 Sources of the Debate: The Globalization of Politics

Globalization and global politics

Globalization can best be understood if it is conceived as a spatial phenomenon, lying on a continuum with 'the local' at one end and 'the global' at the other. It involves a shift in the spatial form of human organization and activity to transcontinental or interregional patterns of activity, interaction and exercise of power (Held et al., 1999). Globalization embraces at least four distinct types of change. First, it involves a stretching of political, social and economic activities across frontiers, regions and continents. Second, globalization is marked by the growing magnitude of networks and flows of trade, investment, finance, culture and so on. Third, globalization can be linked to a speeding up of global interactions and processes, as the development of worldwide systems of transportation and communication increases the velocity of the diffusion of ideas, goods, information, capital and people. And, fourth, it involves the deepening impact of global interactions and processes such that local events can come to have enormous global consequences. In this particular sense, the boundaries between domestic matters and global affairs become fuzzy. In short, globalization can be thought of as the widening, intensifying, speeding up and growing impact of worldwide interconnectedness.

Against this backdrop there has been a marked change in the nature and shape of political life. The distinctive form this has taken can be characterized as the emergence of 'global politics': the increasing reach of political networks, interaction and rulemaking activity, formal and informal. Political events and/or decision-making can become linked through rapid communications into complex networks of political interaction. Associated with this 'stretching' of politics is an intensification of global processes such that 'action at a distance' permeates the social conditions and cognitive worlds (i.e. the ways in which meaning is constructed) of specific places or communities (Giddens, 1990: ch. 2). The idea of global politics challenges the traditional distinctions between the domestic and the international, territorial and non-territorial, inside and outside, as embedded in conventional conceptions of interstate politics and 'the political'. It also highlights the richness and complexity of the processes and connections that link states and societies in the global order. Moreover, global politics today is anchored not just in traditional geopolitical concerns, but also in a large diversity of social, economic and environmental questions. Climate change, pandemics, financial instability and terrorism are among an increasing number of transnational issues which cut across territorial jurisdictions and existing political alignments, and which require international cooperation for their effective resolution.

People, nations and organizations are enmeshed in many new forms of communication, which range across borders. The digital revolution has made possible virtually instantaneous worldwide links, which, when combined with the technologies of the telephone, television, cable, satellite and jet transportation, have dramatically altered the nature of political communication. The intimate connection between physical setting, social situation and politics, which distinguishes most political associations from premodern to modern time, has been ruptured.

The development of new communication systems generates a world in which the peculiarities of place and individuality are constantly represented and reinterpreted through regional and global communication networks. But the relevance of these systems goes far beyond this, for they are fundamental to the possibility of organizing political action and exercising political power across vast distances (Deibert, 1997). For example, the expansion of international and transnational organizations, the extension of international rules and legal mechanisms – their construction and monitoring – have all received an impetus from these new communication systems, and all depend on them as a means to further their aims. The present era of global politics marks a shift towards a multilayered regional and global governance system, with features of both complexity and polycentricity.

The changed landscape of global politics

A number of trends can be identified within the changed landscape of world politics. First, there has been a notable trend involving the integration of the national and the international political spheres (Milner, 1998; Slaughter, 2004). The relationship between national governments and international bodies is no longer unilinear, but rather shaped by overlapping pressures coming from all sides (domestic constituencies, international organizations, global civil society, etc.). From global trade rules to intellectual property rights, from the global financial crisis to climate change, issues are posed for many levels of politics. A second trend that can be observed since 1945 is the emergence of powerful nonstate actors in the development of transborder governance. Nonstate actors such as international nongovernmental organizations, multinational companies and even individuals have always been active agents in political debate, but the manner in which they influence international politics has changed in significant ways (Haas, 1991; Keck and Sikkink, 1998; Betsill and Corell, 2008). For instance, through the direct lobbying of global governance bodies, nonstate actors shape political debate internationally, in turn impacting the behaviour of states from both above and below. Today, the emergence of nonstate actors creates a more complex governance system than one made up of traditional principal–agent relationships between states and purely intergovernmental organizations. This can potentially pose problems of governance fragmentation, but it also broadens the platform for political deliberation and debate (Risse-Kappen, 1995; Anheier et al., 2006; Betsill and Corell, 2008).

Third, there has been a shift in how regulation and governance are enforced. The diverse forms of global governance produce diverse types of regulation intended to influence and delimit the behaviour of states. Traditionally, compliance in international agreements is linked to the possibility of sanctions that penalize violators in order to ensure appropriate conduct. Increasingly, however, trends can be detected that ensure that rules are enforced through alternative means such as voluntary arrangements and initiatives, as well as international standards that are adhered to by actors because of their reputational and coordinative effects (see Kerwer, 2005). Of course, these types of regulation are not sufficient in and of themselves to solve the problem of compliance and enforcement as a spiral of global bads, from global financial market instability to climate change, continues to grow.

Fourth, overlapping with these trends, there has been a proliferation of new types of global governance institutions in the postwar era, and especially since the end of the Cold War (Hale and Held, 2011). These are not multilateral, state-to-state institutions, but instead combine various actors under varying degrees of institutionalization. In some areas of global governance, these kinds of institutions rank among the most important (see Held and Young, 2011). This development has added to the growing polycentricism observed in many areas of global governance. A polycentric approach can have advantages and disadvantages. On the one hand, it can mean that more issues are addressed in effective ways – through specialized bodies qualified to regulate and govern a specific issue area. On the other hand, it can exacerbate institutional fragmentation.

As demands on the state increased following the end of the Second World War, a whole host of policy problems emerged that cannot be adequately resolved without the cooperation of other states and nonstate actors. Accordingly, individual states on their own can no longer be conceived of as the appropriate political units for either resolving many key policy problems or managing effectively a broad range of public functions. Globalization has eroded the capacity of states to act unilaterally in the articulation and pursuit of domestic and international policy objectives; political power, in short, has been reconfigured.

In this context, the traditional questions of political philosophy gain a new inflection. Since early modern times, it has typically been assumed that the political good is inherent in the state. Sovereignty, democracy and social justice, among other concepts, have been deeply contested, but within a fixed normative framework bound to the territorial political community. Yet, with the reconfiguration of political power, further issues arise. In a world of complex interdependence, where social and political processes spill across borders, not only do activities in one country impact others, but they can also escape the control of individual states altogether. What is the appropriate jurisdiction for handling transnational forces and impacts? What is the meaning and relevance of sovereignty, democracy and social justice when some of the most pressing issues of our times pose existential threats, and require new forms and types of cooperative and collective action amongst states; something which they typically have not been good at. Who gets what, where and how, and who the relevant agents are – local, national, regional, global – takes on a new urgency.

Unpacking these concerns has led political philosophy to engage broadly with the global political domain. As we will see below, the links between globalization and the emergence of global political theory defy a formulaic presentation. However, it is still possible to affirm that globalization has challenged the basic framework in which political concepts have been traditionally developed, and in so doing opened up the possibility for a wide array of moral and political concerns and arguments to be developed and discussed.

Globalization and global political theory

There are at least four ways in which globalization has impacted upon normative debates. These, it should be stressed, are not presented here as part of a systematic intellectual history of the debate. Intellectual history is difficult, and we have, accordingly, more modest ambitions. Further, the links between globalization and global political theory are clearly mediated by several cultural, political and intellectual trends that defy a mechanical or formulaic reconstruction. To name just a few: the end of the Cold War, the emergence of the human rights regime and of the responsibility to protect doctrine, and the spread of democratic ideas, etc. Instead, our aim is simply to suggest that the globalization of politics is an important contributing factor to the increased significance that global political theory has gained within the wider discipline of moral and political philosophy.

First, globalization has intensified global and regional patterns of exchange (political, economic, cultural) and thus has made us aware that our actions have implications that do not stop at our own borders, but have wider and more far-reaching effects.

Second, globalization has accelerated the emergence of global collective action problems. Yet, it has also contributed to a new sense of urgency about establishing global cooperation to address them. It is appreciated that to do nothing about financial market risks, terrorism in the Middle East or climate change, among many other global challenges, is to encourage enormous instabilities and to invite lasting damage to the fabric of our institutional lives. There has been the realization that our overlapping collective fortunes require collective solutions – locally, nationally, regionally and globally. And there has also been a widespread acceptance that some of these challenges, if unaddressed, could be apocalyptic in the decades to come.

Third, globalization has increased our awareness of distant suffering. This may seem like a trivial point, but it should not be underestimated. From a purely causal perspective, awareness of a given situation is a necessary condition of our ability to do something about it. But there is more to it than the latter idea suggests. Awareness of suffering, especially through the kind of visual awareness that modern telecommunication technologies allow, can play an important part in the development of empathy and, paraphrasing Peter Singer, in expanding the 'moral circle' (Singer, 2002).

Fourth, globalization has also made us aware of the fact that we can do something about the plight of those who live very far from us. How much we can do for 'distant strangers' is of course a matter of great controversy. Witness the endless debates on the effectiveness of humanitarian and development aid. However, most would accept that our role should not be limited to that of spectators, and that passivity in the face of the suffering of distant others is unacceptable.

The four aforementioned points can be given a more precise interpretation if we look at them through the lenses of the traditional concerns highlighted in moral and political theory. The first and second elements relate to the traditional Rawlsian idea that cooperative activities generate benefits and burdens and that these burdens and benefits have to be distributed in a non-arbitrary fashion. In a similar way, drawing from a broadly democratic perspective, the first and second elements have highlighted the great array of issue areas in which power is exercised without clear accountability mechanisms, and the associated potential for political and economic domination that unaccountable power inevitably generates. The third element, increased awareness of distant suffering, creates the possibility for empathy, which, at least according to a broadly Humean tradition, is a key factor in motivating individuals to act morally. The fourth element, our ability to affect the life prospects of distant individuals, reinforces the motivational pull of empathy by signalling that normative ideas can have significant implications for the real world. Furthermore, the fourth element also partially shapes our reflections about the nature of our moral universe, as it implies that our relationship with distant strangers can be a source of genuinely normative obligations, that is, obligations that specify a set of actions and policies that we may realistically try to implement.

In this section, we have provided an account of the key features of the globalization of politics. Furthermore, we have traced the basic elements that explain the links between globalization and global political theory. Globalization is an important element in explaining the emergence of a political theory with global scope and aspirations. The characterization of the fundamental features of this new philosophical debate is the aim of the next section of the introduction.

2   The Shape of the Current Debate

The cosmopolitan plateau

Ronald Dworkin once famously wrote that all contemporary political philosophy rested on egalitarian foundations (1986: 296–7). Libertarianism, utilitarianism and liberal egalitarianism, the most influential approaches to moral and political philosophy, can all be seen as providing different interpretations of what it means to treat persons with equal respect and concern. The idea of moral equality, in Dworkin's own words, provided 'a kind of plateau in political argument' (1983: 25).

Something similar can be said about the debate in global political theory. Here, we can say that we have reached a cosmopolitan plateau (see Blake, 2013a). Of course, the term 'cosmopolitan' can be interpreted in several ways. Its history is particularly rich and goes back at least to the Stoics (Brown and Held, 2010). For the latter, human beings are better understood as citizens of the world rather than of territorially defined political communities. A second distinctive phase in the history of the term is represented by the Kantian understanding of the universality of human reason. In the Kantian picture, all human beings are part of a shared community, the community of moral argument. In more recent times, the term has also been used to refer to a wide array of approaches, ranging from the cultural, to the legal, to the political. However, the most influential of the contemporary understandings of the term is not related to culture, political institutions or international law. Rather, it relates to our understanding of the moral status of human beings.

Thomas Pogge has provided the most influential definition of moral cosmopolitanism:

> Three elements are shared by all cosmopolitan positions. First, *individualism*: the ultimate units of moral concern are *human beings*, or *persons* – rather than, say, family lines, tribes, ethnic, cultural, or religious communities, nations, or states. The latter may be units of concern only indirectly, in virtue of their individual members or citizens. Second, *universality*: the status of ultimate unit of moral concern attaches to *every* living human being equally – not merely to some subset, such as men, aristocrats, Aryans, whites, or Muslims. Third, *generality*: this special status has global force. Persons are ultimate units of moral concern *for everyone* – not only for their compatriots, fellow religionists, or suchlike. (1992: 48–9; emphasis in original)

Pogge's definition reminds us of what it means to assign a certain status to human beings as moral agents. Most importantly, though, it provides a framework for our political discussions; and it is a framework that is accepted by all those who participate in the conversation of global political theory. It is important to stress the latter point. Some will inevitably complain that a term or label that includes all participants in a given debate may not be particularly useful (Blake, 2013a: 35–7), since it fails to identify any form of serious disagreement. To the contrary, we think that the terminology and the underlying concept that lies behind it still have something to contribute. Namely, they help us delineate the boundaries of reasonable disagreement within our moral debates in a way that is philosophically consistent. They act as a screen to filter the range of plausible moral approaches to the moral understanding of the global political domain. To illustrate, the cosmopolitan plateau tells us that to subscribe to forms of value collectivism, or to deny the equal moral status of all human beings, implies that one's views are beyond the boundaries of reasonable disagreement and thus have no standing in the debate about the moral bases of global politics.

The implications of the cosmopolitan plateau

Of course, to be committed to moral cosmopolitanism is to be committed to a very abstract moral outlook. What are the political and moral implications, if any, of such an outlook? The most important political implication of the cosmopolitan plateau is, in our view, the commitment to basic human rights (e.g. those specified by international legal documents such as the Universal Declaration of Human Rights). Basic human rights have come to articulate the normative focal point of global political theory. They constitute the most important benchmark (though of course not the only one) for the evaluation both of internal and external state conduct, for the actions of global governance institutions, for the norms and principles that constitute international and transnational regimes, for the policies of multinational corporations and for the behaviour of political leaders and public officials. Or, in Henry Shue's words, they articulate what he calls the 'moral minimum', '[t]he lower limits on tolerable conduct, individual and institutional' (1996: xi).

The universal support for basic human rights is best described as an overlapping consensus. This is so for two reasons. First, because to some extent all approaches to the justification of human rights rely, directly or indirectly, on the importance of individual interests, and on the respect that is owed to the basic moral status of human beings (see Vlastos, 1984; Valentini, 2012). In other words, basic human rights are considered by all as deriving, at least in part, from a shared set of 'shallow' but common foundational commitments. The latter implies that emphasis on human rights is not a mere 'convergence'.

Second, however, it is an overlapping consensus because conceptualizations of human rights vary. In the first instance, the common foundational commitment is, as we have just stated, 'shallow'. One can get at this conclusion by asking the following question: what exactly is meant to ground respect for the moral status of human beings? Utilitarians, Kantians and Christians would give decidedly different answers; answers that they would insist go to the heart of their characterization of normative ethics. In a similar way, there is no agreement on how to understand the grounds and justification of basic human rights. Do they reflect the requirement to protect basic needs (Miller, 2012)? Are they drawn from a broader capability framework (Sen, 2005)? Are they to be understood as standards for the articulation of membership in a political community (Cohen, 2004)? Are they an emergent practice in international society to place limits on the internal and external sovereignty of states (Beitz, 2010)? Or are human rights simply a subset of our most fundamental moral rights, which protect the most important human interests (Griffin, 2008)? Or, as Rainer Forst suggests in the opening chapter of this book, do they act as a tool in the emancipatory struggle to end humiliation and to recognise the equal social and political standing of all human beings (see also Buchanan, 2013)?

Of course, these debates have implications for the concrete lists of rights that different authors see as 'real' human rights (see Buchanan, 2013). Yet, they have not, so far, affected agreement across the whole spectrum of theoretical approaches on the fact that a core set of basic human rights is justified and that their protection should constitute the most urgent moral imperative for global political action. Such core entitlements include at least basic rights to political representation (though not necessarily to a fully democratic system), rights against basic forms of discrimination, rights connected to freedom of conscience, religion and expression, and rights to basic subsistence.

At the same time, however, the cosmopolitan plateau has not generated the same type of consensus when it comes to global distributive justice. The best way to characterize the debate is to see the disagreements about global distributive justice as disagreements about the extent to which accepting the idea of moral cosmopolitanism should have implications, beyond respect for basic human rights, for how human beings should be treated. More specifically, the central question, much as for domestic political philosophy, is to what extent notions of equal moral status demand specific forms of equal treatment in the global political context (Blake, 2013a: 41). Put differently, disagreements about global distributive justice should be seen largely as family disputes over different ways of understanding the implications of a broadly liberal outlook for how persons should be treated at the global level.

We shall not proceed to review the different accounts of global distributive justice, nor shall we proceed to a full articulation of the basic differences between them. To do so in the space of a short introductory chapter would be impossible. Furthermore, both topics are developed in the chapters that follow in this volume (see especially Moellendorf's and Blake's contributions). We will instead limit ourselves to two general remarks.

First, something about terminology. The usual terms used to describe the different positions in the debate about global distributive justice are 'cosmopolitans' for those who believe in the extension of demanding egalitarian conceptions of justice beyond the state, and 'statists' or 'nationalists' for those who favour the restriction of egalitarian distributive principles to special forms of association such as the state or national communities. However, as we have claimed above, the term 'cosmopolitan', if understood as 'morally cosmopolitan', encompasses all participants to the debate. So it is more accurate, following Michael Blake (in this volume), to call those who are usually labelled cosmopolitans tout court as 'cosmopolitans about distributive justice'.

To some extent, it is also fair to say that the terms have outlived their usefulness (see Blake, in this volume). Most cosmopolitans about distributive justice concede that allegiance to specific forms of political associations create strong distributive obligations. Conversely, most statists and nationalists would agree that while demanding comparative principles may not apply beyond borders, this does not entail that other less demanding duties of justice do not apply (e.g. sufficientarian duties of justice). The usefulness of these labels, thus, does not lie in their ability to demarcate strongly divergent accounts of global distributive justice. 'Cosmopolitan about distributive justice' and 'statist' or 'nationalist' are not sharp lines in the current philosophical debate. We have, nonetheless, decided to stick to the labels for two reasons. First, while they do not stand for strongly opposing worldviews, cosmopolitanism about distributive justice and statism or nationalism can still be taken to articulate different standpoints in the debate. Put differently, while the difference between the two accounts is not necessarily sharp, the terms still allow us to see what different authors decide to emphasize about distributive obligations beyond the remits of territorially bounded political communities. Moreover, the terms have now acquired historical significance insofar as a great deal of our past and present discussions have been framed through them.

Second, it should be noted that while differences between cosmopolitans about distributive justice and statists or nationalists have been extensively explored in the literature, a number of central issues remain, in our view, under-researched. For example, most of the debates about global distributive justice have concerned the content, grounds and scope of distributive principles, yet there has been much less focus on their relative strength or priority. To illustrate, statists are committed to the idea that comparative distributive principles only apply between co-citizens of a political association like the modern state. However, they are usually also committed to the idea that other, possibly sufficientarian, duties apply beyond borders. How exactly should one characterize the order of priority between these two types of duties? Should they be lexically ordered? Should we give priority to associative obligations towards co-nationals or to the basic needs of foreigners? If so, to what extent? These are, to be sure, difficult questions to answer. And it would be unfair to say that no attempts have been made to provide guidance in answering them (see for example Miller, 2012: ch. 7). Yet, it is also fair to say that, given their importance, they certainly deserve more attention.

Political justice and legitimacy

Debates about distributive justice do not exhaust the remit of global political theory. Similar disagreements and controversies to the ones that characterize the debate on distributive justice are replicated in debates that deal with what we can call global political justice (see Macdonald and Ronzoni, 2012). The distinction between distributive justice and political justice is not clearcut, and the two obviously overlap. To illustrate, a given 'currency' of distributive justice (e.g. Rawls's primary goods) may be partly defined by access to equal rights, including rights to political participation, which, in turn, has implications for the range of permissible forms of political organization. Yet, in our view, the distinction is useful in contrasting questions of institutional design and evaluation from questions relating to specific distributive patterns and about the nature of the goods that are to be distributed accordingly. In this context, we can think of distributive justice as broadly concerned with the patterns of distribution for a range of 'currencies', while political justice refers to the wider question of the institutional context in which such distribution should take place. It follows that we can think of global political justice as a set of normative conceptions meant to specify the institutional architecture of global politics.

The central question in global political justice pertains to the very shape that global politics should take. Should we opt for a system of separate political communities close to those we presently experience, or should we favour some form of radical reshaping of the current system? On the one hand, according to a broadly statist outlook, a reformed state system (a system in which states are internally well ordered and take their international obligations seriously) could, in principle, be just (see Sangiovanni, 2007). It could represent, in Rawls's words, a 'realistic utopia', something towards which we could be reconciled morally speaking. On the other hand, some cosmopolitans argue for deep revisions to the idea of territorial sovereignty (see Pogge, 1992; Held, 1995), while others go as far as advocating the creation of a world state (Cabrera, 2006). As with arguments about global distributive justice, the labels 'cosmopolitans about global political justice' and 'statists about global political justice' do not map precisely on particular or predetermined answers to these questions. More specifically, while all statists are committed at least to the *pro tanto* justifiability of a reformed state system, not all self-defined cosmopolitans are necessarily committed to superseding all forms of territorially defined political communities (see Valentini, 2011).

The issue of global political justice is conceptually close but nonetheless distinct from the issue of legitimacy. Both questions refer to institutional architecture broadly understood. However, at least according to a widely shared intuition, questions of legitimacy are different from questions of justice. At its most basic, the difference between the two lies in the fact that legitimacy seems to allow more latitude, so to speak, compared to justice. In other words, legitimacy is often thought to be a less demanding standard of evaluation for institutions and political arrangements. Justice is about what we think is ideal, while legitimacy is closer to what we think we can accept morally speaking: institutions may be considered to be legitimate even if we do not deem them to be fully just. Legitimacy is also intimately related to the kind of attitudes that one should adopt towards a given institution, namely, the standing that we give to its commands, and the extent to which we consider institutional directives to be authoritative. To say that an institution is legitimate is, at a minimum, to say that one has weighty reasons to comply with its directives (see Buchanan and Keohane, 2006; Buchanan, 2013).

Within the framework of global political theory, the question of legitimacy can be articulated in the following way: what kinds of principles and values should be used as standards of evaluation for international, transnational political and economic institutions? Here too, the literature has developed a series of canonical answers. We will not review these approaches (but see Lefkowitz; Macdonald; and Held and Maffettone in this volume). Instead, we wish to highlight that all of them share something in common, namely, the refusal to accept a background picture in which states are sovereign in the traditional Westphalian sense of the term, and consequently, see their international obligations as only justifiable through voluntariness or consent. To paraphrase Rawls (1999), we now live in a (normative) world where states are no longer considered the originators of all their powers. The upshot is that it is untenable to evaluate international institutions and regimes through the lenses of state consent alone.

Finally, note that while the aforementioned question is, in our view, central, it has not received the attention that it deserves within mainstream debates. The global political theory literature has poured considerable amounts of ink on the scope of egalitarian distributive principles, yet, with the exception of debates addressing the desirability of global democracy (see Held, 1995; Marchetti, 2008) it has paid *comparatively* less attention to the more specific questions pertaining to legitimacy and institutional design (but see Buchanan and Keohane, 2006; Christiano, 2011, 2012). Nonetheless, the reasons to address the topic in greater detail are pressing. The number and range of activities that are shaped or regulated by international and transnational institutions has skyrocketed in the last five decades. Moreover, their role and the pervasiveness of their influence in the internal politics of most nation-states is widely acknowledged. The question of their legitimacy, not simply how they should be optimally designed in order to be congruent with the demands of justice, is thus of central importance.

Further trends in global political theory

So far in this introduction, we have suggested the idea of a cosmopolitan plateau in global political argument. We have seen that the shared acceptance of a broadly cosmopolitan moral landscape, one that considers individuals as moral equals, has translated into a shared commitment to basic human rights, although it has not managed to create consensus on global distributive and political justice. Finally, we have highlighted the relative neglect that questions of legitimacy have suffered in global political theory. In the final part of this section, we explore further significant trends within the debate.

One of the most important discernible trends is undoubtedly the move towards the application of the global political theory approach to diverse issues. While the initial stages of the debate in global political theory were mostly concerned with shared foundational questions, such as the grounds and content of our obligations towards distant strangers and, to a lesser extent, their strength compared to our obligations to co-nationals and co-citizens, the current debate has fragmented into a variety of issue areas.

The number of topics that are addressed by scholars working within the broader framework of global ethics has considerably expanded. To name just a few areas: the justification of trade regimes (James, 2005; Risse, 2007); the distribution of the costs associated with climate change mitigation and adaptation (Caney, 2012; Jamieson, 2014); the nature and justification of territorial rights (Stilz, 2011; Nine, 2012; Ypi, 2014; Moore, 2015); the justifiability of state borders and immigration restrictions (Abizadeh, 2008; Wellman, 2008; Blake, 2013b); the relationship between global justice and future generations (see Gosseries and Zwarthoed in this volume); the ownership of natural resources and its relationship with the resource curse (see Wenar, 2008, and in this volume); and the international intellectual property regime and its relationship to access to health (Pogge et al., 2010).

A second and related trend in the literature is the move towards more applied forms of analysis, closely associated with a specific domain of political activity or with specific empirical problems. Examples include the moral assessments of the current system of capital mobility (James, 2012; Dietsch in this volume); the implications of tax competition for effective tax sovereignty and self-determination (Ronzoni, 2009; Dietsch and Rixen, 2014); the proper aim of structural adjustment programmes (Barry, 2011); and the evaluation of specific global economic institutions such as the WTO (Moellendorf, 2005; Maffettone, 2009). The contributions to these applied debates, it can be noted, show considerable awareness of the underlying empirical complexity that pertains to the technical aspects of the specific topics they address. This is, in our view, one important way in which philosophers can stay closer to where most of the action is, that is, closer to existing political debates and the concerns of policymakers.

A third trend concerns what we here call the cross-fertilization of different areas of the traditional concerns of international ethics. Up until recently, for example, the relationship between just war theory and global political theory has been neglected. Instead, starting with Terry Nardin's work (2004,

2006) we have witnessed a progressive rapprochement between these two areas of inquiry, with specific points of contact pertaining to the relationship between the principles of just war theory and different accounts of distributive justice (see Fabre, 2012; Valentini in this volume), associative duties (Lazar, 2013, and in this volume), and authority and legitimacy (Estlund, 2007; Ryan, 2011).

The cross-fertilization between just war theory and global political theory broadly construed is something to be welcomed for two reasons. The first concerns the potential for interdisciplinary work. To illustrate, according to a widely accepted understanding of justice, the latter concerns enforceable entitlements. Justice, at least when conceived as the first virtue of social and political institutions, is related to what we think we can reasonably impose on others, not simply what we think is commendable in the abstract (see Valentini, 2013). In the same way, principles of *jus ad bellum* are often thought to provide a set of necessary and sufficient conditions for resorting to the use of force at the international level. Thus, the two topics overlap at least insofar as they both require us to investigate the circumstances in which we can reasonably use force or coercion to change or sanction an agent's behaviour. The second reason to welcome this work on cross-fertilization is the potential for restoring the importance of our concerns for war and peace. If we accept, following Rawls (1999), war as one of the great evils of human history, it is crucial to never lose sight of its relevance for global politics and its moral appraisal.

Finally, while we have discussed consolidated or emerging trends in global political theory, it is also important to highlight what, in our view, is missing in this material. The cosmopolitan plateau and all the work on global justice have not generated an equally important body of work on international toleration. One of the most visible features of the global political domain is the great diversity of cultures and political traditions. Yet, global political theorists have not fully developed their views on how exactly to relate to such diversity. The attention that pluralism has received in domestic moral and political philosophy (witness the debate on political forms of liberalism or on multiculturalism) has not been replicated in global political theory (but see Tan, 2000; Blake, 2013c).

With the exception of Rawls's account of international toleration (1999), a great deal of global political theory works under the *assumption* that the only possible way of organizing political society is according to a fully liberal democratic model. This is, in many respects, an attractive ideal for those who share a commitment to liberal values. However, its implications should not be downplayed. To shape every political community according to liberal values requires strong arguments to the effect that no other form of political organization is morally acceptable. Unless these arguments are developed in greater detail, the spread of liberal values cannot straightforwardly be regarded as a form of moral progress.

Useful
Summaries of chapter

3   Plan of the Book

The essays presented in this collection are closely connected to the understanding of global political theory that we have outlined in sections 1 and 2
of this introduction.

In the first chapter, Reiner Forst lays out his conception of human rights.
Drawing on Kant, Forst sees the ground of human rights in the equal moral
standing of all human beings. At its most abstract, such standing entails a
basic right to justification. This is the right to be respected as an equal moral
authority, a right that stems from a conception of persons as moral equals
endowed with a capacity for reason. Yet, Forst also takes his Kantian roots in
the direction of critical theory. According to him, human rights have played
an important emancipatory role – they are part of an historical struggle for
the recognition of the equal political status of all persons. In this account,
human rights are at the heart of a conception of social order where individuals are seen as free and equal citizens, as 'both addressees and authors' of the
rules that structure their coexistence, rather than as subjects dominated and
coerced by various forms of political power. As previously noted, the idea of
human rights is central to global political theory. It is the main political
implication that follows from our commitment to moral cosmopolitanism.
Forst's essay gives us an original and, at the same time, authoritative discussion of one of the central concepts in global political theory.

In chapters 2 and 3, Michael Blake and Darrel Moellendorf, respectively,
explore the two sides of the debate on global distributive justice. Michael
Blake starts by partly challenging the very terms that are used to characterize
the debate about global distributive justice. He goes on to discuss three different approaches to statism (based on community, cooperation and coercion,
respectively) and outlines the types of moral and normative dilemmas that
all statist approaches to global distributive justice need to confront. His
overall conclusion is that the statist position on global distributive justice is
convincing. By confining egalitarian justice to the political relationships
within the modern state, statism is not 'morally perverse', as it is fully compatible, according to Blake, with a genuine commitment to the equal moral
importance of all human beings. These two chapters can be seen as an integrated whole providing researchers, and readers more generally, with an
easily accessible (and yet relatively comprehensive) exposition of the classical
debate on the scope and nature of distributive obligations beyond borders.
Moellendorf starts by reminding us of some of the startling inequalities that
characterize the world in which we live. Such inequalities are not confined
to the distribution of income and wealth, but directly affect persons' basic
opportunities, from education to health. What follows, normatively speaking,
from these facts? Moellendorf argues that persons living across borders stand
in 'relationships of justice with respect to the distribution of wealth, income
and opportunities'. He defends what he calls a 'membership-dependent'

account of cosmopolitan egalitarianism. Put differently, Moellendorf claims that it is the fact that we stand in specific types of social and political relationships that grounds duties of egalitarian justice. Thus, according to Moellendorf, the inequalities of life prospects across borders are not simply a description of our present global political predicament. They are also morally regrettable – a form of injustice that needs to be addressed by an egalitarian conception of global distributive justice.

Chapters 4, 5 and 6 tackle questions relating to institutional structures and the proper normative and evaluative standards that are used as benchmarks to assess them. As we have seen above, one of the features of traditional debates in global political theory is that questions of institutional evaluation have often been neglected. Taken together, chapters 4, 5 and 6 are an attempt to remind ourselves of the centrality of these issues.

In chapter 4, Terry Macdonald provides a conceptual and historical overview of the idea of global political justice. She starts by articulating this idea through different literatures, ranging from international relations to international law and international political theory. She goes on to differentiate the idea of global political justice from the narrower concept of global distributive justice. Macdonald then provides an assessment of different normative concepts and arguments that have been used to frame discussions of global political justice, such as global democracy, law, governance and legitimacy. She concludes by describing what she takes to be gaps in the existing literature that would benefit from further research by global political theorists.

In chapter 5, David Lefkowitz takes a closer look at the idea of the legitimacy of international law. He starts by analysing the concept of legitimacy itself – what does it mean to say that international law is legitimate and what follows from considering aspects of it illegitimate? He goes on to consider different standards for legitimacy assessments pertaining to international law, critically assessing accounts based on democracy, consent, fair play and Raz's 'normal justification thesis'. For each account, Lefkowitz asks whether it can provide necessary and sufficient conditions for understanding the legitimacy of international law, and what one can infer from each about the legitimacy of the current system of norms that presently constitute the international legal order. He argues that none of the aforementioned accounts can show present international law to be fully legitimate. In conclusion, he reminds us of the centrality of legitimacy and suggests that the latter may even take priority over attempts to make the international legal order more just.

In chapter 6, David Held and Pietro Maffettone address the legitimacy of global governance institutions. Their chapter lies at the intersection of the key ideas developed by both Macdonald and Lefkowitz. Global governance institutions are loci where power can be exercised and opportunities provided for coordinating social action in the delivery of collective goals. It is thus not surprising that the question of their legitimacy gathers attention. Held and Maffettone critically survey different approaches to legitimacy, including the consent, democratic and meta-coordination accounts, that have been suggested as the appropriate basis for generating standards for the legitimacy assessment of global governance. They show the consent-based view to be the least convincing approach. They are more supportive of the idea that democratic ideals should play a part in the assessment of global governance even if the precise institutional shape that such ideals should take is not easily settled. Finally, they address the meta-coordination account, put forward by Allen Buchanan, affirming its synchronic and diachronic flexibility, while at the same time noting that fleshing it out will require more work on how the account can be applied to existing global governance institutions.

Chapters 7 and 8 address just war theory. Just war theory, we have claimed, is one of the most important loci of what we have defined as cross-fertilization between more traditional topics in international ethics and recent work in global political theory. In chapter 7, Laura Valentini discusses the relationship between *jus ad bellum* and global distributive justice. Her chapter is crucial to understanding the interplay between justice as a set of coercible normative obligations and *jus ad bellum*'s attempt to provide necessary and sufficient conditions for resorting to (lethal) force. More specifically, Valentini claims that we should integrate our understanding of one of the central elements in *jus ad bellum*, namely, 'just cause', with theories of global justice. In chapter 8, Seth Lazar offers an account of killing in war based on associative obligations. His contribution is important in explaining the relevance of what are often called special relationships and the duties and obligations they generate. The latter idea clearly has an impact on our behaviour towards members of other groups and political communities. While Lazar's focus is on a specific aspect of just war theory, we believe that his chapter forces us to tackle one of the main themes in global political morality, namely, what follows from being members of specific human associations. As the discussion in chapters 2 and 3 highlights, there is widespread disagreement about the relevance of special relationships to the scope and nature of distributive principles. Lazar's chapter allows us to broaden the analysis of the relevance of relationships to basic moral commitments, and, in so doing, shows us, once again, how fruitful cross-fertilization can be.

Chapters 9 to 14, taken as a whole, reflect what we have referred to above as the trends towards diversification of the topics that are addressed by global political theorists and their attempt to offer more applied and empirically informed philosophical analyses. These six chapters can further be divided into three conceptually distinct clusters.

The first cluster, chapters 9 and 10, discusses the issue of territoriality and the related concern for the ownership and sale of the natural resources found in a given territory. In chapter 9, David Miller and Margaret Moore provide

an overview and assessment of different accounts of the nature and justification of territorial rights. Miller and Moore remind us that while globalization
has clearly had an impact on our lives, our politics remains, in their own
words, 'stubbornly territorial'. They defend the model of territorial politics
articulated by the modern state by arguing that the available alternatives are
either undesirable or too unspecified to be credible. They then provide a
sophisticated overview of five different justifications for territorial rights
(utilitarian, Kantian, broadly Lockean, nationalist and based on self-
determination). They conclude by asking whether theories of territorial rights
may help us in answering difficult questions about contested territories. In
chapter 10, Leif Wenar tackles the issue of natural resources. He starts by
observing that natural resources have been highly contested both politically
and theoretically throughout history. He then contrasts two different theoretical accounts of the correct principles that apply to natural resources. The
first interprets such principles as principles of just distribution. The second
sees them as principles that should allow us to avoid dangerous distributions
of power determined by who controls natural resources. Wenar goes on to
provide an overview and assessment of some of the most important contributions to the literature on natural resources, and he concludes his essay by
articulating his favoured approach, namely, popular resource sovereignty.
Wenar's chapter highlights that, much like territory, the concept of natural
resources is deeply political. Who should control natural resources matters
from a fairness perspective, yet, at the same time, who we allow natural
resources to be controlled by has clear implications for how power is exercised by one group of human beings over another.

The second cluster, chapters 11 and 12, explicitly deals with two of the
most important domains in the global economy, namely, international trade
and international capital mobility. In chapter 11, Aaron James starts by discussing the very meaning of 'fair trade'. He distinguishes between interactional (the fairness of trades) and institutional (the fairness of the institutions
composing the international trading regime) approaches. He goes on to
provide an institutional account of fair (international) trade rooted in the
morality of practices. Trade can be considered as one aspect of the international 'market reliance practice' that countries adopt in order to increase
their respective national incomes. Fairness in trade thus concerns the types
of claims that different polities can make to the gains from their shared
cooperative venture in trade. The morality of practices approach presented
by James is closely related to our present historical circumstances and to the
state system as we see it, yet it also provides elements to assess critically the
current system of trade from a normative perspective. In chapter 12, Peter
Dietsch gives us both an overview and an original assessment of one of the
most important aspects of the global economy by addressing the controversial topic of international financial integration. The key question addressed
by Dietsch concerns the normative implications of an internationally

integrated financial system. His analysis discusses the impact of financial integration on a range of important evaluative criteria such as economic growth, the distribution of wealth and income at the national and international levels, and democratic self-determination within the economic sphere. His overall argument is that international financial integration, given prevailing institutional conditions, can pose threats to economic stability and self-determination and thus that substantial reforms are required in order for international financial integration to be morally desirable.

The third and final cluster, chapters 13 and 14, offers the reader a way of understanding the moral aspects of global politics from a different angle by stressing the importance of human interactions with our shared environment and the relevance of our obligations to those who will come after us (but also before us). In chapter 13, Dale Jamieson and Marcello Di Paola set out what it means to do political theory in a different kind of world – one where human beings have dramatically altered the planet's life. Political theory in the Anthropocene, as they call it, may end up being different from 'political theory as we know it'. They trace the potential implications for the discipline of a radical change in philosophical perspective. Living in the Anthropocene, they argue, will affect traditional features of liberal political philosophy such as agency, responsibility, governance and legitimacy. Finally, in chapter 14, Axel Gosseries and Danielle Zwarthoed develop the links between global justice and intergenerational fairness. They distinguish between a comparative and a combinatory way of linking global justice and generations, and adopt the latter approach. They investigate the 'compatibility between global and intergenerational demands', and discuss the question of historical injustice as a specific aspect of the interaction between global and generational fairness. Finally, they conclude by looking at the potential use of migrations as a way of replacing generations. Their contribution links our current moral and evaluative benchmarks to what we owe to those who will come after us and thus effectively gives us a way to think about the future (and past) subjects of global political theory.

References

Abizadeh, A. 2008. 'Democratic Theory and Border Coercion: No Right to Unilaterally Control Your Own Border', *Political Theory* 36: 37–65.
Anheier, H. K., Kaldor, M. and Glasius, M., eds. 2006. *Global Civil Society 2006/7*. London: Sage.
Barry, C. 2011. 'Sovereign Debt, Human Rights, and Policy Conditionality', *Journal of Political Philosophy* 19(3): 282–305.
Beitz, C. 2010. *The Idea of Human Rights*. Oxford: Oxford University Press.
Betsill, M. M. and Corell, E., eds. 2008. *NGO Diplomacy: The Influence of Nongovernmental Organizations in International Environmental Negotiations*. Cambridge, MA: MIT Press.
Blake, M. 2013a. 'We Are All Cosmopolitans Now', in G. Brock, ed., *Cosmopolitanism versus Non-Cosmopolitanism*, 35–54. Oxford: Oxford University Press.
Blake, M. 2013b. 'Immigration, Jurisdiction, and Exclusion', *Philosophy & Public Affairs* 41(2): 103–130.

Blake, M. 2013c. *Justice and Foreign Policy*. Oxford: Oxford University Press.

Buchanan, A. 2013. *The Heart of Human Rights*. Oxford: Oxford University Press.

Buchanan, A. and Keohane, R. 2006. 'The Legitimacy of Global Governance Institutions', *Ethics & International Affairs* 20(4): 405–437.

Brown, G. and Held, D., eds. 2010. *The Cosmopolitanism Reader*. Cambridge: Polity.

Cabrera, L. 2006. *Political Theory of Global Justice: A Cosmopolitan Case for a World State*. London: Routledge.

Caney, S. 2012. 'Just Emissions', *Philosophy & Public Affairs* 40(4): 255-300.

Christiano, T. 2011. 'Is Democratic Legitimacy Possible for International Institutions?', in D. Archibugi, M. K. Archibugi and R. Marchetti, eds., *Global Democracy*, 69–95. Cambridge: Cambridge University Press.

Christiano, T. 2012. 'The Legitimacy of International Institutions', in A. Marmor, ed., *The Routledge Companion to Philosophy of Law*, 380–394. New York: Routledge.

Cohen, J. 2004. 'Minimalism About Human Rights: The Most We Can Hope For?' *Journal of Political Philosophy* 12(2): 190–213.

Deibert, R. 1997. *Parchment, Printing and the Hypermedia*. Ithaca, NY: Cornell University Press.

Dietsch, P. and Rixen, T. 2014. 'Tax Competition and Global Background Justice', *Journal of Political Philosophy* 22(2): 150–177.

Dworkin, R. 1983. 'Comment on Narveson: In Defense of Equality', *Social Philosophy and Policy* 1: 24–40.

Dworkin, R. 1986. *Law's Empire*. Cambridge: Cambridge University Press.

Estlund, D. 2007. 'On Following Orders in an Unjust War', *Journal of Political Philosophy* 15(2): 213–234.

Fabre, C. 2012. *Cosmopolitan War*. Oxford: Oxford University Press.

Giddens, A. 1990. *The Consequences of Modernity*. Cambridge: Polity.

Griffin, J. 2008. *On Human Rights*. Oxford: Oxford University Press.

Haas, P. M. 1991. 'Policy Responses to Stratospheric Ozone Depletion', *Global Environmental Change* 1: 1–21.

Hale, T. and Held, D. 2011. *Handbook of Transnational Governance*. Cambridge: Polity.

Held, D. 1995. *Democracy and the Global Order*. Cambridge: Polity.

Held, D. and Young, K. 2011. 'Crises in Parallel Worlds: The Governance of Global Risks in Finance, Security, and the Environment', in C. Calhoun and G. Derluguian, eds., *The Deepening Crisis: Governance Challenges after Neoliberalism*, 19–42. New York: New York University Press.

Held, D., McGrew, A., Goldblatt, D. and Perraton, J. 1999. *Global Transformations: Politics, Economics and Culture*. Cambridge: Polity.

James, A. 2005. 'Distributive Justice Without Sovereign Rule: The Case of Trade', *Social Theory and Practice* 31: 1–27.

James, A. 2012. *Fairness in Practice: A Social Contract for the Global Economy*. Oxford: Oxford University Press.

Jamieson, D. 2014. *Reason in a Dark Time: Why the Struggle to Stop Climate Change Failed and What It Means For Our Future*. Oxford: Oxford University Press.

Keck, M. E. and Sikkink, K. 1998. *Activists Beyond Borders*. Ithaca, NY: Cornell University Press.

Kerwer, D. 2005. 'Rules That Many Use: Standards and Global Regulation', *Governance* 18(4): 453–475.

Lazar, S. 2013. 'War', in Hugh LaFollette, ed., *The International Encyclopedia of Ethics*, 5379–5393. Oxford: Wiley Blackwell.

Macdonald, T. and Ronzoni, M., eds. 2012. 'Introduction: The Idea of Global Political Justice', *Critical Review of International Social and Political Philosophy* 15(5): 521–533.

Maffettone, P. 2009. 'The WTO and the Limits of Distributive Justice', *Philosophy and Social Criticism* 35(3): 243–267.

Marchetti, R. 2008. *Global Democracy: For and Against*. New York: Routledge.

Miller, D. 2012. 'Grounding Human Rights', *Critical Review of International Social and Political Philosophy* 15(4): 407–427.

Milner, H. 1998. 'Rationalizing Politics: The Emerging Synthesis of the International, American and Comparative Politics', *International Organization* 52(4): 759–786.

Moellendorf, D. 2005. 'The World Trade Organization and Egalitarian Justice', *Metaphilosophy* 36(1): 145–162.

Moore, M. 2015. *A Political Theory of Territory*. Oxford: Oxford University Press.

Nardin, T. 2004. 'Justice and Coercion', in Alex J. Bellamy, ed., *International Society and Its Critics*, 247–264. Oxford: Oxford University Press.

Nardin, T. 2006. 'International Political Theory and the Question of Justice', *International Affairs* 82(3): 449–465.

Nine, C. 2012. *Global Justice and Territory*. Oxford: Oxford University Press.

Pogge, T. W. 1992. 'Cosmopolitanism and Sovereignty', *Ethics* 103(1): 48–75.

Pogge, T., Rimmer, M. and Rubenstein, K., eds. 2010. *Incentives for Global Public Health: Patent Law and Access to Essential Medicines*. Cambridge: Cambridge University Press.

Rawls, J. 1999. *The Law of Peoples*. Cambridge, MA: Harvard University Press.

Risse, M. 2007. 'Fairness in Trade I: Obligations from Trading and the Pauper-Labor Argument', *Politics, Philosophy & Economics* 6: 355–377.

Risse-Kappen, T. 1995. *Bringing Transnational Relations Back In: Non-State Actors, Domestic Structures and International Institutions*. Cambridge: Cambridge University Press.

Ronzoni, M. 2009. 'The Global Order: A Case of Background Injustice? A Practice-Dependent Account', *Philosophy & Public Affairs* 37(3): 229–256.

Ryan, C. 2011. 'Democratic Duty and the Moral Dilemma of Soldiers', *Ethics* 122(1): 10–42.

Sangiovanni, A. 2007. 'Global Justice, Reciprocity and the State', *Philosophy & Public Affairs* 35(1): 3–39.

Sen, A. 2005. 'Human Rights and Capabilities', *Journal of Human Development* 6(2): 151–166.

Shue, H. 1996. *Basic Rights*. Oxford: Oxford University Press.

Singer, P. 2002. *One World: The Ethics of Globalization*. New Haven, CT: Yale University Press.

Slaughter, A.-M. 2004. *A New World Order*. Princeton, NJ: Princeton University Press.

Stilz, A. 2011. 'Nations, States, and Territory', *Ethics* 121(3): 572–601.

Tan, C. 2000. *Toleration, Diversity and Global Justice*. Cambridge: Cambridge University Press.

Valentini, L. 2011. *Justice in a Globalized World: A Normative Framework*. Oxford: Oxford University Press.

Valentini, L. 2012. 'In what Sense Are Human Rights Political?' *Political Studies* 60(1): 180–194.

Valentini, L. 2013. 'Cosmopolitan Justice and Rightful Enforceability', in G. Brock, ed., *Cosmopolitanism versus Non-Cosmopolitanism*, 92–110. Oxford: Oxford University Press.

Vlastos, G. 1984. 'Justice and Equality', in J. Waldron, ed., *Theories of Rights*. Oxford: Oxford University Press.

Wellman, C. 2008. 'Immigration and Freedom of Association', *Ethics* 119: 109–141.

Wenar, L. 2008. 'Property Rights and the Resource Curse', *Philosophy & Public Affairs* 36(1): 2–32.

Ypi, L. 2014. 'A Permissive Theory of Territorial Rights', *European Journal of Philosophy* 22(2): 288–312.

CHAPTER ONE

The Point and Ground of Human Rights: A Kantian Constructivist View

Rainer Forst

1 How To Think About Human Rights

Our thinking about normative concepts is always bound by paradigmatic notions of their primary task in social practice. Human rights are a case in point. Some focus on their moral core as protecting urgent and essential human interests and try to define these; some focus on their being a cross-cultural 'lingua franca' and thus look for definitions and justifications that could be approved from within an 'overlapping consensus' of all cultures and societies – or at least the 'reasonable' ones. Some locate the idea of human rights in international political or legal practice as standards of legitimacy, the violation of which justifies international action or intervention.

Each of these approaches has its advantages as well as its shortcomings, which I will not discuss in detail here (for more in-depth discussion of these approaches, see Forst, 2014: ch. 2). Rather, what I want to argue is that none of them identifies the *political* and *emancipatory* point of human rights properly, the point being that these rights have been (and continue to be) fought for in historical social struggles to establish a legal, political and social status of non-dominated persons within a political normative order – that is, as free and equal persons who are both addressees and authors of the legal, political and social basic structure of their political community. I emphasize that this is the original and primary social context of human rights: the emancipatory struggles and conflicts within particular societies marked by various forms of domination. We only understand the point and ground of human rights if we understand the normative logic of such struggles.

Thus we ought to free ourselves from some all too powerful imaginaries dominating human rights discourse that lead us away from this context. One such misleading imaginary is that of human rights as instruments of the protection of vulnerable persons against threats to their well-being by powerful agents, especially the state (Ignatieff, 2001).[1] Such ways of thinking about human rights focus on persons as primarily *passive* recipients of certain protections and overlook that the full meaning of these rights from the modern political revolutions onward was to achieve an *active* status of non-domination, such that one is not subject to a legal, political and social normative order that denies you standing as an equal; that is, an order that has not been and cannot be properly justified to you as a free and equal member of society. Domination in my understanding (which differs substantially from neo-republican versions)[2] does not mean being denied equal status in the sense of no longer enjoying freedom of choice from arbitrary interference; rather, and more fundamentally, it means being disrespected in one's basic claim to be a free and equal normative authority within the order one is subject to, and that implies the basic right to co-determine the structure of that society. This is the *status activus*, to use Jellinek's term (2011; see also Alexy, 2010: ch. 5), which is a necessary component of human rights: they are not just rights to be protected in one's status as a legally, politically and socially non-dominated person; they are, in a reflexive sense, also basic rights to determine the rights and duties that define that status. Many interpretations of human rights today, even those called 'political', pay insufficient attention to this active, political competence.[3]

The other imaginary to be avoided is the internationalist-interventionist one already alluded to. This defines human rights as international legal rights and implies that, in the words of Charles Beitz, 'the central idea of international human rights is that states are responsible for satisfying certain conditions in their treatment of their own people and that failures or prospective failures to do so may justify some form of remedial or preventive action by the world community' (2009: 13). This way of thinking leads to a number of problems. To begin with, the quote shows that the primary context of human rights is not the international order but, rather, the different states, which ought to realize these rights, and that the international context builds on these state contexts and has the task of establishing procedures to legitimately discover, judge and possibly sanction human rights violations. Thus, human rights are a task for states in the first instance and then for the international community; therefore, the human rights that a state has to realize cannot be reduced to those rights the violation of which the international community finds a sufficient reason to intervene over, given the enormous costs and difficulties of an intervention. Such an argument turns the normative order of human rights on its head: first, we need to know which human rights claims are universally justifiable as claims within states, and then we need to think about legitimate cases and, most importantly, procedures and institutions of intervention – which today are still mostly lacking. Otherwise, we would reduce the core of human rights to those rights the violation of which calls for an intervention, and standard – and in my view essential – human rights like those of gender equality or democratic government would no longer be seen as core human rights because – to cite Beitz – 'the proper inference from the fact that there are circumstances in which the absence of democratic institutions would not generate ... reasons for outside agents to act is that the doctrine of human rights should not embrace such a right' (2009: 185).[4] This view is remarkably at odds with international human rights documents and human rights practice – such as the social practice of demanding human rights to democracy and gender equality and of actively trying to change regimes that deny these. The 'practice-based' internationalist-interventionist paradigm of thinking about human rights, as it is often called, thus focuses on the wrong practice – namely, that of an international regime of human rights rather than that of the critique of states that violate these rights as put forth by members of such societies and by outside agents, even though the latter might not have the power or the legitimacy to intervene. Human rights are one thing, the question of an international politics of intervention is another, conditional on many contingent factors. In other words, if the existing system of international legal human rights were considered the 'heart' of human rights, as Allen Buchanan argues (2013: 274), we would have to look for the 'heart of hearts' to get to the core of human rights and to their justification.[5]

To briefly indicate the further argument I make in this chapter: if I am right about the moral and political *point* of human rights to establish the status of persons within their normative order as legal, political and social equals protected from severe forms of domination, it follows that there is a particular moral *ground* for these rights. Negatively speaking, this is the right not to be subjected to a normative order that denies basic standing as an equal to you and that, reflexively speaking, cannot be justified to you as free and equal; and, positively speaking, it is the right to be an equal normative authority and active agent of justification when it comes to the basic legal, political and social arrangements in your society. This reflexive formulation is necessary, for freedom from domination not just means to be respected as a legally, politically and socially non-dominated equal secured by certain rights; it also means that it is not others who decide without and over you about whether that status is fulfilled or not. Thus, the authority to define non-domination can only lie within a discursive procedure of reciprocal and general justification where all are justificatory equals.

Essentially, the negative and positive formulations used above coincide in the discourse-theoretical, Kantian idea that those subject to a normative order ought to be equal and free *normative authorities* determining that order through procedures and discourses of justification in which all can participate as equals. The main normative concept thus is that of a person as an equal normative authority, having a basic moral claim to be respected in his or her dignity to be such an authority – and thus having the basic moral *right to justification* (see Forst 2012), which in this context means the basic right to be an equal co-author of the (legal, political and social) norms one is subject to, and which define one's basic standing in society. This implies not just political rights of participation, but all those rights that give you the *normative power* to ward off and overcome various forms of domination – that is, of unjustifiable subjection. Thus, it is a particular view of the point of human rights that leads me to reconstruct its moral core and ground in a certain way and locate it in the basic right to justification. In what follows, I will unpack his argument.

2   The Point of Human Rights

An important aspect of the different imaginaries guiding our thinking about human rights is what one considers to be the genealogy of the concept. Those who, like myself, regard them as emancipatory weapons against oppressive regimes and social orders (including feudalism and other forms of economic exploitation – thus the emphasis on *social* non-domination, as I will explain later) locate their origins in the early modern social conflicts in the seventeenth century especially, playing a major role in the revolutions of the eighteenth century and finding their strongest historical expression in the *Déclaration de l'homme et du citoyen* of 1789 (see the historical accounts in Bloch, 1986; Gauchet, 1995; Hunt, 2008). Those who emphasize the international legal character of human rights, however, believe that with the Universal Declaration of 1948 a new conception of human rights as internationally secured protections came into being (Beitz, 2009; Moyn, 2012; Ratner, 2015). Whereas the first conception is guided by powerful images of modern revolutions, the second has no less of a powerful image to relate to: namely, the horrors of fascist tyranny and genocide as social evils to be avoided. The first see human rights as not just constraining, but constituting legitimate political power (Habermas, 1974; Besson, 2015); the second regard them as bulwarks against extreme forms of oppression and suffering.

Still, as I said above, if one looks at the Universal Declaration of 1948 and other covenants and, last not least, international practice, one must recognize that in the idea, as well as the practice, of human rights, states are the main context of their realization (which does not exclude the idea of realizing them in a world state), and the international institutions are only secondary (but of increasing importance) in that regard. Furthermore, it is not just in Article 21 that the Universal Declaration stresses the right to democracy; in its Preamble, it also makes reference to the revolutionary, democratic tradition of human rights by saying that human rights ought to be secured, 'if man is not to be compelled to have recourse, as a last resort, to rebellion against tyranny and oppression' (see Gearty 2014).

To fix ideas about an active (or activist[6]) political imaginary of human rights as an alternative to the internationalist-interventionist as well as the passive notion of the avoidance of suffering, let me use an image. There is an excellent collection of photographs taken during the 'Arab Spring' in 2011 on Tahrir Square, compiled by Karima Khalil (2011).[7] The pictures all show people holding signs asking President Mubarak to leave and to hand over power to a democratic government; some simply say 'freedom' or 'justice'. There is one picture (taken by Hossam el Hamalawy) that shows a man holding a sign that says 'Enough Humiliation' (Khalil, 2011: 87).[8] According to my interpretation, the picture does not just tell us a lot about the notion of dignity grounding human rights (which I will come back to in the next section). It also tells us something important about the point of human rights. For how shall we understand – and now of course I embark on a rational reconstruction and hermeneutic interpretation of my own, though I hope to be true to what the demonstrator meant – the kind of humiliation the activist has had 'enough' of?

The picture helps us place the demand and the politics of human rights in the primary political context in which we have to see them: the struggle for basic forms of respect as legal, political and social agents who do not 'deserve' to be ruled autocratically by a corrupt and oppressive regime. The humiliation that is decried and for which there is a demand that it end is not just a particular form of being denied access to the labour market or to certain social institutions; rather, it is being denied a proper recognition as a legal, political and social authority with certain powers, as someone who 'counts' at least to the extent that it is not others who tell him or her what his or her proper place in society is. (There are also many photographs in the book of women holding similar signs, and needless to say – as not just the post-revolutionary developments in Egypt showed – the dialectic of liberation and of oppression has many facets and is still ongoing, from the rule of the Muslim Brotherhood to the military rule that followed it.) What is more, the protest sign does not just express the claim to be respected as a person with such powers, usually formulated as rights; it also expresses the claim to be a normative authority when it comes to deciding which rights or duties citizens have. This is the full meaning of an emancipatory claim – it is not just a claim to this or that right or social opportunity, but a right to have a say in the institutional regime one is subject to. The humiliation to be overcome is, if you will, a comprehensive experience, and the claim to overcome it has a comprehensive character of becoming a rights agent with the full right to determine the structure of rights to which you are subject.

This implies that we must not understand human rights vertically as rights or privileges granted to subjects by a ruler or a government; this is the older tradition of gaining status recognition from a monarch as the feudal lords did when they wrested the Magna Carta from King John in 1215. Rather, the emancipation from political humiliation implies that the rights one has are rights that members of a society mutually recognize and accord *each other*, based on their mutual respect as equal normative authorities within their social order. So the non-domination aimed at does not just mean having certain important rights, but being the authority to co-determine and secure these rights: a horizontal understanding of human rights (Habermas 1996, ch. 3; Günther 2009). The domination and humiliation to be overcome are twofold: the domination of being denied certain rights that human beings ought to have as legal, political and social equals, and the domination of having no say, no right to justification, within the normative order to which you belong. If you look at the French Declaration, and also at what protesters in human rights struggles demand, this is the full message of those who claim human rights. And that is why the right to democracy is essential to any conception of human rights. For this right expresses the basic right to be a constructive normative agent; and it is only in the discourse among political equals that a justifiable and concrete human rights regime can be determined and realized (see also Tully 2014).

It is not merely Kantian-style political philosophers who describe human rights movements in the thick normative language of dignity or justice; rather, it is the social agents themselves who use such language to express their demands for full respect and human rights – as a fundamental claim of justice among normative equals who are not just takers but also makers of the rights they have, on the assumption that they are free and equal in claiming as well as 'constructing' these rights in political discourse. The claims to be respected as rights-bearers and normative authorities are addressed to the regime one is subject to, to be sure; but what they imply is that it is not up to the regime to deny these claims or to determine their meaning. In a certain sense, they are already part of a process of horizontal justification among those equals who gather in the square (and beyond it, as the community of all subjected). This is why human rights can be formulated (generally and abstractly) in declarations – because among those who respect each other as justificatory equals, there can be no good reason to deny them.

This is the normative power the protesters are backed by when they write such signs. They already 'have' these rights, though they are denied their collective political-legal realization.

3   The Ground of Human Rights

The consideration of the emancipatory point of human rights shows how an historical and sociological reflection on human rights as emancipatory claims and tools links up with a moral and even a transcendental reflection. For we have to recognize not just the comprehensive character of human rights as realizing a fundamental status as legally, politically and socially non-dominated (and in this sense equal) persons, but also that their normative force implies that, among persons who respect each other morally and who aim to materialize this kind of respect in law, these rights are to be seen as justified horizontally between moral equals. They spell out what it means to be such an equal in the social world – and which rights this implies. So these are rights the possession of which equal justificatory authorities can always claim and can never deny each other – as addressees and authors of such claims and of such rights. The moral ground of these rights is the basic right to justification, or the right to be respected as an equal moral authority, and the substance of these rights comes in when it is determined (in discursive practice) what it means to be recognized as an equal and free normative authority in the legal, political and social realm. I will explain in section 4 how such discursive construction is to be conceptualized. But here it is important to understand that these rights, even though they aim at a legal, political and social status and can only be justifiably realized in a democratic regime, have a 'ground' that is both moral and, if you will, transcendental: the autonomy of persons with a right to justification as a normative authority equal to all others. Human or basic rights are constructed on that basis, where the agents of construction are autonomous persons, and the principles of construction are principles of justification among equals (see O'Neill, 1989; Rawls, 1993, ch. 3). Here we arrive at the transcendental, reflexive truth about the ground of human rights: they are rights of and between autonomous equal authorities in the realm of normative reasons, expressing the respect for such autonomy and authority, materialized and justified with respect to the legal, political and social world (and the many dangers of domination). But their ground is the respect for each other as moral equals and as justifying beings (using practical reason), who are bound to nothing but what they as justificatory equals can claim from each other. They are bound and, at the same time, free as autonomous agents of justification – bound to each other as justificatory equals and to the principle of reason as the principle of general and reciprocal justification for reciprocally and generally valid norms (Forst, 2012: chs 1 and 2). So the 'ultimate' justification of these rights is the principle of justification itself.

It is only in Kant's philosophy that we find the appropriate connection between the prior and 'inviolable' moral status of persons that grounds human rights and the activist, constructive aspects of this status as being a law-maker and not a mere law-taker with a claim to protection. Kant's notion of the *dignity* of autonomous persons, with its twofold character of calling for unconditional moral respect as equals and for its operationalization in the mode of discursive justification[9] between legislators in the space of reasons, combines morality, law and politics in the right way to ground human rights (Habermas, 2010: 469; Forst, 2014: ch. 4). It can explain why the Preamble of the Universal Declaration of 1948 starts with the principle that 'recognition of the inherent dignity and of the equal and inalienable rights of all members of the human family is the foundation of freedom, justice and peace in the world', and what the terms 'inherent' and 'inalienable' are supposed to indicate without making reference to a quasi-religious ground for this status.[10] What it means is that the basis for human rights is the respect for each other person as a moral equal who need not qualify for this status or respect in any other way than by being human. To be respected in that way is, as Kant (2009: 6:237) says, an 'innate right' of humans.

The notion of the innate right to independence is Kant's way of bridging the gap between morality and law. In the realm of morality, Kant explains the status of persons as an 'end in themselves', that is, as beings whose purposes have to be respected equally (within the bounds of reciprocity) and must not be ignored or instrumentalized by others, with the 'idea of the *dignity* of a rational being, who obeys no law other than that which he himself at the same time gives' (1997: 4:434). The beings with such dignity are all equally law-givers in the 'kingdom of ends' and thus have to rule over themselves and each other with reciprocally and generally justifiable norms, as the categorical imperative says:

> Our own will insofar as it would act only under the condition of a possible giving of universal law [*allgemeine Gesetzgebung*] through its maxims – this will possible for us in idea – is the proper object of respect, and the dignity of humanity consists just in this capacity to give universal law, though with the condition of also being itself subject to this very lawgiving. (1997: 4:440)[11]

To understand why Kant uses the notion of dignity here, it is essential to focus on the 'worthiness [*Würdigkeit*] of every rational subject to be a law-giving member in the kingdom of ends' (1997: 4:439). By this term, Kant emphasizes the status or rank[12] of persons as moral equals and as active law-givers – that is, as normative authorities subject to no one or no other values than those that can be justified according to the categorical imperative of their own rational will. The imperative asks persons to respect each other as justificatory equals, because being respected as an end in itself means not to be subjected to actions or norms that cannot be justified to each person as an equal. As Kant explains in the *Groundwork*, treating another as a means by making, for example, a false promise, means that the other 'cannot possibly agree to my way of behaving toward him, and so himself contain the end of this action' (1997: 4:429f.). Hence, the moral duty of justification and the right to justification (here duty and right are co-original) express what it means to respect others as ends in themselves and as equal normative authorities in the realm of justifications or norms. So it is not that dignity is the first 'ground' of human rights (see also Waldron, 2015); rather, it is the term to express the status of every moral person as an equal and autonomous normative authority; as Kant affirms, autonomy 'is the ground of the dignity of human nature' (1997: 4:436). Dignity, equal status and normative authority are all concepts that form a unity based on the idea of the moral autonomy of persons with a basic right to justification (within a reconstruction of the principles and ideas of practical reason as justificatory reason) (Forst 2012: ch. 1). This basic claim, to be respected in one's dignity as a normative justificatory equal and not be ignored or oppressed in that standing, explains the notion of freedom from 'humiliation' that the man in the picture demands. He asserts that no government has a normative authority over him that he cannot share in as free and equal.

For the grounding of human rights, this means that every person has a non-deniable claim to all the rights protections and powers that free and equal persons have to grant and guarantee each other who recognize the need to materialize their standing as equal normative authorities in the world of law and politics. Thus Beitz's worry that the right to justification as the ground of human rights is too abstract and dissolves into 'a generic idea of moral standing' (2013: 279) is misplaced, as this ground is necessary but not sufficient for any specification of that standing with respect to the status of being a legally, politically and socially non-dominated person. Human rights secure such status in the legal, political and social world, and thus there is a clear relation between a general moral ground and a more specific context of justifying and theorizing human rights.

In my Kantian view, the right to justification operates between the moral and the legal-political level. Thus it performs the same function as Kant's 'innate' or 'original' right of persons. Kant introduces this right as the only 'natural' right of persons and as the ground of every justifiable form of law imposed over free and equal members of a kingdom of ends; thus, before explaining the innate right, he stresses the natural legal duty to regard oneself and others as ends in themselves (2009: 6:236). In this connection, he introduces the innate right thus: 'Freedom (independence from being constrained by another's choice), insofar as it can coexist with the freedom of every other in accordance with a universal law, is the only original right belonging to every man by virtue of his humanity' (2009: 6:237). This right to independence under general law has rightly been interpreted as a right to non-domination by Arthur Ripstein (2009: ch. 2), and in this connection one needs to stress *both* aspects discussed by Kant under the headings of private and public right: the right to legally protected independence and the corresponding right to partake in the making of the general law that will bind all. These are the two aspects of the moral right to justification in the realm of law and politics: to be only bound by strictly reciprocally and generally valid laws and to be the co-author of these laws, as Kant stresses in his republican theory.

I cannot go into the details of how Kant constructs a system of legal and political justice – and the rights entailed by that – on this basis. What is most important in this respect is not whether we find an explicit account of human rights in Kant's theory; what is essential is, rather, that in his view the form and justification of all rights or rightful claims has to be strictly reciprocal and general, in accord with the general concept of right which means 'the sum of the conditions under which the choice of one can be united with the choice of another in accordance with a universal law of freedom' (2009: 6:230). The natural right to freedom thus is not a ground for a 'derivation' of a list of rights or duties or principles of justice, but entails the moral criteria of justification of any rights or justice claim as well as the principle of the free and equal status of all those who are subjects of the law. This is why the right to freedom – or, in my interpretation, the right to justification – is a foundation for a procedural – and in that sense 'non-foundationalist' – construction of basic human rights.[13] Any constructivist view that entails basic moral criteria of the justification of the constructions as well as of the standing of the constructing agents must be based on a reflexive notion of the moral right to justification among equal normative authorities; and the innate right expresses that standing and such criteria. It is thus formal and substantive at the same time, a ground of autonomous constructions of right(s) and yet not a basis of their non-discursive derivation.[14] A constructivist view always entails two different kinds of normative argument – or two kinds of normativity. First, the normativity of the principles and ideas of practical reason, to use Rawls's language (1980; 1993: ch. 3) – that is, in my account, the principle of reciprocal and general justification and the moral notion of free and equal persons as equal normative authorities with a right to justification. And second, the normativity of the norms (or 'laws') generated by the constructivist or discursive procedure, be it the categorical imperative or a notion of free and equal discourse. In a Kantian view, it is essential that practical reason, in my understanding justificatory reason, is the basis for the principles and ideas used – but practical reason understood as a rational and, at the same time, moral capacity, that is, of not just knowing how to justify norms, but also knowing that one is under a duty to do so. That is why the duty of and the right to justification are co-original. In other words, the theory I suggest uses the principle of justification itself as the justifying ground for a theory of human rights. That is why I call it a reflexive theory: no other ground is used than the normative principle of justificatory reason.

It is important to see that the normativity of constructed norms depends on the normativity of the principles and the normative standing of the agents of construction. One can only get so much normativity out of a procedure as one invests in it from the start; that is why categorical imperatives presuppose one basic categorical imperative, and that is why the duty and right to justification are basic for any justified norm. For the context of justifying rights, this means that any construction of human rights must rest on a basic right itself, as the moral right to justification or the innate right in Kant's theory. We can call this the principle of the *conservation and production of normativity*: human rights can only be grounded on a fundamental notion of a right to have all those rights that free and equal normative authorities cannot reciprocally and generally deny each other if they want to secure and operationalize that status (as the status of discursive authority and non-domination) in the legal, political and social world. If human rights are rights such that free and equal persons cannot with good reasons deny them to each other, then their status as free and equal – and the right to it – is basic; and only such a basis can generate the normativity of such rights. The ground of human rights must not be weaker than their own validity claim; rather, it must contain and transmit its normativity to such rights as rights no one can reasonably reject between moral-political equals.

This is why, to make a long argument short, an interest theory of rights cannot sufficiently ground human rights without adding the normativity-generating factor of justification by and through moral equals. An interest theory of rights says, to use Raz's formulation, that a person has a right if an aspect of his 'well-being (his interest) is a sufficient reason for holding some other person(s) to be under a duty' (1986: 166). This leaves open the criterion for which aspects of well-being, or for which interests, are a sufficient reason to ground a right, and thus attempts are made to narrow down 'essential' interests or aspects of well-being to ground rights.[15] Raz himself gives a value-based account of such interests, arguing that 'the value of the right to its possessor is its ground' (2015: 221). Thus, his approach would better be called a value theory of rights. In order to justify human rights, then, which affirm 'the moral worth of all human beings' and distribute 'power away from the powerful to everyone' (2015: 226), universalizable essential values of the good life have to be identified. But again, in order for these values to have such normative force, they have to not just reflect the equal moral status of every person, but also express it by being non-rejectable between such persons who seek to establish their status as legally, politically and socially non-dominated (as Raz's characterization of these rights entails) by way of securing human rights. And if this is right, then the normativity of these rights does not rest on some prior account of values, but resides in their justifiability between equals who confer their justificatory power to these rights by finding them to be non-rejectable given these persons' moral status as equals and what it requires to secure this status legally, politically and socially. It is the commonly arrived at justification by equal normative authorities that grounds the normativity of human rights. Justificatory equals combine their normative force in and by justifying these rights.

That is why we should see human rights as *congealed and solidified justifications that can withstand normative doubt* (which they need to be able to prove if challenged) and that express the status of moral equals in the legal, political and social world. A number of normative historical experiences and justifications are sedimented when it comes to basic rights to, say, freedom of religion, political participation or access to education. To claim such rights means to use these congealed justifications as normative powers in a contested space of justification and to be able to use them as a package, so to speak, without having to justify these claims anew every time. They provide a safe and secure status or standing in the social world. The basic right to justification gives persons the possibility to own these justifications and use them to ward off illegitimate power claims – but also to contest these justifications if one-sidedness, or narrowness, is feared. So the right to justification, as a 'veto right' against false justifications, is always in place, whereas the content of basic human rights is fixed to some extent, but still the possible object of questioning. Yet every such questioning is bound to the criteria of reciprocity and generality as criteria of practical reason. In a moral-political sense, especially within a constitutional regime, human rights thus serve as veto rights against legal or social arrangements that are unjustifiable and violate these rights; but they can only have such normative force by expressing the basic right of justification. This is why declarations and formulations of human or constitutional rights have a higher-order status, yet one that is not immune to questioning or revision. Whether there is a right to personal property and whether it entails a right to own means of production are part of that discourse, as well as what the right to the free exercise of religion entails with respect to the education of one's children, for example. None of their formulations or interpretations are 'absolute'; yet the justificatory threshold of criticizing them is high.

To summarize my main grounding argument: respecting persons as equal normative authorities in the realms of morality as well as law and politics is basic, and that respect implies that every person (whether capable of exercising the faculty of justification or not)[16] has a right to justification in the relevant contexts of moral action or political normative orders. This is what it means to respect the dignity of human beings as ends in themselves, to use Kantian language. Since moral and basic legal norms claim to be generally and reciprocally binding for all persons equally, the principle of practical reason says that all those subjected to the norms have to be equal justificatory agents when it comes to their justification heeding the criteria of reciprocity and generality. Reciprocity means that no one may make demands he or she denies to others and no one may impose his or her non-generalizable views, interests or values on others. Generality means that all those over whom norms claim to be valid have to be equally involved.

Human rights are not simply general moral rights, but a subset of reciprocally and generally justifiable rights that establish the status of persons as equal normative authorities within a normative order and protect persons from being subject to legal, political or social domination. These rights are based on the basic right to justification, which in this context means to be the co-author of all the justifiable rights and duties that apply to you. This is the equivalent of Kant's innate right to freedom (and rights) under generally justifiable law. But the formulation of the right to justification captures the ideas of equal personhood under law and of being a political co-author of laws, as well as the status of being free from social domination in a more complex way than in Kant's version.

4   Constructing Human Rights

Given what I said so far, I shall define the *concept* of human rights such that they are morally grounded, legally and politically guaranteed rights of free and equal persons who have a basic claim not to be socially or politically dominated or mistreated by states or other agents, and – what is of particular importance – to be the normative authorities of the regime of rights and duties they are subject to.[17] Human rights reflect the insight that the status of being free and equal and not being subjected to the arbitrary power of others needs to be secured by law in a twofold sense: the persons in question must be both the authors and the addressees of the law. Thus, these rights are justified horizontally as those rights that free and equal normative authorities could not deny each other; based on that, they have a vertical justification as rights that no political or social agent or institution may violate and which the state must secure. Their moral core consists in the fact that they confer the status of being a justificatory equal who must not be subjected to others' domination; and their justification lies in identifying those rights that are necessary to secure that egalitarian status in the social world. This implies rights to life, liberty, security, to social and material resources and to the political co-determination of the rights and duties you have.

This approach stresses the moral core of mutual respect essential for human rights, as well as their particular subset function, namely to include only those rights that are required for being secure as a non-dominated, free and equal person in the social and political realm. Classical 'liberal' rights protect this status as much as political rights or social rights that provide protection against political or social domination. This view implies non-arbitrary guidelines for the way in which a specific *conception* of human rights has to be constructed, namely by way of a discursive construction in which all those subjected are involved as justificatory agents – in practice as well as in a critical counterfactual dimension. This means that any conception of human rights for a particular context needs to be justified in a discursive manner guided by the criteria of reciprocity and generality, where no one – to repeat these criteria – may make a claim he or she denies to others (reciprocity of content) and where no one may impose his or her interests, needs, perspective or convictions on others who could reasonably reject these (reciprocity of reasons). Finally, no subjected person may be excluded from the relevant justification community (generality).

Several contexts of such constructions of human rights need to be distinguished. The first context in which a conception of human rights is to be justified is the moral-political context of a basic list of general human rights which contains all the rights that, given human experience of various forms of domination thus far, would be non-deniable between free and equal persons who share a political and legal order. The reference to historical experience is important, as every concrete conception of human rights is the result of an open-ended learning process; again, there is no deduction or derivation of human rights based on the foundation of the right to justification. The list of human rights is the product of a discursive construction and is necessary as a major reference point for any dispute over whether a certain right is actually a human right. As much as these rights are required in particular, concrete contexts, they must have a moral basis, and if they do, there is a list of such basic rights that substantiate the normative core concept named above. This list is general and vague and needs to be discursively concretized through political-legal constructions; yet, at a universal level, a general moral-political conception of these rights is indispensable. A severe dispute over human rights always goes back to this level.[18] The construction of that basic conception of human rights is and remains a moral-political, reflexive matter; in this form of constructivism, we gather and test the best moral arguments for certain rights to secure the standing of persons who are free from domination and are equal normative political-legal authorities within their normative order.

The second context of constructing a conception of human rights is the political context of a state that has the task of securing basic human rights and also of ensuring that the concrete determination and interpretation of these rights is justifiable to all those subject to it. This does not mean to merely 'apply' or 'mirror'[19] a fixed set of morally preconstructed human rights; rather, the political constructions of basic rights on this level determine and interpret what it means in a given political community to have freedom of speech, the right to political participation, to a decent social status and so on. Human rights are determined by way of discursive political constructivism here, and it is important to note that this is a democratic, moral-political form of justification by the participants themselves. When it comes to basic rights, all must be involved in the determination of these rights as political equals and as critical participants who think reflexively about their own status and that of others, and who may transcend given legal and political forms in order to improve them. So human rights are at the same time the ground for such constructions as they are their result: in abstract form, they are the ground for such constructions because the general moral-political conception provides the justificatory background for any legal-political determination, both in procedure and substance, such that a political community has to determine what it means to realize and secure rights no person can justifiably be denied (which includes the rights of non-members). The result is a concrete conception of human rights for a political community. However, this conception must be in tune with the general moral conception and must be criticizable from that standpoint. Non-deniable core human rights provide something like a discursive veto against unjustifiable constructions of basic rights: persons or groups thus have the normative power to reject a determination of a basic right – say, of gender equality – when a majority in a political community believes that, for example, forced marriage is in line with this general right, or when a political community thinks that it can ban minarets and still respect the human right to religious liberty. In every such political context, non-arbitrary forms of legal interpretation and adjudication of basic rights disputes have to be devised; this is implied by the human right to be protected as a person with equal legal standing.

While there are many such political contexts of discursive construction where participatory equals determine their normative order in a non-arbitrary and constructivist way, being open to reflexive improvement and critique, another moral-political construction is taking place on the international and supranational levels. This is the third context to be analysed. Here the construction of a conception of human rights is required that is laid down in international declarations, treaties and covenants, where these norms – and possible sanctions for violating them – are understood to be legally binding. In these contexts, the agents of construction are states with particular conceptions of basic rights as well as persons who make particular claims, possibly dissenting from their states' conceptions. The conceptions to be found on this international level therefore may reflect a thinner notion of human rights as compared to the political conceptions within states. Thus, for example, no particular model of democratic organization can be formulated here apart from the general right to democratic participation. Yet, that there is such a right must be stressed within the general moral conception as well as all particular political conceptions and the international conception. Otherwise, the point of human rights – namely, not to be forced to live in a normative order where you are not part of the relevant justification authority as a justificatory equal – would be lost. At this level, a reflection on which rights violations ought to lead to which sanctions, and by which prior procedure and through which agent, needs to be included. Yet it is a mistake to combine this reflection with the basic arguments for human rights on any of the other levels.

I cannot go into further details at this point about such an institutional scheme of international sanctions or into a more detailed discussion of the general list of human rights and how, from that angle, the meaning of such rights changes, given that the persons who claim these rights are seen as active political agents and not just as subjects to be protected or nourished. Just to give one example: the right to social goods such as food, housing and medicine is then no longer primarily a right to certain means of subsistence, but is a right to a social standing as an equal at least to the extent of being a full member of society and not an easy victim of social exploitation.

Above all, the reflexive point of human rights needs to be kept in mind: if human rights are essentially founded on the basic right to be secure in the status of being a normative authority free from political and social domination and co-determining the normative order one is subject to, then they must be rights constructed by their bearers themselves. This has implications both for the concept and for the various conceptions (and how they are interpreted). It means that human rights protect and express the autonomy of free and equal law-givers and law-addressees. This account is equally true to the historical meaning and function of human rights, to past and contemporary political struggles for human rights and to a moral and transcendental grounding indicated by such terms as 'human dignity'. That grounding is of a reflexive nature: if we look for a firm basis for reciprocally and generally justified human rights, the very principle of reciprocal and general justification and the right to justification is the right place to look for such a ground.[20]

References

Alexy, R. 2010. *A Theory of Constitutional Rights*, trans. J. Rivers. Oxford: Oxford University Press.

Beitz, C. R. 2009. *The Idea of Human Rights*. Oxford: Oxford University Press.

Beitz, C. R. 2013. 'Human Dignity in the Theory of Human Rights: Nothing But a Phrase?', *Philosophy & Public Affairs* 41(3): 259–290.

Benhabib, S. 2011. *Dignity in Adversity: Human Rights in Troubled Times*. Cambridge: Polity.

Besson, S. 2015. 'Human Rights and Constitutional Law: Patterns of Mutual Validation and Legitimation', in R. Cruft, M. Liao and M. Renzo, eds., *Philosophical Foundations of Human Rights*, 279–299. Oxford: Oxford University Press.

Bloch, E. 1986. *Natural Law and Human Dignity*, trans. D. F. Schmidt. Cambridge, MA: MIT Press.

Buchanan, A. 2013. *The Heart of Human Rights*. Oxford: Oxford University Press.

Flikschuh, K. 2015. 'Human Rights in Kantian Mode. A Sketch', in R. Cruft, M. Liao and M. Renzo, eds., *Philosophical Foundations of Human Rights*, 653–670. Oxford: Oxford University Press.

Forst, R. 2012. *The Right to Justification: Elements of a Constructivist Theory of Justice*, trans. J. Flynn. New York: Columbia University Press.

Forst, R. 2013. 'A Kantian Republican Conception of Justice as Non-domination', in A. Niederberger and P. Schink, eds., *Republican Democracy*, 154–168. Edinburgh: Edinburgh University Press.

Forst, R. 2014. *Justification and Critique: Towards a Critical Theory of Politics*, trans. C. Cronin. Cambridge: Polity.

Forst, R. 2015. 'Transnational Justice and Non-Domination: A Discourse-Theoretical Approach', in B. Buckinx, J. Trejo-Mathys and T. Waligore, eds., *Domination Across Borders*, 88–110. New York: Routledge.

Forst, R. forthcoming. 'Human Rights in Context: A Comment on Sangiovanni', in A. Etinson, ed., *Human Rights: Moral or Political?* Oxford: Oxford University Press.

Gauchet, M. 1995. *Die Erklärung der Menschenrechte. Die Debatte um die bürgerlichen Freiheiten 1789*. Reinbek: Rowohlt Verlag.

Gearty, C. 2014. 'Human Rights: The Necessary Quest for Foundations', in C. Douzinas and C. Gearty, eds., *The Meanings of Rights. The Philosophy and Social Theory of Human Rights*, 21–38. Cambridge: Cambridge University Press.

Griffin, J. 2008. *On Human Rights*. Oxford: Oxford University Press.

Günther, K. 2009. 'Menschenrechte zwischen Staaten und Dritten', in N. Deitelhoff and J. Steffek, eds., *Was bleibt vom Staat? Demokratie, Recht und Verfassung im globalen Zeitlater*, 259–280. Frankfurt/M.: Campus.

Habermas, J. 1974. 'Natural Right and Revolution', in *Theory and Practice*, trans. J. Viertel, 82–120. London: Heinemann Educational Books.

Habermas, J. 1996. *Between Facts and Norms: Contributions to a Discourse Theory of Law and Democracy*, trans. W. Rehg. Cambridge, MA: MIT Press.

Habermas, J. 2010. 'The Concept of Human Dignity and the Realistic Utopia of Human Rights', *Metaphilosophy* 41(4): 464–480.

Hunt, L. 2008. *Inventing Human Rights: A History*. New York: Norton.

Ignatieff, M. 2001. *Human Rights as Politics and Idolatry*. Princeton, NJ: Princeton University Press.

Jellinek, G. 2011. *System der subjektiven öffentlichen Rechte*. Tübingen: Mohr Siebeck.

Kant, I. 1997. *Groundwork of the Metaphysics of Morals*, ed. and trans. M. Gregor. Cambridge: Cambridge University Press (citations are according to the Academy edition).

Kant, I. 2009. *The Metaphysics of Morals*, ed. and trans. M. Gregor. Cambridge: Cambridge University Press (citations are according to the Academy edition).

Kateb, G. 2011. *Human Dignity*. Cambridge, MA: Belknap Press.

Khalil, K. 2011. *Messages from Tahrir: Signs from Egypt's Revolution*. Cairo and New York: American University in Cairo Press.

McCrudden, C., ed. 2013. *Understanding Human Dignity*. Oxford: Oxford University Press.

Moyn, S. 2012. *The Last Utopia: Human Rights in History*. Cambridge, MA: Harvard University Press.

O'Neill, O. 1989. *Constructions of Reason: Explorations of Kant's Practical Philosophy*. Cambridge, MA: Cambridge University Press.

Ratner, S. 2015. *The Thin Justice of International Law. A Moral Reckoning of the Law of Nations*. Oxford: Oxford University Press.

Rawls, J. 1980. 'Kantian Constructivism in Moral Theory', *Journal of Philosophy* 77(9): 515–572.

Rawls, J. 1993. *Political Liberalism*. New York: Columbia University Press.

Raz, J. 1986. *The Morality of Freedom*. Oxford: Clarendon Press.

Raz, J. 2015. 'Human Rights in the Emerging World Order', in R. Cruft, M. Liao and M. Renzo, eds., *Philosophical Foundations of Human Rights*, 217–231. Oxford: Oxford University Press.

Ripstein, A. 2009. *Force and Freedom: Kant's Legal and Political Philosophy*. Cambridge, MA: Harvard University Press.

Rosen, M. 2012. *Dignity: Its History and Meaning*. Cambridge, MA: Harvard University Press.

Sangiovanni, A. 2015. 'Why there Cannot be a Truly Kantian Theory of Human Rights', in R. Cruft, M. Liao and M. Renzo, eds., *Philosophical Foundations of Human Rights*, 671–690. Oxford: Oxford University Press.

Sangiovanni, A. forthcoming. 'A Third Account of Human Rights: The Broad View', in A. Etinson, ed., *Human Rights: Moral or Political?* Oxford: Oxford University Press.

Talbott, W. 2005. *Which Rights Should Be Universal?* Oxford: Oxford University Press.

Talbott, W. 2010. *Human Rights and Human Well-Being*. Oxford: Oxford University Press.

Tully, J. 2014. 'Two Traditions of Human Rights', in M. Lutz-Bachmann and A. Nascimento, eds., *Human Rights, Human Dignity, and Cosmopolitan Ideals. Essays on Critical Theory and Human Rights*, 139–158. London: Ashgate.

Waldron, J. 2012. *Dignity, Rank, and Rights*. Oxford: Oxford University Press.

Waldron, J. 2015. 'Is Dignity a Foundation of Human Rights?', in R. Cruft, M. Liao and M. Renzo, eds., *Philosophical Foundations of Human Rights*, 117–137. Oxford: Oxford University Press.

Ypi, L. 2012. *Global Justice and Avant-Garde Political Agency*. Oxford: Oxford University Press.

CHAPTER TWO

Global Distributive Justice: The Statist View

Michael Blake

All philosophical labels are problematic, but *statist* is perhaps more problematic than most. Why should anyone put states at the heart of their thinking about global justice? It is a philosophical commonplace that theories of justice that have stood the test of time are, at their heart, interpretations of a common ideal: that of the moral equality of persons (Dworkin, 1987, 2000; Sen, 1992). Those of us who care about this ideal have good reason to examine how the notion of equality of persons might be understood at the global level, rather than simply within the confines of a territorial state. Why, then, would anyone focus on *states* – those arbitrary, bureaucratic and frequently violent political bodies – rather than directly on persons? Is a *statist* view not silly at best, and morally perverse at worst?

This chapter will show how the statist viewpoint can defend itself against natural criticisms such as these. It will not attempt to offer a dispositive defence of the statist view as superior to its opponents, real or potential; such a task would require more space than is available here. This chapter will, instead, try to do something comparatively more modest: it will define what constitutes a statist view of global distributive justice, and offer some reasons to think that such a view is capable of presenting itself as a reasonable and attractive view of global politics. Far from being immediately ruled out by a global ideal of moral equality, it is instead a particular interpretation *of* that ideal – one on which people who share liability to a common state owe each other particular duties of justice, precisely because the equality of persons would command those particular duties be applied in that context. If there is a primary thesis to this chapter, it is this: that the statist view is, rightly understood, a particular vision of what the global equality of persons entails. It is not incompatible with the equality of persons, but one particular vision of what that equality would demand. A secondary thesis, though, would call the entire notion of statism into question. Dividing the world of theorists into *statists* and *cosmopolitans* only makes sense in a particular argumentative context, in which philosophers are primarily interested in whether or not the egalitarian distributive norms developed within the domestic context hold equal sway within the global context. Increasingly, I think, we are beginning to ask more complex questions than this one; and, accordingly, we may require more fine-grained philosophical taxonomies than those offered by labels such as statist.

I will make this case in three parts. The first will offer a preliminary definition of statism, and make some initial remarks about what that label entails. The second will discuss several dilemmas with which any statist will have to come to terms, along with some difficulties common to all statist views. The final section will discuss three prominent forms of statism – those views that begin with, respectively, community, cooperation and coercion – and will provide some ideas about difficulties encountered by these forms of statism.

1 Statism: Definitions and Implications

We might begin, then, by examining the concept of statism itself. What marks out a view of global justice generally – and of global distributive justice in particular – as a statist view? There is, to my knowledge, no canonical definition of statism; there is no particular text nor thinker who can be put forward as the founder of statism, nor one who has defined its boundaries. What there is, instead, is a broad agreement as to who can be *categorized* as a statist about distributive justice. The definition I favour is one that begins with the question of those individuals over whom comparative principles of distributive justice hold sway. Theorists of justice, after all, must decide at the outset about the boundaries of the group within which comparative principles of distributive justice will have normative force; Arash Abizadeh (2007) calls this the *scope* of distributive justice, while A. J. Julius (2008) simply calls it 'the justice relationship'. If this is taken as our first question, then a statist is properly defined as someone for whom the most stringent norms of distributive justice are restricted in their application to fellow members of a territorial state. This is compatible, of course, with some other duties – often, but not always, focusing on absolute well-being, rather than on relative distributive shares – holding in the global context (see Blake, 2013b). The key, though, is that the statist reserves the most powerful – and, in general, egalitarian – duties for use in the domestic context. In contrast, those views understood as *cosmopolitan*, in the context of global distributive justice, insist that the most powerful duties – understood, again, in terms of some duty towards equalization in some particular space – must be applicable at the global level.

We can take this, then, as a rough definition of a statist, for purposes of our discussion: a statist is someone for whom the most stringent comparative duties of distributive justice must be applied within the state, rather than at the global or international level. There are, I think, several things that might be noticed right away. The first is that the statist view is associativist; it argues that some particular form of association is a prerequisite for the application of the norms of egalitarian distributive justice (see Gilabert, 2012). Not all associativists are statists, in the sense discussed here; some figures have used associativist ideas to ground powerful global duties of distribution (see, in particular, Beitz, 1979; Pogge, 1989, 2002; Moellendorf, 2009). Nor are all views understood as *cosmopolitan*, in the distributive sense, associativist; some theorists have pushed forcefully for the idea that no particular association is required before duties of distributive justice are applicable (see, in particular, Tan, 2004; Caney, 2006; Gilabert, 2012). All statist views, though, are associativist views, and the association they take to be most central for distributive purposes is that of fellow citizenship before the state.

A second thing to note, though, is that it is not always a simple matter to describe a particular view as *statist* or as *cosmopolitan*. There are, of course, views that are easily ascribed to one camp or another; a view like Thomas Nagel's (2005), on which there are no duties of justice towards non-citizens, clearly counts as statist, given its stark contrast between duties within the state and duties outside it. (It is, for that matter, possible to find a relatively pure cosmopolitan, in which all notions of local duties are morally suspect; see Nussbaum's (1994) discussion of the Greek cynics.) Most theorists, though, have more complex moral analyses, and include multiple theoretical stories, on which there may be *both* reasons to insist upon distributive principles within the state, *and* powerful distributive norms that must be applied transnationally. Simon Caney, for example, is generally understood as a cosmopolitan, but accepts the principle that distinct duties of distributive justice might apply only within the contours of the territorial state; these duties will be distinct from powerful norms of transnational justice, but for all that they will not be negligible (Caney, 2008). Mathias Risse (2012), in contrast, is often taken as a statist, but includes state-based duties of distributive justice held only between fellow citizens as compatible with global duties of redistribution that begin with territorial rights, the imposition of a global financial system, membership in the global order and, indeed, common humanity itself. I believe what this should tell us is that the simple vision of statism described above – in which a statist is one who places demanding duties of distributive justice at the state level, while the cosmopolitan does so at the global level – is increasingly an oversimplification of the true range of theoretical disagreement (Blake, 2013a). If we are to keep the label *statist*, and use it to discuss present theories, I think it is best to keep in mind that this label is best understood as a range conception; to the extent that a given view insists upon more demanding distributive duties in the local context than in the global one, that view is rightly understood as statist. In contrast with pregnancy, for example, it *is* possible to be just a little bit statist.

The third thing I would highlight about the label *statist* is that there is no inherent contradiction between the statist and the *moral* cosmopolitan. We must be careful with the use of the term *cosmopolitan*: on one construction – which I will call the distributive cosmopolitan view – it implies an explicit rejection of statism. On this vision, the most powerful egalitarian norms of distributive justice must apply at the global, rather than the local, level. Another version of cosmopolitanism, though, refers to moral norms, rather than to norms of distribution or institutional design. The moral cosmopolitan, on one influential definition, insists upon the idea that *all* people matter; that *only* people (rather than collectives, or institutions) matter *directly*; and that people should be the focus of attention for *everyone* (Sangiovanni, 2007; see also Pogge, 1992). This definition, though, is not incompatible with a view that those who share liability to the state may have distinct duties towards one another. Indeed, the core of the moral cosmopolitan ideal is that like cases must be treated as like; a moral cosmopolitan must, on pain of absurdity, admit that the individual to whom I have made a promise must be treated by me as unlike the individual to whom I have not made a promise. Saying this, though, acknowledges that the specific things we have done to one another can make a difference in what we owe to one another. This is not hostile to moral equality; it is, instead, what it means to respect that equality in practice. The one to whom I have made a promise has special rights to insist upon my compliance – rights not held by humanity generally – and this fact does not tell against the idea that people are alike in moral dignity. So, too, with the state, on the statist view. If there is something special that we do to one another when we share a state with them, then we have special duties to those individuals, ones not shared with humanity generally. To move beyond the distributive context: it is a grave injustice if a French citizen resident in France is not permitted to vote in French elections. It is not obviously unjust, though, for a resident of Seattle, with no legal relationship to the polity of France, to be so excluded. The cosmopolitan might disagree; the onus is on her, though, to explain why there is any moral reason here to think that such local duties are inherently unjust. But these local duties are not understood by the statist as denials of moral equality; they are instead, particular instantiations of what that ideal means. The statist, then, is likely to regard herself as entitled to use both the terms *cosmopolitan* and *statist* to apply to her own view, so long as the cosmopolitan here is understood in the moral sense. The *cosmopolitan about distributive justice* may regard her view as implied by her moral cosmopolitanism; the statist, though, may rightly understand her own view to be equally grounded in the equality of persons.

Particular (distributive) cosmopolitans have, of course, attempted to block this purported move, and so have sought exclusive rights to the legacy of moral cosmopolitanism. Thomas Pogge (2013) has suggested that moral cosmopolitanism would require direct political instantiation, with individual agents whose responsibility as political actors is to the globe, rather than to any particular society. Kok-Chor Tan (2013), in contrast, has argued that only a view that insists upon the equality of some particular good at the global level could count as *cosmopolitan* – and, on this view, no statist view could ever count as cosmopolitan, whether moral or otherwise. These arguments are, though, seemingly rather stipulative; they often depend upon unstated assumptions about the limits of possibility or the nature of moral equality – and the statist can speak back to each. A statist might think that a world in which there is no global government, but instead a loose federation of just democracies, would provide all humans with what moral cosmopolitanism demands. Pogge's response to this seems simply to assert that no such beast would be possible. Tan's view, similarly, seems simply to assert that there must be some defeasible link between moral equality and equality of some particular good; this linkage, though, will appear wrong to those of us who think that the space between moral equality and equality of *stuff* must be argued for. Other lines might be adduced, of course, but I am inclined to think they would not fare much better. My conclusion, then, is that statism is entitled to regard itself as a particular vision of the equality of persons: the idea that individuals owe especially strong duties of distributive justice to all and only their fellow citizens may or may not be *right*, but it cannot be rejected simply by pointing to the equality of persons. Those who want to dismiss statism, then, will have to do more than simply compare it with cosmopolitanism.

The final thing I want to notice about statism is the simple fact that this term arises in a particular context, at a particular time. I mean to highlight, here, not that the term arises in a world in which there are states, although that much is true; it would be difficult to be a statist before the emergence of the state system. I mean, instead, to note that the term arises in a context in which there was a central research question guiding much of our philosophical argumentation: namely, do the norms of distributive justice as we understand them apply in the global context? If this is our question, then it makes sense to divide theorists into two groups: those who say *yes* are termed cosmopolitan, and those who say *no* are termed statist. The problem, though, is that this is not the only question we might have asked to guide our research. The question is, in particular, rather limited in how it conceives of even domestic justice; alternative perspectives on distributive justice, such as the libertarian, are not even possible to conceive of in terms such as *cosmopolitan* or *statist*. What, after all, would it mean for a libertarian to be a statist? Debates on global distributive justice began largely with the question of whether Rawls's principles of distributive justice could be scaled up to the globe, and libertarian views were simply ruled off the table (Hassoun, 2014, is a welcome exception to this). More centrally, though, it seems now as if many figures in global justice are arguing for distinct forms of duties at the global and domestic levels, so that there can be duties of global justice that are not simply the scaled version of the domestic duties, but which are significant and powerful sources of normativity. Mathias Risse (2012), as discussed above, identifies several distinct grounds of distributive justice, many of which work at the global and transnational levels; he refers to this as 'pluralist internationalism', which explicitly implies a rejection of the statist-versus-cosmopolitan distinction. Helena de Bres (2012), similarly, calls for pluralism about global justice, rejecting both the statist privileging of the state, and the cosmopolitan refusal to take the state seriously as a source of moral duty. The term *statist*, in sum, may now be the product of a debate whose time is rapidly departing. In this respect, I think the term is a bit like the label *communitarian*, as used in a previous generation of theorizing. A communitarian, we might think, is someone who – in that previous decade – emphasized the moral importance of culture, the local community and the unchosen ties of place and language. A liberal, in contrast, was someone who emphasized legal and moral equality before the state. Our reaction now, of course, is to insist that a valid analysis of political morality must include *both* of these. Few of us who write political philosophy now think that the concerns of the communitarians, or of their opponents, can be safely ignored. We want, instead, something that includes *both* equality *and* community. So too, I think, with statism. Increasingly, I think we are inclined to demand that a valid theory of global political justice must include *both* global duties of justice *and* particular duties that begin within the context of the state.

We may, then, have arrived at the doorstep of what might be called a *post-statist* view of global distributive justice. I do not think, though, that we are entirely there yet, and, for the purposes of this chapter, I will continue to use *statist* in the manner discussed above – to refer, that is, to those theories of global distributive justice that make the most powerful norms of distributive justice applicable only within the context of the state. Even if my worries about the term are true, after all, *statism* might continue to be a useful taxonomic shorthand for a particular sort of tendency within thinking about global justice. So: let's imagine that a statist view can be identified. What must the holder of such a view come to terms with, in order to vindicate – or, more minimally, explain – her view, and its appeal?

2   Statism: Questions and Difficulties

So: we may take statism as involving the claim that the most powerful and most egalitarian duties of distributive justice will be found within the context of the domestic state; these duties are distinct from whatever duties might be found within other forms of association, or between people considered simply as human beings. What, then, must a statist explain, in order to fully explicate her view?

In this section, I will examine three such questions and indicate three broad corresponding categories of criticism, each of which must be dealt with for the statist to explain how her view succeeds. Each question asks the statist to explain her view of the international realm. The first is perhaps rarely asked explicitly, but is enormously significant: are states, as we know them, inevitable? What I mean by this question is that a full description of the statist project must explain whether the existence of the state system itself is a proper subject of normative theorizing. Many theorists, after all, would regard the issue of what sorts of institution there ought to be as the first, and most important, question of global political philosophy. Institutional cosmopolitans, for instance, might defend the proposition that some forms of global government, mirroring to a greater or lesser degree the attributes of a territorial state, ought to be brought into existence for justice to be possible at the global level (see Cabrera, 2005; see also Ronzoni, 2009). Is the statist, to put it bluntly, committed to the eternal presence of *states*?

There are, of course, different answers to these questions, and different statists will find different answers appealing. Some theorists will regard states as inevitable, and morally necessary. Anna Stilz (2011), for instance, argues that a state is required for the abstract moral rights of Kantian politics to be given lived form and particular content. Mathias Risse (2012), in contrast, simply notes the absence of any viable alternative to the territorial state, and the enormous risks we would take by innovating in the absence of a clear vision. Other statists, though, are more open in principle to the possibility that the state system itself might eventually be utterly transformed; they regard their acceptance of the state system as reflecting the need for political guidance in our present circumstances, not a demand that circumstances such as these continue forever (Rawls, 1999; James 2005; Blake, 2013b). Neither answer is obviously ruled out by the statist vision, nor by liberalism itself; nonetheless, there are potential costs that are invoked by this insistence on the continued existence of states, as I will shortly discuss.

The second question to be asked involves the nature of agency in the transnational world. This question is perhaps more difficult to get a precise handle on – but one way of doing so is to ask whether global institutions, in the forms in which they exist right now, ought to be considered as political agents in their own right, or as something else. Think, for instance, of a global hegemonic superpower that simply sets the terms of trade for others, but which creates a nominally independent treaty body through which this task is accomplished. Is that treaty body a political agent, to which duties of justice apply, or is it simply the letterhead on which the superpower writes the rules that other societies must follow? Which way we answer, of course, may make a difference as to what moral conclusions follow. We would not, for example, think that the world described here is *just* in either case – but *why* it is unjust would be rather different in the two cases, and the appropriate agent to which principles of justice apply would be different as well. Some statists regard states as the primary agents of international politics, to the exclusion of most other forms of agency (Rawls, 1999; Freeman, 2006a; Blake, 2013b). Other statists are willing to accept a plurality of agents, but regard the state as having unique and central importance (Valentini, 2011; Risse, 2012). A statist can, in other words, be more or less open to the possibility that nonstate agents genuinely exist as agents to which principles of justice can directly apply. Taking this possibility seriously, of course, would require a fundamental change in the methods and questions of political philosophy; we would have reason to ask about how justice constrains not only explicitly political bodies like states, but also complex forms of association such as corporations and NGOs. A statist is not precluded from asking these questions; her commitment is to the idea that the state is a central form of human association – not that it is the only relevant one.

The third question I want to ask is the most important of all: why do states matter, in the manner statists assume? Again, it is clear that not all statists will have the same story about why states matter; one can be a statist while still disagreeing with other statists about what is special about the territorial state. The important thing, though, is that the statist is able to explain *why* the state matters, and why those who share liability to that state have distinct duties of distributive justice. This question is important enough that I will give it its own section, below. For the moment, I want to note something else about this question: those opposed to statism may simply reject the bare possibility of any statist story being morally persuasive. It is open to those who are hostile to the possibility of shared citizenship's being relevant to distributive justice to simply reject all such stories at the outset.

This is, perhaps, a good point at which to shift gear, and examine some common difficulties with statist arguments. I will here discuss only three difficulties, each of which corresponds with the questions discussed above. These difficulties are charges that statism is inevitably *conservative*, in an objectionable way; that it is descriptively *inaccurate* for the world in which we live; and that it is morally *perverse*. These arguments are not, of course, exclusive – the borders between them are somewhat porous – but they represent ideal types of common charges against which a statist must defend herself.

We can start with the idea of conservatism. As discussed above, the statist must have some story about why we have no need to challenge the division of the world's population into sovereign and independent states, of wildly varying power, size and population. Some statists will regard the state as a necessary part of any legitimate system of governance; others will simply accept that it is part of *our* world, and that theories that abstract away from that fact will be less useful than those that do not. It is open to the statist's opponent, though, to simply reject the thought that either of these is sufficient to justify the statist reliance upon the continued existence of states. Some theorists, then, will simply regard the statist as having begged the most important questions about global justice, by assuming a world in which justice could not possibly hold sway (Cabrera, 2005; see also Held, 2010). The statist, of course, can simply rely on the reasons she has chosen to assume the continued existence of the state; but at some point it seems likely that we ought to regard the debate between the statist and her opponent as relying on competing visions of the purposes of political theory, or competing visions of what is attainable in the realm of practical politics, or both (Blake, 2012). The charge here, though, is one the statist must find a way to address: why is it necessary for our theorizing to begin with states, when we might instead decide whether or not we even want such creatures to exist?

The second broad criticism of statism begins with the second question discussed above – that of international agency. Many statists believe that nonstate institutions in the world right now are, in Samuel Freeman's words, 'secondary' institutions, whose powers and acts are rightly attributed to states (Freeman, 2006b; see also Blake, 2013b). If our first criticism argued that the state focus reveals a lack of imagination, the second criticism argues that this story ignores the reality of the world in which we are now situated. Allen Buchanan (2000) captures this thought nicely, describing Rawls's statist vision in *The Law of Peoples* as a set of rules for a vanished Westphalian world. Others, such as Josh Cohen and Charles Sabel (2006), have broadened this analysis, to describe the ways in which much of the content of domestic law is influenced by (and in some cases utterly determined by) transnational deliberative bodies (see also Julius, 2008). If the world right now contains rulemaking bodies at both the domestic and international levels, goes this argument, then it is simply wrong to think that there is something special about the state that licenses distributive duties only between residents of that state. This is, again, a powerful worry about the statist vision. It is not, of course, a dispositive disproof of statism itself. Statists can say that their opponents here have perhaps overestimated the power and independence of transnational bodies; even the United Nations, the most nominally inde-pendent and powerful transnational entity, depends upon states for its funding, and grants veto rights to those states that were victorious during the Second World War. In light of facts like these, it is open to the statist to argue that the independence of transnational bodies has been rather exag-gerated. The United Nations, after all, has no independent executive power, nor its own military, nor even its own financial resources, except insofar as states provide (Blake, 2013b). All this, though, points to one central truth about the dispute between statists and their opponents: much of this debate will turn upon empirical political science, and so will depend upon the con-tributions of empirical political scientists. The statist must, if it turns out that the world is fundamentally unlike what she thinks it is, adjust her view. Her only consolation, of course, is that the same must be true for her oppo-nent. It is worth noting, finally, that these two criticisms are strikingly similar: both involve the idea that the statist has fundamentally misread the set of possibilities open to us, by misreading what we might do together, or by misreading what we have – at the global level – already built together. They might be answered together by the statist, as well, either by insisting that we have moral reason to privilege a world of states, or that the world we have built is perhaps more state-focused than the cosmopolitan some-times supposes.

The third broad category of objection to statism is the most basic; namely, the idea that there is a deep perversity in the attempt to ground the most powerful norms of distributive justice in arbitrary facts such as nationality and shared citizenship. Many theorists have sought to reject statism even before a justification for the moral importance of the state could be brought forward, by arguing against any possible justification. Simon Caney (2006), for example, has argued that any plausible theory of justice must be 'human-centered'; it must not allow the course of human lives to be determined by arbitrary forms of human relationship (see also Gilabert, 2012). More recently, Kok-Chor Tan (2012) argued that the egalitarian impulse ought to be applied to all forms of human institution, and that any form of human institution that transforms human difference into human disadvantage is presumptively wrong. Views such as these would, in distinct ways, argue that we need not even ask the question about what the state is; we need only see that the world as a whole has winners and losers, and that the distribution of these is not made in accordance with any defensible norms of justice. The statist can, of course, argue against these views; many statists would, indeed, regard views like Caney's and Tan's as simply relying upon an unpromising notion of why (and when) inequality matters (Blake and Risse, 2008). The fact remains, though, that this objection must be addressed, and addressed by all statists.

These three worries about statism, then, are standing difficulties with the statist vision. They will form the backdrop of many more specific worries about particular forms of statism. My own view is that the statist project is capable of defending itself against these charges; I have given some reason for thinking that this defence is possible. What I want to do now is examine some more specific forms of statism, to see how particular statists have developed their methodologies.

3   Three Forms of Statism: Community, Cooperation and Coercion

The third question asked above – what, exactly, is so special about the state? – is one that has proven to be an essential part of any statist view. The statist owes us an account of what it is about the state that allows these demanding norms of distributive justice to be ascribed within, but not without, that state's jurisdictional limits. There are, of course, any number of possible answers; I will focus here only on three particularly influential ones. We can call these, respectively, the argument from community, the argument from cooperation and the argument from coercion. These are not, it should be noted, entirely distinct from one another; an advocate of one argument may well be attracted to the others, and some theorists may not fit neatly within any particular category. Nevertheless, these forms of argument seem to describe three important forms of justification for the statist project, and the rest of this chapter will focus on how these arguments work – and on how they might be challenged.

We can begin with the argument from community. The argument here begins with some thought that abstract liberalism – understood in the universalist terms its proponents often employ – is simply too abstract and bloodless a vessel on which to rest the institutions and duties that are required for the adequate protection of human lives. This is, of course, susceptible to being interpreted in different ways. Some theorists, like David Miller, have argued that the particular moral vocabulary and traditions of a particular community must be supported and defended from within that community; accordingly, it is morally right that this community's traditions be made the subject of duties of support and allegiance not applicable to humanity generally (Miller, 1995, 2008). This particularism can be phrased in terms of the development of a particular form of moral language and moral community, as it is both in Miller's work and that of Michael Walzer (Walzer, 1986). Other forms of particularism, though, might begin instead from the simple need for a community to gain adherents to its particular projects and local rules. Anna Stilz (2011), as discussed above, argues that the state must be the subject of particular duties held only by members, given the need in the modern state for particularistic affiliation with that state for it to flourish. These ideas, of course, are often part of a wider project, that of the nationalist rejection of abstract liberalism (Taylor, 1989; Tamir, 1993), but they can also serve to ground a rejection of the distributive cosmopolitan position, as they do in both Stilz and Miller. In both cases, the argument comes down to the legitimacy of particularistic duty, and the inadequacy of cosmopolitan duty to provide what is needed for politics as a lived experience to continue and flourish over time.

The argument from community is susceptible to several criticisms. Some of these echo what has been said above: the moral cosmopolitan who is not associativist, in particular, is likely to simply reject the thought that particularist attachments are all that morally fundamental. More broadly, though, these tendencies might be rejected by a liberal who is convinced that the link between the *state* and the *community* is drawn rather closer in the statist's theory than it is in reality. It is, after all, rarely true that the borders of a state link up neatly with the borders of a discursive community; most existing states contain plural communities of discourse within themselves, and the idea of the nation-state is an abstraction more than an empirical truth (Kymlicka, 1995). Why, then, should we think that we have reason to favour our own fellow citizens, in virtue of these supposed obligations to support the members of our own discursive communities? The statist whose statism begins with community can reply to these worries, of course – it is, after all, enormously difficult to run a democratic society unless *some* forms of linguistic or cultural practice are held in common (Song, 2012). The argument, though, continues. The relationship between the felt communities of language and culture, on the one hand, and the legal community of the state, on the other, is a vexed one, and both statists and their opponents have had occasion to examine this relationship in recent years.

The argument from community is susceptible to being understood as an argument for the legitimacy of partiality – although many of its proponents would instead regard it as circumscribing the boundaries within which impartiality has moral weight (Miller, 1995). The next two arguments, though, are not even capable of being understood as arguments for partiality; they are, instead, arguments that the best notion of impartiality includes particular (and particularly demanding) duties of justice within the state. The argument from community, that is, emphasizes duties of justice as special duties, more powerful than any universal duties we might insist upon between humans. The arguments from cooperation and from coercion are subtly different; they argue that particular duties of justice are, in fact, the form taken by universal duties of justice within particular contexts. The difference, roughly, is that between a permissible favouritism, and a complex and contextual analysis of what the absence of favouritism would demand.

We can start, then, by looking at the argument from cooperation. The idea that animates this vision of statism is that the state itself is not an entity, but a practice; it is something created by, and deployed by, particular individuals, who build that state together and live within the legal framework it provides. These individuals have duties towards one another to use that framework in a manner that respects the rights of the other cooperating individuals in the process of state-building and state-using. This idea is often developed with reference to the idea of *reciprocity*: those who share the burden of creating and sustaining a state have obligations to their fellow creators and sustainers that they do not have to other individuals. This idea can be cashed out by noticing that the state purports to act in the name of the individuals it constrains, and so must provide them with the particular forms of equality required for equal control of that process (Nagel, 2005; see also Blake, 2001; Freeman, 2006a). It might, instead, focus on the broad idea that the state as an ongoing process requires individuals to be able to reciprocally accept both the burdens and benefits it requires, while still understanding themselves as moral equals (Sangiovanni, 2007). What is key to these visions is that the state is a distinct kind of thing in the world, one that represents a sort of *relationship* more than simply an agent; but only those relationships that can be understood as respectful of the freedom and equality of persons, though, can be justified. This process of justification, finally, entails certain demands for egalitarianism in distribution. Reciprocal justification, after all, is likely impossible under circumstances in which some individuals are able to simply dictate terms of reciprocal interaction to others.

This last idea begins the criticism of this variant of statism; it is, after all, entirely true that there are forms of political institution at the transnational level, and these institutions seem to impose rules on agents in a manner markedly similar to that of the domestic state (see Pogge, 1989, 2002; Cohen and Sabel, 2006; Julius, 2008; Moellendorf, 2009). Why, then, can we not simply say that duties of reciprocity apply globally, as well as locally? The associativist cosmopolitan, in particular, would simply regard the statist here as ignoring empirical reality; rules and practices with impact upon well-being are found at the transnational level as well as at the local level, and both kinds would seem to give rise to demands of reciprocity. The statist has rejoinders to this worry, of course; the statist might simply deny that the forms of relationship found at the international level are, in fact, the sort that could give rise to duties of distributive justice between individuals. Mathias Risse (2006), for instance, has argued that such institutions are distinct from domestic legal institutions, in that the latter are *directly* and *pervasively* involved in the shaping of individual life-chances, in a manner that gives rise to particular demands for distributive justice between those individuals. The statist can, then, simply insist that the state continues to have a distinct role in the lives of its citizens, and that it is this distinct role – rather than the broad category of 'cooperation' itself – that gives rise to the need for justification through reciprocity. The argument, though, continues, and the statist must provide a justification for why the state is genuinely unlike the more complex institutions of transnational governance that now exist.

The final justification for statism we will consider is closely allied to the second, but emphasizes the nature of the domestic state as *coercive*. On this analysis, what is morally central about the state is not simply that it is the product of shared agency, but that it is capable of enforcing its commands with coercive force. This coercive force stands in need of justification to those individuals over whom that coercion is exercised; and this justification, in turn, is where the familiar norms of distributive justice might be shown to originate. The idea, to put it in its most simple terms, is that coercion is a *pro tanto* moral wrong, and it must be either eliminated or shown to be justifiable. What would make state coercion justifiable, though, entails that those coerced must have some particular guarantees of equality – including, notably, some guarantees that the property law of that state would be justifiable to individuals conceived of as free and equal, and that those subject to the law must have some reasonably egalitarian share of power to make that law. This means, however, that the domestic state might be understood as the context within which the norms of distributive justice have normative force; the coercion of the state is the prerequisite for specifically distributive justice to have normative force (Blake, 2001; Ronzoni, 2009; Risse, 2012).

This justification faces immediate difficulties, the most vexing of which is the simple fact that the international realm is rife with coercion as well (Arneson, 2009). Some scholars have defended this idea by focusing on the role of international borders in coercively shaping life-chances (Abizadeh, 2008). Others have focused on the role of the international treaties constituting the backdrop to international trade (Cavallero, 2010). If coercion is the sine qua non of distributive justice, the statist must come to grips with the fact that there is more of it about than we might think. Some theorists have responded to these facts by concluding that coercion cannot be quite as central as we might have thought (Sangiovanni, 2007; Caney, 2008). Others – notably Laura Valentini (2011) – have maintained the moral concern with coercion, but asserted that this concern entails global distributive duties, instead of local ones. In face of these worries, of course, the statist is capable of reasserting her statist conclusions. Some theorists have chosen to accept that there is global coercion, while denying that the coercion is of the sort that might be justified with reference to distributive shares. Coercion, after all, must be justified or eliminated, on the view in question; it is always open to the statist to choose the latter disjunct and argue that the sorts of coercive regime found at the global level ought generally to be eliminated (Blake, 2013b; see also Ronzoni, 2009). This fact means, though, that the sorts of duties one might expect the statist to endorse at the global level will now have to be considerably more complex and demanding than the label *statism* at first suggests. The statist is able to assert that specifically egalitarian duties of distributive justice hold sway only between citizens of the same state; she is not, however, able to conclude that the international realm is a realm without significant duties, given the degree to which powerful states coerce and threaten more marginal states with impunity. Statism, in the end, might blossom out into a set of duties rather more demanding than the statist might have expected.

4 Conclusions

It is expected, at the end of this sort of chapter, that some broad sense of what the future might look like will be offered – or, more modestly, what the future of theory might potentially involve. I will end this chapter with two brief ideas, one of which has already been discussed. This idea is that *statism* itself is a label that is increasingly difficult to regard as philosophically significant. It continues to have some meaning, I think, when it is used to describe a counterpoint to the distributive cosmopolitan; the latter want egalitarian distribution of some good thing at the global level, where the statists do not. Increasingly, though, I think we are facing a world of theory in which the moral relevance of the state – and of international institutions, and of common humanity – are not regarded as susceptible to this sort of yes-or-no analysis. We will, I think, continue to disagree with one another about what we owe to the distant poor – but we will be unlikely to use these simple terms to describe what it is about which we disagree.

The second note with which I would end is more speculative: the state itself is, I think, under some pressure in the current world. I believe it is common to overemphasize the degree to which the state has withered away; those who believe that global government is already here are, to my thinking, wildly overstating the case. Nevertheless, it is possible that experimentation and alteration of political forms may soon render *statism* a term without a living referent. For the immediate future, though, I believe states – and statists – will continue to exist. In the long run, I am less confident that either is likely to flourish.

References

Abizadeh, A. 2007. 'Cooperation, Pervasive Impact, and Coercion: On the Scope (not Site) of Distributive Justice', *Philosophy & Public Affairs* 35(4): 318–358.

Abizadeh, A. 2008. 'Democratic Theory and Border Coercion: No Right to Control Your Own Borders', *Political Theory* 36(1): 37–65.

Arneson, R. 2009. 'Do Patriotic Ties Limit Global Justice Duties?', *Journal of Ethics* 9: 127–150.

Beitz, C. 1979. *Political Theory and International Relations*. Princeton, NJ: Princeton University Press.

Blake, M. 2001. 'Distributive Justice, State Coercion, and Autonomy', *Philosophy & Public Affairs* 30(3): 257–296.

Blake, M. 2012. 'Global Distributive Justice: Why Political Philosophy Needs Political Science', *Annual Review of Political Science* 15: 121–136.

Blake, M. 2013a. 'We Are All Cosmopolitans Now', in G. Brock, ed., *Cosmopolitanism versus Non-cosmopolitanism*, 35–54. Oxford: Oxford University Press.

Blake, M. 2013b. *Justice and Foreign Policy*. Oxford: Oxford University Press.

Blake, M. and Risse, M. 2008. 'Two Models of Equality and Responsibility', *Canadian Journal of Philosophy* 38(2): 165–199.

Buchanan, A. 2000. 'Rawls's Law of Peoples: Rules for a Vanished Westphalian World', *Ethics* 110(4): 697–791.

Cabrera, L. 2005. *Political Theory of Global Justice*. London: Routledge.

Caney, S. 2006. *Justice Beyond Borders*. Oxford: Oxford University Press.

Caney, S. 2008. 'Global Distributive Justice and the State', *Political Studies* 56: 487–518.

Cavallero, E. 2010. 'Coercion, Inequality and the International Property Regime', *Journal of Political Philosophy* 18(1): 16–31.

Cohen, J. and Sabel, C. 2006. 'Extra Rempublicam Nulla Justitia?' *Philosophy & Public Affairs* 34(2): 147–175.

de Bres, H. 2012. 'The Many, Not the Few: Pluralism About Global Distributive Justice', *Journal of Political Philosophy* 20(3): 314–340.

Dworkin, R. 1987. *Taking Rights Seriously*. London: Duckworth.

Dworkin, R. 2000. *Sovereign Virtue*. Cambridge, MA: Harvard University Press.

Freeman, S. 2006a. 'The Law of Peoples, Social Cooperation, Human Rights, and Distributive Justice', *Social Philosophy and Policy* 23(1): 29–68.

Freeman, S. 2006b. 'Distributive Justice and *The Law of Peoples*', in R. Martin and D. A. Reidy, eds., *Rawls's Law of Peoples: A Realistic Utopia?*, 243–260. London: Blackwell Publishing.

Gilabert, P. 2012. *From Global Poverty to Global Equality: A Philosophical Exploration*. Oxford: Oxford University Press.

Hassoun, N. 2014. *Globalization and Global Justice: Shrinking Distance, Expanding Obligations*. Cambridge: Cambridge University Press.

Held, D. 2010. *Cosmopolitanism: Ideals and Realities*. Cambridge: Polity.

James, A. 2005. 'Constructing Justice for Existing Practice: Rawls and the Status Quo', *Philosophy & Public Affairs* 33(3): 283–316.

Julius, A. J. 2008. 'Nagel's Atlas', *Philosophy & Public Affairs* 34(2): 176–192.

Kymlicka, W. 1995. *Multicultural Citizenship*. Oxford: Oxford University Press.

Miller, D. 1995. *On Nationality*. Oxford: Oxford University Press.

Miller, D. 2008. *National Responsibility and Global Justice*. Oxford: Oxford University Press.

Moellendorf, D. 2009. *Global Inequality Matters*. London: Palgrave Macmillan.

Nagel, Thomas. 2005. 'The Problem of Global Justice', *Philosophy & Public Affairs* 33(2): 114–147.

Nussbaum, M. 1994. 'Patriotism and Cosmopolitanism', *Boston Review*, 1 October.

Pogge, T. 1989. *Realizing Rawls*. Ithaca, NY: Cornell University Press.

Pogge, T. 1992. 'Cosmopolitanism and Sovereignty', *Ethics* 103: 48–75.

Pogge, T. 2002. *World Poverty and Human Rights*. Cambridge: Polity.

Pogge, T. 2013. 'Concluding Reflections', in G. Brock, ed., *Cosmopolitanism versus Non-cosmopolitanism*, 294–320. Oxford: Oxford University Press.

Rawls, J. 1999. *The Law of Peoples*. Cambridge, MA: Harvard University Press.

Risse, M. 2006. 'What to Say about the State', *Social Theory and Practice* 32(4): 671–698.

Risse, M. 2012. *On Global Justice*. Princeton, NJ: Princeton University Press.

Ronzoni, M. 2009. 'The Global Order: A Case of Background Injustice? A Practice-Dependent Account', *Philosophy and Public Affairs* 37(3): 229–256.

Sangiovanni, A. 2007. 'Global Justice, Reciprocity, and the State', *Philosophy & Public Affairs* 35(1): 3–39.

Sen, A. 1992. *Inequality Re-examined*. New York: Russell Sage.

Song, S. 2012. 'The Boundary Problem in Democratic Theory: Why the Demos Should Be Bounded by the State', *International Theory* 4(1): 39–68.

Stilz, A. 2011. *Liberal Loyalty*. Princeton, NJ: Princeton University Press.

Tamir, Y. 1993. *Liberal Nationalism*. Princeton, NJ: Princeton University Press.

Tan, K.-C. 2004. *Justice Without Borders*. Cambridge: Cambridge University Press.

Tan, K.-C. 2012. *Justice, Institutions, and Luck: The Site, Ground, and Scope of Equality*. Oxford: Oxford University Press.

Tan, K.-C. 2013. 'The Demands of Global Justice: Review Essay', *Oeconomia* 13(4): 665–679.

Taylor, C. 1989. *Sources of the Self*. Cambridge: Cambridge University Press.

Valentini, L. 2011. *Justice in a Globalized World: A Normative Framework*. Oxford: Oxford University Press.

Walzer, M. 1986. *Spheres of Justice*. New York: Basic Books.

CHAPTER THREE

Global Distributive Justice: The Cosmopolitan View

Darrel Moellendorf

We live in a profoundly unequal world. Let's start with wealth. A recent study conducted by Oxfam argues that, by 2016, the combined wealth of the richest 1 per cent of the world's population will be greater than the combined wealth of the remaining 99 per cent. Over the course of the last several years this inequality has been growing. The richest 1 per cent is about to exceed 50 per cent ownership of all global wealth, a share that is up from 2009, when they owned 44 per cent (Oxfam, 2015). Thomas Piketty notes that the wealthiest 0.1 per cent of the global population owns about 20 per cent of all wealth (2014: 438), and he conjectures that the wealth of the wealthiest people in the world has grown 6–7 per cent per year over the past three decades (2014: 435). Global health inequalities are stark. According to the World Health Organization, the average life expectancy in low-income countries is just 57 years, while in high-income countries it is 80. Children in the poorest quintile globally are nearly twice as likely to die before their fifth birthday as children from the richest quintile (WHO, 2011). Educational inequalities are also terrible. In the wealthiest countries almost no one aged 20–24 has less than four years of schooling. In many of the poorest countries of the world the majority of the population that age has had less than four years of schooling. In Niger, the worst case, a full 78 per cent of all people aged 20–24 have had less than four years of schooling (WIDE). Cosmopolitans typically argue that global inequalities such as those in wealth, health and education are unjust. In this chapter, I defend the cosmopolitan view. I discuss some of the arguments made by cosmopolitans in support of their view as well as some of the disagreements that exist among cosmopolitans about when duties of justice exist and about the content of justified principles of distributive justice. I also discuss some cosmopolitan reforms to the existing global order; reforms that would serve to reduce global inequality.

1 What is Cosmopolitan Distributive Justice?

I shall call 'a relation of justice' the relationship between two or more persons in which at least one person has a claim of social justice and at least one other has duty in virtue of that claim. Cosmopolitans hold that relations of justice may extend across state borders; relations of justice are not necessarily limited to compatriots; and all those persons who stand in relations of justice are moral equals. Cosmopolitans can allow that compatriots stand in special relations of justice to one another; but cosmopolitans deny that the limit of relations of justice is the compatriot relationship. The form of cosmopolitanism that I shall focus on concerns distributive justice. It is characteristic of these cosmopolitan views that the requirements of the duties of distributive justice are generally no less substantial than the requirements of distributive justice among compatriots, even if they might be different or have a different justification.

I shall assume that, as a first approximation, what matters for distributive justice is the distribution of wealth, income and opportunities. This corresponds to the two parts of John Rawls's second principle of justice (1999: 266). I shall not deny that there might be something more fundamental, say, human capabilities that ultimately matter most of all. But I shall assume that the distribution of wealth and income can serve as a rough approximation for whatever matters most to distributive justice, if it is not ultimately wealth and income. Amartya Sen (1979) criticizes John Rawls's focus on wealth and income by pointing out that two people might be equal in terms of wealth but have very unequal capability sets because the one is able-bodied and the other disabled. One response that Rawls offers to Sen – a response I endorse – is not to deny the force of Sen's point that equality of resources does not ensure that relations are equal in the morally relevant way, but instead to claim that the focus on resources is appropriate at least at a certain level of abstract when the discussion is focused on the design and structure of the basic distributive institutions, and not their day-to-day functioning, which is fine-tuned by legislation and policy (Rawls, 1999: 47–52; 2001: 168–76).

The cosmopolitanism that is under discussion in this chapter, then, holds that persons across state borders stand in relationships of justice with respect to the distribution of wealth, income and opportunities. One remaining characteristic of this view is important. Among the duties that are governed by distributive principles, should there be a case of conflict between what is owed to compatriots and what is owed to non-compatriots, it is not necessarily the case that priority is given to compatriots, on grounds that they are compatriots. A view that held that there were duties of distributive justice that extend across state borders, but which privileged compatriots, would not be in the class of views that I am a discussing as cosmopolitan (Miller, 1998). Cosmopolitanism may allow that there are special duties of justice to compatriots, but it does not allow that among the duties that apply to compatriots as well as non-compatriots, relations between the former necessarily have some feature that requires privileging those who stand in that relation over those who do not stand in that relation to us.

But what does cosmopolitan distributive justice concern? As a matter of distributive justice, the evaluative terms 'just' and 'unjust' are sometimes thought to apply both to the actions of individuals and to institutions. Such accounts might be called 'interactional' even though they include interactions and institutional effects. An example of an interactional account is G. A. Cohen's argument (2008) that it would be unjust of people to demand higher remuneration as a condition of doing work that would benefit the least advantaged as the application of the difference principle only to institutions allows. I employ a more limited use of the terms 'just' and 'unjust' such that they apply primarily to the effects of institutions and derivatively to the policies that operate within the scope of institutions. Accounts that take justice to apply primarily to institutions are often referred to as 'institutional'. These views hold that what matters to justice is how people fare under institutions, not what their pre-institutional circumstance are, and not how individuals behave within the permissible scope of institutions. There are several responses to the interactional account. One relies on the importance of fair public rules for justice in conditions in which persons endorse a plurality of reasonable moral outlooks (Williams, 1998). And Kok-Chor Tan (2012) lays weight on the value of moral pluralism. The idea is that if institutions are arranged justly, as long as people constrain their actions to the rules of the institutions, they are morally free to pursue a variety of morally licit goals, which might range from benefiting their family and friends to developing their talents and pursuing their interests.

2   Arguments for Cosmopolitan Distributive Justice

There are two different broad approaches for justifying duties of cosmopolitan distributive justice. I distinguish these as 'non-membership-dependent' and 'membership-dependent'. Simon Caney makes an extended non-membership-dependent argument in defence of duties of cosmopolitan distributive justice. Often, arguments of this kind claim that the conditions that justify egalitarianism domestically are applicable globally as well. Here is an outline of Caney's argument:

1   '[V]alid moral principles apply to all those who are similarly situated in a morally relevant way' (cf. Caney, 2005: 36).
2   The best arguments for egalitarianism in distributive justice 'all invoke a universalist moral personality' (cf. Caney, 2005: 121).
3   According to a universalist conception of moral personality, a 'person's entitlements should not be determined by their nationality or citizenship' (cf. Caney, 2005: 122).
4   Hence, insofar as the best arguments for egalitarian distributive justice among compatriots are plausible, so then is an argument for egalitarian distributive justice globally.

We can call this 'the similarly situated argument'. The effect of the similarly situated argument is to recruit the domestic egalitarian to the cause of cosmopolitan egalitarianism. The argument obviously does not appeal to those who believe that the case for egalitarianism also fails at the domestic level. But if it succeeds there, then, according to the similarly situated argument, it should apply globally as well.

The similarly situated argument involves an ambiguity about the nature of the justifying conditions. Premise two invokes moral personality. We affirm domestic egalitarianism (if we do) at least in part because we affirm the equal moral personality of all citizens. But that claim and premises one and three entail the conclusion only if equal moral personality is a sufficient condition for distributive egalitarianism. Premise two speaks of egalitarianism 'invoking' universal moral personality, not entailing it. Moreover, it is precisely the entailment claim that will be resisted by those domestic egalitarians who also reject global egalitarianism. They will argue that egalitarianism is justified by such equality only under special relations, such as coercion (Blake, 2001, 2011; Nagel, 2005) or reciprocity (Sangiovanni, 2007), which conditions do not exist between non compatriots.

Membership-dependent accounts of cosmopolitanism invoke features of our partially globalized world to draw the connection between fundamental human equality and distributive egalitarianism. This is sometimes done in explicitly Rawlsian terms by claiming that global interdependence produces conditions relevantly similar to the basic structure of domestic justice. For example, Charles Beitz claims: 'Assuming that Rawls's arguments for the two principles are successful, there is no reason to think the content of the principles would change as a result of enlarging the scope of the original position so that the principles would apply to the world as a whole' (1999: 151). As we shall discuss below, we can distinguish the question of whether the existence of interdependence gives rise to duties of distributive justice from the question of whether the appropriate principle of justice is the difference principle.

I also defend a membership-dependent account of cosmopolitan egalitarianism (Moellendorf, 2009). The outline of the argument is as follows:

1 Justificatory respect requires that the principles that structure the institutions of associations, which generate duties of justice among members, be principles that could be reasonably endorsed by the persons participating in the associations.

2 Associations give rise to duties of justice among members if they meet the following four conditions: they are (i) sufficiently strong, (ii) largely non-voluntary, (iii) constitutive of a significant part of the background rules that govern members' public lives and (iv) can be brought under the collective control of members.

3 If the members of an association, which gives rise to duties of justice goods, by their joint efforts produce goods and powers, useful to the members, to which goods and powers no person has a pre-associational

moral entitlement, justificatory respect entails a defeasible presumption in favour of egalitarian rules regulating the goods and powers.

4 Among the kinds of associations that satisfy premises two and three (and thus also one) is the global economy.

5 Therefore, there is a defeasible presumption in favour of egalitarian rules regulating the goods and powers produced by the global economy.

Each of the four premises requires significant clarification and defence. I turn now to discussing them.

Premise one invokes the idea of justificatory respect. Let's assume that persons possess equal inherent dignity as expressed in the preambles of the major human rights documents of the twentieth and twenty-first centuries. The relationship between the rights enumerated in these documents and the foundational commitment to inherent human dignity is that respecting the latter consists in recognizing the former, which protect and enable dignity. An interpretation of human dignity is required to make this claim plausible. I suggest the following one. Human dignity consists in, among other things, our capacity to act in ways that are responsive to the reasons we have for acting; human rights, by protecting and enabling certain forms of acting (including deliberating and thinking), serve the aforementioned capacity. The freedoms of conscience and association and entitlements to education and medical care all serve the human capacity for practical reason.

The human capacity to act in ways that are responsive to reasons is also respected when the institutions, which constitute the association, are structured by principles that could be reasonably endorsed by persons who participate in the associations constituted by the association. To impose on persons institutions (which are sufficiently robust) that could not be justified to those persons whose conduct is regulated by them would be to fail to respect the dignity of these persons (see also Forst, 2007). It would be to fail to respect their capacity to act in ways responsive to reasons because it would allow their agency to be manipulated by policy in ways that they might reasonably reject.

Premise two delimits the kind of associations that are constrained by justificatory respect. Not all associations are concerns of justice, which require that their constituting institutions be justifiable to the members. Voluntary associations, such as many churches in liberal societies, or clubs of various sorts, would usually be ruled out. When one freely joins such a club, one usually cannot complain of an injustice in its governing structure if one is not treated as an equal member. Four conditions are individually necessary and jointly sufficient for the associations to generate duties of social justice. First, the association should be sufficiently strong, where strength is measured according to the following three indices: how enduring the association is, how comprehensively its institutions are governed by norms and how regularly it affects the highest-order moral interests of its members. This would not include many clubs organized around common interests. Second, the association should be non-voluntary in the sense that there is no reasonable alternative to participation in the association. Many religious organizations and clubs would not satisfy this condition. Third, the association should be constitutive of the background rules that regulate members' public lives. Rules that regulate what one can do as member of a club would not be included. And fourth, the rules must be able to be brought under the control of the members. If there were nothing that could be done to change the rules, then they would not be appropriate concerns of justice.

The second premise of this argument states an important part of what I call 'the principle of associational justice'. That principle holds that duties of justice exist between persons who have a moral duty of equal respect to one another if those persons are co-participants in an association of the requisite kind, one that is relatively strong, largely non-voluntary, constitutive of a significant part of the background rules for the various relationships of their public lives, and governed by institutional norms that may be subject to human control.

The principle of associational justice makes a controversial claim, namely that people can come to bear special duties through non-voluntary relations. Samuel Scheffler summarizes two kinds of objections to that claim. One is 'the voluntarist objection' (2001: 54). According to this objection, if there are associative duties in virtue of membership it is only insofar as membership can be adequately characterized as an instance of a contractual relation broadly understood. A worry that supports this objection is that the existence of non-voluntary associative duties would seem to constrain what some people, but not everyone, are at liberty to do. Some people are picked out as bearing duties that others do not bear, and they are picked out by considerations other than those that they voluntarily chose to assume. When a person makes a promise, it is widely agreed that she has a special duty to the promisee, a duty others do not have, to fulfil the promise. That duty arises out of the voluntary action of the promiser. Now, the principle of associative justice claims that special duties owed by members to other members of certain kinds of associations can arise non-voluntarily. In response to the voluntarist objection: first, it seems to be a moral feature of the world that non-voluntary special duties can morally constrain people. That idea conforms with common-sense morality in a number of ways, for example that family members have special duties to one another. Second, to focus only on the moral constraints imposed by these non-voluntary relations is to miss an important part of the picture. Each duty bearer is also normally an entitlement bearer as well. She has good moral reason to expect that, as a member of the relation, she will be able to claim that other members fulfil their duties to her. And as the example of the family suggests, the moral constraints that exist as a result of non-voluntary special duties are not necessarily regrettable, since they may constitute morally valuable relations.

The second objection noted by Scheffler is 'the distributive objection' (2001: 56). The worry here doesn't have to do with the burdens on the duty bearer, but with the benefits to the person owed the duty. Associative duties pick out some people as beneficiaries, but not others. Against a background commitment to egalitarianism, this feature of associative duties might seem worrying. The person who is a beneficiary does not seem to deserve special benefits, nor does she necessarily have greater needs. How then can the benefits be justified? The question can also be asked in the case of the person who benefits as a result of the fulfilment of special duties in a voluntary relationship. In that case, it might suffice to answer that the beneficiary voluntarily contracted with another person, who, as a result of the contract, owes the beneficiary a good or a service not owed to others. Regardless of whether that answer is sufficient, it's not available in the cases covered by the principle of associational justice, which applies in particular to non-voluntary relationships. Still, the force of the distributive objection depends upon the content of the background commitment to egalitarianism. The principle of associational justice assumes a background duty of equal respect. Now, as long as that commitment alone does not entail strict distributive egalitarianism, and according to the argument under discussion the commitment does not, then the principle of associative justice is compatible with the background commitment to equal respect. Moreover, as noted in the previous paragraph, part of what a person loses in virtue of being bound by duties of justice, she regains as being a beneficiary as well.

The third premise states that justificatory respect establishes an egalitarian presumption regarding the distribution of the goods and powers produced by members of an association if the association generates duties of justice and if the association is what I call 'a common good association'. A common good association is one in which there are no pre-associational valid claims on the goods and powers produced by the joint efforts of the members. The idea is that the only kind of distribution that could be justified to members of a common good association is one that is presumptively egalitarian. If a justification must be made to everyone, then there would be a strong, but defeasible, presumption in favour of equality. The presumption could perhaps be defeated, if there were morally relevant differences in needs or capacities, if persons acted in ways – say criminally – to forgo equality, or if, following Rawls's difference principle, it were to the advantage of the least well-off. Recall the worry of the distributive objection: if equal respect for persons alone entailed duties of egalitarian distributive justice, then the principle of associative justice would seem to contradict the requirements of equal respect. I am now denying the antecedent of that conditional. The connection between equal respect and egalitarian distributive justice is characterized here as requiring both associations that satisfy the principle of associative justice and that are common good ones. This makes explicit the way that the distributive objection is deflected.

The line of reasoning that holds that equal respect entails egalitarian distributive duties only under conditions that satisfy the principle of associational justice and the requirements of a common good association provides a plausible response to Pablo Gilabert's claim that the universal scope of the moral equality of persons affirmed by cosmopolitans requires that the scope of requirements of justice also be universal (2011: 589). As my discussion of premise four will suggest, I agree with the likes of Gilabert and Caney, who defend cosmopolitan principles of distributive justice. But, for the reasons just canvassed, I think that they are wrong in claiming that cosmopolitan principles of distributive justice follow from a commitment to the moral equality of persons without consideration of the nature of the association in which people are related. We do not violate the moral equality of persons when we maintain that we have special duties only to some persons, and that we may claim special entitlements from some persons and not others. As it happens, given the contingencies of globalization we have special duties of distributive justice that have global scope.

The fourth premise simply states that the four conditions laid out in premises two and three apply to the global economic association. I now adumbrate some reasons for believing that this is plausible for each of the four conditions of premise two. With respect to the first condition, the global economic association seems strong in light of the three indices of strength. The association created by the processes of economic globalization is enduring. It is a structural feature of capitalist economic development that has gathered pace recently with technological changes, but that has been observable since at least the early colonial area. Additionally, it is governed primarily by the norm of competition for market share that requires firms to innovate ceaselessly and to reduce production costs. But norms of governance are also in place, especially through the regulatory framework established by the WTO (World Trade Organizaton) and the municipal exclusionary property regimes that are implicitly recognized in all international trade. The globalization of trade, investment and finance has had profound effects on the highest-order interests of persons, including spreading market norms that dictate whether and how a state may succeed in poverty-eradicating human development and imposing rules of governance through the WTO that affect, for example, a state's ability to succeed in development by means of trade. Finally, the effects of the international economic crisis perpetuated by the home-lending crisis in the USA in 2007–8 illustrates the manner in which the highest-order interest of persons are affected by the international economic association. For example, according to the World Bank, net capital flows to developing countries fell 20 per cent in 2009 to $598 billion and were a little over half the 2007 peak of $1.11 trillion (World Bank, 2011: 1).

Consider the second of the four conditions of the principle of associational justice, namely non-voluntariness. There is no reasonable prospect for extensive economic development and growth other than adopting a capitalist economy (Cohen, 2001: 207–15). And the gains from international trade can be immense. Moreover, although states are formally free either to join the WTO or not, the overwhelming majority of states see no reasonable prospect to development outside the WTO. Regarding the third condition, there is no longer any doubt that the pressures of global competition constrain the regulatory regimes of states, and that the constraints affect a range of issues, from employment opportunities and job security to the intellectual property law of a state. These are associated with highest-order human interests in well-being, security and health. The fourth condition requires that norms be subject to control. Market competition can, of course, be limited, directed or counterbalanced by deliberate public policy. And obviously, WTO rules can be amended.

There seems to be plenty of empirical evidence to support the claim that the global economic association satisfies this condition. (See also Tan, 2012: 155 for an abbreviated form of this kind of argument.) This argument does not deny the existence of special duties of justice between compatriots in virtue of their co-membership in either a national economy or a state. It is not an argument that duties of egalitarian justice exist exclusively at the global level (see also Moellendorf, 2011a).

The argument above differs from a prominent kind of anti-cosmopolitan argument that seeks to limit relations of egalitarian justice (Blake, 2001, 2011), or perhaps of social justice generally (Nagel, 2005), to the state on grounds that a necessary condition of such relations is that the persons in them share membership in a coercive state structure. These might be called 'coercion accounts'. Michael Blake and I have had an extended debate on these points, but I cannot fully summarize the arguments here (see Blake, 2011; see also Moellendorf, 2009, 2013). Suffice it to say that Blake's considered opinion is that the best explanation for why distributive egalitarianism is required within states is that states are vertically coercive, in the sense that the coercive agency is established by citizens; that kind of coercion cannot be removed and, instead, it requires justification; and the existence of distributive egalitarianism renders the vertical coercion justified. Internationally, states coerce one another horizontally, that is with respect to the norms of the international system. In principle, that kind of coercion can be eliminated, so rather than justifying it we should seek means to eliminate it (Blake, 2011). In contrast, I argue that the power of egalitarianism to justify coercion, if one supposes that it does do that (which I doubt), does not entail that coercion is necessary to make the case for egalitarianism (Moellendorf, 2009, 2013). I argue that international investment, production, trade and finance bring people into a common good association of the kind characterized by the principle of associational justice; and that suffices for duties of egalitarian distributive justice, assuming justificatory respect (Moellendorf, 2009). A different kind of response to Blake would be to argue that the kind of coercion relevant to relations of justice exists in international institutions as well as in the state (Abizadeh, 2007; Hassoun, 2012). I do not dispute that claim, but nor do I rely on it, because I am not convinced that the existence of vertical coercion is necessary to justify the duties of egalitarian distributive justice.

As discussed above, Caney favours a non-membership-dependent account of cosmopolitan distributive justice. He rejects accounts of cosmopolitan egalitarian distributive justice, like the account I have defended above, on grounds that they face an unsatisfactory dilemma (2011: 523–5). Either they draw a sharp line between the associations in which duties of distributive justice exist and associations in which they do not, or they allow duties to vary with features of the association. The first horn is implausible, he claims, since failing to satisfy the appropriate requirements in only one way would make the association one in which there are no distributive duties. But, according to Caney, the second horn permits gradual variance of duties of justice as associations become more robust, rendering the account necessarily imprecise and incomplete. Hence, any such view is implausible.

How do I reply? Premise two of my argument above takes the existence of duties of justice to depend on the following four conditions: (i) the strength of the association, (ii) its lack of voluntariness, (iii) the association constituting a significant part of the background rules that govern members' public lives, and (iv) that it can be brought under the collective control of members. These requirements are all threshold empirical conditions. The view might be thought of, then, as falling on the first horn of Caney's dilemma. But it could avoid doing so, if beyond some low threshold, satisfaction of the empirical requirements admits of degrees and the moral principles are scaled to the degree of satisfaction. I claim that strength depends on how enduring the association is, how comprehensively its institutions are governed by norms, and how regularly it affects the highest-order moral interests of its members. These considerations admit of degrees, even after the point at which the association is sufficiently strong. There could be more and less strong associations beyond the threshold. The same claims apply also to the constitution of a significant part of the background rules of public life and being subject to collective control. Both may be fulfilled in degrees beyond the satisfaction of a low threshold. My argument seems rather to fall upon the second horn of Caney's dilemma. But how much damage does that do? A. J. Julius offers a reply that seems to deflect the force of the charge: any account of distributive justice that does not register the importance of both national economies and partial global integration seems insensitive to morally important facts of the current global condition. 'A continuous transition between the standards succeeds in acknowledging both circumstances even as it ensures that the international difference principle eventually displaces the national one' (Julius, 2006: 191). Caney may be right that all such accounts currently lack precision and completeness, but what is lost in that regard seems to be made up for in registering the morally relevant features of our partially globalized world.

3 Distributive Principles

Cosmopolitans often defend the global application of the difference principle (Pogge, 1989; Beitz, 1999; Moellendorf, 2002). Brock contends that this is mistaken. Cosmopolitans should rather endorse a basic needs principle, which would ensure that everyone is 'adequately positioned to enjoy the prospects for a decent life' (Brock, 2009: 52). Brock claims that experimental evidence refutes Rawls's original position argument in support of the difference principle. People in a number of different countries were put in simulations modelling the original position, and they consistently ranked the difference principle lower than a basic needs principle. The trouble with Brock's rejection of Rawls's justification, however, is that it does not address Rawls's arguments for why the difference principle would be chosen (Moellendorf, 2011b: 263). Nor is there any assurance that the experimental subjects understood and sought to evaluate Rawls's arguments. Hence, their choice in experimental conditions should not be considered a decisive refutation of the Rawlsian arguments for the difference principle.

Nonetheless, there may be other reasons to doubt the appropriateness of the difference principle for global distributive justice in current circumstances. The requirement of the principle of associational justice is that the rules of the association must be subject to collective control. There is a certain lack of capacity for doing that in conditions of partial globalization. Global and international political capacity to regulate the terms of international trade, investment and finance is significantly weaker than domestic power to do so within home markets. More than that, the political organizations that might legislate that capacity do not even exist. Hence there is reason to doubt the power to arrange municipal property law, international trade treaties, and the institutions of international investment and finance so as to ensure that they approximate a distribution that is, over time, to the maximum benefit of the least advantaged.

The trouble with the difference principle is that it does not offer a plausible norm against which to judge current distributions, because, in a partially globalized world, we lack the capacity to arrange institutions in a way that would seem to be even close to satisfying it (Moellendorf, 2009). Still, as Julius seems to suggest in the quotation cited above, assuming the process of continual global integration, the eventual satisfaction of the difference principle could be a moral goal worthy of our allegiance insofar as it will one day be possible to arrange institutions to approximate it, and justificatory respect would demand that. The greatest collective control currently exists in matters where state capacity can be used and where international institutions are strongest. In these areas, the case for duties that seek to reduce inequalities seems the strongest, even if satisfying the difference principle may not be required.

An alternative principle of distributive justice is fair equality of opportunity. Sometimes, cosmopolitans endorse a globalized version of that principle as well (Caney, 2001; Moellendorf, 2009). Equality of opportunity requires equalizing opportunities to possess goods of some specified kind among persons with approximately equal endowments of some specified sort. Typically, the ideal requires the mitigation of inequalities of wealth and educational access inherited due to social circumstance at birth in order to ensure approximate equality of opportunities for success among the equally talented. Usually, egalitarians argue that the relevant social circumstance to mitigate is the social class of the child's family. But in the global context, the circumstances might include country of origin as well.

Gillian Brock argues that attempts to extend the principle of fair equality of opportunity globally face a dilemma (2009: 61–2). Either they must employ a version of equality of opportunity that relies on favoured social positions from a particular culture without appropriate global scope, or they must allow cultural variation about what counts as a favoured position, which produces an account of equality of opportunity that is too weak to rule out significant disadvantages and discrimination. I believe that there is a viable third horn, namely to identify positions, powers and goods, which are drawn from an interpretation of the association in which the question of justice arises, and which therefore have a broader relevance than merely to participants of a particular culture. This requires an interpretive argument about the position, powers and goods that the association distributes (Moellendorf, 2009: 73–7). If there are such association-specific positions, powers and goods, they constitute the material for egalitarian concern that is established by justificatory respect applied to the common good global economic association.

As an alternative to equality of opportunity Brock supports a principle requiring that there be a decent set of opportunities for all. She seeks to support the principle by contrasting it with equality: 'If faced with the option of equal but poor life options, or a situation in which, though there is some inequality of access, everyone has access to developing a range of skills sufficient for earning a living (or meeting needs) with dignity and delight, we should choose the second situation' (2009: 62). This, however, does not seem relevant. The issue between egalitarians and Brock does not concern the choice between whether boys and girls should have equally poor access to education, or better but unequal access. Rather, it concerns the choice between the latter – better educational opportunities for boys but still decent ones for girls – and the option of equal opportunities for boys and girls to a good education. In rejecting equality of opportunity, Brock would seem to be indifferent between those two options. In contrast, the proponent of equality would defend the option of equalizing opportunities to a good education for boys and girls.

4   Four Cosmopolitan Reforms

Several feasible reforms to both states and international organizations would promote greater global equality and therefore would appear to be required by cosmopolitan distributive justice, unless there prove to be compelling reasons of justice that militate against them. I discuss three such reforms below. One attractive feature of cosmopolitan distributive justice, in contrast to state-centric or nationalist accounts of distributive justice, is that the cosmopolitan accounts have the theoretical resources to pick out these three areas as sites of existing injustice; that, I believe, conforms to many people's considered judgments about these matters. Ultimately, however, remedying global inequality would require a new global institution that has the effect of redistributing wealth from the richest to the poorest. So, I finish by discussing proposals for a global tax.

Legislate liberalized immigration policies

Country of birth confers significant privileges and is therefore an important factor in global inequality. Branko Milanovic's studies of global income distribution show that at least half of the variability in a person's global income percentile rank can be explained by her country of birth's level of human development and the inequality of income within the birth country. If that is correct, there are three ways a person's global income percentile rank might be improved: her efforts might receive greater remuneration; her country might improve its development level; or she might immigrate to a more highly developed country (Milanovic, 2015). Liberalization of immigration restrictions in wealthy countries is fully within the scope of state power. Reducing barriers to immigration could allow people from less developed countries to become better-off. According to a World Bank report, an increase in immigration from developing to high-income countries would increase the labour force of the latter by 3 per cent from 2002 to 2025, and it would generate large aggregate increases in global welfare. When adjusted for prices, the increase in aggregate global income would be $356 billion or 0.6 per cent. Moreover, the disaggregated gains of this policy would go disproportionately to developing countries, where incomes would increase by 1.8 per cent, compared to 0.4 per cent in high-income countries. But for the new immigrants to high-income countries, the cost-of-living-adjusted income gains would increase on average by nearly 200 per cent, due to differences in wages between the countries of origin and destination. And there would be income gains in developing countries due to decreased labour market competition and increased remittances (World Bank, 2006). Immigration liberalization is within the capacity of states to affect; it would promote the equalization of opportunities globally; it is, therefore, required by a cosmopolitan approach to distributive justice.

Prohibit loan conditionality requiring labour market liberalization

Very often, a country's access to finance from the International Monetary Fund (IMF) during times of economic crisis comes with conditions requiring

the country to liberalize its labour markets. The required labour market liberalization takes many forms, including increasing retirement ages, weakening collective bargaining, lowering minimum wages, reducing unemployment
benefits and loosening firing procedures. About one quarter of all IMF loans
since 1987 have required changes that deregulate the labour market of the
borrowing country (Caraway et al., 2012). The IMF justifies labour liberalization as promoting growth and employment (Furceri et al., 2012). That justification, however, is made primarily on the basis of computer modelling
exercises, which lead IMF researchers to make rather hedged prognoses,
especially in light of the experienced negative effects of such policies, including reduced growth, recession and increased unemployment: 'To the extent
reforms enhance credibility and confidence, some of the short-run negative
effects may be countered. In any case, the full impact on growth and employment are likely to materialize only over a medium- to long-term horizon'
(Barkbu et al., 2012: 13). Moreover, whatever the merits of that justification
on its own terms, it simply neglects the more important issue of the distributive effects of the liberalization policies, namely that they tend to increase
inequality.

One comprehensive study employing regression analysis over a 32-year
period of a sample of 110 countries shows that 'even controlling for the fact
that countries participate in IMF programs under bad economic conditions,
the inherent effects of programs are negative on income distribution'
(Vreeland, 2002: 122). Indeed, the programs seem to contain a class bias.
Although labour suffers a decrease in income, capital experiences an increase,
which offsets its losses due to diminished growth (2002: 133). A reform of IMF
policy to prohibit making access to finance during economic crises conditional on labour market liberalization is easily made. And it would stop the
inegalitarian effects of such conditionality. It is, therefore, required by cosmopolitan distributive justice.

Require sequencing trade liberalization to
support developing countries

Although a central aim of the WTO is to liberalize multilateral trade, and
although it claims to prize agreements that give adjustment time to less
developed countries, the WTO has no principled commitment to sequencing
trade liberalization by requiring developed countries to reduce their trade
barriers first. There are, however, good reasons to believe that developing
economies must engage in practices that support and protect their industries,
especially industries producing for export, if these countries are to achieve
higher levels of human development. The classic nineteenth-century argument to this effect is made by Friedrich List (1966) on the basis of an historical
survey, revealing that the development policies of Europe and North America
relied on measures to protect infant industry in almost every successful case

of development. Ha-Joon Chang (2002) provides a twenty-first-century supplement to List's argument with recent studies. Chang argues that Japan and the newly industrialized countries of East Asia all followed the same kind of infant industry support and protection strategy as North America and Europe. Now, trade policies that promote human development are good because the constitutive elements of human development – education, health and income – are valuable. But more can be said about why a trade regime that does not stymie human development is a requirement of cosmopolitan justice. Recall the research of Milanovic (2015) about the importance of the level of human development of a person's country of birth to her income. A trade regime that promotes human development by allowing developing states to protect and support their infant industries is also a concern of justice because it promotes more equal opportunities for income among persons regardless of their country of origin.

Institute a global tax

I began this chapter by citing research that indicates a vast and growing inequality of wealth globally. Although the three reforms discussed above are feasible and would serve to reduce some of the existing global inequalities, primarily by promoting the well-being of some of those who are disadvantaged, they do not seek to reduce inequality by constraining income and wealth. In this final section I consider three proposals that would do that. The financial transaction tax, or Tobin Tax, would tax income made on short-term currency speculation. Milanovic (2005) recommends a global income tax; Piketty (2014) proposes a global, progressive tax on capital.

The Tobin Tax, initially proposed by James Tobin as a disincentive to international currency speculation (1982: 43), involves taxing short-term speculative investments in international money markets. Currency speculation can produce destabilizing fluctuations in the value of currencies in developing countries. Such fluctuations can affect the ability of a country to export its goods, to pay for imports and to pay its debts. Unforeseen fluctuations compromise the capacity to develop rational development plans utilizing export and debt. An appropriately designed tax could serve the development aims of many developing countries to seek to mitigate such fluctuations. And there is no great social good served by short-term currency speculation. So, there is no reason not to deter it.

Tobin and others also suggest that the proceeds that the tax generated could be used for global poverty reduction (Eichengreen et al., 1995). If the tax could be fine-tuned to be applicable only to short-term speculative investments in currency, it would not deter long-term capital investment that serve development ends. There is reason to believe that a very low tax could be effective at generating considerable revenue. Since the benefits of global poverty reduction would be derived from an activity that produces negative economic externalities, there seem to be good moral reasons to support it. The feasibility of the tax is not entirely clear. A Swedish tax on the sale and purchase of equity securities and fixed income securities was dropped a few years after implementation because revenues were low and the volume of trading declined significantly. But the causes of these events are not entirely clear (Wroebel, 1996). A forthcoming European-wide experiment will be interesting: 11 EU states have agreed to implement it in early 2016. The Tobin Tax might serve important aims of cosmopolitan justice, by facilitating development and combatting poverty. If the European experiment demonstrates that it can work successfully, then it should be supported on grounds of cosmopolitan justice.

Milanovic proposes a progressive global income tax scheme that could be expected to be effective in reducing global inequality because of both the burden it places on high earners and the distribution it directs to low earners (Milanovic, 2005: 159–62). Milanovic's income tax proposal involves the coordination of state institutions for taxation. Participating states with high per capita GDPs add a small levy to their already existing income tax schemes. The funds are collected by participating rich states and transferred to an international organization, which oversees their distribution to participating per capita poor states. Transfers of this sort would lay a responsibility on persons who have been successful in using their natural or social good fortune to their market advantage.

There is, however, a potential drawback to the arrangement outlined above. In states that have lower than average per capita GDPs, but high inequality, there may be some persons who are wealthier than persons in states with higher than average per capita GDPs. So, a scheme that simply sent tax revenue from the higher than average per capita countries to the lower than average could carry out regressive transfers from a poorer person in a rich state to a richer person in a poor state. In order to reduce the possibility of this, Milanovic advocates transfers from per capita rich countries only to per capita poor ones that are also relatively egalitarian. This would render it less likely that there would be rich people who would benefit from the transfers of the poor in a more wealthy country. Milanovic's proposal avoids the injustice of regressive taxation, then, at the price of failing to be entirely global in scope. The poor who have the misfortune of living in very inegalitarian states, such as Brazil and South Africa, have no entitlement under the scheme against the rich of the per capita rich states. This limitation, however, may not be all bad. It could have positive effects on political developments within states. It provides an incentive for political elites to address inequality, and it gives an additional argument to domestic social movements on behalf of egalitarian causes.

A proposal that involves taxing politically powerful high earners probably suffers more severely from problems of political feasibility than the Tobin Tax, especially since the latter is also likely to affect a smaller class of people.

The feasibility problems of the global income tax are somewhat mitigated by the fact that the tax could be partially implemented before all of the per capita rich countries participated in it. The successful example of partial implementation might build political support for the proposal. The proposal is certainly worthy of support on cosmopolitan grounds, although it is unclear whether the potential political problems are surmountable.

The central attraction of Piketty's proposal for a global tax on capital is that the tax could get to the main source of inequality far more effectively than an income tax. Because the very wealthy only take a very small proportion of their wealth as income, typically much smaller than the percentage by which their wealth grows, inequality of wealth can grow even with a progressive income tax (2014: 525). What is more, given the high levels of private wealth, even a tax at a modest rate would bring in significant revenue for social welfare policies that support people living in poverty and with low incomes. In Europe, a tax of 2.5 per cent would generate revenues equivalent to 2 per cent of Europe's GDP (2014: 528).

Piketty readily admits that the idea of a global, progressive wealth tax is utopian, since it would require all countries to cooperate by agreeing to, and enforcing, a tax schedule applicable to wealth everywhere. But it is nonetheless useful to consider for a number of reasons. Because presumptively it would be very effective at reducing global inequality in wealth, it can serve as a standard against which to measure the effectiveness of other proposals (2014: 515). Moreover, even a modest tax, Piketty claims, would have important virtues. It would generate reliable information about the global distribution of wealth by requiring the reporting of wealth (2014: 518–19) and by requiring states to broaden their agreements about sharing banking data (2014: 520). The latter would remove the possibility of hiding money away in remote countries. Finally, the aim of moving to a global, progressive tax on capital could possibly be served by first developing regional capital taxes, say in the European Union (2014: 527–30).

Since the political feasibility of a global, or even regional, tax on capital is uncertain, it's not plausible to claim that cosmopolitan justice requires this institution. But it certainly would be desirable. So, there are good reasons of cosmopolitan justice to advocate for such a tax. And should successful campaigning for a global or regional tax on capital sufficiently improve its feasibility, then justice would require that it be instituted.

5   Conclusion

Our world is remarkably unequal. Cosmopolitans typically reject this inequality. They seek a more egalitarian world. According to the account discussed most fully in this chapter (Moellendorf 2009), the requirement of equality derives from respect for the equal inherent dignity of all persons. Respect for this dignity requires that the social order be justifiable to those who are its members. Justice is about that kind of respect. The institutional order that permits the massive inequalities of our world could not possibly be justified to the great many people who fare so poorly while a very small percentage does so fabulously well. According to cosmopolitans, our world is not only remarkably unequal, it is deeply unjust.[1]

References

Abizadeh, A. 2007. 'Cooperation, Pervasive Impact, and Cooperation: On the Scope (not the Site) of Distributive Justice', *Philosophy & Public Affairs* 35(4): 318–358.

Barkbu, B., Rahman, J., Valdés, R., et al. 2012. 'Fostering Growth in Europe Now', International Monetary Fund. https://www.imf.org/external/pubs/ft/sdn/2012/sdn1207.pdf.

Beitz, C. R. 1999. *Political Theory and International Relations*. Princeton, NJ: Princeton University Press.

Blake, M. 2001. 'Distributive Justice, State Coercion, and Autonomy', *Philosophy & Public Affairs* 30(3): 257–296.

Blake, M. 2011. 'Coercion and Egalitarian Justice', *The Monist* 94: 555–570.

Brock, G. 2009. *Global Justice: A Cosmopolitan Account*. Oxford: Oxford University Press

Caney, S. 2001. 'Cosmopolitan Justice and Equalizing Opportunities', *Metaphilosophy* 32: 113–134.

Caney, S. 2005. *Justice Beyond Borders: A Global Political Theory*. Oxford: Oxford University Press.

Caney, S. 2011. 'Humanity, Associations, and Global Justice: In Defence of Humanity Centered Cosmopolitan Egalitarianism', *The Monist* 94: 506–534.

Caraway, T. L., Rickard, S. J. and Anner, M. S. 2012. 'International Negotiations and Domestic Politics: The Case of IMF Labor Market Conditionality,' *International Organization* 66: 27–61.

Chang, H.-J. 2002. *Kicking Away the Ladder: Development Strategy in Historical Perspective*. London: Anthem Press.

Cohen, G. A. 2001. *Karl Marx's Theory of History: A Defence*, exp. edn. Princeton, NJ: Princeton University Press.

Cohen, G. A. 2008. *Rescuing Justice & Equality*. Cambridge, MA: Harvard University Press.

Eichengreen, B., Tobin, J. and Wyplosz, C. 1995. 'Two Cases for Sand in the Wheels of International Finance', *Economic Journal* 105: 161–72.

Forst, R. 2007. *The Right to Justification: Elements of a Constructivist Theory of Justice*. New York: Columbia University Press.

Furceri, D., Bernal-Verdugo, L. E. and Guillaume, D. M. 2012. 'Crises, Labor Market Policy, and Unemployment', International Monetary Fund. https://www.imf.org/external/pubs/cat/longres.aspx?sk=25754.0.

Gilabert, P. 2011. 'Cosmopolitan Overflow', *The Monist* 94: 584–92.

Hassoun, N. 2012. *Globalization and Global Justice: Shrinking Distance, Expanding Obligations*. Cambridge: Cambridge University Press.

Julius, A. J. 2006. 'Nagel's Atlas', *Philosophy & Public Affairs* 34(2): 176–92.

List, F. 1966. *The National System of Political Economy*. New York: Augustus M. Kelly.

Milanovic, B. 2005. *Worlds Apart: Measuring International and Global Inequality*. Princeton, NJ: Princeton University Press.

Milanovic, B. 2015. 'Global Inequality of Opportunity: How Much of Our Income Is Determined By Where We Live?', *Review of Economics and Statistics* 97: 452–60.

Miller, R. W. 1998. 'Cosmopolitan Respect and Patriotic Concern', *Philosophy & Public Affairs* 27(3): 202–24.

Moellendorf, D. 2002. *Cosmopolitan Justice*. Boulder, CO: Westview Press.

Moellendorf, D. 2009. *Global Inequality Matters*. Basingstoke: Palgrave Macmillan.

Moellendorf, D. 2011a. 'Cosmopolitanism and Compatriot Duties', *The Monist* 94: 535–54.

Moellendorf, D. 2011b. 'Why Global Inequality Matters', *Journal of Social Philosophy* XLII: 99–109.

Moellendorf, D. 2013. 'Human Dignity, Associative Duties, and Egalitarian Global Justice', in G. Brock, ed., *Cosmopolitanism versus Non-Cosmopolitanism*, 222–238. Oxford: Oxford University Press.

Nagel, T. 2005. 'The Problem of Global Justice', *Philosophy & Public Affairs* 33(2): 113–17.

Oxfam. 2015. 'Even it Up: Time to End Extreme Inequality'. https://www.oxfam.org/sites/www.oxfam.org/files/file_attachments/cr-even-it-up-extreme-inequality-291014-en.pdf.

Piketty, T. 2014. *Capital in the Twenty-First Century*. Cambridge, MA: Harvard University Press.

Pogge, T. 1989. *Realizing Rawls*. Ithaca, NY: Cornell University Press.

Rawls, J. 1999. *A Theory of Justice*, rev. edn. Cambridge, MA: Harvard University Press.

Rawls, John. 2001. *Justice as Fairness: A Restatement*. Cambridge, MA: Harvard University Press.

Sangiovanni, A. 2007. 'Global Justice, Reciprocity, and the State', *Philosophy & Public Affairs* 35(1): 3–39.

Sen, A. 1979. 'Equality of What?' *The Tanner Lecture on Human Values*. http://tannerlectures.utah.edu/_documents/a-to-z/s/sen80.pdf.

Scheffler, S. 2001. *Boundaries and Allegiances*. Oxford: Oxford University Press.

Tan, K.-C. 2012. *Justice, Institutions, and Luck*. Oxford: Oxford University Press.

Tobin, J. 1982. 'A Proposal for International Monetary Reform', in *Essays in Economics: Theory and Policy*, 488–94. Cambridge, MA: MIT Press.

Vreeland, J. R. 2002. 'The Effect of IMF Programs on Labor', *World Development* 30: 121–39.

WHO (World Health Organization). 2011. *Ten Facts on Health Inequalities and Their Causes*. http://www.who.int/features/factfiles/health_inequities/en/.

WIDE (World Inequality Database on Education). http://www.education-inequalities.org/.

Williams, A. 1998. 'Incentives, Inequality, and Publicity', *Philosophy & Public Affairs* 27(3): 225–47.

World Bank. 2006. *Global Economic Prospects: Economic Implications of Remittances and Migration 2006*. New York: The World Bank. http://www.worldbank.org/content/dam/Worldbank/GEP/GEParchives/GEP2006/343200GEP02006.pdf.

World Bank. 2011. *Global Development Finance: External Debt of Developing Countries*. New York: The World Bank. http://data.worldbank.org/sites/default/files/gdf_2011.pdf.

Wroebel, M. G. 1996. 'Financial Transaction Taxes: The International Experience and the Lessons for Canada', Canadian government publication. http://publications.gc.ca/collections/Collection-R/LoPBdP/BP/bp419-e.htm.

CHAPTER FOUR

Global Political Justice

Terry Macdonald

Introduction

The political governance of any society – whether local or global in scope – depends upon fundamental institutions that constitute, control and distribute political power,[1] in support of collective goals. On the one hand, political institutions must control existing social power, to restrain the escalation of conflict into violence, and the conversion of power into domination.[2] This can be described as the provision of political *order*, and is often regarded as the most fundamental of prerequisites for social life (Williams, 2005; Hurrell, 2007; Bull, 2012). But at the same time, political institutions must constitute and distribute those additional powers required for the collective pursuit of more complex social values (including social justice); this entails the creation of political procedures for collective decision-making, as well as functionally complex governance capabilities. This second function can be described as the facilitation of political *collective action*, and it subsumes and builds upon the first.

In this chapter, I refer to normative questions about the design and reform of global institutions with these fundamental political functions as questions of *global political justice* (GPJ) (for related usages of the label, see Beitz, 2011; Macdonald and Ronzoni, 2012; Buckinx et al., 2015). The label of GPJ is not routinely applied in exactly this way; rather, normative analysis of global political power has been spread across multiple loosely intersecting literatures in political theory, international relations and international law – and has been mostly framed in terms of narrower institutional concepts like global democracy, law, sovereignty, authority, governance, accountability, legitimacy and so on. Moreover, the methodologically hybrid character of these intersecting literatures gives questions of GPJ a somewhat ambiguous disciplinary status, with a sometimes awkward relationship to other international political theory debates now dominated by work with narrower roots in moral and political philosophy.

A central aim of the analysis in this chapter, accordingly, is to draw the complementary insights generated within these intersecting literatures together into a more cohesive dialogue, by applying the unifying conceptual frame of GPJ. To meet this aim, the discussion proceeds in three steps. First, I specify in more depth the *key normative questions* concerning global political power that are linked here through the concept of GPJ, and I distinguish these from the narrower distributive questions that have received greater attention to date within global justice debates. In the following two sections, I map the varying concepts and arguments through which the key questions of GPJ have been answered in existing literatures: those framed in terms of the idea of global democracy; and those framed in terms of ideas of law, governance, and legitimacy. In conclusion, I point briefly to some remaining gaps in this established body of work, and identify some priorities for future theoretical research on the institutional problems of GPJ.

1   Global Political Justice: Understanding the Key Questions

To clarify the key questions that mark out GPJ as a distinctive topic of theoretical inquiry, it is helpful to examine them in three dimensions: the concrete *institutional problems* on which these questions are focused; the *historical development* of these institutional preoccupations in theoretical scholarship; and the relationship of GPJ debates to the moral questions of *socioeconomic or distributive justice* that dominate many other areas of global political theory.

Institutional problems of global political justice

The topic of GPJ is concerned at its core with the normative question of how best to design the fundamental institutions through which political power is constituted, controlled and distributed within global society, as a basis for global governance (or, viewed in more conservative terms, which existing such institutions are worthy of ongoing support, and on what basis). To begin concretely, we are arguing about matters of GPJ when we debate institutional questions of the following kinds.

In general terms, what political agents should be *institutionally recognized as members of global society* and, correspondingly, what *special rights and powers* should be institutionally accorded to them? Such agents may include, for example, sovereign states and nations, individuals, international organizations and courts, and other nonstate groups and organizations. In more specific terms, these controversies focus on three interdependent sets of institutional issues.

First, how should global 'public powers' – that is, political powers to make and enforce laws and political decisions, or, more broadly, to govern global society (Hurrell and Macdonald, 2012) – be *institutionally constituted*? Should global public powers be vested principally in sovereign states, as on a traditional internationalist or Westphalian model of international society? Or should these traditional state powers instead be distributed across a range of other political and legal institutions (at global, regional, transnational or intrastate levels), in accordance with some alternative 'postnationalist', 'cosmopolitan' or other such model of global social order? What role should be played by legal versus non-legal forms of authority in constituting global public power and discharging key functions of global governance? To the extent that global political authority is to be legally constituted, should it possess a constitutionalized or a non-constitutionalized structure? Should global public powers be territorially or functionally organized? To what extent must global public power be backed by coercive or other political enforcement mechanisms, and what kinds of global agencies might best enforce authoritative global rules?

Second, how should global public powers of these varying kinds be *institutionally controlled (or regulated)* in order to guard against their capture and abuse by powerful special interests, and ensure instead that they are discharged in the service of some more inclusive 'public' or 'collective' global purposes? Competing institutional models for the regulation of global public power reflect deep controversies, in particular, about how public purposes can be identified – and correspondingly what regulative institutional arrangements will be required to ensure they are appropriately advanced.

Third, how should political power be *distributed* within global institutions to ensure that an appropriate range of political interests is represented and empowered? This broad and complex question can be unbundled into several narrower ones: *whose interests* should be served by political institutions – or, in other words, how should global political constituencies be delineated? Who should be recognized as entitled to *define* these interests? How should *competing political interests* be weighed, balanced, aggregated, reconciled or transformed (in reaching collective decisions under conditions of social conflict or competition)? And how should material political powers be limited and distributed among agents in light of diverse and competing interests, in order to curtail opportunities for global institutions to be captured by, and directed to the service of, narrow and powerful interest groups?

The historical development of global political justice debates

Debates on questions of these kinds concerning the institutional constitution, control and distribution of global political power have developed in close dialogue with parallel debates focused at the level of the state – and normative analysis of power within state institutions has been a key topic of inquiry throughout the modern history of political thought. From Hobbes's *Leviathan* onwards, a significant body of political theory has evaluated varying institutional schemes of state-level governance in relation to their functional capacities: to minimize social violence through centralized coercive state institutions (as in a Hobbesean realist tradition), to limit abuses of state power through constitutional restraints (as in a Lockean liberal tradition), and to facilitate collective political decision-making and action within states through wider participatory, deliberative and sometimes more thickly democratic institutions (as in a Rousseauean democratic tradition).

Although much of this modern political theory has focused on the *domestic* characteristics of sovereign state institutions, there has been some historical recognition of the deep functional interdependence of domestic and international dimensions of sovereign state institutions, and the consequent importance of analysing the *international* institutional preconditions for sustaining state capacities. States have always depended for their viability on the institutions of a Westphalian international society of states, which recognizes and provides external support for domestic sovereignty through its practices of international law and diplomacy (just as the Westphalian international institutional system depends, conversely, on viable domestic state institutions). While theoretical analysis of this domestic and international institutional interdependence has not been extensive within the modern political theory canon, some notable analyses can be found there.

Arguably, the most historically influential normative analysis of these matters can be found in Kant's essay *Perpetual Peace*, first published in 1795, and within subsequent liberal internationalist literatures building on its insights (see Kant, 1970). In this essay, Kant famously advocated an institutional order incorporating international economic cooperation and some federalist international decision-making structure, operating alongside domestic 'republican' state institutions. Subsequent liberal theorists – in particular, the liberal idealists writing during the early twentieth century (Long and Wilson, 1995) and later democratic peace theorists (Doyle, 1983; Brown et al., 1996) – elaborated and developed these arguments in defence of a variety of international political institutions. These have included the emerging League of Nations and United Nations, as well as strengthened governance structures for supporting international economic integration and promoting state-level democratization.

Additional analyses of domestic and international institutional interdependence can be found elsewhere – for instance in scattered writings of Rousseau (Hoffmann et al., 1991), Burke (Welsh, 1995) and Hegel (Linklater, 1996), among others (Clark and Neumann, 1996; Boucher, 1998). Further important normative analysis of global political power – with a particular focus on normative problems of political order, law and legitimacy – has been developed within a somewhat distinct tradition of international theory linking early writings of international jurists such as Grotius (Bull and Kingsbury, 1992), Vitoria (Ortega, 1996), Pufendorf (Boucher, 1998: 223–54) and Vattel (Hurrell, 1996) with more contemporary work by 'English School' international relations theorists and theorists of international law.

Notwithstanding these important historical contributions, normative work on global political power prior to the 1970s remained fragmentary, and lacked a unifying conceptual framework for systematic inquiry. This began to change following the publication of John Rawls's *A Theory of Justice* (1971) and the subsequent emergence of a more cohesive field of normative international political theory framed in terms of the unifying concept of global or international justice. Although this new body of international theory has focused primarily on problems of global socioeconomic distribution, and relied heavily on methodological tools drawn from moral philosophy, its concern with fundamental international institutions has incorporated some space also for normative analysis of global political power – and more broadly has created a hospitable environment for new scholarship focused more directly on the institutional problems of GPJ.

The burgeoning of new scholarship on GPJ was led by influential proponents of cosmopolitan democracy, such as David Held and Daniele Archibugi in the 1990s (discussed in more depth below), and has since expanded to include not only democratic theories of global political power, but also theoretical work framed in relation to normative ideals of global law, governance, accountability, legitimacy and so on (for further discussion, see contributions in this volume by Lefkowitz and by Held and Maffettone). These new GPJ literatures generally rely less heavily than global distributive justice (GDJ) scholarship on analytic methods drawn from moral philosophy; instead, they combine the application of moral principles with hybrid modes of institutional analysis informed variously by insights from social theory, law, international relations and political science. While the last two decades have fostered much productive dialogue between GPJ and GDJ scholarship, some tensions and ambiguities persist regarding the conceptual and methodological relationships between them. To clarify the position of GPJ debates within the wider global political theory literature, it is thus helpful to give some direct attention to this relationship.

The relationship between questions of global 'political' and 'distributive' justice

Debates about GPJ and GDJ share certain important areas of overlap: both are concerned with the normative assessment of some set of fundamental global political institutions, and both can be framed in the language of 'justice' insofar as moral considerations play an important role in their institutional analyses. They can be distinguished, however, by the specific normative questions about global institutions upon which each is focused. Debates about GDJ are preoccupied primarily with the value of fairness in the distribution of benefits and burdens produced through global social cooperation; debates about GPJ, in contrast, are concerned with how best to design the fundamental institutions through which political power is constituted, controlled and distributed, as a basis for cooperative global political governance. Questions of GPJ and GDJ thus understood do share some common institutional terrain: both are concerned with a range of moral questions that relate to the control and distribution of political power within global institutions. But the full range of institutional concerns of each extends out from this shared terrain in different directions (for further discussion of the overlapping 'currencies' of global normative analysis, see Held and Maffettone's Introduction to this volume).

The institutional concerns of GDJ theories are broader than those of GPJ insofar as they extend to the fair distribution of socioeconomic burdens and benefits as well as that of political power. Conversely, the institutional concerns of GPJ theories are broader than those of GDJ insofar as they are concerned not only with how institutions can distribute power fairly, but also with the prior questions of how the statuses and powers of different members of global society should be constituted and controlled, in order to create functional institutional capacities for securing order and facilitating collective action, as preconditions for cooperative and productive global social life. Theories of GDJ do not generally tackle these background institutional questions; they take the structure and functional capacities of global society's fundamental political institutions as an assumed starting-point for normative arguments about distributive fairness, rather than as a subject of normative analysis in itself. This is what is meant by the claim made by many theorists of GDJ that duties of distributive justice arise at the global level only insofar as the 'global circumstances of politics' are already established, as institutional background conditions for the application of distributive justice principles (for further discussion of this point, see Macdonald and Ronzoni, 2012).[3]

A crucial consequence of these differences in the scope of theories of GPJ and GDJ is that the analytic methods employed for the normative assessment of global institutions vary somewhat in each case – in particular with respect to the role accorded to empirical analysis. Theorists of GDJ tend to employ empirical analysis of institutions principally in considering how moral principles relating to distributive fairness should be applied or interpreted in particular institutional contexts (for arguable exceptions, see James, 2005; Sangiovanni, 2008). Theorists of GPJ, in contrast, tend to engage less in fine-grained philosophical argumentation about the content and justification of moral principles, and more in messier hybrid forms of institutional analysis, which draw together moral considerations alongside complex empirical models of the dynamics of, and preconditions for, salient institutional functions.

Some GPJ theorists – such as some proponents of cosmopolitan democracy and law – have tried to ground their institutional arguments firmly in principles derived from moral philosophy (as discussed further below). But others – such as English School writers on international order and legitimacy – have self-consciously eschewed engagement with philosophical moral arguments, and instead sought to identify guiding normative principles through interpretive analysis of international history, culture and institutional practices (for further discussion, see Hurrell and Macdonald, 2013: 67–8). The grounds and structure of these various analytic methods are not always clearly specified, and raise larger questions about the methodologies most suitable for GPJ analysis. But before these methodological questions can be examined further, it is necessary to lay out in more detail the substance of the various institutional controversies that are the focus of inquiry; this is the task I turn to next.

2   Democratic Institutional Models of Global Political Justice

In GPJ debates on the question of how best to design the fundamental institutions through which global political power is constituted, controlled and distributed, the key controversies centre on the elaboration and evaluation of competing institutional models. Since some of the most prominent theoretical debates have focused on the justification and critique of global institutional models of international, cosmopolitan or transnational *democracy*, I will discuss these first.

The political ideal of democracy embodies the most widely endorsed institutional model for achieving political justice in contemporary world politics. Democratic models of political governance can vary widely in many dimensions (Held, 2006), but all are organized at a basic level around the concept of collective self-rule: democracy is an institutionalized system of power (from the Greek, *kratos*) exercised collectively by a political community or people (from the Greek, *demos*). Democratic models of political governance thus straightforwardly incorporate each of the elements of an institutional model of political justice outlined above. First, democracy requires an institutional framework of *public power* (paradigmatically, but not necessarily, a state), which constitutes the special powers, offices and so on required to create capacity for effective political governance. Second, democracy requires a regulative institutional framework for ensuring that the wider *democratic people* (or demos) can effectively control these institutions of political rule through some suitable mechanisms for political participation, representation, deliberation and so on. An overarching regulative ideal of *political equality* further plays an essential role in this latter dimension, by defining the status of individuals within the demos that is empowered collectively to exercise this political control (Beitz, 1989).

International democracy

Until very recently, the main role accorded to democratic institutions within theoretical frameworks of GPJ was as a basis for domestic political governance within a wider liberal internationalist model of global political institutions. The old argument that democratic governance should be confined to the domestic contexts of nation-states has been carried on and developed in more recent literature by nationalist democrats, including most notably David Miller, among others (Miller, 1995, 2007; Tamir, 1995; Moore, 2001). According to contemporary democratic internationalists, global political governance should be pursued by sovereign democratic nation-states, working cooperatively to preserve this internationalist order (and on some accounts also promote basic human rights) with the support of a thin framework of global institutions operating under the control of democratic states.

Theoretical justifications offered for this democratic internationalism rest on a range of grounds. Some justifications are *endogenous* to the democratic ideal – beginning with assumptions about the content of democratic values, and then arguing that internationalist democracy embodies the best way of realizing these values in practice. Miller (1995), for instance, assumes commitment to a 'civic republican' democratic ideal, and then argues that the forms of wide public deliberation and participation in collective political decision-making, which are essential elements of this ideal, can be more readily satisfied within nation-states than globally. Others argue that effective institutions of public power – the essential instruments of political governance that are key constituents of any democratic system – cannot be sustained on the scale of global politics, and so democratic governance should be confined to the level of the nation-state where it can function most effectively (Dahl, 1999).

Democratic internationalism is also sometimes defended on grounds that are *exogenous* to the democratic ideal – for instance, via the argument that it is the best means of satisfying the moral demands of communitarian social justice – namely, the right of national communities to political self-determination as a means to living in accordance with their local conceptions of justice (Miller, 1995; Walzer, 2008). Contemporary 'democratic peace' theorists, working within the disciplinary field of international relations, argue further that democratic internationalism can be justified as an institutional framework for global political governance insofar as it effectively supports international peace – linked closely to the fundamental political value of order (Doyle, 1983; Russett, 1994), alongside broader moral values.

Cosmopolitan democracy

From the post-Cold War 1990s onwards, this political ideal of democratic internationalism has been challenged by the development of a rival model, committed to the idea that democratic values and institutions should be applied directly on a global scale, rather than confined to domestic political spheres. Conducive social conditions for the emergence of this new global democratic ideal were created, through this period, by both the state-level democratization in former communist countries that accompanied the end of the Cold War, and the acceleration of broader forms of global social integration associated with the phenomenon of 'globalization'. Against this background, a new wave of democratic theorists – led by David Held and Daniele Archibugi – devised and advocated institutional models labelled as 'cosmopolitan democracy', aimed at building democratic governance on a global scale (Held, 1995; Archibugi and Held, 1995; Archibugi et al., 1998). Models of cosmopolitan democracy incorporate institutional prescriptions both for constituting a cosmopolitan structure of global public power and for regulating the exercise of this power through the democratic empowerment of a cosmopolitan demos.

Cosmopolitan authors offer varying accounts, first, of how global public power should be institutionally constituted. Some propose a strong world state structure, with constitutionalized cosmopolitan law, formal global citizenship rights and functional capacity for centralized world government (Cabrera, 2005). Others advocate the development of more loosely integrated legal and political institutions at local, regional and transnational as well as global levels, unified by some thin overarching legal framework of global constitutionalism and world citizenship, but without the strong centralization of political power associated with world government (Pogge, 1992; Held, 1995; Archibugi, 2008; Habermas, 2013). Some authors further emphasize the importance of viewing cosmopolitan democracy as a developmental political process rather than as a firm institutional blueprint, and, accordingly, a willingness to adapt democratic institutional structures to the possibilities and constraints arising across varying global political contexts (Archibugi, 2004, 2008).

These proposals for building cosmopolitan institutions of public power are accompanied, moreover, by proposals for empowering new cosmopolitan political communities to exercise collective democratic control through these institutions. Although details vary, most of these cosmopolitan authors endorse the empowerment of democratic communities at multiple levels within a cosmopolitan framework of global political governance. Here, varying rights of political participation and representation are to be accorded at global, regional, local and functional levels – corresponding with the boundaries of shared political interests and interdependencies, which Held (1995) has described as 'overlapping communities of fate'. The highest of these levels of democratic membership on all models is the global community of cosmopolitan citizens, though the substantive legal and political rights linked to membership in this overarching global 'demos' are specified in thicker or thinner terms by different authors, and are sometimes left open as matters for further exploration.

Justifications for cosmopolitan democracy as a framework for global political governance have been advanced on a range of normative grounds. The most straightforward justifications are endogenous to the democratic ideal – beginning with a simple commitment to some specific conception of democracy itself, and then arguing for cosmopolitan democracy as the best means, under contemporary political circumstances of globalization, for realizing these democratic values. Both David Held and Daniele Archibugi advance justifications of this kind – with Held (1995) invoking liberal democratic principles of political autonomy and equality and Archibugi (2008) invoking three democratic values, of political equality, popular control and nonviolence, as grounds for justificatory arguments. Some other cosmopolitan authors seek justificatory grounds for cosmopolitan democratic institutions that are exogenous to the democratic ideal – arguing, for instance, that cosmopolitan democracy is justified as the best means of satisfying the broader moral demands of cosmopolitan global justice (Cabrera, 2005; Marchetti, 2008).[4]

Disagreements between proponents of internationalist and cosmopolitan democratic models can thus be explained to some degree by their different normative starting assumptions – with proponents of the two models respectively embracing communitarian versus cosmopolitan conceptions of justice, civic republican versus liberal conceptions of democracy, and so on. But not all disagreement on institutional models can be traced back to these principled differences. Internationalist and cosmopolitan models also differ as a result of their polarized views on empirical questions concerning the *feasibility* of establishing and sustaining each democratic model under prevailing global political conditions. On the one hand, democratic internationalists argue that the scale, complexity and pluralism of global politics would make cosmopolitan democratic politics infeasible, in terms of both sustaining effective cosmopolitan governance structures and building a cohesive global demos. On the other hand, cosmopolitans not only defend the feasibility of their preferred democratic model (Koenig-Archibugi, 2010; List and Koenig-Archibugi, 2010), but further argue that it is infeasible to achieve strong democratic self-determination at the level of nation-states, given the degree of international interdependence, mutual vulnerability and social integration experienced by nation-states under conditions of globalization.

Transnational democracy

While internationalist and cosmopolitan democrats adopt polarized positions on these complex empirical questions, a third family of democratic institutional models – which can be described as *transnational* – builds on a middle ground between these opposing empirical analyses. Proponents of transnational democracy adopt varying normative premises in building and justifying their institutional models: some begin with commitments to particular normative conceptions of democracy, including deliberative (Dryzek, 2006), republican (Bohman, 2007) and liberal representative (Macdonald, 2008) democratic ideals; others begin with commitments to particular moral conceptions of global justice, and understandings of the terms on which democratic institutions should be subject to these moral principles (Gould,

2004). But all are unified by the empirical assessment that existing patterns of global social and political interdependence are highly complex and uneven, and not now feasibly transmutable into *either* the nationalist *or* the globalist structures required for the realization of internationalist or cosmopolitan democratic models (Christiano, 2010).

Instead of pursuing either of these ideals, then, transnational democrats propose an approach to the democratization of global political governance that is more partial and piecemeal – attempting to build and strengthen institutions of democratic governance that extend beyond the boundaries of nation-states, albeit lacking either the inclusive global scope or the structural unity of cosmopolitan models. Institutional models of transnational democracy are distinctive, first, in embracing the development of *transnational institutional structures of public power* as instruments of global political governance. These transnational institutions are thought to develop not primarily as a result of rational institutional 'design', but rather through the politicization and developmental reform of more organically emergent transnational governance capabilities, involving nonstate as well as state and international actors (Macdonald, 2008; Zürn, 2014). The result, in contrast to a formal constitutional framework for cosmopolitan global governance, is a fluid and uneven transnational framework of governance institutions – adapted dynamically to a 'partially joined-up world' (K. Macdonald, 2011).

Transnational democratic models further prescribe the empowerment of transnational political communities – or 'demoi' – to exercise some meaningful democratic control over these governance processes. To accommodate the shifting and uneven political structures of these institutions, transnational democrats propose democratic recognition and empowerment of multiple transnational 'demoi' (Bohman, 2007) in place of a unified global 'demos' made up of cosmopolitan citizens. It is most commonly argued that these transnational constituencies should be delineated either on the basis of shared 'stakeholder' interests in (that is, being significantly affected by) particular transnational decision-making processes (Gould, 2004; Macdonald, 2008),[5] or on the basis of shared capabilities to contribute valuable perspectives, ideas and arguments to deliberative processes of transnational political decision-making (Young, 2002; Dryzek, 2006; Erman, 2013). Different transnational democratic models further offer varying proposals for the political empowerment of these transnational demoi – including models for strengthened transnational deliberation (Dryzek, 2006), political participation (Nanz and Steffek, 2004; Gould, 2004) and (mostly non-electoral) representation (Kuper, 2004; Macdonald, 2008).

Although transnational democratic institutional models are arguably the most capable (compared with internationalist and cosmopolitan alternatives) of accommodating empirical facts about the complex transnational structure of global power and social integration in the present political era, these models have greater difficulty in demonstrating their normative credentials when judged against traditional democratic ideals of collective self-rule – and in particular the ideals of *political equality* embodied within them. The key difficulty is that transnational democratic models lack not only a commitment to any formal status of equal democratic citizenship for all individuals, but also any strong legal or political mechanisms for ensuring that all individuals can equally access opportunities for effective political control over the transnational forms of public power that impact upon their lives (Marchetti, 2011). The egalitarian credentials of transnational democratic models can perhaps be defended by arguing that democratic conceptions of equality should be interpreted in realistic rather than idealized terms, and accordingly that strengthening equality to the greatest feasible degree under prevailing circumstances is the best that can be expected of any democratic system (T. Macdonald, 2011). But irrespective of the persuasiveness of such arguments, these criticisms highlight the important and open question of whether and how the persistent tensions between normative ideals of democracy, and practical obstacles to their global realization, can be resolved.

3 Non-Democratic Institutional Models for Advancing Global Political Justice

In light of these difficulties with devising theoretically justifiable and practically workable models of democratic global political governance, some authors have suspended the assumption that democracy is the only (or necessarily the best) normative framework for understanding GPJ. Instead, they have pursued the core question of GPJ – concerning what are the best institutions for constituting, controlling and distributing political power within global society – by focusing on alternative framing concepts for normative institutional analysis. More specifically, they aim to prescribe institutional frameworks for global political justice organized not around normative ideals of global *democracy*, but rather varying ideals of global *law, governance* and *legitimacy.*

Global law

Normative ideals and institutional models of *law*, first, comprise one of the oldest analytic frameworks for thinking about how power should be constituted, controlled and distributed in social life. The ideal of democracy, as just discussed, prescribes that power should be channelled into an institutional scheme of *collective self-rule*, via constituting two kinds of collective political agency (public power, and a demos or demoi) and setting them in mutual regulatory political relations. The ideal of law, in contrast, prescribes that power should be channelled into an institutional scheme of *authoritative public rules*, via specifying some special authoritative *sources* for public rules (which mark out these rules as 'legal' in character), and then constituting institutions empowered to legislate, adjudicate and on some accounts also enforce them.

Normative theories of law differ widely in their views of what special sources mark out rules as legally 'normative' and 'authoritative', ranging from moral principles through varying social and political processes; not all legal theorists regard normative legal authority as grounded in moral principles, and among those who do, not all regard principles of justice, specifically, as the relevant moral standards. Controversies on these matters are especially marked in debates about the normative character of *international* legal authority (Slaughter et al., 1998; Besson, 2010; Lefkowitz, 2010, and in this volume). But even if normative legal authority itself is viewed as deriving from sources other than moral principles of justice, authoritative legal institutions can nonetheless be viewed as instrumentally central to the pursuit of political justice, insofar as well-designed legal institutions have a special capacity to create political order through regulating violence and to facilitate collective political action through codifying rules for complex social coordination. Normative questions about the design of authoritative legal institutions within global politics can be viewed as central to the wider debate on GPJ, then, based on either intrinsic or instrumental accounts of the connection between normative legal authority and the moral value of political justice.

Most debates about the role of law in building GPJ do not focus directly, however, on elaborating such views about the moral value of legal institutions. Theoretical controversies tend to focus instead on more specific disputes about the best institutional structure for legal authority in the context of contemporary global political life (with various views on the moral value of these legal institutions being invoked as background assumptions to these debates). More specifically, these institutional disputes concern the questions: which agents should have authoritative powers to make, adjudicate and enforce law in global politics, and on what should these powers be conditional? And what should be the scope of authoritative legal powers in global politics, with respect to the jurisdictions, bindingness and enforceability of the legal rules to which these powers apply?

Key debates here focus on whether and how powers to make, adjudicate and enforce laws in global politics should be structured by the institution of state sovereignty. According to the Westphalian internationalist model of global legal authority, these legal powers should be accorded solely to multiple sovereign state agents – defined as political regimes with internationally recognized and politically effective control of designated territories and their populations. But this Westphalian model of global legal authority is controversial in several important dimensions.

First, controversies surround the question of what the political conditions should be for the international recognition of political agents as sovereign states with these special legal powers. Internationalist legal models have often been backed by arguments that legal authority in global politics should rest on its capacity to facilitate the political autonomy of *national* communities or 'peoples' – whether or not these are democratically organized – and to promote international peace and stable political order (Walzer, 1980; Rawls, 2001). This nationalist view has been strongly countered by arguments that the special legal claims of sovereign states should be contingent in some way instead on their willingness and capacity to protect fundamental human rights within their territories (Buchanan, 2003, 2014).

Further controversies surround the question of what should be the *territorial scope* of state-like authoritative legal institutions. Some endorse the preservation of status quo sovereign state borders in order to uphold not only the forms of national autonomy noted above, but also the stability of the political order currently built around this internationalist legal structure (Wendt, 1999). Other authors, however, have argued that some supplementary forms of state-like legal authority should be built at global or other supranational levels in order to strengthen state-level governance capacity (Ronzoni, 2012), achieve global security in an era of 'security interdependence' (Deudney, 2007) or combat the emergence of dominating or unjust forms of political power emerging at transnational levels, beyond the regulatory control of individual sovereign states (Ronzoni, 2009; Pettit, 2010).

Finally, these various sovereignty-based models of global legal authority have been challenged by legal theorists arguing that various structural features of state-like legal authority are unsuitable for regulating the socially complex and pluralist global political sphere. These include, most importantly: sovereignty's constitutionally unified and hierarchical ordering of relationships among different authoritative agents and jurisdictions within the legal system; sovereignty's closed formal procedures for legal rule-making and adjudication; and the firmly binding and coercively enforceable status of sovereign legal rules. Under conditions of global social complexity and pluralism, some international legal theorists have argued, the important social values supported by global legal institutions can better be served by authoritative legal structures that are more 'liquid' in these dimensions (Krisch, 2015), resulting in a global legal order that is *pluralist* rather than unified in its authoritative agents and jurisdictions (Krisch, 2010); *informal* in its processes for legal rule-making and adjudication, with increased participation in particular by private and nonstate actors operating at transnational levels (Cutler, 2003; Kingsbury et al., 2005); and *soft* rather than hard in the bindingness and enforceability of its rules (Abbott and Snidal, 2000).

Global governance: accountability and pragmatic experimentalism

An important difficulty with this shift away from traditional sovereign structures of international legal authority is that it can become harder in some contexts to see how rules emanating from pluralist, informal and soft global rule-making processes can retain the special normative status and regulatory political functions of *law*. Since legal rules support GPJ in virtue of their special normative authority and political bindingness, the weakening of these distinctive features of sovereign legal structures blurs the divisions between legal and non-legal forms of global rule-making and political regulation. In recognition of this, many theorists prefer to focus normative analysis conjointly on legal and non-legal systems of global social control and coordination, via the alternative concept of global 'governance'. As James Rosenau has influentially characterized it, global *governance* subsumes all institutional systems of global political rule that occur 'through both the co-ordination of states and the activities of a vast array of rule systems that exercise authority in the pursuit of goals and that function outside national jurisdictions' 2000: 172).

While these broad global governance processes can support global political order and collective action in ways that share some functional equivalence to more traditional sovereignty-based processes of legal regulation, governance processes taken in themselves lack the special legal sources of special normative authority. As such, *normative* political theories of global governance – of the kind that can be viewed as contributions to the theory of GPJ – need to supplement functional empirical analysis of the regulatory capacities and roles of global governance institutions with some additional account of what alternative normative standards they must satisfy in order for them to attain political authority. While many different normative standards can be applied to global governance institutions – including the normative ideals of democracy discussed above, and the broader normative standards of political legitimacy below – two standards in particular are perhaps most strongly associated with the conceptual framework of 'governance' analysis.

The first of these is the normative ideal of accountability, which has been widely endorsed as a regulative standard for global governance institutions in lieu of stronger democratic forms of political control. While accountability is a 'complex and chameleon-like term' (Mulgan, 2000), which has been applied quite differently across varying international relations and public administration literatures, its conceptual core denotes an institutionalized relationship in which one agent has special entitlements and powers to question, direct, sanction or constrain the actions of another (Mulgan, 2000; Bovens, 2007; Goodhart, 2014).

A range of institutional models for strengthening accountability in global governance has been proposed by different writers (Grant and Keohane, 2005; Held and Koenig-Archibugi, 2005; Goodhart, 2014). Models differ first in prescriptions for the political agents to whom governance institutions are to be held accountable – with some advocating accountability to those affected by powerful governance institutions, and others proposing alternative 'horizontal' accountabilities among various powerful agents within governance regimes. They differ further in their underlying normative justifications for imposing these accountability demands, drawing variously on liberal values of limited power (Grant and Keohane, 2005), democratic values of public control (Held and Archibugi, 2005; Goodhart, 2011) and moral values of social justice (Rubenstein, 2007).

An alternative regulative standard for global governance institutions that has been proposed in some recent literatures is that of pragmatic experimentalism, which can be understood in broad terms as an institutionalized process of inquiry-based problem-solving (Dorf and Sabel, 1998; Sabel and Zeitlin, 2008). Whereas early theoretical work on experimentalist governance was focused on building designs for embedding experimentalist mechanisms within the administrative structures of democratic states (Dorf and Sabel, 1998), adaptations of experimentalist institutional models to transnational governance contexts adopt a looser structure for participatory collective problem-solving, 'in which the problems (and the means of addressing them) are framed in an open-ended way, and subjected to periodic revision by various forms of peer review in the light of locally generated knowledge' (De Búrca et al., 2014: 477).

Although the origins of experimentalist governance models are closely associated with the democratic theory of classical American pragmatist John Dewey, their normative justifications can be linked to a broader pragmatic instrumentalism, whereby they are justified as means of solving the concrete political problems of particular transnational populations, on the terms that these groups themselves experience and define their problems. In these experimentalist problem-solving governance processes, political goals are not taken as predefined; rather, the aim of governance processes is to facilitate 'workable cooperation by continuously exploring different understandings of means and ends' among actors within a governance process (Dorf and Sabel, 1998: 314).

Global political legitimacy

While institutional mechanisms for fostering accountable and experimentalist governance offer robust normative grounds for designing certain elements of global political institutions, a weakness is that they do not explain where piecemeal accountability or experimentalist mechanisms should fit within a more comprehensive framework of global institutional order. Some view these mechanisms as potential building blocks for, or stepping stones towards, more comprehensive liberal or democratic ideals of institutionalized global power. But in lieu of an assumed normative commitment to such an ideal, along with a belief in the feasibility of realizing such an ideal in practice under current global political conditions, some broader normative concept is required for framing inquiries focused on these higher system-level institutional questions.

Against this background, a number of authors now examine the concept of normative political *legitimacy* as fit for this kind of wider analytic purpose

– through the development of new normative theories of legitimacy for application to global political institutions (Zürn, 2004; Buchanan and Keohane, 2006, Buchanan, 2010; Tasioulas, 2010; Macdonald, 2016; Erman, 2015).[6] Political legitimacy is a highly complex concept, and, as such, scholars from different disciplinary backgrounds tend to emphasize varying dimensions of it in their theoretical formulations; but at its most generic level, normative political legitimacy is a virtue of institutions whereby some set of political agents has sufficient justifying reasons to support them (Macdonald, 2016). The key tasks of a normative theory of global political legitimacy, then, are to specify the set of agents who must have reasons to support a political institution in order for it to be judged legitimate and to specify the content of the justifying reasons that would count as sufficient for supporting it.

While these questions can certainly be answered by inserting the constitutive values of other political ideals (such as democracy or distributive justice) to specify the relevant agents and reasons, doing this effectively makes the concept of legitimacy redundant (since calling an institution 'legitimate' in either case would then amount to the same thing as calling it 'democratic' or 'just'.) If the normative theory of legitimacy is to do any independent work, then it has to supply an independent account of the agents that must support an institution, and the reasons for which they must support them, in order for it to count as legitimate.

Varying provisional attempts have been made to offer such an account within existing literatures. Most notable are those identifying reasons of legitimacy with: the value of solving complex institutional coordination problems within a global society characterized by conflicting interests and moral values (Buchanan and Keohane, 2006); the value of functional institutional capacity to support collective political action (Macdonald, 2016) or deliberative decision-making (Steffek, 2003); or the protection of certain fundamental moral values distinct from those of either democracy or distributive justice (Erman, 2015; Buchanan, 2010). Overall, though, this normative literature on global political legitimacy is still in an early phase of development, and much further work remains to be done to develop and build upon these preliminary contributions; here, there is significant potential for dialogue with emerging new 'realist' theories of political legitimacy, which draw directly on the political values of order and (empirical) political acceptability in institutional design and justification (Williams, 2005; Rossi and Sleat, 2014).

4 Conclusions: Towards a More Integrated Research Agenda on Global Political Justice

In this chapter I have applied the conceptual lens of GPJ to highlight some important theoretical links among a set of closely related literatures within the broad field of international political theory, all of which are concerned with the constitution, control and distribution of global political power.

While these literatures frame their normative inquiries through different conceptual lenses – linked to ideas of democracy, law, governance and legitimacy – they are nonetheless unified by their substantive engagement with deeply interconnected prescriptive questions of global institutional design. Applying the overarching conceptual framework of GPJ can be analytically useful insofar as it helps bring these intersecting normative analyses into closer dialogue, and in doing so helps produce a more integrated theoretical understanding of the complex normative considerations that should be brought to bear in the evaluation and design of fundamental global political institutions.

A more systematic integration of the insights from across these normative literatures, however, would require more than just the application of a shared conceptual framework of this kind. The varying conceptual frameworks associated with the several literatures I have surveyed here (of democracy, law, governance and legitimacy) do not merely supply *vocabularies* for analysing common institutional problems. More fundamentally, their divergent vocabularies denote varying underlying assumptions on many foundational – normative, empirical, meta-normative and social-ontological – theoretical matters, which together underpin methodologies for institutional design and justification.

These different frameworks vary, first, in their foundational *normative* commitments – with some close associations between particular framing concepts and foundational political values. Instances of such pairings include the concept of democracy and the value of equality, the concept of law and the value of impartiality, the concept of governance and the value of common interest, the concept of legitimacy and the value of public justification and so on. Second, these frameworks vary in their underlying *empirical* assumptions concerning what institutional functions are required to support these foundational values, and what range of political motivations and material capabilities must be fostered and harnessed to perform these functions successfully. While there is extensive divergence within as well as across theoretical frameworks on these complex empirical questions, some framings favour particular empirical views more strongly than others: governance framings, for instance, tend to emphasize the importance of harnessing political self-interest through incentive structures and communication infrastructures, whereas law and legitimacy framings tend to emphasize the importance of harnessing moral and solidaristic motives through institutionalized political socialization and argumentation.

Third, the frameworks vary in their *meta-normative* assumptions concerning the role of empirical claims in the normative analysis of global political institutions, and relatedly the binding character or 'normativity' of the theoretical principles of GPJ intended to guide institutional design and justification. Some theories within each conceptual framework – such as those grounded in commitments to liberal morality – view principles of GPJ as straightforwardly moral (that is, justified in terms of moral values or reasons). Within these theories, empirical claims enter normative analysis only in supporting instrumental calculations about how institutional models can most effectively realize moral values. Other theories, however – such as those grounded in commitments to pragmatist, deliberative or realist conceptions of political justification – can view GPJ principles as possessing some more autonomously 'political' form of normativity, corresponding with a more foundational reliance in normative analysis on empirical facts about political beliefs, motivations, material capabilities, institutional functions and so on.

Finally, the frameworks vary in their *social-ontological* assumptions – in particular those concerning the character of the political communities and collective agencies that animate global political institutions. Democratic theories invoke two types of collective agencies – agents of public power, and demoi or a demos; legal theories invoke law-makers (authorities) and law-takers (legal subjects), which include many collective agents such as states and corporations; governance theories invoke a wide range of collective agencies, including not only those discharging governance functions, but also principals and agents in accountability relationships, problem-solving communities of inquiry in experimentalist governance frameworks and so on; and theories of legitimacy draw on diverse assumptions about the structure of collective political belief, communication, problem-solving, decision-making and action, in supporting their varying models of legitimate global institutions.

Disagreements at these foundational theoretical levels are by no means confined to literatures on GPJ, and live debates persist on these matters also within other areas of moral, political and legal philosophy. But the disparity of views and assumptions is arguably much wider across the range of literatures surveyed here than within other normative theoretical fields; and without significant convergence on these matters it is much more challenging to reach theoretical agreement on suitable methods of normative inquiry and argumentation for answering substantive normative questions of GPJ. While significant progress on the questions of GPJ can still be made within each of the disparate conceptual frameworks of global democracy, law, governance and legitimacy, their contributions stand to be enriched and augmented by further engagement across and synthesis of their separate insights. To this end, further work is still required not only to develop the unifying conceptual framework of GPJ, but also to advance our understandings of the underlying theoretical and methodological issues through which this conceptual framework can be put to work in the normative analysis of global political power.

References

Abbott, K. and Snidal, D. 2000. 'Hard and Soft Law in International Governance', *International Organization* 54(3): 421–456.

Archibugi, D. 2004. 'Cosmopolitan Democracy and Its Critics: A Review', *European Journal of International Relations* 10(3): 437–473.

Archibugi, D. 2008. *The Global Commonwealth of Citizens: Toward Cosmopolitan Democracy.* Princeton, NJ: Princeton University Press.

Archibugi, D. and Held, D., eds. 1995. *Cosmopolitan Democracy: An Agenda for a New World Order.* Cambridge: Polity.

Archibugi, D., Held, D. and Köhler, M. 1998. *Re-imagining Political Community: Studies in Cosmopolitan Democracy.* Stanford, CA: Stanford University Press.

Beitz, C. 1989. *Political Equality: An Essay in Democratic Theory.* Princeton, NJ: Princeton University Press.

Beitz, C. 2011. 'Global Political Justice and the "Democratic Deficit"', in R. Wallace, R. Kumar and S. Freeman, eds., *Reasons and Recognition: Essays on the Philosophy of T. M. Scanlon*, 231–255. Oxford: Oxford University Press.

Besson, S. 2010. 'Theorizing the Sources of International Law', in S. Besson and J. Tasioulas, eds., *The Philosophy of International Law*, 163–186. Oxford: Oxford University Press.

Bohman, J. 2007. *Democracy Across Borders.* Cambridge, MA: MIT Press.

Boucher, D. 1998. *Political Theories of International Relations.* Oxford: Oxford University Press.

Bovens, M. 2007. 'Analysing and Assessing Accountability: A Conceptual Framework,' *European Law Journal* 13(4): 447–468.

Brown, M., Lynn-Jones, S. and Miller, S. 1996. *Debating the Democratic Peace.* Cambridge, MA: MIT Press.

Buchanan, A. 2003. *Justice, Legitimacy, and Self-Determination: Moral Foundations for International Law.* Oxford: Oxford University Press.

Buchanan, A. 2010. 'The Legitimacy of International Law', in S. Besson and J. Tasioulas, eds., *The Philosophy of International Law*, 79–96. Oxford: Oxford University Press.

Buchanan, A. 2014. *The Heart of Human Rights.* Oxford: Oxford University Press.

Buchanan, A. and Keohane, R. 2006. 'The Legitimacy of Global Governance Institutions', *Ethics & International Affairs* 20(4): 405–437.

Buckinx, B., Trejo-Mathys, J. and Waligore, T. 2015. *Domination and Global Political Justice.* New York: Routledge.

Bull, H. 2012/1977. *The Anarchical Society: A Study of Order in World Politics.* London: Palgrave Macmillan.

Bull, H. and Kingsbury, B. 1992. *Hugo Grotius and International Relations.* Oxford: Oxford University Press.

Cabrera, L. 2005. *Political Theory of Global Justice: A Cosmopolitan Case for the World State.* London: Routledge.

Christiano, T. 2010. 'Democratic Legitimacy and International Institutions', in S. Besson and J. Tasioulas, eds., *The Philosophy of International Law*, 119–138. Oxford: Oxford University Press.

Clark, I. and Neumann, I. 1996. *Classical Theories of International Relations.* Houndmills: Macmillan.

Cutler, A. 2003. *Private Power and Global Authority: Transnational Merchant Law in the Global Political Economy.* Cambridge: Cambridge University Press.

Dahl, R. 1999. 'Can International Organizations Be Democratic? A Skeptic's View', in I. Shapiro and C. Hacker-Cordón, eds., *Democracy's Edges*, 19–36. Cambridge: Cambridge University Press.

De Búrca, G., Keohane, R. and Sabel, C. 2014. 'Global Experimentalist Governance', *British Journal of Political Science* 44(3): 477–486.

Deudney, D. 2007. *Bounding Power: Republican Security Theory from the Polis to the Global Village*. Princeton, NJ: Princeton University Press.

Dorf, M. and Sabel, C. 1998. 'A Constitution of Democratic Experimentalism', *Columbia Law Review* 982: 267–473.

Doyle, M. 1983. 'Kant, Liberal Legacies, and Foreign Affairs', *Philosophy & Public Affairs* 12(3): 205–235.

Dryzek, J. 2006. *Deliberative Global Politics: Discourse and Democracy in a Divided World*. Cambridge: Polity.

Erman, E. 2013. 'In Search of Democratic Agency in Deliberative Governance', *European Journal of International Relations* 19(4): 847–868.

Erman, E. 2015. 'Global Political Legitimacy beyond Justice and Democracy'. *International Theory*. DOI: 10.1017/S1752971915000196.

Goodhart, M. 2011. 'Democratic Accountability in Global Politics: Norms, Not Agents', *Journal of Politics* 73(1): 45–60.

Goodhart, M. 2014. 'Accountable International Relations', in M. Bovens, R. Goodin and T. Schillemans, eds., *Oxford Handbook of Public Accountability*, 289–304. Oxford: Oxford University Press.

Gould, C. 2004. *Globalizing Democracy and Human Rights*. Cambridge: Cambridge University Press.

Grant, R. and Keohane, R. 2005. 'Accountability and Abuses of Power in World Politics', *American Political Science Review* 99(1): 29–43.

James, A. 2005. 'Constructing Justice for Existing Practice: Rawls and the Status Quo', *Philosophy & Public Affairs* 33(3): 281–316.

Kant, I. 1970. *Kant's Political Writings*, ed. H Reiss, trans. H. Nisbet. Cambridge: Cambridge University Press.

Habermas, J. 2013. 'A Political Constitution for the Pluralist World Society?', *Journal of Chinese Philosophy* 40(1): 226–238.

Held, D. 1995. *Democracy and the Global Order: From the Modern State to Cosmopolitan Governance*. Stanford, CA: Stanford University Press.

Held, D. 2006. *Models of Democracy*. Cambridge: Polity.

Held, D. and Koenig-Archibugi, M., eds. 2005. *Global Governance and Public Accountability*. Oxford: Blackwell.

Hoffmann, S., Rousseau, J. and Fidler, D. 1991. *Rousseau on International Relations*. New York: Oxford University Press.

Hurrell, A. 1996. 'Vattel: Pluralism and Its Limits', in I. Clark and I. Neumann, eds., *Classical Theories of International Relations*, 233–255. Houndmills: Macmillan.

Hurrell, A. 2007. *On Global Order: Power, Values, and the Constitution of International Society*. Oxford: Oxford University Press.

Hurrell, A. and Macdonald, T. 2012. 'Global Public Power: The Subject of Principles of Global Political Legitimacy', *Critical Review of International Social and Political Philosophy* 15(5): 553–571.

Hurrell, A. and Macdonald, T. 2013. 'Ethics and Norms in International Relations', in W. Carlsnaes, T. Risse and B. Simmons, eds., *Handbook of International Relations*, 57–84. London: Sage.

Kingsbury, B., Krisch, N. and Stewart, R. 2005. 'The Emergence of Global Administrative Law', *Law and Contemporary Problems* 68(3/4): 15–61.

Koenig-Archibugi, M. 2010. 'Is Global Democracy Possible?', *European Journal of International Relations* 17(3): 519–542.

Krisch, N. 2010. *Beyond Constitutionalism: The Pluralist Structure of Postnational Law*. Oxford: Oxford University Press.

Krisch, N. 2015. 'The Structure of Postnational Authority'. http://papers.ssrn.com/sol3/papers.cfm?abstract_id=2564579.

Kuper, A. 2004. *Democracy Beyond Borders: Justice and Representation in Global Institutions*. New York: Oxford University Press.

Lefkowitz, D. 2010. 'The Sources of International Law: Some Philosophical Reflections', in S. Besson and J. Tasioulas, eds., *The Philosophy of International Law*, 187–204. Oxford: Oxford University Press.

Linklater, A. 1996. 'Hegel, the State, and International Relations', in I. Clark and I. Neumann, eds., *Classical Theories of International Relations*, 193–209. Houndmills: Macmillan.

List, C. and Koenig-Archibugi, M. 2010. 'Can There Be a Global Demos?: An Agency-Based Approach', *Philosophy & Public Affairs* 38(1): 76–110.

Long, D. and Wilson, P., eds. 1995. *Thinkers of the Twenty Years' Crisis: Inter-War Idealism Reassessed*. Oxford: Oxford University Press.

Macdonald, K. 2011. 'Global Democracy for a Partially Joined-Up World. Toward a Multi-Level System of Public Power and Democratic Governance?', in D. Archibugi, M. Koenig-Archibugi and R. Marchetti, eds., *Global Democracy: Normative and Empirical Perspectives*, 183–209. Cambridge: Cambridge University Press.

Macdonald, T. 2003. 'Boundaries Beyond Borders: Delineating Democratic "Peoples" in a Globalizing World', *Democratization* 10(3): 173–194.

Macdonald, T. 2008. *Global Stakeholder Democracy: Power and Representation Beyond Liberal States*. Oxford: Oxford University Press.

Macdonald, T. 2011. 'Citizens or Stakeholders? Exclusion, Equality and Legitimacy in Global Stakeholder Democracy', in D. Archibugi, M. Koenig-Archibugi and R. Marchetti, eds., *Global Democracy: Normative and Empirical Perspectives*, 47–68. Cambridge: Cambridge University Press.

Macdonald T. 2016. 'Institutional Facts and Principles of Global Political Legitimacy', *Journal of International Political Theory*.

Macdonald, T. and Ronzoni, M. 2012. 'Introduction: The Idea of Global Political Justice', *Critical Review of International Social and Political Philosophy* 15(5): 521–533.

Marchetti, R. 2008. *Global Democracy: For and Against: Ethical Theory, Institutional Design and Social Struggles*. London: Routledge.

Marchetti, R. 2011. 'Models of Global Democracy: In Defence of Cosmo-Federalism', in D. Archibugi, M. Koenig-Archibugi and R. Marchetti, eds., *Global Democracy: Normative and Empirical Perspectives*, 22–46. Cambridge: Cambridge University Press.

Miller, D. 1995. *On Nationality*. Oxford: Oxford University Press.

Miller, D. 2007. *National Responsibility and Global Justice*. Oxford: Oxford University Press.

Moore, M. 2001. *The Ethics of Nationalism*. Oxford: Oxford University Press.

Mulgan, R. 2000. '"Accountability": An Ever-Expanding Concept?', *Public Administration* 78(3): 555–573.

Nanz, P. and Steffek, J. 2004. 'Global Governance, Participation and the Public Sphere', *Government & Opposition* 392: 314–335.

Ortega, M. 1996. 'Vitoria and the Universalist Conception of International Relations', in I. Clark and I. Neumann, eds., *Classical Theories of International Relations*, 99–119. Houndmills: Macmillan.

Pettit, P. 2010. 'Legitimate International Institutions: A Neo-Republican Perspective', in S. Besson and J. Tasioulas, eds., *The Philosophy of International Law*, 139–160. Oxford: Oxford University Press.

Pettit, P. 2012. *On the People's Terms: A Republican Theory and Model of Democracy*. Cambridge: Cambridge University Press.

Pogge, T. 1992. 'Cosmopolitanism and Sovereignty', *Ethics* 103(1): 48–75.

Rawls, J. 1971. *A Theory of Justice*. Cambridge. MA: Harvard University Press.

Rawls, J. 2001. *The Law of Peoples: With 'The Idea of Public Reason Revisited'*. Cambridge, MA: Harvard University Press.

Ronzoni, M. 2009. 'The Global Order: A Case of Background Injustice? A Practice-Dependent Account', *Philosophy & Public Affairs* 37(3): 229–256.

Ronzoni, M. 2012. 'Two Conceptions of State Sovereignty and their Implications for Global Institutional Design', *Critical Review of International Social and Political Philosophy* 15(5): 573–591.

Rosenau, J. 2000. 'Change, Complexity and Governance in a Globalizing Space', in J. Pierre, ed., *Debating Governance*, 167–200. Oxford: Oxford University Press.

Rossi, E. and Sleat, M. 2014. 'Realism in Normative Political Theory', *Philosophy Compass* 9(10): 689–701.

Rubenstein, J. 2007. 'Accountability in an Unequal World', *Journal of Politics* 69(3): 616–632.

Russett, B. 1994. *Grasping the Democratic Peace: Principles for a Post-Cold War World*. Princeton, NJ: Princeton University Press.

Sabel, C. and Zeitlin, J. 2008. 'Learning From Difference: The New Architecture of Experimentalist Governance in the EU', *European Law Journal* 14(3): 271–327.

Sangiovanni, A. 2008. 'Justice and the Priority of Politics to Morality', *Journal of Political Philosophy* 162: 137–164.

Slaughter, A., Tulumello, A. and Wood, S. 1998. 'International Law and International Relations Theory: A New Generation of Interdisciplinary Scholarship', *American Journal of International Law* 92(3): 367–397.

Steffek, J. 2003. 'The Legitimation of International Governance: A Discourse Approach', *European Journal of International Relations* 92: 249–275.

Tamir, Y. 1995. *Liberal Nationalism*. Princeton, NJ: Princeton University Press.

Tasioulas, J. 2010. 'The Legitimacy of International Law', in S. Besson and J. Tasioulas, eds., *The Philosophy of International Law*, 97–116. Oxford: Oxford University Press.

Walzer, M. 1980. 'The Moral Standing of States: A Response to Four Critics', *Philosophy & Public Affairs* 9(3): 209–229.

Walzer, M. 2008. 'On Promoting Democracy', *Ethics & International Affairs* 22(4): 351–355.

Welsh, J. 1995. *Edmund Burke and International Relations: The Commonwealth of Europe and the Crusade Against the French Revolution*. London: Palgrave Macmillan.

Wendt, A. 1999. 'A Comment on Held's Cosmopolitanism', in I. Shapiro and C. Hacker-Cordón, eds., *Democracy's Edges*, 19–36. Cambridge: Cambridge University Press.

Williams, B. 2005. *In the Beginning was the Deed: Realism and Moralism in Political Argument*. Princeton, NJ: Princeton University Press.

Young, I. 2002. *Inclusion and Democracy*. Oxford: Oxford University Press.

Zürn, M. 2004. 'Global Governance and Legitimacy Problems', *Government & Opposition* 392: 260–287.

Zürn, M. 2014. 'The Politicization of World Politics and Its Effects: Eight Propositions', *European Political Science Review* 6(1): 47–71.

CHAPTER FIVE

The Legitimacy of International Law

David Lefkowitz

The conduct of international affairs is subject to three kinds of normative standards. The first of these is prudence or rational self-interest, and its most common manifestation in international affairs involves reference to a state's national interest as a basis for defending or critiquing its international conduct. Justice provides a second metric for assessing the international conduct of states, and sometimes other actors, and a set of normative concepts including freedom, equality and fairness with which to argue for or against particular acts or policies. Law, including both international law and the foreign law of particular states, provides the third normative framework commonly employed by those engaged in or otherwise concerned with international affairs. Thus an international act, such as one state's invasion of another, can be criticized as imprudent, and/or as unjust and/or as illegal. As normative claims, each of these criticisms purports to give the invading state a reason to desist, and at least in the case of the second and third criticisms, entails that the invaded state and perhaps other actors (for example, other states) have a reason to treat the invading state in ways they would not otherwise be justified in doing. The focus of this chapter is on how international law performs this function; that is, it aims to explain why and when the fact that an act would violate international law in itself provides an actor with a reason, indeed a moral obligation, not to perform it. The answer, I shall argue, is that international law does so if and only if it is legitimate.

I begin in the first section with an analysis of the concept of legitimacy. What does it mean to attribute legitimacy to international law, or to characterize the legal framework that constitutes, say, the World Trade Organization (WTO) as illegitimate? Sections 2–3 consider a number of possible grounds for international law's legitimacy, including the contributions it can make to its subjects' ability to act as they have most reason to act, the consent of those it claims as subjects, considerations of fair-play, and its democratic credentials. My focus in each case is twofold: first, with arguments for thinking that a particular ground is either necessary or sufficient for international law's legitimacy; and, second, with the implications the account in question has for international law's present claim to legitimacy. As will become clear, none of the grounds for international law's legitimacy considered herein, separately or in combination, show the existing international legal order to be fully legitimate; indeed, it likely falls well short of that (perhaps ideal) standard. Still, just as the failure of any existing social order to realize a conception of justice does not by itself provide a reason to reject that conception, so too the failure of the international legal order to qualify as legitimate according to some standard of legitimacy does not by itself provide a reason to reject that standard. I conclude in section 4 by offering a number of reasons why we should care about international law's legitimacy; indeed, why from a moral point of view increasing the international legal order's legitimacy might even take priority over making it more just.

1   The Concept of Legitimacy

Judgments of political legitimacy concern attempts to rule or govern. A attempts to rule or govern B with respect to some domain of conduct if and only if A maintains that B ought to defer to A's judgment regarding what B may, must or must not do; that is, if and only if A claims practical authority over B.[1] When A does so, she maintains that her directives provide B with content-independent and exclusionary reasons for action. So, if A claims authority over B and she directs B not to Φ, then she maintains that B has a reason not to Φ simply because A instructed him not do so, a reason that makes no reference to the content of A's direction to B (i.e., what Φ-ing is). Moreover, she maintains that B ought to treat A's instruction not to Φ as a reason to exclude from his deliberation some or all of the reasons he might have to Φ. From B's perspective, to treat A's directive as a content-independent and exclusionary reason just is to defer to A's judgment; that is, to recognize her as having practical authority over him.

A's attempt to rule over B is *legitimate* if and only if A has a right to rule B, a right that correlates to B's duty to obey A. Strictly speaking, what the subject of a legitimate authority owes her is not conduct, but a certain form of deliberation or practical reasoning, one that treats the authority's directives as content-independent and exclusionary reasons for action. In terms of Hohfeld's (1919) well-known typology of rights, then, the right to rule should be understood as a moral power rather than a claim-right, with the authority's subjects bearers of a moral liability (to have their deliberation shaped by the authority's directives) rather than a duty. Particular conduct may also be owed to the ruler, but it need not be. For example, and in Hohfeldian terms, B may have a duty not to damage C's property, one correlative to C's property right, and a liability to A's judgment regarding what counts as damage to C's property (i.e., what the content of C's property right is), correlative to A's moral power to direct B's conduct (vis-à-vis C's property). Getting clear on this conceptual point is important if we are to avoid the common but mistaken assumption that a successful theory of legitimacy must explain how those subject to a putative authority can owe *it* conduct in accordance with its directives. Nevertheless, and at the risk of inviting this confusion, I will continue to speak of subjects' duty to obey an authority, since this is the language commonly employed in discussions of legitimacy.

To claim the right to rule is not to have it. If A's attempt to rule over B is illegitimate, then while A may claim that B ought to treat her instruction not to Φ as a content-independent and exclusionary reason, B has no duty to do so. Note, however, that B may still have prudential or moral reasons not to Φ, perhaps even conclusive ones; the denial of a putative authority's legitimacy is neither equivalent to, nor entails, the claim that an agent should not act as the putative authority would have him act. Moreover, A's attempt to rule over B may correctly be judged to be good, or at least better than the likely alternatives, even if A has no right to rule B. Both of these points bear emphasis, since, as will become clear below, at present international law often lacks the authority it claims; that is, it is illegitimate. A mistaken understanding of what follows from this conclusion may explain why some theorists argue that we ought to use a less demanding conception of legitimacy, one that correlates to duties of support and non-interference but not to a duty to obey, and/or employ more easily satisfied criteria to justify claims to legitimacy when theorizing international law than we do when theorizing municipal or state law (Buchanan, 2010). Once we recognize that agents can have compelling reasons to support illegitimate institutions, to work for their reform rather than their elimination or wholesale replacement, we should find unpersuasive this rationale for introducing different conceptions of legitimacy, or different standards for when legal institutions enjoy it.[2]

Some theorists maintain that, in addition to the right to issue authoritative directives, the concept of legitimacy includes the right to enforce those directives, or more generally the right to impose costs on those who fail to act as directed or to grant benefits to those who do. The tendency to do so may reflect the common description of certain uses of force as legitimate or illegitimate, or the fact that much theorizing about the concept of legitimacy takes as its subject modern states' attempts at governance. Whatever the cause, we should reject this characterization of legitimacy and instead treat enforcement, or the imposition of costs or granting of benefits more generally, as simply another form of conduct over which authority may be exercised, but not conduct in which an agent must engage in order to qualify as an authority. To claim authority over the enforcement of authoritative directives is simply to claim the authority to determine who may use force against those who fail to act as directed, when they may do so, and what form the use of force may or may not take. In the modern state, those authorized to enforce the law are often legal officials; that is, legislative and judicial officials authorize officials of the executive branch of government to execute or enforce the law. But this is not always the case; for example, modern states authorize private actors to use force in self-defence, in light of which we often describe such acts as legitimate. Within the international legal order, almost all law enforcement takes the form of legally authorized self-help. For instance, the WTO enforces the ruling of its dispute settlement body by authorizing the party that brought the complaint to impose limited countermeasures against the party found to be in violation of its legal obligations as a member of the WTO. We appear to have good reason, then, to characterize the *concept* of legitimacy solely in terms of the exercise of authority, even if the *justifiability* of a putative authority's claim to legitimacy depends on its ability to reliably impose costs on the disobedient and grant benefits to the obedient.

In crafting public international law, states and international organizations assert that those subject to the law have a duty to obey it. The fact that a state has an international legal obligation to forbear from armed intervention in another state's territory except under very specific conditions is alleged to provide it with a content-independent and exclusionary reason not to do so. Similarly, as a signatory to the WTO a state has an international legal obligation not to impose tariffs on select goods imported from other WTO members (again, except under very specific conditions), a legal obligation that is alleged to provide it with a content-independent and exclusionary reason not to perform these acts. What these legal obligations purport to exclude is a state acting on its own judgment that armed intervention or the imposition of tariffs will advance its national interest or promote justice. Whether these judgments are true or false, if the international legal norms that create the aforementioned obligations are legitimate, then states are not free to act on those judgments, but must defer to the law's judgment that such acts ought not to be performed.

With a clearer understanding of the concept of legitimacy, we can now consider the conditions under which agents, and in particular international legal officials, possess it. By 'international legal officials', I mean state officials engaged in crafting or applying international law, as well as officials in international legal institutions such as the WTO and the International Court of Justice (ICJ). International legal officials attempt to exercise authority by issuing general rules or specific decisions that are intended to guide international legal subjects. Questions regarding the legitimacy of international law, then, are questions about when and why these attempts to exercise authority succeed or fail – or put another way, when and why international legal subjects should or should not treat their legal obligations as providing them with content-independent and exclusionary reasons for action.

2   The Instrumental Argument for International Law's Legitimacy

What makes international law legitimate?

Justifications of authority fall into one of two categories: those in which deference to authority is instrumental to the just treatment of others, and more broadly to acting as one has reason to act, and those in which deference to authority is (also) constitutive of the just treatment of others. In contemporary debates, the first of these approaches is most closely associated with the philosopher Joseph Raz, with John Tasioulas and Samantha Besson among those who have drawn on Raz's work to offer an analysis of international law's legitimacy (Raz, 1979, 2006; Besson, 2009; Tasioulas, 2010). According to Raz, law is legitimate, or has a justified claim to authority vis-à-vis its subjects, when the following two conditions are met:

1 The Normal Justification Condition (NJC): The subject would better conform to reasons that apply to him anyway (that is, to reasons other than the directives of the authority) if he intends to be guided by the authority's directives than if he does not.
2 The Independence Condition (IC): The matters regarding which the first condition is met are such that, with respect to them, it is better to conform to reason than to decide for oneself, unaided by authority (Raz, 2006: 1014).

A's claim to authority over B is justified, then, if B is more likely to act as he has most reason to act by deferring to A's judgment regarding what he should or should not do than by acting on his own judgment, except in cases where it is more important that B decide for himself what to do than that he decide correctly (i.e., than that he do what he has most reason to do). In such cases, A enjoys a right to rule B, and B has a duty to obey A's directives.

Some theorists contend that the NJC does not suffice to justify one agent's claim to authority over another. They argue that the mere fact that B will do better at acting as he has most reason to act if he defers to A's judgment does not entail that A has a right to rule B (e.g., Buchanan, 2010: 85). Raz concedes this point in some cases, namely those where it is more important that an agent act on his own judgment than that he act in accordance with right reason. When and why this is the case is a point over which theorists may disagree without disputing Raz's general account of when one agent's claim to authority over another is justified. Moreover, it is not merely the fact that an agent will do better at acting on the reasons that apply to him by deferring to the law that renders the law legitimate. Rather, it is that fact in conjunction with the nature of the reasons that apply to the agent independently of the law that does so. In the most general terms, if B has a moral duty to treat C justly, a reason for action that exists independently of the law, and if B is more likely to fulfil that duty by obeying the law than by acting on his own judgment, then those two facts suffice to establish the law's right to rule B. If, in fact, B is more likely to treat C justly if she defers to A's judgment regarding what that requires than if she acts on her own judgment, then it is hard to see why that does not suffice to establish A's right to rule B properly conceived; that is, as A enjoying a moral power to determine the reasons for action B ought to consider vis-à-vis her treatment of C, a power A exercises by issuing directives that provide B with content-independent and exclusionary reasons for action.

Some argue that satisfaction of the NJC cannot suffice to establish the law's authority over an agent because, if it did, then even a deeply unjust state could be legitimate (see, e.g., Christiano, 2008: 234). The fact that state officials or some of its subjects stand ready to perpetrate even greater injustices if an individual does not act as the law directs may give the individual a reason to treat the law as authoritative, but surely it does not entail that the state has a *right* to rule the individual; that is, that it enjoys *legitimate* authority. In response, it is important first to keep in mind that on Raz's instrumental account the duty to obey (some of) the laws of an unjust state is owed not to the state, but to those individuals a person is more likely to treat justly by obeying the law than by acting on his or her own judgment. But second, we should distinguish between the NJC being satisfied and an agent having good reason to believe that it is. Subjects of a deeply unjust state will often have little reason to believe that either its law or its legal institutions aim to improve their conformity to the independent (moral) reasons that apply to them; that is, that the law represents a good faith effort to satisfy the NJC. Therefore, they will have little or no reason to treat it as authoritative – that is, as providing them with content-independent and exclusionary reasons for action. This is likely to be so even where, as a matter of fact, the law of a deeply unjust state does satisfy the NJC, at least vis-à-vis some of its subjects. In such cases, while the individuals in question ought to defer to the law rather than act on their own judgment, they will likely not be blameworthy for their failure to recognize that this is the case.

Suppose, *arguendo*, that the independence condition is met, and consider how international law might help those over whom it claims jurisdiction to improve their conformity to right reason, as I will label an agent's acting as he, she or it has most reason to act. One way it may do so is by correcting for ignorance or mistaken beliefs. Tasioulas offers as an example international legal rules created via the enactment of multilateral treaties (2010: 101). The process whereby such rules are crafted makes it likely that they reflect information that any single party to the convention would fail to acquire on its own, and so fail to take into account when deciding how to act (e.g., what particular foreign policy or domestic legal regime to adopt). Moreover, negotiations over multilateral treaties can serve as a useful corrective to biases that undergird parties' mistaken beliefs, once again facilitating practical reasoning that is better informed and so likely to more closely approximate or conform to right reason than would unilateral decision-making. In some cases, international law may also provide some of its subjects with access to expertise they cannot produce domestically.

International law can also protect its subjects against what Tasioulas labels volitional defects. For example, state officials may come under great pressure from more powerful states, representatives of multinational corporations, or domestic interest groups to engage in conduct that promotes those actors' perceived interests or vision of justice but that is contrary to right reason. International law provides a mechanism for resisting such pressure. International law's ability to steel its subjects against temptation is particularly important given the general human disposition to impatience, the tendency to treat oneself or one's circumstances as exceptional, and the fact that the interests of legal officials in remaining in power may diverge from both the long-term interests of the state's present and future members and the demands of justice.

Finally, and perhaps most importantly, international law can enhance its subjects' conformity to right reason by solving collective action problems (Buchanan and Keohane, 2006: 107–8; Besson, 2009: 352–7, 366–70; Tasioulas, 2010: 102). In some cases, it may do so by rendering more determinate a shared but vague standard of right conduct, where the parties are rightly indifferent between any of a number of possible ways in which the abstract standard may be made more concrete. Far more common, however, is disagreement over what justice requires, forbids or permits with respect to the use of force, international migration, trade in goods, financial transactions, the use of and control over the oceans or the earth's atmosphere, etc. In all these cases, international actors are generally likely to do better at approximating justice by conforming to common standards set out in international law than by acting on their own judgment. In some cases, such as addressing climate change, this may be because justice can only be achieved via the cooperation of (nearly) all states. In other cases, the attempt by a state or international organization to act on its own understanding of what justice requires, and contrary to international law, may result in an immediate gain in justice in one place, and/or vis-à-vis one type of conduct, but a longer term and greater reduction in justice in that place or in others, and vis-à-vis that type of conduct or others. One reason this is so is that one state's genuinely just war or trade regime may frequently appear to another to be an act of aggression or protectionism. A second reason is that state officials acting in bad faith may offer the example of another state's just but illegal conduct as cover for their own unjust conduct. Each of these arguments points to the likely bad consequences of deviating from the common standards of right conduct set out in international law. I consider below additional, non-instrumental, justifications for the claim that actors have a duty to obey international legal norms that facilitate justice-enhancing collective action.

International law can successfully address the problem of collective action raised by differing understandings of justice only if most of those whose cooperation is needed, especially the most powerful, take it to be authoritative. If other international legal subjects do not, then each party has little reason to assume that conformity to international law per se is the best means for it to approximate the just treatment of others and its own just treatment by them. Thus, where international law's legitimacy is a function of its facilitating justice-approximating collective action, international law's *de facto* legitimacy is a necessary condition for its *de jure* authority (Raz, 2006: 1036). It follows, Tasioulas notes, that 'in order to maintain this source of legitimacy…public international law must not stray too far from implementing values that resonate widely with its would-be subjects' (2010: 102). As a consequence, at a given point in time the content of international law may diverge considerably from what justice truly requires. Yet as long as international legal subjects are more likely to act justly (or, perhaps better, less likely to act unjustly) by obeying international law than by acting on their own judgment, they have a duty to do so.

The instrumental account entails that international law's legitimacy may be piecemeal. For any particular international legal norm or legal regime, the NJC may fail to establish its authoritativeness vis-à-vis some or even all of the actors whose conduct it purports to direct. Generally speaking, existing international law hews quite closely to the interests of powerful states (or elites within those states), and gives highest priority to the preservation of peace and stability, often at the expense of justice. As a consequence, its dictates may often diverge from what right reason requires precisely because it is the result of legislative activities that are not undertaken on the basis of a good faith effort to identify it. A full defence of these assertions would require both an argument for a substantive conception of international or global justice and a careful empirical analysis of existing international law, neither of which I can carry out here. Still, even those who maintain that international law is not merely the product of power and interest acknowledge that those two factors play a considerable role in determining its content. If so, then on the instrumental account a fair bit of scepticism regarding the extent of international law's legitimacy seems warranted.

How can we identify legitimate international law?

Thus far I have focused on the various ways in which international law can satisfy the NJC. Yet a theory of the legitimacy of international law should do more than explain the normative basis of international law's legitimacy – that is, what *makes* it authoritative. It should also offer guidance on how to *identify* legitimate international law, reasons to believe that international law or international legislators meet the normal justification condition. The complex standard of legitimacy for global governance institutions advocated by Allen Buchanan and Robert Keohane (2006) provides an excellent starting point for developing such an account (see also Kumm, 2004).

The complex standard consists of a set of substantive and procedural requirements that, when met, provide compelling evidence for the legitimacy of a global governance institution's attempt to rule.[3] The former include not persistently violating the least controversial human rights, not forgoing institutional changes that would provide greater benefits than existing ones and that are both feasible and accessible without excessive transition costs, and not intentionally or knowingly engaging in conduct at odds with the global governance institutions' purported aims and commitments. The latter include mechanisms for holding global governance institutions accountable for meeting the aforementioned substantive requirements as well as mechanisms for contesting the terms of accountability; that is, the ends that global governance institutions ought to pursue and the means they should employ in doing so. To be effective, mechanisms for holding officials accountable must be broadly transparent. This includes making information about how the institution works not only available, but accessible to both internal and external actors, for example inspectors general and nongovernmental organizations, as well as the provision of public justifications for the most consequential efforts at governance.

What unifies the various elements of the complex standard is that they all provide the legal subjects of global governance institutions with reason to believe that officials in these institutions are making a good faith effort to determine what justice requires. The point may be clearer if we consider the converse: the absence of one or more elements of the complex standard of legitimacy gives those subject to an attempt at global governance reason to doubt that the putative rulers aspire to enhance their subjects' conformity to right reason. Instead, subjects may suspect, and perhaps rightly so, that governance is being exercised in pursuit of other goals, such as the national interest of powerful states or the private interests of businesses or religious groups, and contrary to the demands of justice. Consider, for example, the substantive elements of the complex standard: no attempt at international governance, either by global governance institutions or by states that persistently violated 'the least controversial human rights' or that systematically discriminated in the application and enforcement of international legal norms, could plausibly claim to be making a good faith effort to enhance its subjects' conformity to right reason. The procedural elements that comprise the complex standard evidence a good faith effort to determine what right reason requires partly because they militate against efforts to deploy international law for private interest rather than the public or common good, and partly because they improve the quantity and quality of the information on the basis of which global governance is conducted. As the first of these claims implies, the complex standard's procedural elements are desirable not only for their epistemic value but also because they are likely to facilitate efforts at governance that actually succeed in being legitimate; that is, that actually meet the normal justification for authority. As an example of the second claim, the requirement that global governance institutions facilitate effective engagement with external epistemic agents such as Human Rights Watch and the International Committee of the Red Cross likely leads to more informed and less biased rules and decisions than either these institutions' officials or those they directly or indirectly govern would achieve on their own.

3 Non-Instrumental Arguments for International Law's Legitimacy

International law's value as a means for enhancing its subjects' conformity to right reason is not the only ground theorists have offered for its legitimacy. Many have sought instead, or at least in addition, to defend non-instrumental accounts, according to which obedience to legitimate international law constitutes the just treatment of others. At least since the nineteenth century the most prominent such account used to justify international law's claim to authority has been state consent. More recently, theorists have identified considerations of fair play as a basis for international law's legitimacy, or maintained that the justifiability of international law's claim to authority rests on it being democratically enacted. I consider each of these approaches in turn.

Consent

Consent involves a minimum of two parties: an agent who grants another a claim-right or power and thereby acquires a correlative duty or liability, and an agent who acquires the right. For example, in signing and ratifying a treaty setting out the terms that will govern their use of a river that runs through or along both of their territories, two states may be said to grant one another rights to conduct that conforms to those terms, and to acquire obligations to act as the treaty directs. Similarly, in joining the WTO, states consent to its authority to resolve their disputes regarding compliance with their obligations under that treaty. In conforming to the terms of a treaty to which they have consented, states uphold their duties to one another, which is to say that in at least one respect they treat one another justly. They may also treat one another justly because the content of the treaty reflects or determines what justice truly requires vis-à-vis the use of a common resource, trade, the use of force, etc. This need not be the case, however; a state that has consented to govern its conduct according to certain terms may not unilaterally disregard them simply because it believes that justice or its national interest require contrary conduct.[4] Rather, the state owes its obedience to the other party or parties to the agreement, or, in other words, the state's consent makes the norms that comprise the agreement authoritative.

Consent's attraction as a basis for a duty to obey the law rests on its ability to reconcile a conception of agents as morally free and equal with their submission to authority. If an agent chooses to place himself under a duty to another, then those duties are the product of the agent's control over his life, not requirements imposed upon him or a facet of his subjugation to the will of another agent. If consent is to manifest this kind of control, it must be free and informed; agreements that are made involuntarily or as a result of fraud generate neither moral duties nor moral rights. Moreover, one agent may consent on another's behalf only if the latter authorizes him to do so, since only then will the resulting obligations be properly characterized as a product of the obligated agent's control over his life. Finally, the moral freedom and equality of all agents places limits on the obligations that any can acquire via consent; even when free and informed, agreements to commit murder, theft, fraud, etc. are null and void.

Each of the foregoing conditions on the generation of moral obligations via consent provides a basis for challenging consent-based arguments for international law's legitimacy. First, in light of the costs their citizens are likely to suffer if they refuse, the consent of economically and militarily weak states to bilateral or multilateral treaties frequently fails to qualify as voluntary. Even where the costs of non-participation do not rise to the level necessary to render agreement non-voluntary, if the distribution of benefits and burdens set out in the agreement reflect unrectified past injustices committed by one party against another, then the agreement may still be at odds with the commitment to the treatment of all as free and equal that underpins consent-based accounts of legitimacy. Second, states increasingly consent to general frameworks that are then filled in by treaty-based but partly autonomous bodies that exercise quasi-legislative and/or quasi-judicial powers (Kumm, 2004: 914). As a consequence, states may find themselves subject to obligations they did not intend nor even suspect they would acquire when they consented to the original framework. Generally speaking, while an agent need not know the precise details of the obligation she is acquiring via consent, the greater her ignorance of these matters the less compelling it will be to describe the agent's consent as the exercise of control over her life rather than as an abdication of control to another. Insofar as a treaty permits signatories to withdraw their consent to its terms, as many do, it might be argued that a state's decision not to do so constitutes its tacit or ongoing consent to specification of its terms by semi-autonomous international organizations such as the WTO or the International Criminal Court (ICC). Of course, this argument works only if the costs of withdrawal from the treaty are not so high as to render continued submission to it non-voluntary.

Second, the current governments of some and perhaps even many states lack the legitimate authority to consent to obligations on behalf of the political communities they claim to represent. Clearly this is true if a necessary condition for state officials having the standing to obligate their citizens under international law is that the state be sufficiently democratic and respectful of some core set of its subjects' rights. It may still be true of a fair number of states even if we should employ a somewhat broader understanding of what it is for state officials to adequately represent their citizens. Whether democratic or not, states may consistently fail to represent the interests of certain domestic minorities, such as indigenous peoples. The existence of persistent minorities challenges any state's claim to the standing to acquire obligations on behalf of all its subjects. Finally, some theorists point to the fact that much international law-making is carried out not by states' legislators, but by members of their executive branches, as a reason to doubt that those who purport to acquire international legal obligations on their citizens' behalf have the moral standing to do so. In some cases, such as legislative ratification of treaties negotiated by a state's executive branch, those who are empowered by a state's constitution to make law have some say in its acquisition of international legal obligations. Where that amounts to little more than an up or down vote on terms negotiated entirely, and perhaps secretively, by the executive, there may be reason to doubt that legislative consent suffices to render the resulting duties consistent with the treatment of the political community's members as free and equal.

Third, if any international legal norm or regime requires conduct that treats people in a manner incompatible with a proper understanding of their moral status as free and equal, then no state's consent to abide by those norms generates a genuine moral duty to do so. Thus, if Thomas Pogge is right to maintain that the WTO, the IMF, and the World Bank systematically contribute to the persistence of severe global poverty, and if in doing so they fail to treat the global poor as a proper understanding of their moral status as free and equal requires, then no state's consent to rule by these organizations gives rise to a moral obligation to act as they direct (Pogge, 2010). Much depends on what the proper understanding of people's moral status as free and equal is, of course. However defined, though, if consent matters because, and to the extent that, it enables agents to control or shape their lives by altering their rights, duties, powers, and immunities vis-à-vis others, then it cannot render permissible – let alone obligatory – conduct at odds with a proper appreciation for any agent's moral freedom and equality.

The foregoing arguments suggest that even where consent seems most likely to justify international law's claim to legitimacy, namely with respect to treaty-based law that applies to states, its success is likely to be piecemeal at best. This conclusion is only strengthened when we consider customary international law (CIL). Where CIL is a product of longstanding state practice, then those states that voluntarily and knowingly engage in the practice, or that at least do not persistently object to it, might be said to tacitly consent to the norms that structure that practice. Once again, though, this conclusion does not follow for those states whose participation or failure to object is nonvoluntary; for example, postcolonial states subject to customary international legal norms developed largely by European powers prior to or during the colonial era. Consent also appears to be an inadequate basis for the legitimacy of international legal norms that apply directly to individuals. These observations are typically offered to support the conclusion that at best consent offers an incomplete ground for international law's legitimacy, but it is worth noting the possibility of drawing the opposite conclusion, namely that the truth of the moral view that underpins consent-based accounts of legitimacy simply shows significant portions of international law to be illegitimate.

Thus far I have focused on the extent to which (state) consent actually provides a successful justification for international law's claim to authority. A more basic question, though, is whether consent is even a necessary condition for international law's legitimacy. If all agents necessarily owe certain moral duties to non-compatriots, and if they can discharge those duties only by treating international law, or at least certain international legal norms and institutions, as authoritative, then it follows that they have a moral duty to do so. The necessity of obedience to international law for the discharge of an agent's natural moral duties may be empirical and contingent, as Raz maintains, or it may be a conceptual truth, as Kant argued. In circumstances characterized by disagreement over what counts as rightful conduct, Kant claimed, agents have a moral duty to subject themselves to a common juridical order; that is, one in which all are governed by common standards, rather than each being free to act on his or her understanding of what counts as the treatment of persons as free and equal (Kant, 1996/1797: 456). For Kant, then, justice can only be (fully) realized through the rule of law, or, more precisely, a multilevel legal order composed of both the domestic law of a republican state and an international law governing relations between such states (and their citizens).

Fair play

The principle of fair play offers an alternative basis for states' and perhaps other international actors' duty to obey international law (Lefkowitz, 2011). On one common interpretation, the principle states that agents who benefit from others' participation in a cooperative scheme have a duty to contribute their fair share to its operation, as long as they rank receipt of those benefits at the cost of contributing their fair share to the scheme's operation over not enjoying those benefits and not bearing the costs of contribution to the scheme. An agent who fails to contribute his or her fair share when these conditions are met free-rides on the contributions of others; he or she takes unfair advantage of others' good faith sacrifices of their liberty or discretion. As noted above, international law frequently functions to facilitate mutually advantageous collective action among states and other international actors. If these actors take the benefits they enjoy as a result of others' deference to these legal norms to outweigh the costs of deferring themselves, then they have a fair-play duty to obey the law. In contrast to the aforementioned instrumental argument for the legitimacy of international legal norms that facilitate morally mandatory collective action, the fair-play argument treats deference to such norms as constitutive of the fair treatment of other international actors and required for that very reason, independent of any effects free-riding on others' obedience to international law may have.

Democracy

At the domestic level, some form of democratic decision-making, understood in individual-majoritarian terms, is widely viewed as at least a necessary condition for legitimacy, so much so that few rulers feel able to go without at least the façade of democratic rule. It may seem natural, therefore, to conclude that the legitimacy of global governance institutions and international law more generally requires that they become more democratic. Whether this is so depends, however, on the manner in which democracy contributes to law's legitimacy. Like legitimacy, democratic governance may be defended on both instrumental and non-instrumental grounds. As an example of the former, individual-majoritarian decision-making may have epistemic advantages over the feasible alternatives (Goodin, 2003; Estlund 2009). Depending on how substantive a conception of democratic decision-making we employ, it may result in greater collective deliberation than would otherwise take place. Several important points follow from this observation. First, democracy's instrumental value contributes to its legitimacy only insofar as it increases the probability that democratically enacted law meets the NJC – that is, improves its subjects' conformity to right reason. Second, if democracy is valuable only because its output satisfies the NJC, then there is little reason to think democracy is a necessary condition for law's legitimacy. In some cases, non-democratic decision-making procedures may serve equally well or better at producing legitimate law; for example, where democratic decision-making procedures systematically lead to unjustifiable discrepancies in the weight or importance given to the interests of some over others, as state-level democratic governance may do vis-à-vis the interests of citizens and non-citizens (Buchanan and Keohane, 2006: 415–16). Indeed, even if democratically enacted law best satisfies the NJC, non-democratically enacted law will still be legitimate if no democratic decision-making procedure exists and those over whom the law claims authority do better by deferring to it than by acting on their own judgment. In short, if democracy's value is entirely instrumental, then international law's democratic deficit need not preclude its legitimacy.

Many of those who defend democratic decision-making as a necessary condition for the legitimacy of domestic law do so on non-instrumental grounds, however. Thomas Christiano (2008), for example, argues for democratic authority on the grounds that in circumstances characterized by diversity, cognitive bias, and fallibility, the treatment of all as moral equals requires that agents be able to see that the shared institutions that structure their common lives together treat them as equals. Legitimacy depends on public equality. This requires in turn that each agent has an equal say in the shaping of those institutions; or, in other words, that the legal order that frames their interactions with one another be the product of, or at least subject to control by, a democratic assembly. Yet Christiano resists the extension of this last claim to the international legal order. In part he worries that a global peoples' assembly would fail to be sufficiently democratic; for example, it might too readily produce persistent minorities and thereby fail to instantiate a public commitment to the moral equality of all (2010: 133–4). More intriguing, though, is his argument that, at a global level, the public treatment of all as equals does not call for democratic governance, and need never do so (2010: 130–3). Rather, Christiano maintains that a form of democratic governance in which each individual has an equal say in shaping political and legal institutions is called for only among those who share a common world, defined as one in which there is a great deal of interdependence among agents' interests and where each has a roughly equal stake in the normative order produced or sustained by the institution's rule.

Consider the latter point first. If a system of rules will affect two parties to very different degrees, with one party's life barely impacted while the other's plans and prospects are deeply dependent upon the content of these rules, then it would be unfair to give them an equal say in settling what those rules should be. To do so would give the first party too much control over the second, with the latter unable to view the process as one that publicly treats all parties as moral equals. But why does the public equality argument for democratic rule apply only when there is a great deal of interdependence among agents' interests? Why not treat each interest or issue separately? Christiano replies that 'since democratic decision-making must be taken by majority rule, it is important that there be many issues so that those who come up losers on some issues be winners on others' (2010: 131). In the absence of recurring decision-making on a bundle of issues, losers in a majority-rule process have little reason to view it as publicly treating them as equals. Like permanent minorities, they have no procedural evidence, namely victories in the decision-making process, that they can point to as reason to believe that the governing institution is truly committed to the equal treatment of all those it rules.

Christiano acknowledges a few instances of interdependence among the interests of all individuals around the world, as in the case of climate change. However, he maintains that international legal institutions governing trade and the environment typically impact individuals' interests far less than domestic legal orders do, and, at least by implication, not enough to meet the first of the two conditions for the existence of a common world. Moreover, even when international legal norms do impact the lives of individuals around the world, they do so to very different degrees. The life plans and prospects of some individuals may depend a great deal on international trade, while for others the impact may be quite small. Were all to exercise an equal say in determining the international rules that ought to govern cross-border trade, then those whose lives depend heavily upon those rules could rightly complain that the procedure for governing global trade did not publicly treat them as moral equals.

Christiano rightly rejects the inference from the fact that the conduct of people in one state affects the interests of those living in other states (or, more narrowly, affects those interests that ground human rights) to the conclusion that the former can treat the latter justly only by submitting to a common legal order whose laws are enacted by a directly elected global parliament. However, the arguments he offers to support this conclusion elide the fundamental error in the inference, namely that if it is possible for agents to treat one another justly by limiting their interactions so that they do not threaten to setback one another's fundamental interests, then they are not morally required to submit to a common set of rules that govern these interactions. Instead, the decision to do so is one over which agents exercise moral discretion. The question of whether agents are morally required to submit to a common set of rules regulating some type of conduct is prior to the question of how the rules of such an order ought to be made if they are to be legitimate. The principle of public equality provides an answer to the latter question, but to answer the former, Christiano needs a version of the affected interests principle, namely one that holds that agents have a duty to submit to a common legal order if and only if doing so is necessary to avoid setbacks to their own and/or to others' fundamental interest in judgment.

Rather than a global democratic assembly, Christiano maintains that efforts to establish international law's legitimacy should focus on making it the product of, or subject to control by, a fair system of voluntary association among highly representative states, or a fair democratic association (2010: 126–9). In principle, at least, state-level democratic procedures could offer individuals a voice in the shaping of international legal norms, and in practice they might better serve this end than would other legislative mechanisms, even if they fell well short of the ideal. An international legal order in which all states' commitments were genuinely voluntary, and in which the procedures for legislating, applying, and enforcing international legal rules and decisions did not reflect unjustifiable asymmetries in bargaining power, would be one whose product or operation could be viewed by all individuals as committed to their equal treatment. Moreover, the justification of international law's legitimacy in the moral ideal of a free and equal association of internally legitimate democratic states provides a non-consensual basis for the legitimacy of those international legal norms that rule out conduct at odds with such an ideal – for example, the *jus cogens* prohibitions on slavery, genocide and aggressive war. Were the conditions for fair democratic association met, all individuals would have compelling reason to believe that both the domestic and the international institutions of collective governance to which they were subject were committed to the equal treatment of all, and so their efforts to rule them legitimate.

It may be worth emphasizing that Christiano does not deny that some existing international legal norms and practices enable agents residing in one state to violate the basic rights (or setback the fundamental interests) of people living in other states. Nor does his argument necessarily entail that the morally optimal world is one in which states, or the common worlds they constitute, exist as independent islands subject only to international legal rules that aim to preserve their independence. Rather, Christiano maintains only that efforts to reform the existing international legal order so that it satisfies the principle of public equality, and therefore enjoys legitimacy, should be in the direction of creating a free democratic association, not a global democratic parliament.

Yet the fair democratic association model of global governance confronts a serious difficulty. If voluntary agreements are to conform to the principle of public equality, they must be negotiated and entered into in free and fair conditions. Securing such conditions, however, requires a public law whose legitimacy cannot itself depend upon voluntary agreement. A legitimate public international law consists in a set of impartial rules that aim at the common good, and such rules cannot themselves be the product of agreements in which parties act partially, that is, to advance their own interests. This is true even if actors seek to advance their interests only within what they take to be the moral limits on doing so, for the very reasons that Christiano offers when defending the legitimacy of a liberal democratic state's domestic law.[5] The conclusion Christiano draws is that realizing the conditions for a free democratic association 'seems to drive us in the direction of global institutions, which in turn must be evaluated in terms of democratic principles' (2011: 92). This appears to leave us at an impasse, unable to ground international law's legitimacy in either its enactment by a global democratic legislature or in a voluntary association of democratic states.

4   Why Care About Legitimacy?

The foregoing discussion suggests that, at present, international law enjoys less, and perhaps far less, legitimacy than it claims (or that some claim on its behalf). Does that matter? Yes and no. As I mentioned earlier, one conclusion we should be careful not to draw from the illegitimacy of international legal norms or global governance institutions is that agents have no moral reasons to support them, including in some cases acting as they require, or to work for their reform rather than their replacement. Crucially, though, the sort of arguments that can be offered in support of complying with illegitimate rules and institutions differs from the one available when rules and institutions are legitimate, namely that one has a moral duty to obey those rules and institutions. Moreover, where international law's illegitimacy owes largely to its being an instrument for the unjust advancement of national or special interests by the relatively powerful, the less powerful may have little choice but to play by the existing legal rules. Doing so may be the right thing to do not only prudentially but also morally, if conduct that violates those rules is either unlikely to bring about a more just world or, possibly, if there are limits on the setbacks to their own interests that agents must bear in order to combat injustice.

Nevertheless, there are compelling reasons to pursue the goal of a more legitimate international legal order. First, greater legitimacy entails an increase in justice. This conclusion follows necessarily from Raz's account of what makes law legitimate; a world with more legitimate law is one in which actors more often conform to right reason than they do in a world with less legitimate law. Empirically, we have compelling evidence that mechanisms of accountability, transparency, and participation in the crafting of law and in governance more generally typically lead to outcomes widely viewed as just, or at least as more just than those produced by governance in the absence of such mechanisms. Second, it seems plausible to maintain that an increase in the actual or *de jure* legitimacy of international law will lead to an increase in its *de facto* legitimacy, which will in turn increase international law's actual legitimacy by making it more effective at guiding its subjects conduct.[6] The converse point may be even more powerful; the failure to pursue greater legitimacy for the international legal order may lead to more injustice as justifiable cynicism erodes some of the advances in, for example, managing conflicts, promoting human rights, and protecting the environment to which international law has been a significant contributor. Third, it may be possible to reach greater agreement regarding when international law enjoys legitimacy than when it is just. Recall in this regard Christiano's argument that democratic governance allows individuals to see the political institution that rules them as committed to the equal advancement of all its subjects' interests even when the substance of some of its laws offers reason to doubt it. Legitimacy also requires less than justice, both in terms of what it takes for an agent to enjoy legitimate authority and in terms of the duty it imposes on agents. In particular, an agent may concede the law's legitimacy while working to change it (perhaps even by acts of civil disobedience), which may make actors more willing to concede a norm's legitimacy than its justice. Finally, it may be that we should be more concerned with the legitimacy of international law than with its justice. The aforementioned possibility that we are more likely to achieve widespread agreement on legitimacy than on justice provides a pragmatic reason to draw this conclusion. Although justice is the ideal, legitimacy may be the best we can do, and therefore, at the very least, we should be extremely hesitant to risk a diminution in international law's legitimacy for an increase in its justice. There is also a principled argument for focusing more on legitimacy than on justice, however, namely the one associated with Kant and briefly mentioned above, according to which just relations between agents can only be realized within a particular kind of legal order.[7] Only in a republican legal order can agents enjoy freedom as independence or non-domination, meaning lives in which they neither exercise arbitrary control over others nor are subject to such control themselves. If these are the terms in which we ought to understand justice, then the pursuit of global justice requires nothing more, but nothing less, than the realization of a fully legitimate international legal order.

References

Besson, S. 2009. 'The Authority of International Law: Lifting the State Veil', *Sydney Law Review* 31: 343–380.

Bodansky, D. 2013. 'Legitimacy in International Law and International Relations', in J. L. Dunoff and M. A. Pollack, eds., *Interdisciplinary Perspectives on International Law and International Relations: The State of the Art*, 321–342. New York: Cambridge University Press.

Buchanan, A. 2010. 'The Legitimacy of International Law', in S. Besson and J. Tasioulas, eds., *The Philosophy of International Law*, 79–96. New York: Oxford University Press.

Buchanan, A. and Keohane, R. O. 2006. 'The Legitimacy of Global Governance Institutions', *Ethics and International Affairs* 20(4): 405–437.

Christiano, T. 2008. *The Constitution of Equality: Democratic Authority and Its Limits*. Oxford: Oxford University Press.

Christiano, T. 2010. 'Democratic Legitimacy and International Institutions. In S. Besson and J. Tasioulas, eds., *The Philosophy of International Law*, 119–138. New York: Oxford University Press.

Christiano, T. 2011. 'Is Democratic Legitimacy Possible for International Institutions?', in D. Archibugi, M. Koenig-Archibugi and R. Marchetti, eds., *Global Democracy: Normative and Empirical Perspectives*, 69–95. New York: Cambridge University Press.

Estlund, D. 2009. *Democratic Authority*. Princeton, NJ: Princeton University Press.

Goodin, R. 2003. *Reflective Democracy*. New York: Oxford University Press.

Hohfeld, Wesley. 1919. *Fundamental Legal Conceptions*, ed. W. Cook. New Haven, CT: Yale University Press.

Kant, I. 1996/1797. 'The Metaphysics of Morals', in M. J. Gregor, ed., *The Cambridge Edition of the Works of Immanuel Kant: Practical Philosophy*, 353–604. New York: Cambridge University Press.

Kumm, M. 2004. 'The Legitimacy of International Law: A Constitutionalist Framework of Analysis', *European Journal of International Law* 15(5): 907–931.

Lefkowitz, D. 2011. 'The Principle of Fairness and States' Duty to Obey International Law', *Canadian Journal of Law and Jurisprudence* 24(2): 327–346.

Peter, F. 2014. 'Political Legitimacy', *The Stanford Encyclopedia of Philosophy*, ed. E. N. Zalta. http://plato.stanford.edu/archives/win2014/entries/legitimacy/.

Pogge, T. 2002. *World Poverty and Human Rights*. Malden, MA: Polity.

Pogge, T. 2010. 'The Role of International Law in Reproducing Massive Poverty', in S. Besson and J. Tasioulas, eds., *The Philosophy of International Law*, 417–435. New York: Oxford University Press.

Raz, J. 1979. *The Authority of Law*. Oxford: Clarendon Press.

Raz, J. 2006. 'The Problem of Authority: Revisiting the Service Conception', *Minnesota Law Review* 90: 1003–1044.

Tasioulas, J. 2010. 'The Legitimacy of International Law', in S. Besson and J. Tasioulas, eds., *The Philosophy of International Law*, 97–116. New York: Oxford University Press.

CHAPTER SIX

Legitimacy and Global Governance

David Held and Pietro Maffettone

Introduction

This chapter will explore the idea of legitimacy in relation to global governance institutions by critically assessing three of the major accounts available in the field: the state consent, democratic and meta-coordination accounts.[1] The argument will be that the state consent account generates a number of major difficulties and cannot be readily adapted to the complex and changing circumstances of global politics. While the democratic approach to legitimacy fares considerably better, it leaves open a number of major questions, which need further examination. The third approach, the meta-coordination view set out by Allen Buchanan, makes a number of important advances and offers much needed flexibility and adaptability in relation to the diversity of global governance institutions. However, Buchanan's view needs to be further developed in order to provide robust guidance on how to assess different types of global governance institutions.

Two concepts are central to our discussion: legitimacy and global governance. We understand legitimacy to refer, broadly speaking, to the difference between the imposition of rules or norms and their acceptance because of sound normative reasons. Legitimacy entails that rules and institutional arrangements are in some sense worthy or just, and thus should be followed for reasons other than expediency or the threat of sanctions. Furthermore, legitimacy confers a certain standing on institutions. There are different ways of portraying the precise nature of this standing, but we think that it is best to conceive it as a kind of respect for institutional directives. The latter idea can be contrasted to the much narrower use of the term that is often employed in technical discussions within political philosophy. In more technical language, political legitimacy is often understood as the claim of an agent to have a right to rule over some other agent with respect to a given domain. A right to rule correlates to a duty to obey. A duty to obey can be understood in different ways, but it usually entails that those who have such a duty consider the directives issued by the legitimate authority as providing them with content-independent reasons to follow them (see Lefkowitz in this volume for a more detailed treatment). When we use the term legitimacy in this chapter, we refer to the broader definition of the term. Employing what we have called the technical definition would, for our purposes here, unduly narrow the discussion (see section 2 for a fuller discussion).

By global governance, we refer to a complex mixture of multilateral and transnational governance arrangements. Global governance is multilayered insofar as the making and implementation of global policies can involve a process of political cooperation and coordination between suprastate, national, transnational and often substate agencies. It is a highly differentiated sphere: the politics of global trade regulation is, for instance, distinct from the politics of climate or peacekeeping. Rather than being monolithic or unitary, the global governance system is best conceived as sectoral or segmented. Moreover, many of the agencies of, and participants in, the global governance complex are no longer simply public bodies; it is a multiactor complex in which diverse agencies participate in the formulation and conduct of global public policy. The complexity and polycentricity of global governance is an important backdrop to the discussion below.

1   The State Consent Theory of Legitimacy

According to the consent-based approach to legitimacy, an institution is legitimate only if its subjects-to-be have consented to it. This view, originally associated with the work of Hobbes, Grotius, Locke and Pufendorf (see Hampsher-Monk, 1993), has been more recently revived by Simmons (2001). The basic idea is that what binds us to an institution is the voluntary acceptance of its authority. From an historical perspective, the idea that consent grounds legitimacy constitutes a strong departure from traditional Christian perspectives as developed in Western Europe. In this Christian worldview, human beings are part of an immutable order of nature. Their subjection to political authority is coextensive with their subjection to God. The consent approach to legitimacy provides a dramatic transformation of the way we conceptualize the political sphere. If we accept the consent view, it is the individual who determines his or her political obligations. The focus in this section is, of course, the state consent theory of the legitimacy of global governance institutions. This theory essentially transposes the traditional consent-based view and applies it to the realm of international politics. According to this account, a global governance institution is legitimate if it has been created via the consent of the states that will be subject to it (see Held, 2002).

A consent-based account of global governance institutions fits closely with the traditional conception of Westphalian sovereignty. Reflecting on the intense religious and civil struggles of the sixteenth century, Bodin (1992) argued for the establishment of an unrestricted ruling power competent to overrule all religious and customary authorities. In his view, an 'ordered commonwealth' depended on the creation of a central authority that was all-powerful. While Bodin was not the first to make this case, he developed what is commonly regarded as the first statement of the modern theory of sovereignty: that there must be within every political community or state a determinate sovereign authority whose powers are decisive and whose powers are recognized as the rightful or legitimate basis of authority. Sovereignty, according to him, is the undivided and untrammelled power to make and enforce the law and, as such, it is the defining characteristic of the state.

The doctrine of sovereignty developed in two distinct dimensions: the first concerned with the 'internal', and the second with the 'external' aspects of sovereignty (see Hinsley, 1986; Cassese, 1995). The former involves the claim that a person, or political body, established as sovereign rightly exercises the 'supreme command' over a particular society. Government – whether monarchical, aristocratic or democratic – must enjoy the 'final and absolute authority' within a given territory. The latter involves the assertion that there is no final and absolute authority above and beyond the sovereign state. In the traditional conception of external sovereignty, nothing but the will of the sovereign can effectively bind the state. It follows that international institutions can only be legitimate if they can rely on the consent of the subjects over which they claim authority, namely, sovereign states.

This 'classic' conception of sovereignty envisages the development of a world community consisting of sovereign states in which states are, in principle, free and equal; enjoy supreme authority over all subjects and objects within a given territory; form discrete political orders with their own interests; engage in diplomatic initiatives and ensure cooperation between states, if and only if this cooperation is in their mutual interest and reduces transaction costs. Territorial sovereignty, the formal equality of states, non-intervention in the domestic affairs of other recognized states and state consent become the basis of international legal obligation and the core elements of international law (see Crawford and Marks, 1998). Of course, this conception of sovereignty was often ignored by leading powers seeking to carve out particular spheres of influence. The reality of classic sovereignty was often messy, fraught and compromised (see Krasner, 1999). But this should not lead one to ignore the systematic shift that took place in the principles underlying political order with the rise of the modern sovereign state.

Yet, right from the beginning, the state consent theory of legitimacy exhibited a number of problems. The first and most obvious is that to conceive of consent as both necessary and sufficient for legitimacy may be deeply counter-intuitive if what is consented to is grossly immoral (Estlund, 2009). One could call this the 'immoral consent' problem. An example of this is that most people would feel uncomfortable with the idea that an institution is legitimate if its members have consented to it while, at one and the same time, the institution operates in a way that violates basic human rights. As the old adage goes, the fact that something is accepted need not be a good guide to what is acceptable.

This is not, of course, to claim that consent is irrelevant to the legitimacy of an institution. In a democratic age, the latter claim would be highly implausible. However, it tells us that a completely procedural view of the legitimacy of an institution based on consent intuitively runs counter to our considered convictions about both sufficient and necessary conditions for legitimacy.

Second, according to most accounts of the consent theory of legitimacy, the normative force of consent can only be obtained if consent has been genuinely given. This is contrary to the Hobbesian view that norms and institutions can be legitimate even if they are accepted through coercion, manipulation, substantially asymmetric bargaining circumstances or lack of epistemic awareness. Valid consent is always *free* and *informed* consent. The idea of free and informed consent needs to be qualified in some respect. In the first instance, it is reductive to imagine that the only properties that can be attached to 'consent' are binary distinctions such as 'free/unfree' and 'informed/uninformed'. For example, Held (2006: 155) develops a typology based on seven different ways in which consent can be given. To mention just two options, consent can be given as a result of unreflective choices based on tradition, or because we lack specific preferences in relation to what we consent to. Furthermore, even accepting the relevance of the aforementioned binary distinctions, the latter rely on epistemically and normatively loaded concepts. How much information is enough to justify the label 'informed'? And what counts as a freely undertaken choice? For example: up to what point are market transactions freely undertaken given the background of unemployment and financial constraints that some market actors face? Similarly, voters regularly express their political preference and cast their ballots without necessarily being fully aware of the nature of the political options available to them; nor, often, do they have a satisfactory epistemic understanding of the technical issues linked to various economic and social policies proposed by different parties and coalitions. Is the average voter's ballot an expression of informed consent? Can we say it meets the standards of deliberative reasoning (Fishkin, 1991; Offe and Preuss, 1991)? Needless to say, these are questions that we will not be able to settle here.

Thus, while stating that valid consent must be free and informed seems a sound way of putting restrictions on what constitutes valid consent, the claim is not necessarily very helpful. As such, these restrictions do not easily help us to specify concretely which instances of consent are genuinely free and genuinely informed. They do provide a benchmark, but only a very abstract one. The presence of largely grey areas, and difficult cases, should not, however, preclude the assessment of more clear-cut scenarios. Some instances of consent are easy enough to classify: consenting to the highway robber who 'asks' for our money in return for our lives is not what most of us would consider as free consent. In the same way, young children cannot enter into contractual relations because we believe that their age precludes them from fully understanding what they would be agreeing to.

One way to take the argument forward is to note that what seems to be central in all the aforementioned cases are the background circumstances under which consent is given, such as the extent to which those who have consented knew what they were consenting to, or the implications, from a moral point of view, of not consenting. Given that background circumstances are important to determine the nature of consent, how does the state consent approach to the legitimacy of global governance institution fare? A significant number of international interactions and agreements, in the first instance, clearly run afoul of the ideas of free and informed consent. Having a seat at a negotiating table in a major international organization or at a major conference does not ensure effective representation; even if there is a parity of formal representation, it is often the case, for example, that developed countries have large delegations equipped with extensive negotiation and technical expertise, while poorer developing countries often depend on one-person delegations, or even have to rely on the sharing of a delegate (see Held, 2004: 95–6). The latter example enables us to portray what we can call the 'uninformed consent' problem that plagues global governance institutions. A substantial number of their members are simply unable to process all the relevant information that would allow them to be fully informed about the agreements they are subscribing to. In the same way, given the bargaining asymmetries that characterize international negotiations, the state consent theory is unlikely to provide a satisfactory general account of the legitimacy of global governance institutions. If consent must be 'free' in order to be valid, the large imbalances in economic and political power between negotiating parties clearly cast a shadow on its validity. Put differently, global governance institutions suffer from a 'coerced consent' problem.

These concerns are also reinforced by the development of the international system from the 1960s onward. As Robert Jackson (1990) has argued, decolonization has allowed a large number of former colonial countries to become independent. However, their formal independence, what Jackson labels as negative sovereignty, was often not matched by their substantive ability to govern themselves and to become institutionally and politically self-standing, or what should otherwise be understood as positive sovereignty. In other words, the international system after the decolonization process can be described as an arena where a large number of players are essentially unable to stand on their own, and are instead 'territorial jurisdictions supported from above by international law and material aid' (Jackson, 1990: 5). In a world of 'quasi-states', the state consent theory seems a peculiarly unsound guide to the legitimacy of global governance institutions. Quasi-states lack both the bargaining power and, often, the technical capabilities to consent genuinely to the way in which global governance institutions are run.

There are two further limitations found in the state consent view of the legitimacy of global governance institutions. The first is that global governance is increasingly difficult to capture simply through the lens of state-to-state interactions (Weiss and Wilkinson, 2014). Call this the 'scope' problem. The massive growth of transborder governance arrangements has transformed the very way in which we conceptualize global politics. The global political domain is still the stage for power politics between states. However, it certainly cannot be fully captured simply through a state-to-state lens. The latter idea is based on the appreciation of what we take to be two central structural changes in the global political domain since the Second World War (see Held, 2014). First, global governance has been characterized by the proliferation of influential nonstate actors. From multinational corporations (MNCs) to international nongovernmental organizations (INGOs), the global political landscape has evolved and become more complex, with a vast array of agents actively participating in the formation of global policy. Second, and relatedly, global governance arrangements have been increasingly characterized by new types of institutional arrangements. In many issue areas, and to different extents according to the issue area, global governance institutions are not simply constituted by state-to-state interactions. The case of global finance stands out in this regard (e.g. the Basel Committee on Banking Supervision, the Financial Stability Board), but other examples include global health governance (e.g. the Global Fund, the GAVI alliance, and polio eradication efforts) and climate governance (which seeks to coordinate diverse actors in relation to a single norm – 2 per cent as the agreed limit placed on climate change) (Held, 2014: 65).

In short, the contemporary global governance system has features of both complexity and polycentricity, as noted above in the Introduction. Such features are, simply put, impossible to assess if we remain anchored to a view of the global political domain that is based solely on the actions and interactions among political communities. In this respect, then, the state consent view is incomplete and unable to function as a tool for the critical scrutiny of the legitimacy of existing global governance institutions. Or to put the point differently, even if one accepted the normative correctness of the state consent theory, the latter would be irrelevant when it comes to legitimacy assessments concerning many global governance institutions.

Of course, those who subscribe to the state consent view may reply that our objection cannot really demonstrate that the state consent approach is inadequate. It is, they could say after all, a normative view about how global governance should be, and not a descriptive account. At best, the scope problem can show that some global governance institutions are illegitimate given that they are not subject to state consent. Such a position would have implications for large parts of contemporary global governance arrangements, indicating that they cannot have an authoritative role in the spheres in which they operate. If this judgment were taken seriously, however, it could have profound negative implications for the efficacy of global governance.

Those who favour the state consent view might reply that we do not need to consider an institution legitimate in order to believe that following its directives is, 'all things considered', required. Put differently, even illegitimate institutions may generate directives that we have independent reasons to comply with. While, theoretically, this is certainly an option, it is not one we find appealing. First, note that, in this context, nothing much seems to follow from the fact that an institution is illegitimate. Second, it is unclear how exactly one can generate effective forms of institutional cooperation if one denies the legitimacy of a substantial part of global governance and leaves the decision to comply with global governance institutions to a case-by-case approach.

Finally, and perhaps most importantly, the state consent theory of legitimacy becomes increasingly less tenable to the extent that withholding consent may have severe externalities. Call this the 'externalities' problem. This seems to be the case for global governance institutions that serve, in principle, the purpose of solving collective action problems, or addressing 'global public bads' such as climate change, pandemics, financial instability and nuclear proliferation. These global public bads are indicative of three core sets of challenges we face – those concerned with (a) sharing our planet (climate change, but also biodiversity losses and water deficits); (b) sustaining our humanity (global pandemics, but also conflict management and prevention); and (c) developing our rulebook (nuclear proliferation treaties, but also global international trade and taxation regimes) (see Rischard, 2002). In our increasingly interconnected world, these global problems cannot be solved by any one nation-state acting alone. They call for collective and collaborative action (Held, 2004: 11–12). The state consent view of legitimacy essentially gives unlimited opting-out powers to states and, yet, given the global collective action problems we currently face, withholding consent from even reasonable attempts at their solution may imply imposing severe costs on others. Put differently, consent must be limited by the type of externalities it generates. Of course, it is open to those who favour the state consent view to claim that the latter contention is not very informative without a clear account of the externalities in question and, in the present context, without a clear picture of what kind of externalities we may permissibly impose on others. We cannot fully address this point here. However, we think that at least for a central class of cases that are at the heart of global governance, such as climate change, prudential financial regulations and nuclear proliferation, the types of externalities involved would, in the absence of cooperation, have important implications for the basic interests of humankind. Accordingly, they would be part of any plausible account of the kind of externalities we are not allowed to impose on others.

In this section, we have argued that the state consent theory of legitimacy is not a credible position. We have highlighted what we take to be five important problems with the state consent view, namely immoral consent, uninformed consent, coerced consent, scope and externalities. The first three problems are relatively familiar in traditional discussions of the consent view of legitimacy. They arise because consent is a procedural notion that provides no indication about the content of what is consented to and because the background conditions under which agents consent to something often invalidate the normative relevance of what is agreed to. The remaining two problems pertain to the extent to which the state consent position, as an application of the more general position that consent legitimizes institutions, is a plausible guide to the legitimacy of global governance institutions. They emerge because we live in a world where globalization has altered the types of agents that actively participate in the formation of global governance norms and regimes, and in which withholding consent can effectively represent, at least in the long run, an existential threat to the whole planet. These two objections to the state consent view of the legitimacy of global governance institutions tell us that even if we were to accept the moral justification linked to consent-based approaches to legitimacy, the current conditions of global politics make it an implausible candidate to judge global governance institutions.

Given the problems highlighted, it is natural to look elsewhere for a satisfactory account of the legitimacy of global governance institutions. The most important alternative suggested in the literature on the legitimacy of international and transnational institutions is democracy. Democracy often appears to legitimate modern political life: rulemaking and law enforcement often seem justified and appropriate when they are 'democratic'. Of course, it has not always been so. A general commitment to democracy is a very modern phenomenon and the extension of the idea of democracy to the global domain is an even more recent phenomenon, marking a shift from a world of national communities of fate to a world of overlapping communities of fate – where the fortunes of countries are densely interwoven (Held, 2006). However, the idea of extending democracy beyond national communities has recently been subjected to a number of criticisms. Many have argued that democracy is inadequate to provide us with a relevant normative benchmark to assess global governance institutions. In the next section, we address what we believe to be some of the most sophisticated versions of these arguments. Our provisional conclusion is that, while such critiques are insightful, they do not provide conclusive reasons to abandon the democratic account in all respects.

2 The Democratic Account

Given the success of democratic forms of governance at the domestic level, it is hardly surprising that democracy has been proposed as a form of benchmark for the assessment of the legitimacy of global governance institutions. There are different ways of conceiving both how democratic decision-making confers legitimacy on institutions in general and how democracy can be understood as a relevant standard for global governance institutions.

Some accounts of democratic legitimacy rest exclusively on the empirical claim that democratic forms of governance are uniquely placed to produce good outcomes or decisions, while other accounts claim that the legitimacy of democratic institutions is the result of the democratic character of the decision-making procedure (for a discussion of the distinction and its relevance to legitimacy, see Peter, 2010; see also Christiano, 2008). Others still (see Peter, 2008; Christiano, 2012b) argue that the two dimensions (i.e., substantive and procedural) are irreducible to one another and, thus, that a successful account of the legitimacy conferring properties of democratic governance will rest on some form of combination between the two.

The idea of a democratic conception of the legitimacy of global governance is also closely connected to the idea of global democracy. Needless to say, there is more than one account of global democracy, and hence it is useful to say something more specific about what we mean by a democratic account of the legitimacy of global governance institutions. One characteristic way of classifying different models of global democracy is to analyse the different conceptions of the demoi upon which such models are built (Archibugi et al., 2011; Held, 1995, 2006; see also Marchetti, 2008). The first model of global democracy is based on intergovernmentalism and views global democracy as an international form of association based on the membership of democratic states. The second, transnational model, is based on the idea of stakeholdership and constitutes global democratic demoi through the application of the all-affected principle. The third model is the most inclusive and considers all human beings as members of a global demos qua individuals, rather than as national citizens or affected parties. In the latter model, a necessary condition for global governance institutions to be legitimate is that every human being should have an equal say in how these institutions operate and function. Accordingly, each model of global democracy offers a different account of the democratic bases of the legitimacy of global governance institutions.

In what follows we will not take a stand on which account of democratic legitimacy is the correct one. Our discussion below will be largely compatible with a number of ways of understanding what grounds democratic legitimacy. Rather, we will assume a specific account of *global* democracy, namely, the global demos model. This is for two reasons. First, we consider the latter to be the most inclusive and coherent one in order to assess the plausibility of democracy as a standard for global governance; and, second, most of the arguments we address below use, implicitly or explicitly, the global demos model as a critical target.

Several criticisms have been levelled against the democratic account of the legitimacy of global governance institutions. In what follows we assess two of them. The first considers the democratic principle as grounded on specific assumptions about background political conditions, some of which, so the argument goes, are absent in global politics. In other words, democratic rule presupposes a very specific set of empirical circumstances in order to be morally justified. In turn, the absence of at least a number of these empirical presuppositions invalidates the use of democracy as a benchmark for legitimacy assessments. Thomas Christiano (2010) has developed a powerful version of this argument. The second objection, initially developed by Allen Buchanan and Robert Keohane (2006), contends that the democratic model of legitimacy is constructed on the features of the traditional territorial state and thus is simply not applicable to institutions (i.e., global governance institutions) which are different in several normatively salient respects. We are broadly sympathetic to the overall concerns raised by Christiano. However, we contend that the way in which global politics is currently articulated makes the applicability of Christiano's arguments to global governance institutions precarious. In a similar way, we tentatively agree with Buchanan and Keohane that the complexity of global governance institutions may put pressure on the appropriateness of the applicability of the democratic standard. Having said this, we want to suggest that the democratic approach is more 'flexible' than they contend and thus that it may still have a role to play.

Christiano has put forward a sophisticated critique of the global demos account of the legitimacy of global governance institutions (2010, 2011, 2012a). More specifically, his argument highlights several conditions that need to be met if democracy can be considered an appropriate mode of governance at the global level. According to him, democracy is founded on the principle of public equality and can only realize public equality if very specific background conditions are in place. Adopting democratic forms of governance can only be justifiable when:

> 1. A number of important issues…arise for the whole community. 2. There [is] a rough equality of stakes among persons in the community concerning the whole package of issues. 3…the community is [not] divided into discrete and insular groups with distinct preferences over all the issues in the community so that one or more substantial groups always lose out in majority voting…4.…when it protects at least the fundamental human rights of all the persons in the community. 5.…when the issues with which it deals are not primarily of a purely scientific or technical character. 6.…[when] there [is] a dense network of institutions of civil society that connect[s] individuals to the activities of the democratic legislative power. (2010: 130)

In Christiano's view, conditions 2 and 3 on the list are closely related to the assessment of democracy as a standard of legitimacy for global governance. Condition 2 allows us to understand the specificity of the global political domain. It enables us to see that domestic and global politics may be different in a normatively salient way. Condition 3 highlights a general risk that democratic rule can face, but one that is likely to be higher if the idea of democracy is extended to the international system. Appreciating the relevance of both aforementioned conditions, in turn, renders the democratic account of legitimacy inappropriate for global governance institutions.

Let us call conditions 2 and 3 put forward by Christiano the *equality of stake* objection and the *persistent minorities* objection, respectively. The equality of stake objection seeks to provide a rebuttal to one of the most commonly used arguments in favour of some version of democratic global governance, namely, that an increasing number of social, political and economic problems have made persons around the globe more closely interdependent than they once were. Such interdependence is then taken to justify some form of global democratic system insofar as some mechanism of political and institutional accountability is required to regulate political decisions that have significant spillover effects across many jurisdictions. However, Christiano argues that the latter idea is not enough to justify the recourse to democratic forms of accountability. Democracy is justified not simply by interdependence, but by interdependence characterized by a rough equality of stakes between those who participate in the democratic process. By 'stake', Christiano refers to 'the susceptibility of a person's interests or well-being to be advanced or set back by realistically possible ways of organizing the interdependent group' (2010: 131). Given this definition, the requirement of equal stakes can be interpreted as a fairness-based one: it is simply unfair to give, as democracy does, equal influence over decision-making to people who are affected in radically unequal ways by the outcomes of such decision-making. Or, in Christiano's words: 'If one group of persons has a very large stake in a community, in which there is interdependence of interests, and another has a fairly small stake, it seems unfair to give each an equal say in decision-making over this community' (2010: 131). However, this is precisely what would happen, he argues, if we simply applied the democratic principle beyond the nation-state. While the modern nation-state has immense institutional capacity and thus impacts individuals' interests and welfare to such a degree that the equal stakes condition applies (i.e., the stakes are comparable because they are very high for all citizens), the same cannot be said for international laws and institutions, since the latter 'play a fairly small role in the lives of people throughout the world' (2010: 132).

The problem highlighted by Christiano is clearly one that goes at the heart of democratic theory, and he should be credited with raising it in the context of global governance institutions. Nonetheless, we are not convinced that the unequal stakes argument is as damaging to the supporters of global democracy as Christiano seems to suggest. First, there is, clearly, an empirical dimension to the argument. At least at first sight, the presence/absence of equality of stakes seems to rest on the empirical appraisal of concrete political circumstances. While there is no doubt that, prima facie, the vast majority of domestic political communities feature a reasonable equality of overall stakes internally and, less so, when such stakes are compared to the global level, the latter judgment needs to be qualified by the appreciation of some of the most pressing global problems we currently face. Humanity is increasingly confronted by political challenges that are momentous if not existential in nature. From climate change and environmental degradation to nuclear proliferation, pandemics, financial instability, terrorism and failed states, global problems are becoming politically disruptive for the whole of humankind. Apocalypse may be an abused term, and yet it is not necessarily out of place to describe what some of the threats we are facing could lead to if they are not properly managed. In this context, equality of stakes is not as remote as one might initially conjecture. It is perhaps less visible and immediate than in everyday domestic politics, and yet all stakes seem to be roughly equal when each stake is close to being infinitely high.

Of course, it could be objected that many problems at the global level, such as terrorism and environmental degradation, often affect different political communities in different ways. For example, oil spills are localized, while restrictions on financial flows that are used to fight the financing of terrorist activities are becoming burdensome on countries that heavily rely on remittances. These points are certainly correct. What is less clear is the extent to which they invalidate our broader argument. Several of the collective action problems we face at the global level are not easily captured by the aforementioned examples. One way to see this is to think about the very idea of how we want to define a 'stake'. If we define it as the actual impact that some specific political event has on a specific set of people, then inequality of stakes may very well be prevalent. If, instead, we broaden the definition of 'stakes' to include the risks that are generated by some political and economic activities, then they are more evenly spread. In the same way, although climate governance regimes, nuclear proliferation regimes, global capital requirements regimes, etc. will, synchronically and taken individually, affect different peoples differently, in time, and taken together, their shape and very existence will affect everyone in a similar way.

These remarks also signal, in our view, the potential to reconcile our arguments with Christiano's position. Accepting that a significant set of global collective goods is congruent with the broad idea of equality of stakes may signal that, at least with respect to those important political questions, equality of stakes cannot be taken to be a decisive objection to the adoption of the global demos model. However, the latter contention is compatible with the idea that several other domains in which global governance institutions operate may not necessarily display the same type of empirical features. In those domains, it could well be correct, following Christiano, to accept that a global demos approach may be inapplicable, as it would give equal weight to unevenly affected groups. We think that the global demos model is flexible enough to accept this kind of approach.

Finally, we should note that there is a potential difficulty connected to the very structure of Christiano's argument concerning equal stakes. The fact that the modern state has immense institutional capacity, to use his words, is not a natural phenomenon. Even accepting, for the sake of argument, that inequality of stakes is prevalent, we need to ask from where, politically speaking, does this inequality originate? Equality of stakes, just like the idea of the modern state, is not a natural condition. It is, instead, the result of institutional choices: for example, the persistent uneasiness and opposition on the part of most states to the delegation of sovereign powers to other forms of organizations. However, if we accept that the modern state has a much larger institutional capacity compared to global governance institutions as a result of past institutional choices by sectional groups and powerful interests, then it becomes less clear why the equality of stakes argument matters: the point is not that equal stakes do not arise at the global level, but rather that they have not been encouraged or even allowed, institutionally speaking. The question then is: should equality of stakes at the global level be something that we should aim for? Whether or not the answer to the latter question is affirmative, it cannot be settled just by looking at the current organization of the global political landscape. To an extent, we think, Christiano could agree with the latter contention. Given his account of the normative core of democracy, he might accept that in a world where stakes were *allowed* to become more 'equal' and people had more say on a wide range of pressing issues at the global level, the equal advancement of human interests is best served. As we have highlighted above, this does indeed seem to be the case for an important class of global collective goods.

The second objection we will discuss highlighted by Christiano is connected to the idea of permanent minorities. Once again, we believe the argument presented by him deserves careful consideration as it is central to the question of the desirability of global democracy. However, while the issue merits attention, and should clearly work as a factor that cautions us against easy transpositions of the democratic mode of governance into global politics, we are also convinced that the empirical picture suggested by Christiano is only partially convincing. He describes the problem as follows:

> If the issues upon which a democratic international institution makes decisions are such that discrete and insular coalitions tend to form (with some forming a majority and some forming minority blocs), then there is a significant chance that some groups will simply be left out of the decision-making process. *And this leaves open the possibility that their lives will be heavily determined by strangers.* (2010: 133; emphasis added)

Christiano goes on to distinguish the problem of permanent minorities from the problem of the tyranny of the majority: while the two often go together, they need not do so conceptually speaking, as it is entirely possible that a permanent majority could treat members of a permanent minority in accordance with human rights even while denying the minority any input into the decision-making process (2010: 134). Christiano also qualifies his concern for the formation of global permanent minorities by observing that we cannot know in advance whether such a problem would in fact occur, and that even if it occurred it could, at least potentially, be addressed through the same types of institutional mechanisms that are used within domestic democratic settings. However, he concludes that the prospects for such institutional solutions to emerge are poor given the comparative weakness of global civil society (2010: 134).

As we have mentioned above, it is hard to disagree with Christiano about the importance of the problem of permanent minorities: they are certainly an issue. However, at the empirical level, the way in which new global problems are generated by globalization seems to render this critique partly inert. The fact of globalization and the rise of what some have called intermestic issues (see Rosenau, 2002) suggest that there is no way (or at least no sensible way) to retreat from certain domains of international or transnational interaction. Clearly, the latter is not an uncontroversial claim (however, see Held et al., 1999; Held and McGrew, 2007; Hale et al., 2013). Yet it is important to pause and ask ourselves what the truth of such a claim would imply for the permanent minorities argument. The fact that we may consider global democracy as morally unattractive because it might engender permanent minorities seems to rely on the existence of an alternative framework, one in which, by not engaging in democratic forms of global governance, one could avoid the formation of permanent minorities. Such an arrangement could perhaps be one in which all countries retreat to their own political backyard. But how plausible is this alternative background picture? Is it empirically and politically credible? If, for example, as we have suggested, globalization makes the retreat to domestic politics increasingly difficult, then this background picture is simply not one that we can seriously entertain. The most credible alternative scenario, alas, is the one we are facing right now: the existence of permanent political minorities without the (albeit minimal) guarantees of the democratic process. Instead of permanent minorities within shared institutional settings, what we get is peoples with no say over institutions that will affect their lives whether or not they participate in those institutions. Christiano correctly balks at the '*possibility that (people's) lives will be heavily determined by strangers*'. Yet, the world we are facing is, precisely, one in which we witness more than the mere possibility of this happening.

Christiano could argue that to deny that the current system is legitimate is not to provide an argument that supports global democracy. Put differently, the fact that we are experiencing the *de facto* formation of global permanent minorities on several important issues, does not disprove the contention that global democracy would suffer from the same ills. It just tells us that the dangers of permanent minorities formation are shared by the current non-democratic system and the putatively democratic one that global democrats champion. This is a fair point, though not one that is conclusive. The global democracy model could offer some guarantees that the current non-democratic system is not well placed to provide. For example, a global democracy approach could feature standards of formal representation in key global governance institutions that would allow less powerful and currently underrepresented or disenfranchised actors more leverage than they currently have and the opportunity to form coalitions. Comparatively speaking, the global democratic approach could well fare better in the precise sense of providing more political representation and voice to a larger range of actors than we currently witness.

Yet, Christiano could contend that real issue does not concern the comparative effectiveness of different arrangements with respect to the problem of permanent minorities. Rather, the problem is whether the issue is likely to arise again. Improving on what we have may not be enough if the risk of generating permanent minorities is still significant. Christiano (2011) himself has argued for what he calls the 'fair democratic association' (FDA) model. This is essentially an internationalist model based on the consent of democratic states. FDA, he contends, would fare better when it comes to the problem of permanent minorities, since it would allow participants to refuse to enter into treaties and institutions that they would not find acceptable or beneficial. Nonetheless, it must be stressed, as Christiano recognizes, that the price of this ability to withdraw participation is very high, given that it would engender significant problems with externalities imposed on third parties (see above). Furthermore, note that Christiano argues for the FDA model in the context of a discussion of the legitimacy of international institutions. Yet, as we have shown in section 1, global governance is subject to a proliferation of relevant actors and is thus increasingly difficult to capture in terms of state-to-state interactions. This tells us that FDA, even if justifiable as an account of the legitimacy of international institutions, cannot be easily transposed to the broader issue of the legitimacy of global governance. Finally, note that, as argued above, the global demos approach is potentially flexible and can be deployed according to its suitability for specific issue areas. Thus, it is open to global democrats to claim that the problem of permanent minorities should be one factor that cautions against the blanket application of the global democracy approach to all institutions in global governance.

To sum up, the permanent minorities and unequal stakes arguments, while normatively correct in themselves, still rest on empirically disputable accounts of global politics: equality of stakes is often a reality when humanity faces several existential threats and permanent minorities are exactly what the present system of global governance already allows, given that it embeds institutions that are only responsive to the needs of the few and affect the fate of the many.

Finally, we consider a further recent critique of the democratic account of the legitimacy of global governance institutions, namely, the one levelled by Allen Buchanan and Robert Keohane (2006). In order to understand the roots of their critique, it is important to recall a shared feature of the arguments we have put forward to assess both the state consent model and the critique of the democratic account made by Christiano. Throughout this chapter, we have stressed the importance for normative accounts of legitimacy to be isomorphic or congruent with the empirical reality that they are trying to assess. The latter view is, of course, controversial (at least when applied to

debates about the nature of justice and other core moral and political concepts; see, for example, Valentini, 2009). Nonetheless, taking this point of
departure seriously, we are able to put forward what we think is a prima facie
sound criticism of the adequacy of democracy as a standard for the legitimacy
of global governance institutions. The problem is essentially one of fit: fit
between the features of global governance institutions taken generally and
the features of the democratic account of legitimacy. We will not belabour
the point excessively, as it has already been extensively developed elsewhere
(see Buchanan and Keohane, 2006; Buchanan, 2010, 2013). The democratic
account of legitimacy is a demanding one. It has been, at least initially, developed for institutions, political communities broadly understood, which
possess certain important features that are morally speaking salient when it
comes to the types of normative expectations we have about them. Such
features are, among others, the claim to possess a right to rule and to have
exclusive jurisdiction over a given domain, and the ability to attach penalties,
usually physical coercion, to non-compliance. The democratic account of
legitimacy is geared to reflect these features of domestic political communities: from Greek city-states to the modern nation-state, these features were
and are essential elements of our understanding of the exercise of political
power in territorially bound political communities (Held, 2006).

However, political power is not simply the exercise of power by institutions
claiming a right to rule backed by the use of coercion and physical force.
Moreover, many institutions, strictly speaking, neither aim to, nor credibly
exercise, political power in any recognizable meaning that we can attribute
to the notion. This is precisely what we find in global politics. From NGOs to
transnational public and private bodies that issue standards and regulations,
to the various UN agencies and the pillars of the international economic order
such as the IMF and the WTO, the array of characteristics displayed by the
institutions in question cannot be fully captured by traditional ideas concerning the exercise of political power. Many such institutions do not claim a
right to rule, most cannot really attach penalties to their commands, the vast
majority make no claim to exclusive jurisdiction, while even those institutions that come close to claiming a right to rule and attach some form of
enforcement mechanism to their rulings do not rely on the use of coercion
or, at least, do so in a very decentralized and/or indirect fashion. It would
thus be surprising if exactly the same standard of legitimacy applied across
all these types of institutions and if that standard were to be the demanding
one we attach to more traditional exercises of political power, as we experience them in domestic political societies. However, we routinely speak of the
legitimacy of such institutions, and we judge them from a moral and political
point of view. While these institutions have different constituencies, different
goals and different ways of advancing such goals, we nonetheless portray
them as legitimate or illegitimate. Of course, it is entirely possible that, when
describing these institutions as legitimate or illegitimate, we may be using

entirely different concepts altogether. It may be the case that our use of language is simply loose in this respect. However, it is also possible that the very concept of legitimacy is broader than the democratic account suggests alone and that to require every institutional form at the global level to be governed democratically is, simply put, not very useful or appropriate.

As we have initially stated, we are broadly sympathetic to some of the concerns raised by this critique of the democratic account. We also share with Buchanan and Keohane the goal of achieving a more encompassing and, at the same time, a more general understanding of the concept of legitimacy, one that is flexible enough to capture the wide array of institutional forms that populate global governance (more on this below). Nonetheless, we want to conclude this section by making a distinction and by explaining why such a distinction invites caution when it comes to the demise of the democratic model of legitimacy applied to global governance institutions. The distinction is, roughly put, one between democratic institutional forms, on the one hand, and democratic values and ideals on the other. As examples of the former, one can think of the different shapes that the majority principle can take, or of the role of parties in the democratic process. As examples of the latter one can think of political equality, accountability, public deliberation, self-determination and political autonomy. Needless to say, the distinction is not meant to be sharp. Furthermore, it is abundantly clear that the two ideas are intimately related. Yet, it is also patently clear that the two are not one and the same thing. Democracy as an institutional form has been articulated and interpreted in several different and historically contingent ways (see Held, 2006). The same goes for democratic values and ideals. What does this tell us? It tells us that to discuss the appropriateness of democracy as a standard for the legitimacy of global governance institutions is, at least in one important respect, an open-ended exercise in which the choice of target seems to matter as much as the content of one's arguments.

The distinction between the values and ideal of democracy and the institutional forms in which such values and ideals can be embedded suggests, in our view, that the democratic approach is potentially more flexible than many of its critics seem to suggest. For example, even if we do not think that a specific global governance institution should be organized according to the majority principle, we could argue that its governance should be inspired by broadly democratic values and ideals by stressing the importance of transparency and accountability, or the fact that those that are affected by its decisions should have their voices heard. This is something that Buchanan and Keohane (2006) clearly acknowledge when they refer to the idea of 'broad accountability' as a key component of the legitimacy of global governance. Of course, broad accountability cannot be considered equivalent to a majoritarian account of democracy (Buchanan, 2010: 93). However, there is no reason to equate the democratic approach to a specific, majoritarian, model. Rejecting the latter, while plausible, does not allow us to assess conclusively the suitability of the former.

Moreover, just as a democratic country can embody a diversity of types of public institutions, which function according to different conceptions of legitimacy, there is no reason that this could not also be true for global democracy. The argument that institutional types vary is not an argument per se against assigning a role to democratic values at the global level. The ideal of global democracy is compatible with a diversity of types of public institutions that could be evaluated according to normative standards that are not institutionally democratic but still congruent with democratic values and ideals. The latter picture mirrors what many liberals think is the role of conceptions of justice at the domestic level. Conceptions of social and distributive justice are not meant to apply to institutional forms within civil society (nor, for that matter, to all public institutions), and yet they constrain and shape the evaluative criteria that we use to assess such institutions.

Whether these comments wholly rescue the democratic account is something that we cannot settle here. However, we do believe that the rejection of specific institutional instantiations of the democratic model should not necessarily be translated in the rejection of robustly and recognizably democratic values and ideals to be used as benchmarks for institutional evaluations. This is a point worth stressing. The complexity of global governance certainly cautions us against a one-size-fits-all approach. Nonetheless, there is no reason to believe that this is the only option that is open to a democratic approach to the legitimacy of global governance institutions. In the long run, the values and ideals of democracy may still have a part to play in the normative assessments of global governance institutions.

3   The Virtues and Problems of the Meta-Coordination View of Legitimacy

In the first two sections of this chapter, we have critically engaged with the state consent view of legitimacy and with the democratic account. The former is both morally and empirically implausible. The latter fares better, yet we have reason to believe that it too faces problems, at least if it is interpreted too narrowly. In this section, we discuss a recent attempt by Allen Buchanan (2013) to put forward an alternative to the aforementioned traditional accounts of legitimacy. Buchanan aims to provide a general account of institutional legitimacy. He calls this account the meta-coordination view. His analysis starts from two observations. The first one concerns what he calls the 'distinctive practical role of legitimacy judgments'; that is, the fact they are necessary to solve meta-coordination problems. Meta-coordination problems refer to attempts to converge on (normative) public standards that institutions are required to meet in order to be accorded the relevant standing that they need to function effectively (2013: 178). The second concerns the type of conceptual space that our solutions to coordination problems should occupy. In order to be legitimate, we should require these solutions to be in-between two poles: mere advantage compared to a non-institutional benchmark is not enough, and yet full justice and perfect efficiency are simply too much. Between these poles lies our ability to respect institutions normatively and to take their directives as providing, at the very least, weighty reasons to comply. In this framework, legitimacy is clearly a weaker notion than justice and we can give standing to institutions that we do not find to be fully just.

While providing a conceptual location for legitimacy is important, it is of course not conclusive, since, as Buchanan recognizes, there is likely to be more than one set of criteria that satisfy the requirement of being better than non-coordination and less than full justice or optimality. Furthermore, some are bound to be sceptical of the idea that we can confer normative standing on an institution that is not fully just. Buchanan addresses both problems. He provides a set of what he calls variable criteria in order to narrow down the potentially unlimited number of solutions to coordination problems that we can describe as legitimate (2013: 188–90), and, at the same time, he puts forward what, at least in our view, are good reasons to allow institutional standing and full justice to diverge in many circumstances (2013: 180–3).

The criteria suggested are (1) good or at least not seriously tainted origins; (2) the reliable provision of the goods the institutions are designed to deliver (assuming reasonably favourable circumstances); (3) institutional integrity or the match between the institution's justifying aims and performance; (4) the avoidance of serious unfairness; and (5) the accountability of the most important institutional agents (2013: 189). These criteria should not be understood as necessary and/or sufficient to establish the legitimacy of an institution. Rather, they are to be understood as 'counting principles' the satisfaction of which should be seen as a 'good-making' feature of our legitimacy assessments. The reasons why legitimacy should be understood both as a weaker normative requirement than justice and constitute an appropriate benchmark to bestow standing on an institution are broadly connected to the idea that the best can be the enemy of the good – many institutions can provide the distinctive benefits they were designed to provide without excessive and undue costs even when they are not fully just. More specifically, Buchanan highlights how (1) it is unreasonable to expect agreement on what full justice requires and easier to converge on what we should consider to be the worst injustices; (2) in the absence of functioning institutions, what justice requires is often indeterminate because non-institutionalized moral thinking cannot be fully specific or action guiding; (3) justice may not be attainable in the here and now but more often than not will require the existence of functioning institutions in order to make progress towards what justice requires.

In what follows we assess the meta-coordination view. We believe that the position has several important positive features. At the same time, we contend that it also has some drawbacks that call for reflection on its actual potential to deliver the theoretical benefits that it claims to provide. The benefits of the meta-coordination view pertain to what we will call synchronic and dia-chronic flexibility. Its main drawback lies in what we will call latent indeter-minacy. As it is often the case, what is good about something also marks out its limitations. The meta-coordination view is no exception to this general rule: the flexibility that allows it to adapt to the complexity of the current system of global governance has a theoretical price in terms of its ability to elicit determinate legitimacy assessments.

Why do we find the meta-coordination view attractive? Its main virtue is its flexibility, which is both synchronic and diachronic. Synchronically, the position is commendable because, by considering the criteria of legitimacy as variable counting principles, it allows us to adapt our specific conception of legitimacy to different types of institutional structures. If, following Rawls (1971/1999), we accept that the principle for a thing depends on the nature of that thing, then this is no small advantage. For example, it allows us to model our specific conception of legitimacy to different forms of institutions, which have radically divergent ways of operating. To illustrate, many global governance institutions have a technical nature; they fix standards for certain specific types of activities and create the conditions for lower transaction costs in the domains that they oversee (for instance, the International Standards Organisation, the International Maritime Organisation and the Internet Corporation for Assigned Names and Numbers). For these institu-tions, it is plausible to think of institutional integrity (i.e., the degree to which they are able to accomplish the task(s) that they were created to perform) as going a significant way towards establishing their legitimacy, without consent or institutionally democratic requirements entering the frame. This is espe-cially the case if we reject the idea that legitimacy is, necessarily, concerned with the establishment of a moral power (i.e., the power to impose duties), and we allow legitimacy assessments to be more widely construed as the establishment of some form of respect for institutional authority or standing (more on this below). Second, the position allows us to do this in a way that is, in our view, theoretically ecumenical. Insofar as it provides space for both deontological and teleological considerations and, at the same time, takes into account both institutional processes and outcomes, the view provides a unified form of normative assessment that tries to keep together the most important properties and benchmarks that we intuitively connect to legiti-macy assessments.

The implications of such theoretical flexibility and overall ecumenical char-acter are even more important if we think about the current state of global politics. In a world where many important international institutions and regimes are gridlocked (see Hale et al., 2013) the flexibility of the meta-coordination view allows us to be pragmatic without abandoning some our most stringent normative commitments. It allows us to understand, for example, that the benefits that we can, in principle, expect for solving specific coordination problems may be great enough to ensure we have principled reasons to relax the demandingness of the normative requirements that apply to institutional evaluations. This could be an advantage in two respects that are, in our view, morally significant. First, and most importantly, it could allow us to avoid serious harm, and harm that would in all likelihood fall on the weakest and most vulnerable people in the world, by cautioning us not to ask what is not achievable in the immediate future. Second, the meta-coordination view tries to avoid being, to paraphrase Rawls (1996), political in the wrong way. Our desire to relax the normative standards we apply to institutional structures is internal to the very idea of legitimacy, and reflects the complexity of our institutional and political landscape – not the surrender of our normative aspirations. But the meta-coordination view is also diachronically flexible. It allows us to recognize that, as circumstances change and, hopefully, become more favourable to progress towards what justice requires, we can gradually expect more from our institutions. Progress over time and according to circumstances keeps together the moral tension between more just arrangements and the reality of our present political condition.

However, as we have mentioned above, for all that is significant about the flexibility of the meta-coordination view, its flexibility has a price. The price, quite simply, is that, as it stands, it does not yet provide precise enough guidance. While Buchanan's broad position is, as we will see shortly, progress compared to some of the most influential accounts of the legitimacy of global governance institutions and public international law, it still needs to be further developed in order to provide concrete help in assessing existing institutional forms in global politics.

To see why Buchanan's view is progress, consider the Razian approach, which has recently been applied to public international law by John Tasioulas (2010). According to Joseph Raz:

> [T]he normal way to establish that a person has authority over another person involves showing that the alleged subject is likely better to comply with reasons which apply to him (other than the alleged authoritative directives) if he accepts the directives of the alleged authority as authoritatively binding and tries to follow them, rather than by trying to follow the reasons which apply to him directly. (1986: 53)

Raz refers to the latter as the Normal Justification Thesis (NJT). Roughly put, in the Razian picture of the legitimacy of authority, authority is bestowed to the extent that compliance with institutional directives gives those subject to the institution a better chance of acting rightly than does relying on private judgment alone. However, what the Razian account does not seem to provide is a way to recognize the specific conditions that should be met to reasonably believe that an institution realizes the NJT (see Lefkowitz in this volume). Lacking a more definite account of how the NJT can be satisfied hampers our ability to ascertain whether concrete institutions are to be judged as legitimate or not. It is fair to say that, without such an account, the Razian view seems to be almost completely silent about the content of legitimacy assessments. While, in our view, Buchanan's and Raz's accounts are broadly compatible, it should be clear that the meta-coordination view takes us further along the path that goes from the abstract exercise of developing the concept of legitimacy to the concrete assessment of specific institutions by providing a set of easily recognizable standards or criteria of legitimacy.

Nonetheless, some may also argue, as we do, that the meta-coordination view replaces one form of indeterminacy with another: we may have a framework to generate the appropriate types of reasons and criteria to recognize legitimate institutions, but we seem to lack a clear picture for when and how such reasons apply to different institutional types. To see why, it is useful to conceive concrete legitimacy appraisals as the result of three theoretical steps (see figure 1). The first step is the development of a concept of legitimacy, where a view of the nature and function of the very idea of legitimacy are elaborated. The second step takes us from the concept of legitimacy to different conceptions of legitimacy. Conceptions of legitimacy provide relatively abstract evaluative standards that, at least in the position we have advocated here, and which is consistent with Buchanan's view, depend on the features of the institutions we are evaluating. The third and final step gets us from a given conception of legitimacy to a judgment pertaining to a specific institution. Given our conception of legitimacy, can institution X be considered as legitimate?

Buchanan's view takes us further along the process of forming legitimacy assessments for specific institutional types and for concrete institutions. It does so by developing, as we have seen, a list of what Buchanan calls legitimacy criteria. Such criteria, understood as counting principles or

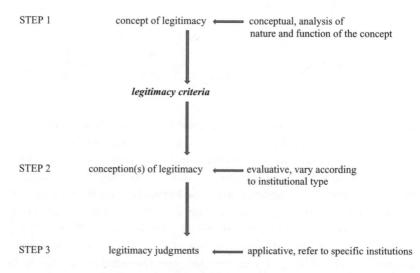

Figure 1 *Legitimacy from concept to judgment*

good-making features of an institution, allow us to create a bridge between the concept of legitimacy and the different conceptions that will apply to different institutional types. However, while the criteria of legitimacy provided by Buchanan are useful and allow us to make progress, we still face a potentially strong form of indeterminacy given the latitude that the meta-coordination view permits. More specifically, what seems to be missing is an account of how exactly we can go from the standards of legitimacy (the variable criteria) to a specific conception of legitimacy that applies to a specific institutional type. Given that such criteria are to be understood simply as 'counting principles', which criteria are *more* salient for which type of institution? Even assuming agreement on the fact that the criteria of legitimacy suggested by Buchanan are correct (something we find plausible), there is bound to be significant disagreement about which criteria are more important for different types of institutions. For instance, should we give more prominence to the fact that institutions should not have tainted origins if the institution itself uses coercive means to ensure compliance with its directives? Should accountability become more important as the interests that are affected by an institution become more significant? In the same way, developing the precise meaning of the variable criteria provided by the meta-coordination view is going to be subject to interpretation, and relies on the understanding of the domain over which an institution operates, as well as its features. Here too, more guidance is needed to ascertain how this interpretive exercise should be conducted. For example, how are we to understand the 'avoidance of serious unfairness' in different contexts such as the setting of technical standards and international economic governance?

Asking the meta-coordination view for more guidance may strike the reader as an unfair request. Perhaps, the reader will add, we are asking something that theory alone cannot provide. Perhaps the only way to be more clearly action-guiding is to allow theory to be complemented by historical and socio-logical argument in order to put forward more specific proposals. Furthermore, once we have accepted that conceptions of legitimacy are linked to the type of institution we are considering and the context in which such institutions operate, then to give guidance cannot mean to provide a formula for each possible institutional type. These are fair points and, to the extent that we can accept them, our criticism of the meta-coordination view should be seen more as an opportunity for further research rather than an open challenge to its validity or desirability. In our view, what is needed, is a framework for generating conceptions of legitimacy. It should be one that provides us with grounds to assess the relative importance and the correct way of interpreting the legitimacy criteria developed by the meta-coordination view, as it applies to some of the main institutional types (i.e., the modern state, major global governance institutions within the economic sphere, transnational institutions which have mainly coordination functions with respect to technical standards, human rights institutions, etc.). Providing this type of framework is no easy task. And it may very well be the case that more empirically informed research is required to make progress. For example, progress could require a large-scale project that analyses the empirical features of a large number of specific global governance institutions to retrieve any generalizable conclusions that pertain to their legitimacy given their domain of action and the type of directives that they generate. Nonetheless, we hold that providing such a framework is an urgent priority if the Buchanan view is to be fully compelling and if it is to be adopted as an important guide for the evaluation of legitimacy of global governance institutions.

4 Conclusion

While the accounts of legitimacy explored in this chapter have different strengths and weaknesses, we have argued that state consent theory is both conceptually weak and a poor fit to the complexity of contemporary global governance; that the democratic theory of legitimacy, although more robust than state consent theory in many respects, too often seeks an inappropriate one-size-fits-all solution to institutional diversity and is too abstract to provide precise judgments of legitimacy in relation to particular organizations; and that the meta-coordination view, while it has distinct advantages of providing greater flexibility and adaptability to the diversity of global governance institutions, is vulnerable to indeterminacy. In a robust general theory of the legitimacy of global governance institutions, we think that elements of both the democratic and meta-coordination views may have a qualified role, but this theory is far from available at the present time.

The case for defending democratic ideals remains very strong in the context of severe existential threats and permanent minorities (perhaps, more accurately, substantial majorities on many issues) effectively excluded from the global and economic political system. Severe global challenges generate equality of stakes that democracy, appropriately embedded, could legitimately address in the long term. Likewise, suitably developed, democracy provides the means to address the problem of minority exclusion and to develop accountability mechanisms that are broadly inclusive. After all, democracy is a system of ideals and practices that seeks to ensure that regulatory structures and rule sets are accountable in the public domain. Yet, in the short term, the meta-coordination view provides important signposts and stepping stones to resolving legitimacy queries which inevitably arise under imperfect political circumstances. A general theory of legitimacy, accordingly, would seek to combine these two approaches.

References

Archibugi, D., Archibugi, M. and Marchetti, R., eds. 2011. *Global Democracy: Normative and Empirical Perspectives.* Cambridge: Cambridge University Press.

Bodin, J. 1992. *On Sovereignty*, trans. and ed. J. H. Franklin. Cambridge: Cambridge University Press.

Buchanan, A. 2010. 'The Legitimacy of International Law, Democratic Legitimacy and International Institutions', in S. Besson and J. Tasioulas, eds., *The Philosophy of International Law*, 79–96. Oxford: Oxford University Press.

Buchanan, A. 2013. *The Heart of Human Rights*. Oxford: Oxford University Press.

Buchanan, A. and Keohane, R. 2006. 'The Legitimacy of Global Governance Institutions', *Ethics & International Affairs* 20(4): 405–437.

Cassese, A. 1995. *Self-Determination of Peoples: A Legal Reappraisal*. Cambridge: Cambridge University Press.

Christiano, T. 2008. *The Constitution of Equality: Democratic Authority and Its Limits*. Oxford: Oxford University Press.

Christiano, T. 2010. 'Democratic Legitimacy and International Institutions', in S. Besson and J. Tasioulas, eds., *The Philosophy of International Law*, 119–138. Oxford: Oxford University Press.

Christiano, T. 2011. 'Is Democratic Legitimacy Possible for International Institutions?', in D. Archibugi, M. Koenig-Archibugi and R. Marchetti, eds., *Global Democracy*, 60–95. Cambridge: Cambridge University Press.

Christiano, T. 2012a. 'The Legitimacy of International Institutions', in A. Marmor, ed., *The Routledge Companion to Philosophy of Law*, 380–394. New York: Routledge.

Christiano, T. 2012b. 'Authority', *The Stanford Encyclopedia of Philosophy*, ed. E. N. Zalta. http://plato.stanford.edu/entries/authority/.

Crawford, J. and Marks, S. 1988. 'The Global Democracy Deficit: An Essay on International Law and Its Limits', in D. Archibugi, D. Held and M. Köhler, eds., *Re-imagining Political Community*, 72–90. Cambridge: Polity.

Estlund, D. M. 2009. *Democratic Authority: A Philosophical Framework*. Princeton, NJ: Princeton University Press.

Fishkin, J. 1991. *Democracy and Deliberation*. New Haven, CT: Yale University Press.

Hale, T., Held, D. and Young, K. 2013. *Gridlock: Why Global Cooperation is Failing When We Need It Most*. Cambridge: Polity.

Hampsher-Monk, I. 1993. *A History of Modern Political Thought: Major Political Thinkers from Hobbes to Marx*. Oxford: Blackwell.

Held, D. 1995. *Democracy and the Global Order*. Cambridge: Polity.

Held, D. 2002. 'Law of States, Law of Peoples', *Legal Theory* 8(1): 1–44.

Held, D. 2004. *Global Covenant: The Social Democratic Alternative to the Washington Consensus*. Cambridge: Polity.

Held, D. 2006. *Models of Democracy*, 3rd edn. Cambridge: Polity.

Held, D. 2014. 'The Diffusion of Authority', in T. Weiss and R. Wilkinson, eds., *International Organization and Global Governance*, 60–72. London: Routledge.

Held, D. and McGrew, A. 2007. *Globalization/Anti-Globalization*, 2nd edn. Cambridge: Polity.

Held, D., McGrew, A., Goldblatt, D. and Perraton, J. 1999. *Global Transformations: Politics, Economics and Culture*. Cambridge: Polity.

Hinsley, F. H. 1986. *Sovereignty*, 2nd edn. Cambridge: Cambridge University Press.

Jackson, R. J. 1990. *Quasi-States: Sovereignty, International Relations and the Third World*. Cambridge: Cambridge University Press.

Krasner, S. 1999. *Sovereignty: Organized Hypocrisy*. Princeton, NJ: Princeton University Press.

Marchetti, R. 2008. *Global Democracy: For and Against*. New York: Routledge.

Offe, C. and Preuss, U. 1991. 'Democratic Institutions and Moral Resources', in D. Held, ed., *Political Theory Today*, 143–171. Cambridge: Polity.

Peter, F. 2010. 'Political Legitimacy', *The Stanford Encyclopedia of Philosophy*, ed. E. N. Zalta. http://plato.stanford.edu/archives/win2014/entries/legitimacy/

Peter, F. 2008. *Democratic Legitimacy*. New York: Routledge.

Rawls, J. 1971/1999. *A Theory of Justice*. Cambridge, MA: Harvard University Press.

Rawls, J. 1996. *Political Liberalism*. New York: Columbia University Press.

Raz, J. 1986. *The Morality of Freedom*. Oxford: Oxford University Press.

Rischard, J. F. 2002. *High Noon*. New York: Basic Books.

Rosenau, J. N. 2002. 'Governance in a New Global Order', in D. Held and A. G. McGrew, eds., *Governing Globalization*, 70–86. Cambridge: Polity.

Simmons, A. J. 2001. *Justification and Legitimacy: Essays on Rights and Obligations*. Cambridge: Cambridge University Press.

Tasioulas, J. 2010. 'The Legitimacy of International Law, Democratic Legitimacy and International Institutions', in S. Besson and J. Tasioulas, eds., *The Philosophy of International Law*, 97–116. Oxford: Oxford University Press.

Valentini, L. 2009. 'On the Apparent Paradox of Ideal Theory', *Journal of Political Philosophy* 17(3): 332–355.

Weiss, T. and Wilkinson, R., eds. 2014. *International Organization and Global Governance*. London: Routledge.

CHAPTER SEVEN

Just War and Global Justice

Laura Valentini

Introduction

The field of international ethics has been growing exceptionally fast since the end of the last century. This is especially true of two areas of inquiry: global justice and just war theory. For the most part, though, scholars working in the former area have taken little notice of developments in the latter, and vice versa. Only recently have international ethicists started to explore the possibilities for cross-fertilization between the two. In this chapter, I reflect on this recent trend, and sketch a systematic framework for integrating debates about just war theory and debates about global justice. I suggest that a central concern of just war theory – namely the just cause for war – can only be adequately addressed by appeal to theories of global justice. In making this suggestion, I revisit and elaborate on a valuable insight by Terry Nardin (2006) – namely, that the justification of coercion might be central to both global justice and the ethics of warfare – the potential of which has been under-appreciated by international ethicists.[1]

The chapter proceeds as follows. In section 1, I sketch the 'orthodox' approach to the just cause for war, and contrast it with recently developed cosmopolitan alternatives. In section 2, I articulate the widely accepted conceptual thesis that principles of justice, in general, set out rightfully enforceable entitlements. In section 3, I show that this thesis offers a conceptual entry point for linking debates about the just cause for war to debates about global justice. On the view I sketch, while principles of justice tell us which entitlements are rightfully enforceable in general, just causes for war focus on a subset of such entitlements: those that are in principle enforceable through lethal means. Making this conceptual move explicit allows us holistically to test theories of global justice against accounts of the just cause for war and vice versa, so as to achieve 'reflective equilibrium' between the two.[2] In section 4, I illustrate the substantive and methodological implications of my analysis by looking at the interplay between just cause for war and three prominent accounts of global justice: cosmopolitanism, statism and public reason theories. Section 5 concludes.

My argument and its conclusions are limited in four respects. First, my analysis is set against the background of contemporary just war theory, and does not engage with the tradition as a whole.[3] Second, my discussion is exclusively confined to the just cause for war, and sets aside other standards for the justification of armed conflict. Third, my exploration of the relationship between the just cause for war and global justice is premised on a broadly liberal perspective on political morality, according to which political conduct is just if, and only if, it is consistent with the fundamental moral equality of persons (see, e.g., Waldron, 1987). Finally, and most importantly, my aim in this chapter is not to defend a substantive view about either the just cause for war or global justice. Rather, my aim is methodological: taking the lead from recent developments in the field of just war theory, I want to sketch a systematic approach for thinking about just war and global justice together, and highlight how doing so enriches both domains of international ethical concern.

1 Just Cause for War: Orthodox versus Cosmopolitan Approaches

Let me begin by briefly explaining what I mean by war. War is what Gallie (1955) termed an 'essentially contested concept'. The stakes are high when it comes to drawing the conceptual boundaries of 'war'. When a conflict acquires the status of a war, particular normative consequences follow – e.g., about the applicable legal and, arguably, moral standards – and this partly explains the concept's contested nature. To keep things simple, I am going to offer a broad definition of 'war' so as to delimit the scope of my inquiry. I do not claim that this definition is optimal, but simply that it captures a large class of phenomena we would intuitively call 'wars'.

War: a conflict involving the use of lethal violence on a large scale.

The component parts of this definition should be further elucidated. First, I take wars to be conflicts characterized by the use of lethal violence – it is the use of lethal violence that renders them both particularly tragic, and justificatorily challenging. Second, the definition I have offered is very general, but in what follows, I shall exclusively focus on war as an international phenomenon – e.g., I exclude civil wars – that is, as a conflict involving agents who belong to different states. That said, I remain open about which sorts of agents may be involved in the relevant kinds of conflicts. These need not be exclusively state officials or representatives, but can also be private individuals, or armed groups that do not represent any given political community. Finally, wars involve the international use of force on a large scale. How large is 'large enough' for a conflict to count as a war is something on which I again remain agnostic. It is obvious, though, that whereas a conflict involving lethal violence between two nationals of different states would not meet the 'large-scale' condition, a conflict involving millions of individuals would. Readers themselves may choose the cut-off point they find most plausible between these two extremes.

Having offered a rough sketch of what I mean by 'war', I now turn to the ethical norms governing it. The ethics of war, or just war theory, is divided into three areas: (1) *jus ad bellum* – concerning the principles governing justified *resort* to war; (2) *jus in bello* – concerning the principles governing the justified *conduct* of war; and (3) *jus post bellum* – concerning the principles governing just peacemaking and reconstruction. In order for a war to be all-things-considered justified, the principles governing all three areas have to be complied with.[4]

In this chapter, I zoom in on one standard of *jus ad bellum*: the just cause for war. A just cause is a *necessary but not a sufficient condition* for resort to war to be justified. In addition to (a) just cause, the following further standards have to be met: (b) legitimate authority, (c) last resort, (d) right intentions, (e) proportionality and (f) likelihood of success.[5] To say that a war has a just cause, then, is to simply rule out one possible ground for the impermissibility of resorting to it; it is far from positively establishing that resort to war is, in any given circumstance, justified. Readers should bear this in mind as my discussion proceeds. In particular, they should not be tempted to draw overall conclusions about the justification of any given war solely based on my reflections about the just cause. Given the limited role played by the just cause condition in this process of justification, overall conclusions are necessarily unwarranted.

So, when is there a just cause for war? On what is sometimes termed the 'orthodox' view – most prominently defended by philosopher Michael Walzer (1977), and generally accepted in contemporary just war practice – war has a just cause only when it is a response to *aggression* (Fisher, 2011: 68–71). On this view, depending on who the target of aggression is, wars with a just cause may be fought:

- in national defence – i.e., the target is the particular state fighting a war;
- in defence of a third-party state – i.e., the target of aggression is a different political community, or
- with humanitarian aims – i.e., the targets of aggression are civilians brutalized by their own government.[6]

Differently put, on the orthodox view, resort to large-scale lethal force at the international level has a just cause only when it is used in defence of the 'bodily integrity' either of individuals – as in the case of humanitarian intervention – or of entire political communities, understood as collective agents – as in the case of wars of national defence. The intuition behind this aggression-centred perspective is, roughly, that in the same way in which an innocent person may rightfully use lethal force to defend herself or another innocent person from a culpable assailant, so too political communities are permitted to defend themselves, and others, from violent aggression.[7]

This 'aggression-centred' view is intuitively plausible, and informs much contemporary just war practice; yet it has not gone unchallenged. Especially – but not exclusively – in recent years, just war theorists of a broadly *cosmopolitan* disposition have started to question the conviction that aggression is the only admissible just cause for war (e.g., Beitz, 1979; Luban, 1980; McMahan, 2005; Fabre, 2012). Two observations appear to motivate this development. First, while aggression of course jeopardizes very important rights – from the physical security of individuals, to the 'bodily integrity' of collective agents – these are not the *only* rights worth defending through lethal means. For instance, as natural law theorists such as Hugo Grotius (1625) and Emer De Vattel (1758) had already remarked in the seventeenth and eighteenth centuries, rights to subsistence (or 'of necessity') – that is, to access the material resources necessary for self-preservation – might also be defended by means of violence (see also S. Miller, 2007).

Second, the aggression-centred paradigm is excessively collectivist, and clashes with the commitments of a normative individualist political morality. In particular, from a normative individualist perspective, it appears to both overgenerate and undergenerate just causes for war. Overgeneration occurs when violations of the 'bodily integrity' of a state do not put into question the fundamental rights of individuals. For instance, the occupation and annexation of an uninhabited, resourceless piece of territory belonging to 'state A' would be an act of aggression and, on the orthodox paradigm, constitute a just cause for war. Yet its impact on the rights of individual members of 'state A' appears too minimal to justify resort to lethal force in response (cf. Rodin, 2002; Fabre, 2012: ch. 2). Undergeneration occurs insofar as internally legitimate states are treated as automatically entitled to their territory and resources, in the way we typically think of human beings as 'automatically' owners of their bodies. But this assumption is morally dubious, especially from a cosmopolitan perspective. In a deeply unequal world, some of the resources possessed by wealthy states, cosmopolitans insist, 'morally' belong to the global poor. This has led some cosmopolitan theorists to suggest – in stark contrast to the orthodox paradigm – that culpably bringing about severe poverty and/or failing to remedy it constitute just causes for war (see, e.g., Luban, 1980; Fabre, 2012: 103; Lippert-Rasmussen, 2013; Øverland, 2013).[8]

This is only a rough (and incomplete) 'snapshot' of current thinking about the just cause for war, and specifically of the division between cosmopolitan and orthodox approaches to the topic. In what follows, I do not wish to evaluate the substantive merits of either of these approaches. Instead, I want to unearth the broader conceptual connections between just war theory and theories of global justice that implicitly underpin them – connections that only cosmopolitan theorists have recently started to explore, and which have far-reaching consequences, beyond cosmopolitan theorizing. Once those connections have been brought to the surface, it will become possible *systematically* to examine the implications of different approaches to global justice for the just cause for war, and vice versa.

2 (Global) Justice and Rightful Enforceability

To appreciate how theories of (global) justice might systematically feed into an account of the just cause for war, we need to gain a firmer grip on the nature of justice as a special type of moral concern for political philosophy.

As is well known, principles of justice differ from other types of moral principles in that they determine persons' *rights*: they tell us who is entitled to what. The claim that I have a duty of justice to X implies that there is some other agent (or group of agents) who has a right to my X-ing. Duties of justice are correlative to rights and therefore *owed* to others. Other duties, by contrast, lack this structure. Take, for instance, duties of charity to help the needy: although their performance is morally required, they are not correlative to rights, and therefore not *owed* to particular others (Buchanan, 1987; Barry, 1991; Valentini, 2013b).

The conceptual space occupied by rights is still broader than that occupied by the justice claims *central to political philosophy*. The latter pick out only a subset of rights, namely those that are enforceable, by which I mean 'rightfully enforceable' – in principle enforceable as a matter of right (O'Neill, 1996; Kant, 1999/1797; Nardin, 2004; Pogge, 2006; D. Miller, 2007: 261; Valentini, 2013a).[9] For instance, promises give rise to rights, yet we do not typically think that they may be rightfully enforced by the state or other agents. To that extent, promise-generated rights may be a matter of 'interpersonal justice', but not a matter of justice in the sense relevant to political philosophy. In what follows, I will use the notion of justice in the narrower, political sense.

To see the connection between justice and rightful enforceability, take the two most prominent contemporary theories of *domestic justice*: Rawls's liberal egalitarianism and Nozick's libertarianism. According to Rawls's (1999a) theory, a society is just if, and only if, its citizens have equal basic liberties and fair equality of opportunity, and if economic inequalities are to the greatest absolute benefit of the worst off. These principles set out citizens' entitlements, which may be rightfully enforced by the state.[10] Nozick (1974), by contrast, holds that, provided entitlements have the right historical pedigree, a just society is compatible with significant levels of inequality. To be sure, such an unequal society, although just, would not be morally optimal. Libertarians like Nozick therefore often acknowledge the existence of duties of charity to help the destitute. Such duties, however, are not correlative to rights and may not be rightfully enforced by the state or any other agent. In sum, despite their substantive differences, both Rawls and Nozick hold that principles of justice are distinctive insofar as they ground rightfully enforceable entitlements.

While the enforceability aspect of justice is explicit in discussions concerning the domestic realm, it is not equally prominent in discussions about global justice – i.e., about what rightfully enforceable entitlements exist beyond borders – probably because of the lack of effective enforcement mechanisms at the global level.[11] But the enforceability of global justice is often implicitly alluded to in the literature, for instance by those who advance proposals for global tax-based redistributive schemes (Pogge, 2008: ch. 8). If the demands of global justice were not enforceable, taxation would not be a legitimate means of fulfilling them.

More generally, if the 'justice' in 'global justice' refers to the same type of moral concern as the 'justice' in 'domestic justice' – which is what participants in the debate on global justice imply – rightful enforceability must be one of its defining features. (Of course, which entitlements may be rightfully enforced through *lethal* means is a further question, which will be discussed below.) The contemporary debate on global justice – involving disagreements between statists, cosmopolitans, nationalists, internationalists and so forth – is thus best understood as a debate concerning people's rightfully enforceable entitlements beyond the state (for an overview, see Valentini, 2011). In sum, it appears plausible to stipulate that justice, whether domestic or global, always concerns rightfully enforceable entitlements. This conceptual stipulation, in turn, gives us a basis for drawing a systematic connection between the just cause for war and theories of global justice. I elaborate on this conceptual connection in the next section.

3   Global Justice and the Just Cause for War: A Framework

War involves the use of lethal force at the international level. The use of force, in general, is *in principle* rightful when utilized to protect our justice-based entitlements. What, then, might constitute a just cause for war? The obvious answer seems to be: the protection of our fundamental (by which I mean 'most important') entitlements. In turn, what our fundamental entitlements are, at the international or global level, depends on the particular theory of global justice to which we subscribe. Once the connection between justice and rightful enforceability is established, we can see the just cause criterion as focusing on rights so important that they may *in principle* be rightfully enforced through lethal means (though, as explained earlier, whether their enforcement via war is actually justified in any given instance depends on its fulfilling further just war criteria).[12]

Thinking of the just cause for war as a *special case* of the general question of global justice – as I am suggesting here – has three distinctive, and related, theoretical advantages. First, in line with Nardin's original suggestion, it allows us to see our thinking about justice in the international realm as being more coherent, parsimonious and well integrated than it is usually perceived to be (2006: 454).[13]

Second, it allows us to put greater discipline on appeals to justice at the global level. The notion of justice is in fact often invoked in discussions about international ethics, mostly because of its rhetorical power. However, the implications of using the language of justice are seldom taken seriously. The conceptualization presented here systematically accounts for the key role played by justice in political philosophy. Matters of justice are of special importance insofar as they concern *rights*, and not just *any* kind of rights, but specifically those rights that may be rightfully enforced. This means that every time we hear the claim 'X is a matter of justice', to evaluate its tenability, we need to ask ourselves (1) whether it is plausible to think that someone is entitled to X and, if so, (2) whether the entitlement to X may be rightfully enforced under suitable circumstances. Moreover, whenever a particular object X is given the status of a 'fundamental demand of justice', we need to ask ourselves whether its defence could ever plausibly count as a just cause for the use of lethal force, including war. If our answer is negative, then X's status as a *fundamental* demand of justice will have to be questioned.

This leads me to the third virtue of the unified approach proposed here. At a deeper level, the approach has the methodological advantage of allowing us to test our views about just war theory against our views about global justice, and vice versa. Most contemporary political philosophers agree that a good theory of justice should be one in which our considered judgments about specific cases stand in 'reflective equilibrium' with the principles advocated. The more the theory allows us to account for, and to illuminate, our considered judgments, the better the theory. Moreover, the more considered judgments the theory encompasses, the more reliable the theory is. As John Rawls (1999a) and, subsequently, Norman Daniels (2013) have pointed out, we should aspire to achieve 'wide' reflective equilibrium, reaching consistency in our judgments across a broad range of interconnected issue areas. The view presented here helps us widen reflective equilibrium across the issue areas of just war and of global justice. Theories of global justice will have to stand in reflective equilibrium with judgments about the just cause for war, and approaches to the just cause will need to stand in reflective equilibrium with judgments about global justice (i.e., about people's and communities' enforceable entitlements at the global level). This is precisely one of the most advantageous methodological underpinnings of the recent cosmopolitan turn in just war thinking. But what cosmopolitans have done – once the conceptual basis for their approach has become transparent – other theorists of global justice can do too.

In fact, *if* the conceptual connection between justice and rightful enforceability is tenable, this is not just what other global justice theorists can do, it is, arguably, what they *should* do. A good theory of the just war (of which the just cause for war is a key component) cannot be developed independently of a theory of global justice, and vice versa. If our theory of the just war presupposes an account of global entitlements that strikes us as implausible, we need to revise it. Similarly, if our theory of global justice establishes entitlements the defence of which has implausible implications for the just war, we have reason to revise it.

In the next section, I give some concrete examples of how theorizing about global justice and about the just war might benefit from this mutual testing. My aim is not to argue for any specific *conception* of the just cause for war or of global justice, but to illustrate the implications of the approach sketched here.

4 Just War and Global Justice: Reaching Equilibrium

From the perspective of this approach, a war has a just cause if and only if it is aimed at protecting fundamental entitlements at the international level. This means that whether defence against aggression is a valid ground for waging war depends on the particular outlook on global justice one subscribes to. The aggression-centred model of the just cause is not to be seen as fundamental to the ethics of war – as it has been until recently – but is instead a by-product of a particular account of international justice. In what follows, I illustrate this point with a few examples, drawing on three distinct accounts of international justice: statism, cosmopolitanism (relational and non-relational[14]) and public reason views. Let me again emphasize that these examples exclusively focus on the *just cause* requirement, which is a *necessary but not a sufficient* condition for justly resorting to war.

Consider, first, the account of the just cause dominant in contemporary international practice, according to which any *de facto* recognized sovereign state may justly fight a war of national defence. If we adopt the 'integrated approach', we must conclude that this account surreptitiously presupposes a particular outlook on global justice. On this outlook, *de facto* sovereign states are entitled to the resources they possess, including the land on which they exist, and may therefore *in principle* rightfully fight in order to protect them. From this perspective, no matter how unequal the distribution of relevant resources between states, no matter whether such unequal distribution prevents some states from building well-functioning communities, attacks on the status quo give rise to just causes for war.[15] That is, any *de facto* state whose territorial integrity and resource possession is threatened by a violent attack has a just cause for protecting itself through equally violent means.

Problematically, this view is status quo biased, and certainly incompatible with a recognizably liberal political morality. It is thus no surprise that even the most 'conservative' liberal outlook on international justice, namely *statism*, holds that international justice requires both respect for the sovereignty of *legitimate* (peaceful and human-rights respecting) states *and* assistance towards *needy* societies (e.g., Rawls, 1999b; Blake, 2001). The duty of assistance, in particular, implies that, whenever a society is 'burdened by unfavourable conditions', and others can help without too much sacrifice, they have an enforceable duty of justice to do so (Rawls, 1999b).[16]

International assistance, understood as an enforceable requirement of justice, appears to make a lot of sense from a liberal perspective, until we consider its implications for the ethics of war. If the integrated approach withstands scrutiny, and the principle of assistance sets out fundamental rights, then destitution – *no matter what causes it* – counts as a just cause for war whenever there are others who could end it at moderate cost. Bluntly put, on this picture, if you fail to help the poor and could do so without too much sacrifice, the poor have a just cause to wage war against you.[17] By moving away from the conservative outlook on justice underpinning aggression-based accounts of the just cause, statists inadvertently end up with a highly revisionary account of *jus ad bellum* itself, one they would probably not be happy to endorse.

Note that I am not making an exegetical claim about what statists *actually* think. In fact, I strongly suspect that they would vocally resist the conclusion I am pressing onto them; and understandably so. My point is that, in order to resist that conclusion, they have to deny that the duty of assistance is a *duty of justice correlative to a fundamental right*. Given the importance of the interests protected by that duty, denying the fundamental nature of the corresponding right might be rather tricky. It would perhaps be easier to deny its character as an enforceable duty of justice, and 'turn it' into one of charity or beneficence. Doing so, however, would also come at a cost: namely leaving the global poor at the mercy of the good will of the world's privileged. In sum, tested against its implications for the just cause for war, statism – as an approach to global justice – might need some revision.[18]

Let us look at how another perspective on global justice, namely *relational cosmopolitanism*, fares with respect to its implications for the just cause. Relational cosmopolitans hold that duties of socioeconomic justice only apply between those who routinely interact with each other, thereby mutually shaping and constraining their life contexts (e.g., Pogge, 1989; Beitz, 1999; Moellendorf, 2002). For relational cosmopolitans, the fact that certain societies and their inhabitants are burdened by unfavourable conditions triggers concerns of international/global justice only when such conditions can be at least partly traced to the agency of outsiders.[19] A particularly influential version of this view is offered by Thomas Pogge (2008).

Pogge argues that the inhabitants of wealthy countries, and their governments, support a global institutional structure that *causes* other societies to be unable to protect their citizens' basic rights. In fact, Pogge goes so far as to assert that the global order, supported mostly by the wealthy of the West, *foreseeably and avoidably* causes millions of people to die from poverty and destitution every year. It is because of this causal/moral link, Pogge argues, that the predicament of the poor may be appropriately regarded as an injustice. This is why the wealthy may be said to *owe* the poor (1) a better-designed global institutional structure, allowing them to build well-functioning societies, and (2) compensation for the harms imposed on them.

If Pogge were right, given the gravity of the injustice at stake, burdened societies and their inhabitants would have a *just cause* for war against the wealthy as a means of enforcing those basic entitlements the wealthy are violating (again, let me emphasize that a just cause would not suffice to render such a war justified). However, unlike in the case of statist assistance, their potential act of violence could be more easily reconciled with the 'aggression-centred' paradigm central to contemporary *jus ad bellum*. There is a sense in which, by (allegedly) supporting deeply unjust institutions, the wealthy are 'attacking' the poor, preventing them from building, and living in, decent states. In other words, the agency of the wealthy is so deeply involved in the predicament of the poor that we can construe a hypothetical war of the latter against the former as a non-paradigmatic instance of defence against aggression (Lippert-Rasmussen, 2013; for a response, see Pogge, 2013; for discussion, see Räikkä, 2014; see also Fabre, 2012: ch. 3; Øverland, 2013, 2014). Once again, let me emphasize that I am not making an exegetical claim about what Pogge is, or relational cosmopolitans more generally are, committed to. Indeed, Pogge (2013) himself strongly insists that he is *not* committed to the conclusion I am envisaging. All I am saying is that *if* we look at relational cosmopolitan theories of global justice from the perspective of the proposed integrated approach, we obtain a particular account of the just cause. This account, in turn, can help us reconcile a liberal commitment to normative individualism in thinking about justice, with the strong (independent) conviction that lethal force at the international level may primarily be used in response to aggression – though, as we have seen, the notions of aggression, and defence against aggression, will have to be broadened here, so as to include some non-paradigmatic instances.

This is only one of the possible outcomes delivered by the mutual testing (between considered judgments about *jus ad bellum* and global justice) I am proposing. Other outcomes are also possible, for instance if we start from non-relational cosmopolitan premises. For *non-relational cosmopolitans*, the egalitarian principles of justice that liberals defend in the domestic arena should apply globally, independently of the existence of particular types of relations across the world's population (Caney, 2005; arguably, Tan, 2004). Specifically, for many non-relational cosmopolitans, justice demands that nobody in the world should be worse off through no fault of his or her own (cf. Temkin, 1993: 17). If remediable luck-based inequalities exist *and* prevent the disadvantaged from leading minimally decent lives, on the integrated approach, it would follow that lethal force could *in principle* be rightfully employed to redress this injustice. Imagine a society hit by a natural catastrophe, whose inhabitants consequently find themselves poor and destitute. To the extent that other, more prosperous societies refuse to assist the disaster-stricken one, its inhabitants would have a just cause for using lethal force to appropriate the resources they need for their own survival (Luban, 1980: 177–8).

Non-relational cosmopolitans might variously respond to the just war implications of their view, under the integrated approach. Some might bite the bullet and simply accept that their account of justice requires a radical revision of the just cause requirement. National and third-party defence are not the only just causes for war; on the revisionary picture, redistribution and subsistence are too. Indeed, this is precisely what the cosmopolitan theorists I have mentioned at the outset conclude (most prominently, Luban, 1980; Fabre, 2012: ch. 3). Others might instead feel uncomfortable with such an expansion of the just cause condition and revise their preferred account of justice in either of two ways. One option consists in switching to relational cosmopolitanism which, as we saw earlier, can arguably more comfortably accommodate both a commitment to normative individualism and a plausible (not too revisionary) account of the just cause for war. The other option consists in modifying the status of non-relational principles of justice. Although this move has not been explicitly made in the debate on global justice, it is a relatively familiar one in the debate on domestic justice, and I illustrate it in what follows.

Faced with the somewhat counterintuitive implications of their views, proponents of so-called luck-egalitarianism – which we can treat as a domestic analogue of non-relational cosmopolitanism – have often responded that their preferred distributive principles are in fact only one ingredient in an overall account of enforceable rights-based morality, that is, what I here call justice (Arneson, 2000; Cohen, 2003, 2008). The principle that nobody should suffer disadvantages through no fault of her own can be factored into an account of justice in at least two ways.

First, it can be said that such a principle needs to be balanced with other principles, including principles of assistance, of efficiency and so forth. Once all the relevant moral considerations have been taken into account (in conjunction with empirical facts), we can devise what Cohen (2003) famously called 'rules of regulation', namely moral norms which should govern society and be enforced by the state. But if justice is, as I have argued, rightfully enforceable morality, then such rules of regulation *are* more aptly termed rules of justice. If non-relational cosmopolitans follow this strategy, they need no longer worry about the implications of their preferred account of justice for the theory of the just war, because what they offer is *not* an account of justice, but only one component of such an account. To that extent, it is unclear what non-relational cosmopolitanism implies for our enforceable entitlements and, consequently, for the theory of the just war and, crucially, *of global justice.*

The second way in which the luck-egalitarian principle underpinning several versions of non-relational cosmopolitanism might be incorporated into a broader account of justice moves us in the direction of what I would term 'public reason theories'. For public reason theories, the demands of justice should be established 'omnilaterally', rather than unilaterally.[20] Within any specific domain of human interaction – the international domain in our case – people reasonably disagree about what justice demands. When reasonable disagreements occur, the morally correct way of determining people's entitlements, public reason theorists suggest, is *procedural*: first by identifying the areas of overlap between different reasonable views, and then by filling remaining gaps through fair (usually democratic) decision-making. Since there exists no global democratic state, a public reason view of global justice will only be able to proclaim as valid those rights which lie in the area of overlap between different reasonable views about global justice – where 'reasonable' is understood (broadly) in terms of consistency with normative individualism.

Following this strategy, the luck-egalitarian (or non-relational cosmopolitan) can simply treat her view as one admissible input to a fair decision-making procedure, the output of which will determine people's enforceable rights. From this perspective, non-relational cosmopolitanism would again not operate at the level of defining what counts as enforceable morality, and would thus have no direct consequences for the theory of the just war.

Whether non-relational cosmopolitans would be happy to endorse either of the two solutions I have described is an open question. Both reduce the significance of non-relational cosmopolitan principles in a way that seems at odds with the self-image of their proponents. However, if non-relational cosmopolitans do feel uncomfortable with the just war implications of their views under my proposed integrated approach, they may have no choice but to scale down their project in the ways I have suggested.

To sum up, in this section, I have illustrated how thinking about just war theory (specifically, the just cause for war) and global justice together opens up further lines of argument in both fields, and allows us holistically to test our views about the former against our views about the latter, and vice versa. So far, only some cosmopolitan theorists have started systematically to work out the implications of a cosmopolitan moral outlook for the ethics of war. But the same can be done in relation to other approaches to global justice, and the direction of argument need not exclusively be 'from global justice to the just cause for war'. The opposite direction is also viable (as, indeed, the method of reflective equilibrium prescribes): we may want to modify our approach to global justice if this turns out to have excessively counterintuitive implications for the ethics of war. Although such mutual testing is likely to lend greater plausibility to certain views about global justice rather than others, my main aim has not been to defend any particular substantive account of our global entitlements or of the just cause for war. Instead, I have endeavoured to illustrate the methodological advantages, and potentially radical substantive implications, of thinking about the two together.

5 Conclusion

In this chapter, taking the lead from Terry Nardin's insight, and reflecting on recent cosmopolitan approaches to the ethics of war, I have tried to unearth the conceptual connections between theories of global justice and theories of the just war. I have suggested that, while theories of global justice establish rightfully enforceable entitlements at the global level, theories of the just war concern the justified use of *lethal* force to secure entitlements across national borders.[21] This understanding of justice and the ethics of war not only unifies our thinking about justice in the international realm, but also allows us to test our ideas about the just war and international justice against one another.

That said, I should again emphasize the limits of my inquiry. As I anticipated at the outset, my focus here has been specifically (and somewhat artificially) on global justice and the *just cause for war* only. This means that my conclusions are both partial and provisional, and need to be supplemented with an analysis of global justice in connection with other criteria of *jus ad bellum*, *jus in bello* and *jus post bellum*. Most importantly, whatever we think about the just cause for war, we should remember that having a just cause is a necessary but not a sufficient condition for justifiably resorting to war. The demands of likelihood of success and last resort also have to be satisfied – among others. Once we bear this in mind, it becomes clear that hardly any 'global-justice' war would be permissible in the world today. Still, reflecting on the connection between global justice and just causes for war has advantages. In particular, it allows us fully to appreciate the gravity of certain injustices, as well as the urgency of remedying them – even if it leads us to rule war out as the 'all things considered' appropriate remedy.

Finally, in this chapter I have not considered whether there are compelling reasons for keeping just war and global justice separate, and specifically for treating war as 'special' and discontinuous with our political-moral thinking more generally. If those reasons exist, they will need to be compared to, and balanced against, the advantages of thinking about just war and global justice together. Here, I have only looked at 'one side' of the balance.[22]

References

Arneson, R. J. 2000. 'Luck Egalitarianism and Prioritarianism', *Ethics* 110(2): 339–349.

Barry, B. 1991. 'Humanity and Justice in Global Perspective', in *Liberty and Justice: Essays in Political Theory 2*, 182–210. Oxford: Clarendon Press.

Beitz, C. R. 1979. 'Bounded Morality: Justice and the State in World Politics', *International Organization* 33(3): 405–424.

Beitz, C. R. 1999. *Political Theory and International Relations*. Princeton, NJ: Princeton University Press.

Blake, M. 2001. 'Distributive Justice, State Coercion, and Autonomy', *Philosophy & Public Affairs* 30(3): 257–296.

Brock, G. 2009. *Global Justice: A Cosmopolitan Account*. Oxford: Oxford University Press.

Buchanan, A. 1987. 'Justice and Charity', *Ethics* 97(3): 558–575.

Caney, S. 2005. *Justice beyond Borders*. Oxford: Oxford University Press.

Christiano, T. 2008. *The Constitution of Equality: Democratic Authority and Its Limits*. Oxford: Oxford University Press.

Coates, A. J. 1997. *The Ethics of War*. Manchester: Manchester University Press.

Cohen, G. A. 2003. 'Facts and Principles', *Philosophy & Public Affairs* 31(3): 211–245.

Cohen, G. A. 2008. *Rescuing Justice and Equality*. Cambridge, MA: Harvard University Press.

Daniels, N. 2013. 'Reflective Equilibrium', *The Stanford Encyclopedia of Philosophy*, ed. E. N. Zalta. http://plato.stanford.edu/archives/win2013/entries/reflective-equilibrium/.

De Vattel, E. 1758. *The Law of Nations*.

Fabre, C. 2012. *Cosmopolitan War*. Oxford: Oxford University Press.

Fisher, D. 2011. *Morality and War: Can War Be Just in the Twenty-First Century?* Oxford: Oxford University Press.

Gallie, W. B. 1955. 'Essentially Contested Concepts', *Proceedings of the Aristotelian Society* 56(1): 167–198.

Grotius, Hugo. 1625. *On the Law of War and Peace*.

Kant, I. 1999/1797. *Metaphysical Elements of Justice: Part I of The Metaphysics of Morals*, trans. J. Ladd. Indianapolis, IN: Hackett.

Lazar, S. 2013. 'War', in H. LaFollette, ed., *The International Encyclopedia of Ethics*, 5379–5393. Oxford: Blackwell.

Lippert-Rasmussen, K. 2013. 'Global Injustice and Redistributive Wars', *Law, Ethics and Philosophy* 1(1): 65–86.

Luban, D. 1980. 'Just War and Human Rights', *Philosophy & Public Affairs* 9(2): 160–181.

Maffettone, P. 2013. 'The Coherence and Defensibility of Rawls' Law of Peoples', PhD thesis, The London School of Economics and Political Science. http://etheses.lse.ac.uk/705/.

McMahan, J. 2005. 'Just Cause for War', *Ethics and International Affairs* 19(3): 1–21.

Miller, D. 2007. *National Responsibility and Global Justice*. Oxford: Oxford University Press.

Miller, S. 2007. 'Civilian Immunity, Forcing the Choice, and Collective Responsibility', in I. Primoratz, ed., *Civilian Immunity in War*, 113–135. Oxford: Oxford University Press.

Moellendorf, D. 2002. *Cosmopolitan Justice*. Boulder, CO: Westview Press.

Nagel, T. 2005. 'The Problem of Global Justice', *Philosophy & Public Affairs* 33(2): 113–147.

Nardin, T. 2004. 'Justice and Coercion', in A. J. Bellamy, ed., *International Society and Its Critics*, 247–264. Oxford: Oxford University Press.

Nardin, T. 2006. 'International Political Theory and the Question of Justice', *International Affairs* 82(3): 449–465.

Nozick, R. 1974. *Anarchy, State, and Utopia*. New York: Basic Books.

O'Neill, O. 1996. *Towards Justice and Virtue: A Constructive Account of Practical Reasoning*. Cambridge: Cambridge University Press.

Orend, B. 2008. 'War', *The Stanford Encyclopedia of Philosophy*, ed. E. N. Zalta. http://plato.stanford.edu/archives/fall2008/entries/war/.

Øverland, G. 2013. '602 and One Dead: On Contribution to Global Poverty and Liability to Defensive Force', *European Journal of Philosophy* 21(2): 279–299.

Øverland, G. 2014. 'Global Poverty and an Extraordinary Humanitarian Intervention', in T. Brooks, ed., *New Waves in Global Justice*, 29–47. Basingstoke: Palgrave Macmillan.

Pogge, T. 1989. *Realizing Rawls*. Ithaca, NY: Cornell University Press.

Pogge, T. 2004. '"Assisting" the Global Poor', in D. K. Chatterjee, ed., *The Ethics of Assistance: Morality and the Distant Needy*, 260–88. Cambridge: Cambridge University Press.

Pogge, T. 2006. 'Justice', in D. M. Borchert, ed., *Encyclopedia of Philosophy*, 4:862–870. Farmington Hills, MI: Macmillan Reference.

Pogge, T. 2008. *World Poverty and Human Rights: Cosmopolitan Responsibilities and Reforms*. Cambridge: Polity.

Pogge, T. 2013. 'Poverty and Violence', *Law, Ethics and Philosophy* 1(1): 88–111.

Rawls, J. 1999a. *A Theory of Justice*. Oxford: Oxford University Press.

Rawls, J. 1999b. *The Law of Peoples: With 'The Idea of Public Reason Revisited'*, Cambridge, MA: Harvard University Press.

Rodin, David. 2002. *War and Self-Defense*. Oxford: Clarendon Press.

Räikkä, J. 2014. 'Redistributive Wars and Just War Principles', *Ratio.Ru* 12: 4–26.

Sangiovanni, A. 2007. 'Global Justice, Reciprocity, and the State', *Philosophy & Public Affairs* 35(1): 3–39.

Tan, K.-C. 1998. 'Liberal Toleration in Rawls's Law of Peoples', *Ethics* 108(2): 276–295.

Tan, K.-C. 2004. *Justice without Borders: Cosmopolitanism, Nationalism, and Patriotism*. New York: Cambridge University Press.

Temkin, L. S. 1993. *Inequality*. New York: Oxford University Press.

Valentini, L. 2011. *Justice in a Globalized World: A Normative Framework*. Oxford: Oxford University Press.

Valentini, L. 2013a. 'Cosmopolitan Justice and Rightful Enforceability', in G. Brock, ed., *Cosmopolitanism versus Non-Cosmopolitanism: Critiques, Defenses, Reconceptualizations*, 92–110. New York: Oxford University Press.

Valentini, L. 2013b. 'Justice, Charity, and Disaster Relief: What, If Anything, Is Owed to Haiti, Japan and New Zealand?' *American Journal of Political Science* 57(2): 491–503.

Waldron, J. 1987. 'Theoretical Foundations of Liberalism', *The Philosophical Quarterly* 37(147): 127–150.

Walzer, M. 1977. *Just and Unjust Wars: A Moral Argument with Historical Illustrations*. New York: Basic Books.

CHAPTER EIGHT

The Associativist Account of Killing in War

Seth Lazar

Introduction

Many of us believe that pacifism is mistaken. Warfare, though it involves intentional killing, can sometimes be justified. At the same time, we believe humans enjoy fundamental moral protections against being deliberately killed – commonly expressed in the language of human rights. The challenge is to render these two commitments mutually consistent. We could argue that in justified wars those whom we intentionally kill are liable to be killed: they have lost or forfeited the protection of their rights, so killing is just, because it is rights-consistent. Or we could concede that warfare necessarily involves violating rights, but argue that weightier reasons can override those rights violations, rendering warfare all things considered justified, though unjust.

Contemporary philosophers of the ethics of war, despite their other profound disagreements, until recently unanimously affirmed the first option. Michael Walzer (2006/1977: 135) argued that 'a legitimate act of war is one that does not violate the rights of the people against whom it is directed'. Jeff McMahan, for all his other criticisms of Walzer, agreed that, with very rare exceptions, intentional killing in war must be justified, if at all, by the target's liability (1994, 2004, 2009; although see also 2014). Likewise, Walzer's supporters (Benbaji, 2008; Steinhoff, 2008; Emerton and Handfield, 2009) and his many opponents (Kamm, 2004; McPherson, 2004; Øverland, 2006; Miller, 2007; Altman and Wellman, 2008; Coady, 2008; Fabre, 2009a; for dissenting views, see Kutz, 2008; Shue, 2008). The dispute between these camps is over who loses their rights in war: Walzerians advocate the 'symmetrist' position that combatants on both sides of any war lose their rights to life, while noncombatants on both sides retain them; anti-Walzerian 'asymmetrists' think that combatants and perhaps some noncombatants whose side went to war unjustifiably – hereafter combatants-U and noncombatants-U – lose their rights against attack, but combatants and noncombatants on the justified side – combatants-J and noncombatants-J – retain them.

I think this endorsement of Walzer's starting assumption is a mistake – at least, if we want to justify a plausible set of armed conflicts, while affirming a plausible theory of the right to life (see Lazar, 2009a, 2010a; for similar views, see Kutz, 2008; Shue, 2010). If all combatants-U must be liable to be killed for warfare to be permissible, we have to set the threshold of responsibility for that liability low enough to ensure that even the most inept, inactive combatant meets it. But if we endorse this low-threshold view, then, at least in modern states, we will render whole adult populations liable to be killed, since we are almost all responsible, if only minimally, for our states' warfighting capacities – through our taxpaying, voting, contribution to war-related industries, and so on. If mere contribution or innocent contribution were sufficient, very few would escape the liability net. Most will find this untenable: they must argue that liability presupposes a 'fit' between the degree of responsibility or contribution and the resulting fate. But once we endorse this high-threshold view, we find that many of the combatants-U whom we need to kill are not sufficiently responsible, or do not contribute enough, to be liable to be killed.

For those who reject collective liability – which includes all the just war theorists mentioned so far – liability can be grounded only in the assessment of each potentially liable individual's behaviour. As his critics argued, Walzer's generalization over all combatants is unacceptable – but so is their generalization over all combatants-U. Considered as individuals, at least on the more plausible high-threshold view of liability, some combatants-J are liable to be killed; not all combatants-U are liable. If individual rights are inviolable, we must ensure that each individual whom we intentionally kill is liable to that fate. Yet warfare is too messy for us ever to fight wars that satisfy this demand. Most killing happens from a distance; the targets are coordinates rather than individuals. The relevant actors frequently cannot discriminate between those who are and those who are not liable to be killed. Any theory of our right to life that is sufficiently indiscriminate to render this carnage consistent with that right is surely not discriminating enough to be a plausible theory of our right to life. In all likely wars, we will intentionally kill and maim many non-liable people. Wars cannot be wholly just. If they must be entirely just to be justified, we should endorse pacifism.

This chapter proposes one strand in an alternative solution – one that affirms the high-threshold view of liability to be killed, and therefore concedes that the rights-respecting war is an unattainable ideal, but maintains that warfare can nonetheless sometimes be justified. I focus on a class of widely neglected reasons. Most of us share a number of morally important relationships with those closest to us – our family, friends and other loved ones. Combatants enjoy similarly significant relationships with their comrades-in-arms. When aggressors attack, they threaten those with whom we share these relationships – our associates. Sometimes we can protect our associates only if we fight and kill. We have duties to protect our associates, grounded in the value of these special relationships. Our armed forces are the executors of those duties. When they fight, those duties may clash with the rights that they must violate to win the war. In some cases, the associative duties to protect can override those rights, thus rendering some acts of killing all things considered justified. I call this the 'associativist account' of (part of) what justifies killing in war.

While contemporary just war theory is almost exclusively impartial in orientation, ordinary understandings of the justification of warfare are characterized by extreme partiality. I think it is commonplace to suggest that, when people justify fighting to themselves, their desire to protect their loved ones, their comrades-in-arms and their community is at the forefront of their reasoning.

> The fighter is often sustained solely by the determination not to let down his comrades … Numberless soldiers have died, more or less willingly, not for country or honour or religious faith or for any other abstract good, but because they realized that by fleeing their post and rescuing themselves, they would expose their companions to greater danger. Such loyalty to the group is the essence of fighting morale. (Gray, 1998/1959: 40)

Similarly, Joanna Bourke finds that 'combatants cited solidarity with the group and thoughts of home and loved ones as their main incentives' (1999: 142). Obviously, it is possible that this is just the sort of chauvinism that morality should condemn – all the more so given how high the stakes are in war. This chapter, however, is motivated by a curiosity as to whether this common-sense partiality has any place in the morality of war.

Notice, though, that the associativist account is not a comprehensive theory of what justifies killing in war. The best such theory will include, alongside the arguments discussed here, a theory of permissible killing in self-defence and other-defence, including a defence of the high-threshold approach to liability, as well as an account of the independent moral significance of goods such as political sovereignty and territorial integrity. My goal here is simply to insist that reasons of partiality be incorporated into that more comprehensive theory.

My argument will be restricted in one further respect. A full defence of the associativist account should invoke duties that we owe to compatriots qua compatriots. I will not argue for these duties here, since doing so is itself a challenging task and the subject of significant debate (though see Lazar, 2010b). Instead, I will argue that the duties that we owe to those with whom we share our deepest, most valuable personal relationships – which often overlap at least with residency in the same territory, if not with co-citizenship – can help justify killing non-liable people in war.

I begin by identifying the relevant class of special relationships and the associative duties that they ground, focusing on family, friendship and fellowship of arms. I then argue that associative duties are both more *stringent* and more *grave* than otherwise comparable general duties – meaning, respectively, that they can exact greater costs from the duty-bearer, and that they weigh more heavily against other moral considerations. In particular, I argue that our associative duties to protect those with whom we share valuable relationships can sometimes override our general negative duties not to harm others.

Having shown that when we fight to protect our loved ones, we are justified in imposing more costs on innocents than when we fight to protect strangers, I go on to show how that view can be operationalized in the morality of war. This involves two tasks: first, showing how soldiers who fight on behalf of their community can justify their actions as the execution of the associative duties that the members of that community owe to protect their loved ones; second, showing that the argument from associative duties can justify the sort of killing that a theory of war's morality particularly needs to justify. I then show how the associative duty to protect is restricted in various ways.

1 Grounding Associative Duties

I understand duties as a kind of moral reason, distinguished by being non-voluntary, having a particular weight, and retaining its force when overridden. Thus, if you have a duty to φ, and no equally weighty moral reason not to φ, then you may not permissibly choose not to φ. Sometimes, however, you have other reasons not to φ, for example a duty to ψ that is incompossible with φing. If the latter duty is weightier than the former, you ought to ψ. And yet, though the φ duty was overridden, it retains its force: with respect to that duty and its beneficiary, you have acted wrongly, even if ψing was all things considered justified.

Impersonal duties are owed to nobody, interpersonal duties to other person(s) and personal duties to oneself. General duties are interpersonal duties owed to everyone, and special duties are interpersonal duties owed to specific people, because of some interaction or relationship. Associative duties are a subclass of special duties that are owed in virtue of a morally important relationship. To demonstrate an associative duty, we must first show that a candidate relationship has properties that are of significant non-instrumental value (i.e., that give strong, direct reasons for action); and then that the duty is either a necessary condition of preserving those properties or is otherwise constitutive of the relationship or of an appropriate recognition of the relationship's value.

The relationships that I think are particularly relevant to the ethics of war are those between family members, friends and comrades-in-arms. I argue at length elsewhere that these relationships can indeed ground associative duties relevant to justifying killing in war (Lazar, 2013). For reasons of economy, here I rely on the intuitive plausibility of that claim. I think that everyone who thinks that there are any associative duties at all should agree that *at least some* intimate relationships such as these are sufficiently valuable to ground them. And anyone who thinks we have associative duties to protect those with whom we share these kinds of valuable relationships must surely think that we have duties to protect them from the kinds of serious threats that arise in war (that is, if you have duties to protect your loved ones from *any* threats, then you surely have a duty to protect them from *being killed*). It's important to stress that *not all* relationships between friends, family members and comrades-in-arms will be valuable in the relevant way. Sometimes, people's most intimate relationships are among their most corrupted and pernicious. All I mean to assert is that *some* relationships such as these can give their members associative duties to protect one another from the threats that arise in war.

But what does it mean for A to have an associative duty to protect B? Suppose A and B share a valuable relationship of the kind described; for A to respond appropriately to the valuable properties of that relationship, he must give greater weight to B's interests in his deliberations than if their relationship did not obtain. That is precisely what it means to view a relationship (and one's associate) as special. The special relationship acts as a moral amplifier.

The strength of duties varies along at least two dimensions: the costs they can justify imposing on the duty-bearer and their relative weight when they clash with other moral reasons. We can call these dimensions stringency and gravity respectively. In my view, special relationships amplify duties along both dimensions. In virtue of his relationship with B, A must bear greater costs to serve B's interests than if there were no relationship: his duties to B are more stringent. And in virtue of that relationship, A's duties to B are more likely to override other moral considerations than if they were not owed to an associate: his duties to B are graver.

The next section substantiates the second claim. Here, I will illustrate the stringency claim. Suppose that A is at the beach and sees B struggling in the water. If A had no connection with B, then he might be required to take on x cost in order to save him. But if B is someone with whom A shares a valuable relationship – his son, say – then the cost that he ought to bear will be greater than x. So, suppose B is caught in a rip, and A judges that he would be risking his life to try to save B. This would not be morally required were B a stranger (suppose), but may be required if A is his father, and they have a valuable relationship. This will of course depend on further details – A's prospects of saving B must be sufficiently high, for example – but the basic point should be clear.

Sometimes this amplification is best described by saying that A's duty to B is more stringent if they share a valuable relationship; sometimes the amplification results in a duty obtaining that would otherwise be absent. Special relationships might generate other duties that cannot be analysed in this way, but these amplifying duties are sufficient for the purposes of this chapter.

What explains this amplification? Suppose you fail to perform a duty owed to your associate, which you would have owed even in the absence of the relationship. You retain the reasons that apply in virtue of your shared humanity – you have damaged the interest protected by the duty and disregarded the victim's moral standing (see Lazar, 2009b). But you have also betrayed a friend and disregarded the value of the relationship between you. This additional reason amplifies the force of the reasons you already have.

2 The Gravity of Associative Duties

We respond appropriately to the valuable properties of our deep personal relationships by giving our associates' interests greater weight in our deliberations than would be justified absent that relationship. This means bearing greater costs to protect their interests than we are required to bear for non-associates. In this section, I defend the more controversial view that we can justifiably impose greater costs on non-associates to protect our associates' interests than would be permissible without that relationship. Indeed, I argue that we can permissibly kill non-associates to save the lives of associates.

To begin with, however, it is helpful to consider the infliction of harms short of death. Suppose a meteor is plummeting from the sky, directly towards B, and will surely kill her if nothing is done. A can deflect the meteor using her surface-to-air heat-seeking missile launcher. But if she does so, fragments of the meteor will hit a non-liable person C. Suppose, for now, that A bears no relation to either B or C. If she lets the meteor fall on B, she must consider the harm that B suffers and the qualitative evaluation of letting B suffer that harm. If she diverts it towards C, she must consider the harm that C will suffer and the qualitative evaluation of diverting that harm towards C. Her two options, in other words, each involve agential and harm-based dimensions. Suppose that intervening in a causal process leading to harm is qualitatively worse than failing to prevent a causal process from resulting in harm. If the prospective harms to B and C are equal, then A ought to do nothing, since letting B die is better in one respect and in no respect worse than killing C. However, if the prospective harm to C is less than the harm to B, then A might be required to divert the meteor – though the agential difference between her options means that the harm to C must be more than marginally less than that to B. But there is some threshold of harm H, such that if the harm to C is less than H, A is morally required to divert the meteor.

I suggest that when B and A share a valuable relationship, the threshold of harm A can permissibly inflict on C to save B's life is higher than if A and B are not associates. This is so for two reasons. First, in virtue of their valuable relationship, A must give greater weight to B's interests than would otherwise be so. Second, the agential dimension of failing to save B is qualitatively worse given their relationship – it amounts to a failure to recognize the value of their relationship. A has weightier reasons to save B's life when they share a valuable relationship, so those reasons can outweigh more harm inflicted on C. In the terms introduced above, A's duty to protect B is graver when B is her associate.

This view contravenes philosophical orthodoxy, according to which our associative duties cannot override general negative duties (McMahan, 1997; Scanlon, 1998; Kolodny, 2002; Pogge, 2002; Scheffler, 2002; Keller, 2007; Seglow, 2010; in the context of war, see Lefkowitz, 2009; for a more sympathetic view, see Kamm, 2004; Hurka, 2005). Breaching negative duties is not lexically worse than breaching positive duties – as though we ought to perform any negative duty, no matter how slender the interests at stake, in preference to any positive duty, no matter how serious. And as the meteor example shows, sometimes it is permissible to breach negative duties as a lesser evil, even in the absence of a special relationship. My contention is simply that our deep personal relationships affect how much harm can be inflicted as a lesser evil.

One might concede this much, yet deny that our associative duties can justify *killing*. However, while killing a non-liable person is clearly a presumptively wrongful act, not all acts of killing are alike. There are important agential differences between killing and letting die, between intentional killing, unintended but foreseen killing, unintended, unforeseen, but foreseeable killing, and unintended, unforeseen, unforeseeable killing. There is a further distinction between eliminative and opportunistic killing. In eliminative killing, the killer derives no benefit from the victim's death that he would not have enjoyed in the victim's absence. In opportunistic killing, the killer does derive such benefits (Quinn, 1989; Frowe, 2008; Quong, 2009; Tadros, 2012). If A diverts the meteor towards C, then while A clearly foresees C's death she does not intend it. Her killing is also eliminative, insofar as she would be no worse off if C were elsewhere (some think that eliminative agency is a subset of intentional agency; I disagree). Contrast this with an alternative, whereby, unless the meteor lands on someone, it will explode and kill B anyway. If A diverted the meteor towards C in this case, she would be using C opportunistically, deriving a benefit that would have been unavailable in her absence. This would be a qualitatively worse killing.

At least in 1:1 cases, the duty to protect one's associates from lethal harm cannot override the general negative duty not to intentionally, opportunistically kill a non-liable person. But, as I now argue, it can override the general negative duty not to foreseeably eliminatively do so.

My argument that A's associative duty to protect B can justify killing C starts with the comparison of three cases, and a commitment to transitivity in ethical reasoning, according to which, if the moral reasons for φing outweigh those for ψing, and those for ψing outweigh those for μing, then the moral reasons for φing outweigh those for μing. While the transitivity of moral reasons has in recent years come under sustained criticism (Dancy, 1993, 2004; Temkin, 2012), it remains the default, common-sense position.

Case 1   A meteor is plummeting towards the earth, and, if A does nothing, will kill five non-liable people. If she uses her missile launcher, however, she can divert it away from the five. If she does so the meteor will land on and kill C.

This is just the standard trolley case, albeit with meteors instead of trams. I am assuming, note, that the cost to each person of dying is the same, and that the costs to others of their deaths are also the same. It is intuitively clear to most that A is at least permitted to divert the meteor. Indeed, anyone who denies that it can be permissible to foreseeably kill an innocent person as a side-effect of saving others (or who thought the ratio had to be much higher than 5:1) would have to be a pacifist. Wars cannot be fought without foreseeably killing innocents.

> Case 2   Two meteors are plummeting towards the earth. One is headed towards a group of five, as in case 1. The other is headed towards A's daughter, B, with whom A shares a paradigmatic special relationship. A has only one missile, and can divert only one meteor. The diverted meteor will land harmlessly in a field.

Again, I think it is intuitively obvious that A is permitted to save B rather than the five. Moreover, I think that A is morally required to save her daughter – she would be acting wrongly if she did not. I offer more discussion of this distinction below.

> Case 3   There is only one meteor again, and it is headed towards A's daughter B. A can divert the missile, but it will subsequently land on and kill C.

I think A ought to divert the meteor, killing C, in order to save her daughter. The argument to reach this conclusion can be stated in two versions, one stronger than the other. The stronger form is this: in case 1, A is morally required to save the five, rather than avoid killing C; in case 2, she is morally required to save her daughter, rather than the five; so, by transitivity, in case 3 she is morally required to save her daughter, rather than avoid killing C. The weaker version is: in case 1, A is permitted to save the five, rather than avoid killing C; in case 2, she is permitted to save her daughter rather than the five; so, by transitivity, in case 3 she is permitted to save her daughter, rather than avoid killing C.

Why should we believe the stronger version of this argument? Some of course will simply share my intuition about case 3, so the argument from transitivity will be otiose. Those who do not initially share that intuition, but agree with my assessments of cases 1 and 2, might be persuaded to change their minds about 3 if they think that A's deliberations in these cases should take the form of weighing her reasons for action to reach a conclusion about what she ought to do, all things considered. We can model this by using numerical values to capture the weight of her reasons – remembering, of course, that the numbers are just a heuristic. Following the model introduced above, we can distinguish between agential reasons against φing, and harm-based or, better, interest-based reasons against φing. For simplicity, let us posit that agential and interest-based reasons are additive.

Suppose the interest-based reasons against killing C (independent of the agential dimension) are of magnitude 100, while the agential reasons against killing her are of magnitude 900. The interest-based reasons against letting each of the five die are also of magnitude 100, while the agential reasons are, for each one, 110. A's reasons to save the five amount to 1050, while her reasons not to kill C amount to 1000, so she ought to save the five by killing C.

On this model, if A is required to save B rather than the five, then the magnitude of her reasons for saving B should be greater than her reasons for saving the five. On my view, A ought to give her associate's interests additional weight in her deliberations. Plus, there is a distinct agential dimension to failing to protect someone with whom she shares a valuable relationship. We could model this by saying that her interest-based reasons to save B amount to 200, while the agential reasons against letting her daughter die amount to 900, giving a total of 1100.[1]

The specific numbers, of course, are arbitrary; they are just a means of modelling A's deliberations. But if this is a sound way for A to deliberate, then the permissibility of her killing C to save B should follow – if her reasons to save B are greater in magnitude than her reasons to save the five, and her reasons to save the five are greater in magnitude than her reasons not to kill C, then, since 'greater in magnitude than' is a transitive relation, her reasons to save B should be greater in magnitude than her reasons not to kill C.

However, this model supports the stronger version of the argument only if A is indeed morally required to save B rather than the five, in case 2. And while I think A is definitely not required to save the five rather than B, I do not have a conclusive argument that she is required to save B rather than the five.

Morality cannot plausibly be so demanding as to require A to sacrifice her chance to save her daughter in order to save the five. The central theme of much non-consequentialist ethics – apparent, for example, in the contrast between eliminative and opportunistic agency mentioned above – is that there is something inherently objectionable about our being made into resources for the advancement of valuable states of affairs or opportunities for others to exploit to their advantage (for a powerful recent statement of this classic view, see Tadros, 2012). Just as A may not use C as a means to save the five, so she cannot be required to make herself into a means to save them, when the cost of doing so is as great as sacrificing her daughter's life (I discuss why in greater depth below).

I am less certain that A is morally required to save B, however. Though I think she certainly wrongs B by failing to save her, she may not be acting wrongly, all things considered. On my view of associative duties, B has a justified claim against A, grounded in their valuable relationship, that A give her interests greater weight than if their relationship did not obtain. By failing to save her, A fails to give B's interests that weight and shows disrespect for their relationship, wronging her. To deny this, while accepting the argument of the previous paragraph, would be to suggest that the moral significance of A's duties to B is exhausted by their contribution to A's well-being. This would effectively reduce those duties to prudential reasons. This is a serious category mistake: our reasons to protect our nearest and dearest are not merely complicated reasons of self-interest. Failing to protect those whom you care about is not merely irrational or stupid – it amounts to a genuine moral failing.

While A wrongs B by failing to save her, there are two interpretations consistent with this judgment. On the first, A simply acts wrongly, all things considered. The second is that, in saving the five, A permissibly breaches her duty to protect B in order to do something supererogatory (Kamm, 1996: 317). Though saving the five is all things considered permissible, it involves *pro tanto* wronging B. If A saves B, then she both fulfils her associative duty to B and acts merely permissibly. This interpretation captures my view that A genuinely owes B a duty to protect her – it is not merely a question of fulfilling her self-interest – while remaining consistent with the conclusion that A is merely permitted to save B, rather than required.

My theory and intuitions strongly favour the first interpretation: A acts impermissibly if she fails to save her daughter. By saving the five at the expense of her daughter, she is not showing an admirable capacity for self-sacrifice, but an objectionable lack of regard for her child and the relationship they share – I liken her to Dickens's Mrs Jellyby, whose concern for the distant needy leads her to neglect her own children. But one could reasonably argue that while it would perhaps be wrong to save one stranger rather than her child, when there are five other lives on the line, it is permissible for A to sacrifice her chance to save her daughter, for the greater good. Those who agree with the first interpretation of the case should be satisfied with the stronger version of the argument; to convince those who affirm the second interpretation, I need to defend the argument in its weaker form.

The weaker version of the argument, however, faces a serious objection: that my purported transitivity fails because the first two cases do not give enough information to draw conclusions about the permissibility of killing C in case 3. Case 1 tells us that the duty to save five is graver than the duty not to kill C, and case 2 tells us something about the stringency of the duty to save five, but nothing about the gravity of the associative duty to save B. So, how can we draw warranted conclusions about either the stringency of the duty not to kill C or the relative gravity of that duty and the duty to save B?

One might respond that the duty not to kill C is less stringent than the duty to save the five just in case the latter duty is graver than the former. But that is quite implausible, as the following trio of cases shows.

Case 4 Two meteors are falling towards the earth, each headed for a group of five people. A can press a button that will fire missiles at each meteor, diverting them. But this will lead to the meteors instead crushing two different people (C_{1-2}).

Case 5   There are three meteors plummeting towards the earth. Two are, as in case 4, each heading for a group of five people, the third for A. She can press a button to fire a missile that will divert the meteor headed at her, or one that will fire two missiles, saving the ten. Either way, the diverted meteor(s) will land harmlessly.

Case 6   There is only one meteor again, and it is headed towards A. A can divert the missile, but if she does so it will land on, and kill, two people (C_{1-2}).

I assume that if diverting the meteor is permissible in case 1, it is permissible in case 4. This could involve the fallacy of composition, but probably does not: if the duty to save five lives is graver than the duty not to kill one, then two instances of the former duty should be graver than two instances of the latter. I also assume that A is permitted to save herself in case 5, even though it means letting the ten die. So the duty to save ten is graver than the duty not to kill two, but not stringent enough to require A to sacrifice her life. If duties' relative stringency can be inferred from their relative gravity, then in case 6, A should be permitted to divert the missile towards C_{1-2}. Her duty not to kill them cannot be more stringent than her duty to save the ten, since it is less grave, as case 4 shows. But it is surely not plausible that A is permitted to kill two to save herself.

To save the weaker version of the transitivity argument, I need either to show how facts about stringency can be inferred from facts about gravity, or argue that the permission to save B rather than the five is more than a reflection on the stringency of the duty to save the five. Recall that, since the stronger version relies only on gravity to make its case, it is untouched by this objection.

I think it would be unusual for stringency and gravity to be either wholly disconnected from one another or connected by some sort of discontinuous relation. The considerations that ground a duty's weight relative to other moral reasons and those that ground its weight relative to the interests of the duty-bearer seem at first sight to be just the same considerations. When we assess the gravity of the duty to save another person, we adduce the moral weight of that individual's interests and the independent significance of her standing relative to the duty-bearer (qua human being or qua associate); when we assess that duty's stringency, we appeal to just the same considerations.

However, one consideration does bear on stringency and gravity in different ways. This is the basic non-consequentialist thesis that there is something inherently objectionable about making people into resources for realizing valuable states of affairs. This 'means principle' (Tadros, 2012), grounds differences in the stringency of positive and negative duties. If A were morally required to sacrifice her own life to save the ten in case 5, morality would make her a means for realizing the best state of affairs, at the cost of her own life. Negative duties, by contrast, do not make us into a means for realizing optimal states of affairs. If A performs her duty not to harm C, in case 3, she does not become a means. She does not thereby save C. Nor does her presence provide C with a benefit she could not have enjoyed in A's absence. Had A not been there, C would have been just fine. Since adhering to negative duties does not make us into a means, there is nothing inherently objectionable about them.

The means principle explains, then, why a given positive and negative duty can be differentially exacting, even when other considerations that ground stringency and gravity are basically the same. And importantly, while the means principle has some bearing on the gravity of positive and negative duties, it does so in quite a different way: it lends additional gravity to duties not to turn others into a means. But while such duties are more likely to be negative than positive, they can also be positive, and plenty of negative duties are not grounded in the means principle. One salient example is the negative duty not to harm a non-liable person eliminatively, with which we are primarily concerned here.

So, even if the other reasons that ground our assessment of a positive and negative duty's relative gravity are identical, they can be differentially stringent because of the means principle's contribution to the stringency of positive duties. Thus we can consistently affirm (in cases 1–3) that it is permissible to save the five rather than not kill the one, permissible to save B rather than save the five, and yet impermissible to save B rather than not kill the one.

The second approach, recall, is to argue that the permission to save B rather than the five is more than a reflection on the stringency of the duty to save the five, hence cases 4–6 are not in fact analogous to cases 1–3. This is because A's permission to save B depends crucially on the duty she owes to protect B from harm, not merely on the great cost to her of not saving B. Since cases 5 and 6 involve only costs to A's well-being, rather than any associative duties, we can consistently deny that killing C_{1-2} is permissible in 6, while affirming that killing C is permissible in 3.

My own view is that even this interpretation of A's position is not quite right. I think that her duty to protect B is graver than her duty to protect the five, which is graver than her duty not to kill C; so her duty to protect B is graver than her duty not to kill C. In other words, I affirm the strong interpretation of the argument. But surely some who reject that view will find this intermediate alternative attractive: there is something fundamentally odd about supposing that the deliberative force of A's reasons to protect B are reducible, in case 2, to the contribution B makes to A's well-being. This chapter is premised on the assumption that our associative duties are genuine moral reasons. If that is true, then it is possible that only when the costs to A are combined with her duties to B is it permissible for her not to save the five, and likewise in case 3 – the moral reasons grounded in A's associative duties to B are a necessary condition of her being permitted to kill C.

The argument that A can permissibly kill C, in the course of saving B's life, should go through for those who agree with the strong interpretation, according to which A is required to save B, at the cost of C's life; and for those who favour the intermediate interpretation, which says that A's associative duties to protect B are a necessary component of the permissibility of her killing C. Those who affirm the weak interpretation may remain unconvinced. For them, one last gambit is possible. At least some will believe that it is permissible for A to kill C (in the manner described in the cases above), when she has no other means of saving her own life. That is, they think the duty not to kill C is not stringent enough to require A to sacrifice her own life rather than take C's. These philosophers should agree that, on the same grounds, it is permissible for A to kill C in the course of saving B in case 3, at least if A would choose to sacrifice her own life to save B, if she could. For if A would make that sacrifice, then she regards death (while B lives) as preferable to life without B. If she cannot be required to bear the cost of death to avoid killing C, then she cannot be required to bear the comparable cost of life without B.

3   Operationalizing Associative Duties

Suppose that war is imminent and that we can do nothing, as individuals, to prevent it: either because we face an implacable adversary or because we cannot alter our government's course of action. We and our closest associates are under threat; necessarily for active combatants, most likely for noncombatants too. Our loved ones face the prospect of grievous damage to their most vital interests. Each of us owes it to our associates to protect them, if we can, against these threats. I have just argued that these duties can override some duties not to harm others, but how are they operationalized, so that they become directly relevant to the justification of killing in war?

Combatants' duties to protect their comrades-in-arms are operationalized automatically by the onset of conflict – in defending their comrades and their associates back home, they are acting (at least) on reasons that apply to them directly. In a *levée en masse*, where erstwhile civilians rise up to defend themselves and their families, the same is true – each person can permissibly fight (and kill), while appealing only to reasons that directly apply to himself. But this is not the whole story. I will argue that combatants can act on behalf of the community of which they are a part, and that their actions can be justified by reasons that apply directly to the members of that community. They act not only on reasons that apply to them qua individuals, but on reasons that apply to them qua representatives of that community, which include the associative duties that are, in part, the very grounds for living together in communities and organizing ourselves for collective defence.

Imagine a village in the state of nature, in which 100 families live. Suppose it lacks any institutional structure besides a few informal public spaces. One day, the village is attacked by a marauding band. The villagers, disorganized as they are, each defend their own families and friends from this murderous crew. It should be uncontentious, I think, that part of what justifies each person in using force to defend his loved ones are the associative duties that they owe to protect them. Perhaps one might think that, if all the marauders are liable to be killed, then the villagers have no need to appeal to their duties to protect their loved ones; simple principles of self- and other-defence will suffice. Suppose, then, that each marauder is on horseback with an innocent human shield tied to the horse, so that the villagers cannot defend themselves without risking harm to innocents. Then we must invoke duties that can override the duties not to harm innocents.

Suppose the villagers successfully fight off the band. After they have treated the wounded and cleared up the damage, they decide that some among them – the most martially adept – should stand guard over the others. Some time after they establish this militia, the marauders come back. Surely whatever reasons justified defence in the first case, where the villagers each fought to defend their own, should also justify defence in the second case, where they have deputed some to fight on their behalf? Why should those reasons disappear merely because the villagers have a more robust way to ensure that their loved ones are protected?

Warfare requires natural attributes of courage and skill, and considerable training. Many people would make ineffective soldiers. Moreover, these differences in ability raise serious problems of fairness. Those who can fight effectively are better able than others to perform their associative duties. Moreover, in most conflicts it will not be necessary for every able-bodied person to fight; indeed, it would probably be counterproductive. Thus non-fighters are able to free-ride on others' military capabilities, which in turn threatens to cause serious collective action problems. We resolve these problems by creating institutions to enable us all to perform our duties to protect – whether associative or general – in a fair and optimal way. The armed forces are the executors of those duties: when soldiers fight, they are not simply responding to reasons that apply to them as individuals, but also to reasons that apply to all of us in the community they represent, on our behalf. And when we assent to and provide for these institutions, we authorize them to defend our associates on our behalf.

This institutionalist argument operationalizes the duties underpinning the associativist account, rendering them directly applicable in war and showing how the associative duties of civilians in a society can justify the killing done by their armed forces. It also forestalls some worries that the account might raise. For example, it allows us to remain agnostic on whether duties to compatriots qua compatriots play an important role in justifying killing in war. Co-citizenship is quite different from the relationships that paradigmatically generate associative duties, but in most political communities, most people will share most of their special relationships with other people who are resident in the same territory. There are obviously exceptions, but the requirement of optimality justifies concentrating on those duties that sub-stantially overlap.

The institutionalist argument addresses another worry about the associativ-ist account. Participating in even a justified war can often damage combat-ants' valuable relationships. Kept apart from their families, and subjected to radically different experiences, rifts can emerge. If their participation in war were justified by reasons grounded in their own relationships, those reasons might in fact mandate not fighting, given the risk to their deep relationships.

This objection invites three responses. First, sometimes combatants ought to put their own special relationships first, and refuse to fight. Second, that injunction must be qualified by the countervailing pull of their duties to their comrades-in-arms.[2] Given the relative threats faced, in some cases protecting their comrades-in-arms will be justifiable even if it means sacrificing their relationships with those back home. Third, combatants are not performing their own associative and general duties alone; they are also the executors of those duties for their whole society. These duties give them powerful reasons to serve, even when they undermine their own relationships by doing so.

The institutionalist move might draw some criticism from those who think that our associative duties, as agent-relative reasons, cannot be transferred like this. My associative duty to protect my wife, for example, does not give you reason to protect her. That I could justifiably φ, because I have agent-relative reason to φ, does not mean that φ-ing is justified for you. However, if you are acting on my behalf – if I have authorized you to be my agent, and you have assented to that authorization – then you should enjoy the same permission that would otherwise apply to my action. In virtue of my being permitted to φ, I have the moral power to authorize you to φ on my behalf, even though, without that authorization, you would not be permitted to φ (see also Fabre, 2009b, for a similar argument). The same dynamic operates in contracts. Suppose I have a right to collect a debt from you and I empower a bailiff to collect that debt. As he is acting as my agent, with my authoriza-tion, he is entitled to respond to the reasons that apply to me. Without that authorization, he would just be some guy trying to take your car.

When their lives are at stake we surely have reason to ensure that our associates are protected, though not necessarily that we specifically be their protectors. The advantages of coordination are so great that it would be absurdly counterproductive to insist on carrying out these duties ourselves.

This shows how the duties that I owe to protect my son (for example) can be relevant to the justification of actions taken, on my behalf, by soldiers defending us against military aggression. The arguments above showed that our duties to protect those with whom we share valuable relationships can override the duty not to kill a non-liable person, at least in 1:1 cases where the victim is killed foreseeably and eliminatively, rather than intentionally and opportunistically. One might nonetheless think that the contribution made by the associativist account to justifying killing in war will necessarily be incomplete. After all, successfully fighting wars surely requires opportunistic and intentional killing, as well as eliminative and foreseen.

I readily concede this objection: our duties to protect our associates cannot, in my view, override duties not to harm others opportunistically when the harms in question are otherwise roughly equal. The associativist account is not intended to be a comprehensive theory of the morality of killing in war, but to contribute one significant piece to that theory. Our reasons to protect our associates probably cannot justify defensive war against purely political aggression (which does not threaten our special relationships); I also concede that they cannot justify the opportunistic killing that war inevitably involves. The best theory of the morality of war will need to appeal to more than associative duties.

That the associativist account is incomplete does not, however, entail its irrelevance. Necessary killing in war covers the gamut; some of it can be justified by appeal to associative duties. In particular, I think that much of the intentional killing in war is qualitatively no worse than the redirection of a meteor in the cases above. Killing innocent people *eliminatively* is no harder to justify when it is intentional than when it is unintentional. Much intentional killing in war is eliminative in the following way: we would confine our attacks to those enemy combatants who are liable to be killed if we could, but we cannot tell the liable from the non-liable. We therefore cannot defend ourselves at all, unless we are prepared to intentionally kill people who may turn out not to be liable. We would be just as well off if the non-liable combatants-U did not exist, indeed better off, for then we could kill the liable combatants-U without the moral cost of killing the non-liable. To see that these killings are equivalent to unintended eliminative killings, consider the following pair of cases (inspired by McMahan, 2011):

Bunker 1   Ten Islamic State militants are taking cover in a bunker. An innocent civilian is trapped nearby.

Bunker 2   The militants have grabbed the civilian and hauled him into their bunker; you're unable to tell them apart.

Suppose that, in each case, your only weapon is a hellfire missile, which will surely kill all 11 people. Then I think it is obvious that it is permissible to proceed in Bunker 1 if and only if it is permissible to do so in Bunker 2. In my view, firing the missile at the bunker, knowing the innocent person is inside counts as intentionally killing the innocent person as well as the militants. But suppose you disagree with that. Now imagine that the only way to kill the militants is with a sniper rifle, and that time is short – if you do not kill them all within the next minute, they will carry out some deadly threat. Then I think you may permissibly kill each person in sequence, on just the same grounds as you could fire the hellfire missile, even though in this case you are intentionally killing each person. Now, one could argue here that this is not the kind of intentional killing to which morality attaches such opprobrium, but that is irrelevant for my purposes. All I need is that this is a kind of intentional killing of the innocent, which is qualitatively similar to the eliminative unintentional killing of the innocent which I have argued can be justified by appeal to associative duties.

But operationalizing the associativist account is not simply a matter of showing that it can justify the kinds of intentional killing that war inevitably involves. It must also not prove too much. In particular, it should not license killing noncombatants (otherwise we are no better off than on a low-threshold, liability-based view). Elsewhere, I show that killing noncombatants in war is more seriously wrongful than killing combatants, so it does not follow from the availability of lesser-evil justifications for killing non-liable combatants-U that we will be able to justify killing noncombatants-U as well (Lazar, 2015).

4   Restricting the Associative Duty to Protect

One might object that the associativist account draws on reasons that are detached from regular morality, offering a distinct source of normativity potentially radically at odds with our standard moral reasons, which might have very troubling implications outside of war. There are three important variants of this objection. First, sometimes our associates are liable to be harmed – sometimes they even deserve it. Does the associativist account ground duties to protect them then? The second variant notes that sometimes really evil people can develop deep relationships with one another. Do they accordingly have associative duties to one another? The third asks whether granting associative duties this degree of gravity might entail troubling conclusions about what ordinary people can do to protect our associates outside of war.

It seems clear that the more liable our associates, the weaker our duties to protect them. Suppose A can defend his associate B from a threat posed by C, which is in response to a threat B posed to C's life. If B is at fault for the threat she poses, then A's duties to protect her are much weakened, and certainly cannot override his duties not to harm C. Notice, though, that B's liability does not obviate all A's duties to protect her. If he could save B without C being harmed, A will have a duty to protect B. Suppose he can interpose his body between B and C, taking the force of C's blow. For some magnitudes of resultant harm, and some relationships, A will have an associative duty to B to bear that harm to protect her, but no general duty to do so because his general duties to protect others are less stringent.

It seems unlikely that we have duties to protect associates from harms they deserve to suffer. Suppose B has murdered someone, and has fled the police. She comes to A seeking shelter. Though A might want to protect her from the threat of capture, he surely has no morally grounded reason to do so. B deserves to be caught and punished, and any duties A has to protect her are defeated by that fact. That noted, although he has no duty to protect her from deserved threats, he perhaps cannot be required to be the agent of retribution. Unless, of course, he has other reasons to be that agent. In Bruce Springsteen's 'Highway Patrolman' (from the album *Nebraska*) a police officer, Joe Roberts, allows his brother Frankie to escape to Canada after a fight in which he murdered another man.[3] This seems an understandable but unjustifiable exaggeration of associativist reasons. Frankie deserves to be caught, tried and punished, so Joe has no duty to protect him and, given his occupation, Joe may not recuse himself in this way. Were he not a police officer, however, I think he would be permitted to connive at his brother's escape.

Our duties to protect our associates from harms to which they are liable cannot weigh to any significant degree against our general duties. These are important constraints on the role of associative duties in morality, but do not undermine the associativist account of killing in war – provided that we combine it with a particular view of what grounds liability to be killed. Theories of liability typically argue that an individual must have made some sort of contribution to an unjustified threat to be liable to be killed, when that is a necessary and proportionate means to avert the threat. On low-threshold views of liability, many combatants and noncombatants in war (at least on the unjustified side, if there is only one) will be liable to be killed. On the high-threshold view – which I affirm – almost all noncombatants will not be liable to be killed, nor will a significant proportion of combatants. It follows that at least some of the associative duties owed by comrades-in-arms to protect one another, and almost all the associative duties owed by noncombatants to protect one another, will be owed to people who are not liable to be killed.

The second worry derives from the possibility that people committed to deeply evil activities might develop deep relationships with one another. A powerful example is reserve police battalion 101, called up during the Second World War by the Nazis, and tasked with exterminating Polish Jews (Browning, 2001). Members of this battalion reported strong feelings of loyalty to one another, which in part motivated their participation in the atrocities. Does the associativist account open the door to this sort of deeply objectionable reasoning?

The first response is that reasons of loyalty were in these cases clearly being abused. Members of battalion 101 were not protecting one another against a threat: their victims were unarmed men, women and children. An appeal to associative duties is as specious as is one to self-defence. Second, they were liable to whatever threats they did face, and indeed probably deserved them. One cannot nonculpably engage in genocide. Thus any associative duties they might have had to one another would have been either defeated or seriously weakened.

A third response more directly questions whether relationships that are predicated on doing evil to outsiders can really generate associative duties. If the relationship's internal qualities were developed through the knowing infliction of wrongful suffering, then any capacity that relationship would otherwise have had to generate strong moral reasons may well be defeated (for a similar argument, see Hurka, 1997). Suppose the members of reserve police battalion 101 went through a lot together, as they murdered thousands of Polish Jews. Perhaps they risked their lives to protect each other against the few people among their victims who still posed a threat. Any property of the relationship deriving from the knowing infliction of such egregiously wrongful suffering loses any potential reason-giving capacity.

The associativist account starts with the belief that neither Walzer nor his critics can justify fighting in wars where we must intentionally kill non-liable people. Since it endorses the high-threshold view of liability to be killed, it asserts that in all likely wars victory depends on intentionally violating some people's rights to life, so we need additional moral reasons to override those rights violations, some of which we can find in associativist morality. In that sense, it offers a perspective on the morality of war different from both Walzerian symmetrists and anti-Walzerian asymmetrists.

For Walzer, soldiers need not ask themselves whether fighting is justified. They know that if they adhere to the standards for just conduct in war, they will fight justly, without violating rights. Thus it is always permissible to participate in wars. For Walzer's critics, this view is both pernicious and inane. As Christopher Kutz puts it: 'if death and destruction matter morally, as they do, and if reasons matter morally, as they do, then differences in combatants' reasons for bringing about death and destruction must also matter morally' (2008: 44). The associativist account agrees: soldiers may fight only if they have very strong reasons for doing so. If they do not have sufficient reason to fight and kill, then they are acting unjustifiably, even if they adhere to the *in bello* code.

However, the associativist account joins Walzer in affirming that combatants on both sides of a war can, in some cases, fight justifiably. Most importantly, it explains how combatants-J can justifiably fight, even though doing so inevitably involves violating rights. Since the primary goal of any theory of the ethics of war that denies pacifism should be to show that soldiers on at least one side in at least some wars can fight justifiably, this is the headline result.

But the associativist account can also give combatants-U reason to fight and kill, insofar as they are performing their own associative duties to protect their comrades-in-arms from wrongful harms, and acting on behalf of a community whose members have duties to protect their associates from wrongful harms (i.e., those that the victim is not liable to suffer). Of course, sometimes the best way for combatants-U to protect their associates will be to surrender. I do not mean to exaggerate the justificatory force of the associativist account, or the merits of warfare as a means of protecting those we care about.

Moreover, combatants-U clearly face a heavy burden of justification, insofar as their fighting contributes to their side's achieving its unjustified goals – this will probably mean that associative duties could only justify genuinely defensive operations, for example. Nonetheless, contra Walzer's critics, combatants-U can sometimes be justified in fighting, and on much the same grounds as combatants-J.

The final worry is that the associativist account will justify egregiously wrongful partiality outside of war. For example, suppose A's associate, B, is dying from organ failure, and the only way to save her is to kill C and transplant his organs. If duties to protect our associates can override general negative duties not to kill innocent people, then why should A's duty to protect B not override his duty not to harm C? Indeed, given the argument about institutionalization advanced in the last section, couldn't we argue that we are justified, as a society, in setting up institutions where doctors routinely harvest organs from some, so that we can perform our associative duties to protect our loved ones from organ failure?

Such an outrageous conclusion neither follows from the associativist account, nor is even plausibly licensed by it. Killing C to transplant his organs is an egregiously wrongful form of killing, and A's duty to protect B does not override his duty not to kill C in this way. Killing C is opportunistic, he is clearly not liable to be killed, he is vulnerable and defenceless, and harming him in no way reflects his choices. Since A would not be permitted to kill C in this way to save B, there are no grounds for applying the reasoning of this chapter to justify institutionalized organ-harvesting or other similarly counterintuitive schemes.

5 Conclusion

The associativist account is not a complete theory of the morality of war. In particular, it cannot justify the resort to war in defence against political aggression, and it cannot justify the intentional, opportunistic killing of non-liable people that warfare inevitably involves. It also depends for its plausibility on giving an independent account of the limits on permissible killing in war, in particular the prohibition on targeting noncombatants. I discuss those in detail in Lazar (2015). However, it can justify some of the intentional killing in war. The foregoing discussion is intended to dispel the instinctive rejection of the associativist account by philosophers who are predictably sceptical about the deployment of reasons of loyalty in moral theory. It has offered grounds for those duties and has argued, against the philosophical orthodoxy, that associative duties can override serious general negative duties, both in peacetime and in war. It has also shown that conceding this point does not mean allowing a tribalist anti-egalitarianism to run amok through morality. It is quite possible to concede the force of associative duties in war, while still restraining their impact, both in war and in ordinary life.[4]

References

Altman, A. and Wellman, C. H. 2008. 'From Humanitarian Intervention to Assassination: Human Rights and Political Violence', *Ethics* 118(1): 228–257.

Benbaji, Y. 2008. 'A Defense of the Traditional War Convention', *Ethics* 118(3): 464–495.

Bourke, J. 1999. *An Intimate History of Killing: Face-to-Face Killing in Twentieth-Century Warfare.* London: Granta.

Browning, C. R. 2001. *Ordinary Men: Reserve Police Battalion 101 and the Final Solution in Poland.* London: Penguin.

Coady, C. A. J. 2008. *Morality and Political Violence.* Cambridge: Cambridge University Press.

Dancy, J. 1993. *Moral Reasons.* Oxford: Blackwell.

Dancy, J. 2004. *Ethics without Principles.* Oxford: Clarendon Press.

Emerton, P. and Handfield, T. 2009. 'Order and Affray: Defensive Privileges in Warfare', *Philosophy & Public Affairs* 37(4): 382–414.

Fabre, C. 2009a. 'Guns, Food, and Liability to Attack in War', *Ethics* 120(1): 36–63.

Fabre, C. 2009b. 'Permissible Rescue Killings', *Proceedings of the Aristotelian Society* 109: 149–164.

Frowe, H. 2008. 'Equating Innocent Threats and Bystanders', *Journal of Applied Philosophy* 25(4): 277–290.

Gray, J. G. 1998/1959. *The Warriors: Reflections on Men in Battle.* Lincoln, NE: University of Nebraska Press.

Hurka, T. 1997. 'The Justification of National Partiality', in R. McKim and J. McMahan, eds., *The Morality of Nationalism*, 139–157. Oxford: Oxford University Press.

Hurka, T. 2005. 'Proportionality in the Morality of War', *Philosophy & Public Affairs* 33(1): 34–66.

Kamm, F. M. 1996. *Morality, Mortality: Volume II.* Oxford: Oxford University Press.

Kamm, F. M. 2004. 'Failures of Just War Theory: Terror, Harm, and Justice', *Ethics* 114(4): 650–692.

Keller, S. 2007. *The Limits of Loyalty.* Cambridge: Cambridge University Press.

Kolodny, N. 2002. 'Do Associative Duties Matter?', *Journal of Political Philosophy* 10(3): 250–266.

Kutz, C. 2008. 'Fearful Symmetry', in D. Rodin and H. Shue, eds., *Just and Unjust Warriors: The Moral and Legal Status of Soldiers*, 69–86. Oxford, Oxford University Press.

Lazar, S. 2009a. 'Responsibility, Risk and Killing in Self-Defence', *Ethics* 119(4): 699–728.

Lazar, S. 2009b. 'The Nature and Disvalue of Injury', *Res Publica* 15(3): 289–304.

Lazar, S. 2010a. 'The Responsibility Dilemma for Killing in War', *Philosophy & Public Affairs* 38(2): 180–213.

Lazar, S. 2010b. 'A Liberal Defence of (Some) Duties to Compatriots', *Journal of Applied Philosophy* 27(3): 246–257.

Lazar, S. 2013. 'Associative Duties and the Ethics of Killing in War', *Journal of Practical Ethics* 1(1): 3–48.

Lazar, S. 2015. *Sparing Civilians.* Oxford: Oxford University Press.

Lefkowitz, D. 2009. 'Partiality and Weighing Harm to Non-Combatants', *Journal of Moral Philosophy* 6(3): 298–316.

McMahan, J. 1994. 'Innocence, Self-Defense and Killing in War', *Journal of Political Philosophy* 2(3): 193–221.

McMahan, J. 1997. 'The Limits of National Partiality', in R. McKim and J. McMahan, eds., *The Morality of Nationalism*, 107–138. Oxford, Oxford University Press.

McMahan, J. 2004. 'The Ethics of Killing in War', *Ethics* 114(1): 693–732.

McMahan, J. 2009. *Killing in War*. Oxford: Oxford University Press.

McMahan, J. 2011. 'Who is Morally Liable to be Killed in War', *Analysis* 71(3): 544–559.

McMahan, J. 2014. 'What Rights May Be Defended by Means of War?', in S. Lazar and C. Fabre, eds., *The Morality of Defensive War*, 115–156. Oxford: Oxford University Press.

McPherson, L. 2004. 'Innocence and Responsibility in War', *Canadian Journal of Philosophy* 34(4): 485–506.

Miller, S. 2007. 'Civilian Immunity, Forcing the Choice, and Collective Responsibility', in I. Primoratz, ed., *Civilian Immunity in War*, 113–135. Oxford: Oxford University Press.

Øverland, G. 2006. 'Killing Soldiers', *Ethics & International Affairs* 20(4): 455–475.

Pogge, T. 2002. 'Cosmopolitanism: A Defense', *Critical Review of International Social and Political Philosophy* 5(3): 86–91.

Quinn, W.S. 1989. 'Actions, Intentions, and Consequences: The Doctrine of Double Effect', *Philosophy and Public Affairs* 18(4): 334–351.

Quong, J. 2009. 'Killing in Self-Defense', *Ethics* 119(2): 507–537.

Scanlon, T. M. 1998. *What We Owe to Each Other*. London: Belknap.

Scheffler, S. 2002. *Boundaries and Allegiances: Problems of Justice and Responsibility in Liberal Thought*. Oxford: Oxford University Press.

Seglow, J. 2010. 'Associative Duties and Global Justice', *Journal of Moral Philosophy* 4(1): 54–73.

Shue, H. 2008. 'Do We Need a Morality of War?', in D. Rodin and H. Shue, eds., *Just and Unjust Warriors: The Moral and Legal Status of Soldiers*, 87–111. Oxford: Oxford University Press.

Shue, H. 2010. 'Laws of War', in S. Besson and J. Tasioulas, eds., *The Philosophy of International Law*, 511–530. New York: Oxford University Press.

Steinhoff, U. 2008. 'Jeff McMahan on the Moral Inequality of Combatants', *Journal of Political Philosophy* 16(2): 220–226.

Tadros, V. 2012. *The Ends of Harm: The Moral Foundations of Criminal Law*. Oxford: Oxford University Press.

Temkin, L. 2012. *Rethinking the Good*. Oxford: Clarendon Press.

Walzer, M. 2006/1977. *Just and Unjust Wars: A Moral Argument with Historical Illustrations*, 4th edn. New York: Basic Books.

CHAPTER NINE

Territorial Rights

David Miller and Margaret Moore

Introduction

In 1891, Henry Sidgwick defined territory as a political concept, inextricably connected with the idea of political jurisdiction. 'The connection between a political society and its territory', he wrote, 'is so close that the two notions almost blend' (1891: 213). On this reading, territory represents the geographical domain of political society and must be distinguished both from land (any physical portion of the earth's surface not covered by water) and from property (which as real estate is land owned and used by individuals or associations, typically under the auspices of, and regulated by, political authorities). This understanding of the concept was hardly surprising: for several centuries prior to Sidgwick's time, the territorial state had been the basic building block of the international order, and its exclusive right to control everything within its territorial borders was central to that order.

In the modern world, there is much talk of globalization and deterritorialization, but the basic organizational structure of the international order remains stubbornly territorial: indeed, the entire usable earth is divided into political units, each claiming jurisdictional authority over a distinct geographical area. States are the paradigm case, but jurisdiction can be held at both higher and lower levels: suprastate entities (such as the European Union) can be said to have territories, and so can substate entities (such as Quebec, Bavaria or Maine). Indeed, any politically organized group capable of exercising jurisdiction is a potential bearer of territorial rights; this includes indigenous peoples who claim as territory the land that they regard as their homeland and over which they claim specific (jurisdictional) rights, such as fishing rights or hunting rights, or other kinds of jurisdictional authority.

The concept of territory is complex in much the same way as is the concept of property. In each case we discover a bundle of different rights – claim rights, liberties, powers and immunities – that when held together with respect to some material thing add up to the fullest form of normative control over that thing (in the case of property, to what Honoré, 1961, in a famous analysis, called 'full liberal ownership') but that are also capable of being parcelled out and held by different agents. Each right within the bundle may call for a separate justification. Central to the idea of territory is the right to jurisdiction, which we understand to mean not only the right to create and enforce laws within the domain in question, but also the power to make changes to the territory's status, for example by incorporating it into some larger entity such as the EU, or by creating subjurisdictions in a federal system.[1] However territorial rights are normally understood to include other rights beyond jurisdiction: rights to control resources within the geographical area, rights to control borders and regulate the flow of people and goods across them and rights to defend the territory against outside aggression (Simmons, 2001; Miller, 2012). These are typically assumed to be inherent in the very idea of a sovereign state, but we can envisage entities that have some rights of jurisdiction but lack other elements in the territorial bundle. This is true of most substate authorities: there are significant jurisdictional powers at the US state level, but no border checks between Massachusetts and New Hampshire, for example; and there can be rights to control resources (which in the Canadian federation are controlled at the substate level, by provinces) in the absence of other dimensions of territory, such as collective rights of self-defence or rights to control the migration of people or flow of goods across provincial boundaries.

Although the territorial state has been central to our international order for several centuries, it faces both practical and philosophical challenges. The most important practical challenges arise from rival claims to the same territory. This can take the form of a secessionist movement, as in Scotland, Quebec, Catalonia, the Basque area of Spain, East Timor, the Kurdish areas of Iraq, Syria and Turkey; military annexation, such as China's occupation of Tibet, Israel's occupation of the West Bank and Gaza, and, for cases of occupation combined with irredentism, Turkey's occupation of the northern part of Cyprus and the Russian occupation of Crimea and the eastern part of Ukraine; boundary disputes between neighbouring states, such as between India and Pakistan over Kashmir or Morocco and Algeria over the Western Sahara; disputed claims to offshore islands, such as between Argentina and the UK over the Malvinas/Falkland islands and between China and Japan over the Diaoyu/Senkaku islands; and, finally, rival claims to unoccupied territory, in the Arctic, the Antarctic and the seabed.

There are also philosophical challenges to territory, which mainly take the form of unpacking the bundle of territorial rights, and criticizing one or more of its elements. The territorial state's claim to monopoly control over the resources found within its domain is challenged by the idea that the world belongs to humanity as a whole, and its bounty should be used to benefit everyone who lives in it; no particular group can make a claim of entitlement or desert to exclusive control of natural resources. The right to control borders is also challenged, on the grounds that the state's right to exclude violates the human rights (to free movement) of those people who are prevented from migrating, and also serves to perpetuate the massive inequalities that currently exist between the inhabitants of rich and poor territories.

1   For and Against the Territorial State

The territorial state has been much criticized, on these and other grounds, but increasingly in terms of its failure to grapple with many of the problems that arise in the world today, which require international or global coordinated responses. In *Leviathan*, Hobbes remarked on the fact that the territorial state system was effectively a state of nature: 'Kings, and Persons of Soveraigne authority, because of their Independency, are in continuall jealousies, and in the state and posture of Gladiators; having their weapons pointing, and their eyes fixed on one another' (1985/1651: 187). Nevertheless, he argued that the sovereign authority was able to provide its citizens with effective security, thus avoiding the miserable condition endured by individual men in the state of nature. We live, however, in an era of much greater interdependence, including global markets, global trade, global flows of ideas and migration. These in turn produce pathologies that require global responses: countries need to act in concert to combat international terrorism and crime, and to agree on effective ways of limiting greenhouse gas emissions in order to reduce harms to the environment, to future generations and to low-lying areas that will be devastated by climate change. Poverty too is exacerbated in many cases by global capitalism, where countries adopt inadequate safety standards, have poor or non-existent environmental regulation and permit child labour and other forms of exploitation, principally because they fear that they are in a competitive 'race to the bottom', as multinational corporations threaten to exit to cheaper, less regulated locations. None of these problems can be tackled by states acting independently. The competitive – indeed gladiatorial – posture of most territorial states is a serious obstacle to arriving at a better, more just global order.

What, then, can be said in favour of the territorial state? Its central feature is that it applies uniform rules and common policies to people living in proximity to one another. It makes sense to apply a single framework of law to people living close to one another, since they will unavoidably have more intense contact, and therefore more occasion for conflict. Such a uniform body of law both provides predictability and makes possible coordinated decision-making. It is superior to law organized on the personal principle, where each individual or each group in a geographical area may be subject to a different legal regime, since by applying laws equally to everyone on the territory, regardless of their status or identity, it advances values such as equal freedom and equality of opportunity. The benefits of a territorial form of organization, in terms of coordination, predictability, equality before the law and the achievement of social justice, are therefore considerable.

As we have seen, however, these benefits come accompanied by significant disadvantages at the global level. So a more complete justification would have to be comparative. What alternatives to a territorially organized state might we envisage? There are at least three.

We could imagine a global free market, in which the protective and other services that people need would be supplied on a contractual basis by organizations that had no territorial limits – so two people might be neighbours but yet buy healthcare, legal protection and personal security service from two entirely different suppliers. All of the goods that states now provide would instead be supplied by competing market-based associations. Some elements of this broadly libertarian vision were articulated by Robert Nozick (1974), though Nozick's own conclusion was that competition between what he called 'protective associations' would lead to one such association becoming the dominant provider of protective services in any given geographical area – so free-market anarchy would eventually culminate in the emergence of an 'ultraminimal state'. Nozick's underlying assumption, however, was that the only grounds on which coercion could be exercised, whether by states or private associations, were to protect individual rights and ensure that contracts and other market transactions are free of force and fraud. So many of the functions that states now perform – whether providing welfare to those unable to work, ensuring equal opportunities in education and the job market, or providing public goods such as roads, parks and museums – would be dispensed with. Thus, there are significant costs attached to abandoning the territorial state, even assuming that the global market in protective services turned out to work efficiently in other respects

A second alternative is a global state. Obviously, a global political order would avoid the static and essentializing effects associated with hard boundaries between territorially distinct political communities, and would allow coordination to solve global problems. However, it is less clear that the global state would be either functional or just. As Rawls argued in *The Law of Peoples*, a world state (which he regards as a precondition for a global scheme of distributive justice) would lead either to tyranny or to lawlessness. Specifically, Rawls writes:

> I follow Kant's lead in *Perpetual Peace* (1795) in thinking that a world government – by which I mean a unified political regime with the legal powers normally exercised by central governments – would either be a global despotism or else would rule over a fragile empire torn by frequent civil strife as various regions and peoples tried to gain their political freedom and autonomy. (1999: 36)

One reason why we might think a global state would degenerate into tyranny is that states are not simply territorial entities that offer coordinating rules and dispense justice: their boundaries also define the demos as part of which the people can make decisions over their collective lives, thus enabling the members of the political community to be collectively self-determining.

Citizen alienation is more likely when individuals cannot see their role in decisions that are made by distant central organs. It is one thing to be one voice in a hundred or a thousand, but quite another to be one vote in seven billion. One may also argue that an important precondition for unalienated citizenship is identification with co-members in a political project, which is unlikely to reach across the globe, but tends to occur in more local settings among people with commonalities of language, values and a shared historical experience of political self-rule.

Is there a third option, neither market nor global state? It is not difficult to find authors who, with the benefit of hindsight, are able to demonstrate the historical contingency of the territorial state, drawing attention to the other forms of political order that it managed to displace (see, for example Ruggie, 1993; Agnew, 1994; Spruyt, 1994). The suggestion here is that if we recognize this contingency, we will be better able to understand how forms of political coordination that lack a territorial basis may emerge – and indeed are beginning to appear in the contemporary world. The problem, however, is that many of these coordinating bodies are either established by states, or depend upon states for their stability (for example, as providers of legal systems that can be used to resolve disputes in the event that these cannot be settled internally). Outlining a fully fledged alternative to the territorial state has proved difficult. The most likely contender would be a functional theory that disaggregates the various tasks that states now discharge and assigns them to different institutions, some local, some regional and some global – so the territorial principle would not be entirely abandoned, but instead different spatial boundaries would be treated as relevant for different functions.[2] By way of illustration, we might consider the concept of 'ecological space' favoured by a number of environmental theorists (see Hayward, 2014), which might be used to mark out the contours of ecosystems that need to be managed collectively by all those whose life plans rely upon them, regardless of whether they exist within or cut across existing territorial boundaries; thus Avery Kolers speaks of 'interstitial settlements' where groups with different 'ethnogeographies' overlap in space, and argues that in such cases individuals can be subject to multiple jurisdictions: 'individuals can be governed under multiple jurisdictions concurrently, with the relevant legal system determined not by location but by activity, or even which computer program they are using' (2012: 341).[3] However, Kolers does not discuss how this understanding of territory can be implemented, in particular how government services can be provided, how legal relationships between different jurisdictions can be understood and conflicts between them sorted out. Others have proposed the partial unbundling of territorial rights: thus Nine (2014) uses the example of rivers whose waters flow between two or more states to argue against exclusive control of territory and in favour of a shared or joint sovereignty arrangement in such areas, and Armstrong (2015) argues against sovereign control of natural resources on the grounds that there are no good reasons to link jurisdiction over land to ownership of the usable or extractable resources that it contains. But in neither case do we find a head-on challenge to territorially based authority as such. At present, then, there is no clearly articulated third alternative, which means that the territorial state remains the principal – indeed, hegemonic – political form in the modern world, both practically and philosophically.

2   Theories of Territory

Showing that the territorial state has certain advantages that its would-be competitors lack does not, however, give us a full theory of territorial rights. Most notably, it does not explain how such a state can legitimately claim to exercise authority over any particular portion of the earth's surface. We need to solve this 'particularity problem' if we are to address the many cases referred to earlier in which territory is contested between rival states. Here we examine five influential theories of territory: utilitarian, Kantian, Lockean, nationalist and self-determination. As we shall see, the last three theories address the particularity question directly, while the first two do not.

Utilitarian theories

We take Sidgwick as our representative of a utilitarian theory of territory that perhaps comes closest to the way territorial rights are currently understood in international law. Its central thesis is that over the area in which a state achieves an effective social order, it has a prima face justified claim to territorial rights. In his view:

> the main justification for the appropriation of land to the exclusive use of individuals or groups is that its full advantages as an instrument of production cannot otherwise be utilised; the main justification for the appropriation of territory to governments is that the prevention of mutual mischief among the human beings using it cannot otherwise be adequately secured. (1891: 239)

But what if two governments each claim that they are able to perform this function in a given area: should the territory be awarded to whichever is likely to create more happiness overall, as the utilitarian standard might suggest? In fact, Sidgwick sets the bar low, in such a way that territorial rights are awarded to any state so long as it is 'exercising a tolerably effective and continuous governmental control' over the territory in question (1891: 242). Thus, when he discusses secessionist claims, he argues that such claims have force only when the secessionists can demonstrate 'some unjust sacrifice or grossly incompetent management of their interests, or some persistent and harsh opposition to their legitimate desires' (1891: 217). Moreover, the preferences of the secessionist group have to be set against 'the dislike of the community from which secession is proposed to lose territory that has once belonged to it, and to which it has a claim recognized by foreigners' (1891: 219). Given the difficulty in weighing up the welfare gains and losses experienced by the two sides, and bearing in mind the disruption that a secession will cause, Sidgwick's position supports the claim of nearly all established states to their territories. At the same time, a utilitarian can raise no objection *in principle* to a successful conquest, and Sidgwick himself was perfectly ready to defend colonialism so long as the material interests of the colonized peoples were adequately protected (1891: ch. 18, §§7–8).[4]

Moving beyond Sidgwick, we can ask how a utilitarian might try to resolve the problem of indeterminacy just identified. Here we can distinguish an act-utilitarian approach that resolves specific territorial disputes by a direct application of the greatest happiness principle, and a rule-utilitarian approach that asks which rule for assigning territorial rights will maximize human welfare in the long run. An act-utilitarian will in particular want to investigate which claimant group will make the *best* use of the disputed land, for example, farming it or developing it economically in the most efficient way. But this might lead to instability, as over time different contenders can make the strongest claim; and it is also likely to be biased against indigenous groups with a close attachment to the land who might wish to use it sustainably but not 'efficiently' in the usual sense (for contrasting views about the appeal to efficiency as a ground for territorial rights, see Moore, 1998; Meisels, 2009). A rule-utilitarian, on the other hand, may want to follow Sidgwick's lead in defending the claims of the current holders, whoever they are, on the grounds that stability of possession gives political communities the strongest incentive to use land responsibly, knowing that it will pass in due course to their descendants. This, of course, provides no guidance in the case of territory that has yet to be occupied by anyone.

Kantian theories

Kantian arguments for territorial rights also proceed at the general level, by justifying the state as necessary to the pursuit of justice. By the same token, they have difficulty in explaining which bits of territory each state ought to have, and, in the same way as Sidgwick's, reject a maximalist interpretation of the principle of justice, opting instead to define a threshold above which a state's territorial claims must be regarded as legitimate.

In Kant's own case, the argument proceeds in three steps.[5] He first defends the right to occupy and appropriate objects as implicit in, and justified by, the exercise of individual freedom. Next, he points out that removing things from common use prevents other people from enjoying the object in question. Since the exercise of my freedom seems unavoidably to involve restrictions on someone else's freedom, the third step involves multilateral recognition of the obligation to respect the acquisition, transfer and use of objects in the external world, which we normally think of as 'rights of property'. In consequence, according to Kant, people who live in close proximity to one another, and therefore cannot avoid interacting, are morally obliged to enter the civil condition and acknowledge a political authority whose coercive law can guarantee their property rights. There is no choice about this, so anyone meeting the proximity condition can be compelled by others to join the state if he refuses. The state's territorial rights correspond to the area over which it exercises jurisdiction. The justification for its exercise of those rights is simply that it thereby replaces 'a state *devoid of justice*' with 'a rightful condition' (Kant, 1996/1797: 90).

This theory fixes territorial rights only in the sense that the principle of proximity marks out a domain in which people are unavoidably interacting with one another, wherever that happens to be. It does not, however, tell us which territorial unit we should join in cases where we stand midway between one group of proximate people who are in the process of creating state A, and a second group who are creating state B; indeed it appears that both the As and the Bs might be justified in compelling us to join their political community, since otherwise we will be left in a lawless condition. Kant's argument cannot address this dilemma. Indeed, he avoids discussion of such a case by appealing to considerations that fall outside the Kantian theory itself: he noted that people tend, as an empirical fact, to be naturally grouped into linguistic or religious collectivities, and that membership in these cultural groups helps to define particular jurisdictional domains (1971/1795: 113–14). This empirical assumption also helps Kant to escape what might appear to be the cosmopolitan logic of his account: without appeal to that purely contingent (and, in his terms, unjustified) fact of people's preference to associate politically with others who speak the same tongue or belong to the same confession, there is no reason internal to the theory why jurisdiction should not be universal, why we would not end up in a global state.

Neo-Kantian theories of territory, such as those of Lea Ypi, Allen Buchanan and Anna Stilz, have had to grapple with at least two problems bequeathed to them by Kant. One is the problem of particularity just identified (what gives *this* state rights over *that* territory, with its specific boundaries?). The other is how to set and defend any given threshold of justice in order to define what counts as a legitimate state capable of holding territorial rights (why not assign territory to whichever state will do the *best* job, not merely an *adequate* job, regardless of the wishes of the current inhabitants?). Neo-Kantians have responded to the latter question by building some democratic requirements into justice. Thus Ypi lists as 'essential criteria' for legitimacy 'the ability to guarantee the rule of law; to protect basic human rights; and to provide sufficient opportunities guaranteeing citizens' democratic participation' (2014: 300). Buchanan's position is more nuanced: his minimal view is that any wielder of political power over a territory is legitimate 'if and only if it (1) does a credible job of protecting at least the most basic human rights of all those over whom it wields power and (2) provides this protection through processes, policies, and actions that themselves respect the most basic human rights' (2004: 247). But he adds to this that where 'institutional resources allow for democratic authorisation', full legitimacy then requires 'all persons to participate as equals in the public processes for determining who shall wield political power', that is, some form of democracy (2004: 256). Stilz's position is nuanced in a different way. Having initially stated that a state's claim to territory requires a system of law that ' "rules in the name of the people", by protecting basic rights and granting the people a voice in defining them' (2011: 578) – which seems to imply democratic government – she later concedes that there may be 'forms of political participation other than democracy that suffice to render a state legitimate'. Thus:

> I would support extending *provisional territorial* rights to nondemocratic regimes that (a) protect basic rights and institute the rule of law, (b) provide meaningful nondemocratic forms of political consultation and contestation, and (c) are reformist regimes, i.e. they aim at reforming the political culture in the long term, in a manner that is supportive of democracy. (2011: 589)

Such nuancing seems unavoidable if neo-Kantians are to avoid the conclusion that most contemporary states have no legitimate claim to the territories they govern. Yet even the basic human rights condition cited by all three authors seems to disqualify many of them (as Stilz admits, citing Zimbabwe, Iran, Sudan, China and North Korea as examples). Thus neo-Kantians have to explain why justice-promoting states should be prevented from annexing or colonizing justice-deficient ones. Might they do this by addressing the particularity problem – the problem of identifying the specific territory that any state, no matter how legitimate, can claim?

Ypi (2014) tackles this issue by laying heavy stress on the *de facto* possession of territory, whatever its origins, but then coupling this with the proviso that full territorial rights can only be established by states subjecting themselves to an international political authority that will adjudicate all territorial claims. This solution draws inspiration from Kant, but appears to extend the powers of the authority more widely than Kant did in his 'league of free states'.[6] In other words, her solution to the particularity problem is a procedural one: states are (conclusively as opposed to provisionally) entitled to whatever the global association says they are. Buchanan does not address the particularity problem directly, but appears to believe that the territorial rights legitimate states currently hold are justified unless the territory in question has been unjustly annexed. His main concern is to attack what he calls 'primary right' theories of secession which would permit territorially concentrated groups within established states to demand independence without having to show that their basic rights were being systematically violated under the status quo (see Buchanan, 2004: ch. 8; also see Buchanan, 2003). Stilz appeals to the fact of occupation to define the group and the territory over which a state may exercise its authority, so long as the occupants in question are there through no fault of their own – that is, they have not unjustly displaced some other group. On this view a state cannot be legitimate if it usurps an already legitimate state, and neo-Kantians rely upon this principle to explain the wrongness of annexation. But they will find it harder to show why a just state could not gain territorial rights from a much less just state if they annex its territory through victory in a defensive war. This of course was precisely the situation of the Allied Powers who occupied Germany in 1945, a case addressed by Stilz (2011: 590-1; for a critical appraisal, see Moore, 2014). To resist the conclusion that the Allies could legitimately incorporate the divided territory of Germany within their various political projects, thereby gaining rights of jurisdiction, rights to resources and so on, she has to invoke the idea of a German 'people' who hold meta-jurisdictional rights over the territory in question – but it's not clear that a Kantian-derived theory, which justifies territorial rights in terms of the enactment of justice, has the conceptual resources to do so.[7]

Locke and neo-Lockean Theories

As we have seen, both Kantian and utilitarian theories of territory are better able to explain what justifies territorial rights *in general* than to explain how states come to have such rights over specific areas of land. Either they end up heavily biased towards the status quo – awarding rights to any political authority that is able to establish a threshold level of social order or rights-protection – or, in the case of some versions of utilitarianism, they recommend awarding rights to groups that appear not to deserve them (such as invading colonizers who can claim that they will increase the productivity of the land they are about to occupy). For a theory that *begins* with landholding and treats territorial rights as derivative from this, we turn to John Locke and contemporary neo-Lockeans.[8] Their common starting point is the Lockean theory of property in land, which claims that, antecedently to any political authority, individual persons may acquire such property by 'mixing their labour' with the land and thereby improving it (Locke, 1988/1689: Second Treatise, ch. 5). Locke then asks us to imagine persons, either individuals, or loosely associated persons (e.g., families), many of whom have property in land, combining together to create a state. Individuals in the state of nature, Locke argued, would consent to majority rule, to obedience to, and support for, law (within the limits of natural law) and, importantly, for this account of territory, consent to incorporate their rightful landholdings into that territory over which the society will have jurisdiction (see Simmons, 2001: 313). The crucial passage in Locke linking the creation of authority over persons and authority over territory is the following:

> By the same Act therefore, whereby any one unite his Person, which was before free, to any Commonwealth; by the same he unites his Possessions, which were before free, to it also; and they become, both of them, Person and Possession, subject to the Government and Dominion of the Commonwealth, as long as it hath a being. (1988/1689: 348)

Legitimate territorial right is established, on this account, through the subjection, by free consent, of persons and their land to state authority. This has the advantage of linking people and land together prior to the creation of political authority. It also explains the domain of jurisdictional authority: the boundaries of the state are coextensive with the set of properties incorporated either by individual owners or the holders of common land (such as parishes) when political society was created. However, it encounters the problem that the domain created in this way might not be continuous. Because individual consent is required to make political authority legitimate, there may be dissenters whose land is interspersed with the properties of those who are willing to sign the social contract. If we think of the territorial state as an institution with fixed and regular boundaries whose laws are applied consistently across the whole of the area within those boundaries, the Lockean theory provides no guarantee that such a state can be (legitimately) established in any given area.[9] Moreover, it might seem that those who initially give their consent might later choose to withdraw it, leaving the state's territory with internal gaps occupied by property-owning dissidents.

Contemporary followers of Locke disagree over whether this should be seen as a failing. We referred earlier to Nozick, whose 'ultraminimal state' tolerates 'independents' living within the area in which one protective agency has achieved dominance. Hillel Steiner defends the right to dismember territory: 'precisely because a nation's territory is legitimately composed of the real estate of its members, the decision of any of them to resign that membership and, as it were, to take their real estate with them is a decision that must be respected' (1996: 144). Others, however, follow Locke himself in arguing that the transfer of land to a Commonwealth, once undertaken, is irrevocable and binds those who might later inherit the property. For instance Simmons claims that, in Locke's theory: 'when people consent to make or join a political society ... their consent should normally be understood as consent to whatever arrangements are necessary for a peaceful, stable society' (2001: 313). This is what justifies Locke's insistence that property once incorporated cannot be detached from the Commonwealth and that 'subsequent holders of that land will also be bound by the obligations of membership, including subjection of the land to state jurisdiction' (Simmons, 2001: 313). Another reading of Locke draws attention to his remark that once political communities have been formed, their territorial boundaries are settled by 'compact' between them, thereby severing the connection between individuals' property rights and states' territorial rights (Van der Vossen, 2015). This, however, would bring Lockean theory into much closer alignment with the Kantian theory discussed above, and deprive it of its distinctive method of determining the legitimate territorial boundaries of states.

Nationalist theories

Contemporary nationalist conceptions of territory begin, like Locke's, by treating the link between people and land as more primitive than the state's.

In this case, however, people are understood collectively as a nation – 'a community (1) constituted by shared beliefs and mutual commitments, (2) extended in history, (3) active in character, (4) connected to a particular territory, and (5) marked off from other communities by its distinct public culture' (Miller, 1995: 27). This builds the idea of a national homeland into the very definition of nationality. The connection between people and land is forged in two main ways. First, by interacting with the land over a long historical period and shaping it so that it better serves the needs and interests of its members as defined in part by the national culture, the nation has a strong claim to enjoy the fruits of its collective labour, which it can only do if it retains possession of the land itself. Second, the particular tract of land that the people have occupied over time acquires a special significance for them, as they bury their dead in certain places, build monuments to significant historic achievements or losses, and so on (see Miller, 2007: 214–21; 2012: 257–62; Meisels, 2009: esp. chs 3 and 7). In light of this intimate connection between the nation and its territory, a state that effectively represents the nation can claim territorial rights in that area so long as it also satisfies general criteria of legitimacy such as those discussed earlier. The nationalist argument is that only a state organically linked in this way to the nation – ideally but not necessarily a democratic state – can ensure that the material and cultural value that the land holds for the people is safeguarded.

This argument has to confront a number of challenges. The most radical asserts that nations are largely fictitious entities, at least if we are thinking about most contemporary states, which are predominantly multicultural and/ or multinational (Brilmayer, 1995; Barry, 1999: 42–3; Watner, 2010: 252–3). Thus there is no culturally homogenous group of the kind that is presupposed when claims are made about land being physically shaped and imbued with cultural significance by the nation. Or, if such a group can be identified, it will turn out to be an ethnic 'core' within the state, with the worrying implication that these are the 'true' owners of the land. A second challenge points out that those who have been responsible for adding material value to the land are not necessarily the same group as those for whom the land has cultural significance. According to Stilz, 'much of the improvement of land that goes on within a national territory – the construction of houses, churches and the like – is not carried out by the nation but by individuals or private associations. "The nation" does not mix its labor with these objects in any sense except metaphorically' (2011: 577). A third challenge points to cases in which rival nations make claims to the same piece of territory, and are each able to advance arguments about physical improvement and cultural significance in support – the city of Jerusalem, for instance. What use is the nationalist theory in these circumstances? In reply, nationalists argue that their approach will still provide guidance, by allowing us to evaluate the relative strength of the competing claims, and that in cases such as this a more complex political arrangement, such as consociationalism or joint sovereignty, may be the solution that the theory prescribes (see Miller, 2014).

A final challenge to the nationalist theory is that it appears to grant nations territorial claims to places that have symbolic meaning to them, whether or not the places in question are currently occupied by co-nationals, and whether or not the territory formed by 'joining the dots' would be continuous or not. Thus, Serbian claims to the territory of Kosovo centre on the site of the battlefield where in 1389 the Serbian Prince Lazar fought against the invading Ottoman army – an event that now marks the most important day in the Serbian national calendar. But this site is now deep in territory occupied by Albanian Kosovans, so in order to reunite the Gazimestan monument that commemorates the battle to Serbia itself, a large chunk of Kosovo would need to be transferred, along with its unwilling population. What this reveals is that the two components of the nationalist argument – the investment of collective labour in transforming the land, and the cultural significance of place – can in some circumstances pull in opposite directions. One way to resolve the conflict is to say that claims of cultural significance only have force in the case of land that either now or in the recent past has been occupied by the nation in question. Otherwise the claims can only be claims of *access* to monuments or sacred sites, not claims to exercise territorial control.

Self-determination theories

Self-determination theories of territory have the same overall shape as nationalist theories, but they seek to avoid the difficulties of assuming culturally homogenous nations by ascribing territorial rights to a 'people' understood as a political rather than a cultural unit. Territory is here conceived as the site of collective self-determination. On Moore's account, states (or substate units) hold territorial rights by acting as a vehicle of self-determination for some group G (Moore, 2015: esp. ch. 3). However not just any group can qualify as a potential holder of territorial rights. Three specific conditions are required: political identity, political capacity and political history. The political identity condition requires that the group is united by a shared aspiration for wide-ranging powers of jurisdictional authority or political control over the territory. The political capacity requirement refers to a predicted and/or demonstrated ability to exercise self-determination and maintain effective forms of governance. The third condition requires that the members of the group have a history of shared practices and mobilization in terms of political projects. Unless these conditions are fulfilled, a group will not be equipped to exercise jurisdictional authority over an extensive territory. The territory itself over which jurisdiction is to be held is determined by the fact of occupancy. Occupancy is more than just physical presence: it requires a stronger connection to land. The group must occupy the land legitimately (meaning that it has not displaced some other group), and it must be rooted in that geographical space by the individual life plans and collective and political projects of the group's members. In short, when group G (which meets the three conditions above) legitimately occupies territory T (understood as geographical space), it can be said to hold territorial rights over T.

There are three important challenges to self-determination theories. First, connection to land, in terms of group occupancy, can identify heartlands of groups, but does not offer precise guidelines for boundary-drawing because, at the fringes, more than one group can claim the same land. It does not therefore provide an easy solution to border disputes. Second, the emphasis on collective self-determination as the value that territorial rights realize seems to apply most straightforwardly to groups that engage in democratic self-determination, because then we can be confident that the state is the vehicle of the group's self-determination. This, however, may seem too restrictive a condition. Third, such a theory, with its emphasis on capacity, cannot assign territorial rights to people who inhabit failed or conquered states.

Self-determination accounts could respond to the last criticism by pointing out that, in contrast to theories that make territorial rights dependent on the state's achieving a certain standard of justice or social order, these theories vest them directly in groups with the requisite political capacity to be self-determining, regardless of whether they are currently able to exercise it. In the case of a failed state, for example, the normative implication is not that external actors are entitled to claim jurisdiction, but that they may have an obligation to help the rights-holding people create the conditions under which they can be self-governing. In reply to the charge that only groups with democratic institutions can be awarded territorial rights, Moore (2015) defends a precautionary principle for institutional design, which entails that where a state governs on behalf of a group, we should assume that it acts as a vehicle of self-determination for that group unless we have good reasons to think otherwise. Even though democratic institutions are usually optimal for achieving self-determination, they are not always necessary.

3 Challenges to the Idea of Territory

In this final section, we ask how theories of territorial rights can respond to the practical and philosophical challenges we identified in our introduction. The main practical challenge concerned contested territories, where the solution will depend on which theory we favour. Take secessionist demands as an example. Utilitarian and Kantian theories, as standardly formulated, are hostile to secession unless it can be shown that the state that the seceders are trying to leave is manifestly failing to protect their rights and legitimate interests. Some neo-Kantians would make an exception for groups that have been incorporated into the state against their will and without just cause. Notice, however, that the status quo bias implicit in these theories has the paradoxical consequence that a secessionist group will lack territorial rights up to the moment at which it succeeds in its struggle for independence, at which point, and providing it creates a political entity that meets the threshold these theories set, it gains full entitlement over the territory it commands. Locke's theory, in its original formulation, is directly hostile to secession, since the initial transfer of jurisdiction over property to the state is irrevocable. In contrast, those such as Steiner who offer a libertarian reading of Lockean theory leave the door wide open to secession by any group able to command a majority in a compact territory (for what this might mean in practice, see Beran, 1988). For nationalist and self-determination theories, the issue is whether the seceding group qualifies as the kind of agent entitled to claim and exercise territorial rights. For nationalists, this will often be complicated by the fact of multilevel identities: if the secessionist region also contains many individuals who identify with the larger nation of which it forms a part, then the case for outright secession (as opposed to some form of devolved government) may be weak (see Miller, 1998). Self-determination theories too may award competent subgroups some forms of non-exclusive jurisdiction as an alternative to full secession.

In responding to the philosophical challenges, we should begin by observing that all the theories we have examined justify territorial rights by appeal to the interests, broadly conceived, of the inhabitants of the territory in question. Thus they are vulnerable in principle to cosmopolitan critics who point out that the interests of those who live outside the territory are ignored. Sidgwick, for example, candidly admitted that his treatment of territorial rights, and associated questions such as the right to immigrate, assumed what he called 'the national ideal of political organization'. If one were to switch instead to the cosmopolitan ideal (which 'is perhaps the ideal of the future') then the state's task would be 'to maintain order over the particular territory that historical causes have appropriated to it, but not in any way to determine who is to inhabit this territory, or to restrict the enjoyment of its natural advantages to any particular portion of the human race' (1891: 308). For Kant, too, a full theory of territorial rights had to recognize the principle of 'cosmopolitan right', deriving from the fact that 'all nations stand *originally* in a community of land' – in other words, that the earth was originally held by the human race in common (1996/1797: 121). Kant drew the relatively modest conclusion that each person had the right to travel abroad for purposes of engaging in commerce, and when he did so 'he must not be treated with hostility, so long as he behaves in a peaceable manner in the place he happens to be in' (1971/1795: 106).

Their underlying cosmopolitanism notwithstanding, neither Sidgwick nor Kant directly challenged the right of a legitimate state to determine who should be allowed to settle permanently within its borders. But others have asked why territorial rights should include the right to prevent strangers from entering. Once again the answer will depend on the precise theory of territory that we invoke, but broadly speaking it will turn on the conditions that are necessary for a territorial state to function effectively. Immigration changes both the set of people who fall within the jurisdiction of the law and, in democratic states, the citizen body that is responsible for making it. If, like Kant, we imagine state representatives deliberating together to establish rules to govern their intercourse, it seems very likely that the right to control borders would be accepted as one such rule, since many internal policy decisions depend on the state's ability to exercise it. Against that might be set the human rights of immigrants who would be denied protection if barred from entering. But this would only establish a limited right on the part of refugees to enter *some* state that could provide them with shelter.[10]

The final challenge we shall consider concerns the natural resources that lie within the boundaries of each territorial state. In some intuitive sense it seems that different groups of citizens are arbitrarily advantaged or disadvantaged by the resources that lie unearned beneath their feet. Yet it is hard to see how jurisdiction can be exercised effectively if it does not include the right to legislate on (and thereby control) the use of resources that fall within the territory. A possible solution to this dilemma is to tax each state for the resources that it either possesses or uses, the funds raised in this way to be distributed either on an equal per capita basis to all of the world's inhabitants (see Steiner, 1994: ch. 8; 1996), or to people living in countries whose per capita income takes them below the global poverty line (see Pogge, 1998; 2002b). But the problem here is to find a way of valuing unimproved natural resources that is impartial in the sense of being independent of any particular political community's beliefs about the appropriate use of a particular resource: what members of one society may regard as a holy site, others may regard as merely a lucrative development opportunity (for an elaboration of this point, see Miller, 2007: ch. 3; Moore, 2012). If territorial rights can be defended, therefore, on one or other of the grounds canvassed in this essay, some degree of arbitrariness in access to resources may be the unavoidable price.

References

Agnew, J. 1994. 'The Territorial Trap, The Geographical Assumptions of International Relations Theory', *Review of International Political Economy* 1: 53–80.

Armstrong, C. 2015. 'Against "Permanent Sovereignty" over Natural Resources', *Politics, Philosophy & Economics* 14: 129–151.

Barry, B. 1999. 'Statism and Nationalism: A Cosmopolitan Critique', in I. Shapiro and L. Brilmayer, eds., *Nomos 41: Global Justice*, 12–66. New York: New York University Press.

Beran, H. 1988. 'A Liberal Theory of Secession', *Political Studies* 36: 21–31.

Brilmayer, L. 1995. 'The Moral Significance of Nationalism', *Notre Dame Law Review* 71: 7–71.

Buchanan, A. 2003. 'The Making and Unmaking of Boundaries: What Liberalism Has to Say', in A. Buchanan and M. Moore, eds., *States, Nations, and Borders: The Ethics of Making Boundaries*, 231–261. Cambridge: Cambridge University Press.

Buchanan, A. 2004. *Justice, Legitimacy, and Self-Determination: Moral Foundations for International Law*. Oxford: Oxford University Press.

Hayward, T. 2014. 'Equality and Ecological Space', JWI working paper series no. 2014102. Edinburgh: Just World Institute.

Hobbes, T. 1985/1651. *Leviathan*, ed. with an introduction by C. B. Macpherson. Harmondsworth: Penguin.

Honoré, A. 1961. 'Ownership', in A. G. Guest, ed., *Oxford Essays in Jurisprudence*, 1st series, 107–147. Oxford: Clarendon Press.

Kant, I. 1971/1795. 'Perpetual Peace: A Philosophical Sketch', in *Kant's Political Writings*, ed. H. Reiss. Cambridge: Cambridge University Press.

Kant, I. 1996/1797. *The Metaphysics of Morals*, trans. M. Gregor. Cambridge: Cambridge University Press.

Keane, J. 2003. *Global Civil Society?* Cambridge: Cambridge University Press.

Kolers, A. 2009. *Land, Conflict and Justice: A Political Theory of Territory*. Cambridge: Cambridge University Press.

Kolers, A. 2012. 'Floating Provisos and Sinking Islands', *Journal of Applied Philosophy* 29: 333–343.

Kuper, A. 2004. *Democracy Beyond Borders: Justice and Representation in Global Institutions*. Oxford: Oxford University Press.

Locke, J. 1988/1689. *Two Treatises of Government*, ed. P. Laslett. Cambridge: Cambridge University Press.

Meisels, T. 2009. *Territorial Rights*, 2nd edn. Dordrecht: Springer.

Miller, D. 1995. *On Nationality*. Oxford: Clarendon Press.

Miller, D. 1998. 'Secession and the Principle of Nationality', in M. Moore, ed. *National Self-Determination and Secession*, 62–78. Oxford: Oxford University Press.

Miller, D. 2007. *National Responsibility and Global Justice*. Oxford: Oxford University Press.

Miller, D. 2011. 'Property and Territory: Locke, Kant and Steiner', *Journal of Political Philosophy* 19: 90–109.

Miller, D. 2012. 'Territorial Rights: Concept and Justification', *Political Studies* 60: 252–268.

Miller, D. 2014. 'Debatable Lands', *International Theory* 6: 104–121.

Miller, D. 2016. 'Is There a Human Right to Immigrate?', in S. Fine and L. Ypi, eds., *Migration in Political Theory: The Ethics of Movement and Membership*, 11–31. Oxford: Oxford University Press.

Moore, M. 1998. 'The Territorial Dimension of Self-Determination', in M. Moore, ed. *National Self-Determination and Secession*, 134–157. Oxford: Oxford University Press.

Moore, M. 2012. 'Natural Resources, Territorial Right and Global Distributive Justice', *Political Theory* 40: 84–107.

Moore, M. 2014. 'Which People and What Land? Territorial Right-Holders and Attachment to Territory', *International Theory* 6: 121–140.

Moore, M. 2015. *A Political Theory of Territory*. New York: Oxford University Press.

Nine, C. 2008. 'A Lockean Theory of Territory', *Political Studies* 56: 148–165.

Nine, C. 2014. 'When Affected Interests Demand Joint Self-Determination: Learning from Rivers', *International Theory* 6: 157–174.

Nozick, R. 1974. *Anarchy, State, and Utopia*. Oxford: Blackwell.

Pogge, T. 1998. 'A Global Resources Dividend', in D. Crocker and T. Linden, eds., *Ethics of Consumption, the Good Life, Justice, and Global Responsibility*, 501–536. Lanham, MD: Rowman and Littlefield.

Pogge, T. 2002a. 'Cosmopolitanism and Sovereignty', in *World Politics and Human Rights*, 168–195. Cambridge: Polity.

Pogge, T. 2002b. 'Eradicating Systemic Poverty: Brief for a Global Resources Dividend', in *World Poverty and Human Rights*, 196–215. Cambridge: Polity.

Rawls, J. 1999. *The Law of Peoples*. Cambridge, MA: Harvard University Press.

Ruggie, J. 1993. 'Territoriality and Beyond, Problematizing Modernity in International Relations', *International Organization* 47: 39–74.

Sidgwick, H. 1891. *The Elements of Politics*. London and New York: Macmillan.

Simmons, A. J. 2001. 'On the Territorial Rights of States', *Philosophical Issues* 11: 300–326.

Spruyt, H. 1994. *The Sovereign State and its Competitors*. Princeton, NJ: Princeton University Press.

Steiner, H. 1994. *An Essay on Rights*. Oxford: Blackwell.

Steiner, H. 1996. 'Territorial Justice', in S. Caney, D. George and P. Jones, eds., *National Rights, International Obligations*, 139–148. Boulder, CO: Westview Press.

Stilz, A. 2011. 'Nations, States, and Territory', *Ethics* 121: 572–601.

Van der Vossen, B. 2015. 'Locke on Territorial Rights', *Political Studies* 63: 713–728.

Watner, C. 2010. 'The Territorial Assumption: Rationale for Conquest', *Journal of Libertarian Studies* 22: 247–260.

Ypi, L. 2014. 'A Permissive Theory of Territorial Rights', *European Journal of Philosophy* 22: 288–312.

CHAPTER TEN

Natural Resources

Leif Wenar

Natural resources have been contested by force throughout history – and sometimes, it seems, with equivalent intellectual force throughout recent theory. Theorists battle over which principles correctly apply to natural resources, over how to understand their value, even over what the term 'natural resources' should rightly be understood to refer to. It is sometimes thought that this scholarly fight over resources is just a proxy war between those who favour 'ideal' and 'non-ideal' theorizing. However, ideal and non-ideal theorizing are not intrinsically opposed. The battle over natural resources, rather, at first appears more to be fought by methodological camps so antagonistic that they cannot even agree what the problem about natural resources should be taken to be.

On one side of this methodological battle, the central problem that theorists solve is one of distributive justice. From this perspective, natural resources currently yield a *distribution of value that is unjust*. On the other side of this battle, political theory should primarily focus on power. From that viewpoint, the problem with natural resources is that they currently yield a *distribution of power that is dangerous*. Partisans of the first view might tendentiously characterize the war as between 'valuable' and 'valueless' theory; from the other side, the contrast would be between 'powerful' and 'powerless' theory.

Yet, as we will see, that contrast gives too neat a description of the contest among philosophers. The current scholarly situation is in fact less like the Cold War, where two large and fundamentally opposed superpowers vied for supremacy. The Thirty Years War – with its chaotic clashes, its partial and ever-shifting alliances – is the more accurate comparator. 'Theories of distributive justice' and 'theories of power' define points on a spectrum, and actual theorists are spread across this spectrum according to how loyal they are to one side or the other.

Here we will survey the work of theorists across this spectrum, giving more attention to the 'power' end since the 'distributive' end is better-known among academic philosophers. Before beginning the survey, it is worth noting that the extremes on the spectrum fight on common ground. Just as Catholics and Protestants during the Thirty Years War at least shared a view on Jesus' divinity, so all Western theorists who write on resources share the heritage of Grotius, Locke and Pufendorf and the idea that in some sense the world's natural resources are naturally an asset for all of humanity. As Michael Blake and Mathias Risse put it: 'Since the earth is simply *there*, with no one deserving credit for it, a plausible view on original ownership is that all humans have *some* sort of symmetrical claim to it' (2009: 134).

However, as with Catholics and Protestants in the seventeenth century, the shared doctrinal area here is modest. What Western theorists agree on is a negative premise: that no human being is (as was believed in pre-modern times) born with rights over any particular natural resources – so the ancient apologies for the divine right of kings over lands, such as those of the English political theorist Robert Filmer, are surd. Theorists also share a justificatory environment in which respectful positive principles recognizing the inherent political equality of all humans must be the starting point. The contest, which has been vigorous, is over what positive principles fill this area.[1]

1   The Distributive Justice Perspective

At one end of the spectrum of theories of distributive justice we find the egalitarian theory of Hillel Steiner, who calls his redistributive mechanism the 'Global Fund':

> The Global Fund is a mechanism for the global application of the Left Libertarian conception of distributive justice. As a form of luck egalitarianism, this conception confers upon each person an entitlement to an equal share of all natural resource values, since natural resources – broadly, geographical sites – are objects for the production of which no person is responsible. Owners of these sites, i.e. states, are liable to a 100% Global Fund tax on their unimproved value: that is, their gross market value *minus* the value of the improvements added to them by human effort. (2011a: 328)

Steiner's left libertarianism draws a hard line between choices (for which individuals are responsible) and natural resources ('for the production of which no person is responsible'). Since no one is responsible for producing natural resources, all have equal rights to their value. The goal of redistribution by the Global Fund is then to ensure that all receive the value to which they are entitled.

David Miller, however, has challenged Steiner over his use of market values of resources within his left libertarian theory. Miller says that Steiner, by his own lights, should be concerned only with the 'unimproved' value of resources – not with their market values, which also reflect the choices (to invest, improve, etc.) that individuals have made with regard to those resources. Miller notes that it would be frightfully difficult to know what the unimproved value of resources actually is, but that, in any case, using market values as the metric for the *distributandum* must be unfair, since market values register both choices and circumstances (2007: 57–60). Steiner (2011b) has engaged Miller in this debate.

Joseph Mazor admits these difficulties, but looking more from the 'power' end of the spectrum argues that there are nevertheless particular advantages to taxing the market value of natural resources. There are many social goods for which egalitarian redistribution might be warranted, Mazor says, but redistributing the value of natural resources is less dangerous and costly than redistributing other goods. For a coercive authority to attempt to determine what natural endowments persons have, and what choices they have made, could be quite intrusive and expensive. By contrast, taxing the market value of holdings of natural resources is much less invasive (Mazor, 2009: 119–28; see also Mazor, 2010). And, as Paula Casal (2011) adds, resource taxes are less likely to disincentivize productive work than income taxes do – and since natural resources seem to many to be something like manna from heaven, taxes on them may be more willingly accepted.

In Steiner's fuller left libertarian theory of distributive justice, it is not only 'geographical sites' that are included among 'natural resources' in the sense of things for the production of which no person is responsible. Each individual's germ-line genetic information also counts as a natural resource in this sense: 'natural resources' are not only around us, but part of who we are. Accordingly, the value of each person's 'natural endowment' is also subject to the egalitarian norm and so taxation or supplementation as required (Steiner, 2004). Indeed, for Steiner, every 'non-produced' thing is, by definition, in the category called 'natural resource'. Here we see the theory of distributive justice defining the object of theoretical concern so that it aligns with the concerns of the theory itself – the *distributandum* ('natural resources') is defined by this distributive theory's focus on the choice–circumstance divide.

Other theorists have also started with their favoured distributive theory and then attempted to expand the class of objects of theoretical concern in a way that bears on the distribution of natural resources (in a more ordinary sense). This was the path of reasoning of those who interpreted John Rawls's justice as fairness as being primarily concerned with rectifying advantages that are 'arbitrary from a moral point of view'. If 'arbitrary from a moral point of view' marks out the category of Rawlsian concern, then natural resources must fit within this category. Thus Charles Beitz, in the first edition of his seminal book *Political Theory and International Relations* (1979), argued in a Rawlsian mode that, just as Rawls saw personal natural endowments as arbitrary from a moral point of view in his domestic theory, so he should have seen national endowments of natural resources as arbitrary from a moral point of view in his international theory.

Beitz thus argued for a resource redistribution principle that (analogously to Rawls's difference principle) would allow inequalities in value of resources only to the extent that these were to the greatest benefit of those least advantaged by the inequality (1999/1979: 141). Brian Barry (1981, 1982) argued similarly, outside the Rawlsian framework. The fact that some states have more natural resources within their borders, Barry said, unjustly favours those states – especially since the borders themselves are often the relics of injustice. So a tax should be placed on resource extraction from the resource-favoured countries, and the revenues given to the resource-disfavoured countries, in order to achieve a distribution of advantages that is more just from an egalitarian perspective.

Rawls himself took a different position on the value of natural resources: that they have none, or, more specifically, that their value is not relevant to an international theory that aims to give an account of a justifiable distribution of advantages among nations (1999: 108–9, 116–17). Noting that resource-poor countries like Japan have done well, while resource-rich countries like Argentina have struggled, Rawls asserts that the wealth of a people turns on 'their political culture and in the religious, philosophical, and moral traditions that support the basic structure of their political and social institutions, as well as in the industriousness and cooperative talents of its members, all supported by their political virtues' (1999: 108). Beitz's resource redistribution principle, therefore, aims to redistribute something that is, from the correct theoretical perspective, irrelevant. Thomas Pogge (1994) has argued energetically against Rawls on this point.

Rawls is often thought to be an exemplar of a theorist of distributive justice, on the leftward extreme of our spectrum of theories. But this is a mistake. Rawls himself tells us that the primary concern of his international theory is not distribution at all:

> Two main ideas motivate the Law of Peoples. One is that the great evils of human history – unjust war and oppression, religious persecution and the denial of liberty of conscience, starvation and poverty, not to mention genocide and mass murder – follow from political injustice, with its own cruelty and callousness…The other main idea, obviously connected with the first, is that, once the gravest forms of political injustice are eliminated by following just (or at least decent) social policies and establishing just (or at least decent) basic institutions, these great evils will eventually disappear. (1999: 6–7)

What Rawls is primarily concerned with, as he says here, are the distributions of power that are dangerous. Realizing just distributions of value is not, as this passage explains, an end in itself. Just distributions are, at most, merely a means to produce a better world – a world in which the great evils of abuse of power no longer occur.

Political scientists who study natural resources have gone even farther than Rawls's 'no value' position. Consider, for instance, this passage from Michael Ross's book *The Oil Curse*:

> Since 1980, the developing world has become wealthier, more democratic, and more peaceful. Yet this is only true for countries without oil. The oil states – scattered across the Middle East, Africa, Latin America, and Asia – are no wealthier, or more democratic or peaceful, than they were three decades ago. Some are worse off. From 1980 to 2006, per capita incomes fell 6 percent in Venezuela, 45 percent in Gabon, and 85 percent in

> Iraq. Many oil producers – like Algeria, Angola, Colombia, Nigeria, Sudan, and again, Iraq – have been scarred by decades of civil war…Today, the oil states are 50 percent more likely to be ruled by autocrats and more than twice as likely to have civil wars as the non-oil states. They are also more secretive, more financially volatile, and provide women with fewer economic and political opportunities. (2012: 1–2)[2]

Far from giving unjust advantage that is ripe for redistribution, in our world some natural resources actually appear to have negative value because of the power they give to authoritarians, civil warriors, and so on. Some distributive theorists have acknowledged this point (Beitz, 1999: 206). Yet it leaves their treatment of natural resources in something of a bind.

Recall Miller's internal critique of Steiner: that it is difficult to ferret out the 'unimproved' value of natural resources within their market values – and that the theory cannot use market values because they incorporate a factor (choice) that the theory is not meant to be sensitive insofar as it is redistributive. Here, distributive theorists are in an even more difficult situation. It is difficult for them correctly to represent the value of natural resources in the world as it is, because the actual value of possessing resources turns on a factor (power) that theory is not meant to be sensitive to. So these theorists have two bad options. They must either ignore a part of the world – natural resources – that they feel intuitively must be valuable and so subject to redistribution. Or they must produce a redistributive theory that gives counterintuitive results, such as that the value of resources must be distributed away from poor, strife-torn but resource-rich countries and distributed to peaceful, wealthy resource-poor countries.

So far we have been surveying conflicts around theories like those of Steiner and Beitz, which say that an unjust distribution of resource value is the problem, so redistribution of resource value must be the solution. The distributive theories we have seen so far have been egalitarian, but of course there are internal battles within the distributive camp about which principle should be deployed for the distribution of resources. Casal (2011), for instance, advances a prioritarian principle.

These egalitarian and prioritarian theorists emphasize the normative importance of redistributing the value of resources among the states that currently control those resources. Another group of theorists instead emphasizes the values that justify leaving resources under the control of national groups.

Theorists who bring out the values that justify leaving resources under the control of nations include, for example, Rawls, who says that leaving resources under national stewardship promotes their effective management and conservation (1999: 8, 38–9). Another such theorist is Margaret Moore:

> [There is] a connection between control over natural resources and the moral value of collective self-determination. On this view, collective control, in the form of jurisdictional authority over resources, is an important dimension of collective self-determination,

particularly the cultural dimension of different rules regarding land. The idea here is that, if we assume reasonable pluralism about the good life, we might expect that different societies would favour different property regimes or different approaches to the treatment of land and potential resources...Control over natural resources is an important part of collective self-determination. If people lack this kind of control, then, to that extent, they lack robust forms of collective self-determination. (2012: 87–8)

Avery Kolers (2009) goes further than Moore along this line, to say that what even counts as a 'resource' is a matter on which different groups will have different views. 'Resource' is for Kolers an agent-relative concept, and inhabitants of different 'geospaces' must be respected in their own interpretations of the value of their natural surroundings. This means also leaving these group agents with substantial control over what they see as the resources around them, the true value of which only they understand.

David Miller argues in favour of national control over resources on the ground that national communities have, through history, added to the value of the resources under their control. Nations do not, after all, merely benefit from resources by scooping up manna from heaven – their people labour to cultivate the land, redirect rivers, prospect for minerals. Moreover, national peoples very often form special attachments to features of the natural environment within which their communities have historically been in symbiotic relations, giving those features a deep symbolic significance (Miller, 2012). These kinds of attachments may go very deep into the identity of the group members, who may think of themselves as dwellers in a particular forest or hunters on a specific range or the inhabitants of some island (Miller, 2007).

Other theorists deploy related arguments to argue for significant 'local' control over natural resources. Cara Nine, for example, calls on a Lockean 'desert-for-value-added' argument in support of resource rights in collectives with demonstrable capacity to add value by establishing legitimate political authority within the geographical area in which they have historically been located (2008; 2012: ch. 6). Simmons (2001) takes a more individualistic Lockean approach, where the resource rights of groups are just a function of the consensual agglomeration of the rights of individuals who have legitimately appropriated resources themselves.

The theories mentioned that emphasize the value of national control have been subject to powerful contestation, notably by Anna Stilz (2009, 2011) and Chris Armstrong (2014, 2015). Readers interested in following through on those debates are invited to start with their rebuttals.

2 The Power Perspective

Instead of pursuing the 'distributive' debate further, we will take Locke as a pivot for the transition between the perspective on resources that is primarily distributive and the perspective that is primarily concerned with power. From the 'power' perspective, natural resources are important, because controlling them can boost the power either of those who already have more (hence their danger) or of those who currently have less (making them an instrument not of power, but of 'counter-power'). Those who look at natural resources in this second way do not see principles for control over resources as expressing eternal truths about just distributions, but rather as principles for countering power in particular, often historically-specific contexts. The role of resources in what real people can do – and cannot do – to each other is what really matters.

From this perspective, Locke's own arguments about property rights in resources and 'the common ownership of the earth' were essentially counterpowerful. For Locke, who had to flee in fear for his life from the sovereign of his native England, the power that needed countering was that of a monarch who was claiming to be absolute. Locke was opposing the divine right of kings. In the *Two Treatises of Government*, he first counters the divine right thesis by arguing that even if God did give the whole world to Adam, this could not be a basis of absolute political power today because *property rights cannot be that strong* (Locke, 1988/1689: I, sections 41–43). Locke then argues that political power cannot be absolute today because, starting from common ownership of the earth, we can prove that in society *no one's property can rightly be taken without the consent of the people or their representatives* (1988/1689: II, section 140).

Locke's property arguments were influential in his day because they were counterpowerful. His was a philosophy to embolden the rising parliamentary forces to assert their rights against the high-handed monarchs. Locke's philosophy was then taken up by the American colonists, who fought their own battle against the British monarch's 'absolute Despotism' in the century following.[3] It continues to inspire those who oppose excessive state power today as well.

More power-minded contemporary philosophers, such as Mathias Risse and Thomas Pogge, invoke 'the common ownership of the earth' much in the spirit of Locke – as a principle that should constrain powerful institutions, only, this time, nations considered as wholes. Accepting that nations should have primary control over their natural resources, they say, the common ownership of the earth requires that the international system should also work to meet the basic needs of all persons. For Risse, common ownership grounds a human right: the right of each person to have opportunities to meet his or her own basic needs (2012: 89–151).[4] For Pogge, common ownership requires that nations should be forced to pay into a global fund whenever they extract natural resources, with that fund being used to meet the basic needs of the world's poor (1994; 2008: ch. 8; 2011).[5] For both these philosophers, national control over resources need not be replaced – it needs to be constrained by a 'common ownership' principle so that the international system works for the good of the poor everywhere.

The values that these philosophers emphasize are weighty ones. Satisfying basic needs will indeed be a priority for any justifiable international system;

this is not controversial. Moreover, 'common ownership' might well be a useful principle for guiding institutional design in some areas – especially for uninhabited regions such as the deep seabed and outer space, where ideas like 'the common heritage of mankind' already appear in treaties.[6] The common ownership of the earth's atmosphere is also a promising starting point for property-based proposals to reduce greenhouse-gas emissions.[7]

Principles that countered power in centuries past, however, may not do so now. And principles that countered power within English-speaking countries may not do so when stretched over the earth. It all depends on the reality: on who has too much power and how the opposition can claw some away. 'Common ownership of the earth' may not be a counterpowerful principle for natural resources today; in fact, invoking it may be counterproductive. From the perspective of power, what is crucial is to attend to the world as it is now.

Between the Second World War and the end of the twentieth century, philosophers forgot the world – at least mainstream English-speaking philosophers did. With a few noble exceptions, there was very little sustained attention to issues affecting what was then called the 'Third World'.[8] Indeed, insofar as international issues were discussed by English-speaking philosophers at all, the discussions centred on Western preoccupations. Philosophical hawks scrutinized the confrontation with the Soviets; doves worried about human rights and the famines seen on television.

What no leading English-speaking philosopher theorized was the main narrative of most of humanity: the struggle of peoples to gain control over their own countries, and not least over their natural resources. The determination of peoples to control their own fates was, for most of the world, the most important political story of the twentieth century – much more important than the rise of human rights, more important even than the Cold War. Yet the great drama of the century hardly registered in Anglophone philosophy. For philosophers in America and other former British colonies, 'victory over the empire' was very old news. For the British, a sense of imperial loss kept eyes down and lips shut.

This is part of the 'great forgetting' of how recent the victories of popular sovereignty have been – and how aspirational this step away from the world of colonialism and absolute monarchs still remains for many peoples. One can hear both the pain of the battle and the yearning for popular sovereignty in the Namibian constitution of 1990:

> We the people of Namibia – have finally emerged victorious in our struggle against colonialism, racism and apartheid; are determined to adopt a Constitution which expresses for ourselves and our children our resolve to cherish and to protect the gains of our long struggle; desire to promote amongst all of us the dignity of the individual and the unity and integrity of the Namibian nation among and in association with the nations of the world; will strive to achieve national reconciliation and to foster peace, unity and a common loyalty to a single state; committed to these principles, have

resolved to constitute the Republic of Namibia as a sovereign, secular, democratic and unitary State securing to all our citizens justice, liberty, equality, and fraternity.[9]

And also in the South African constitution of 1996:

We, the people of South Africa, Recognize the injustices of our past; Honor those who suffered for justice and freedom in our land; Respect those who have worked to build and develop our country; and Believe that South Africa belongs to all who live in it, united in our diversity.

We therefore, through our freely elected representatives, adopt this Constitution as the supreme law of the Republic so as to: Heal the divisions of the past and establish a society based on democratic values, social justice and fundamental human rights; Lay the foundations for a democratic and open society in which government is based on the will of the people and every citizen is equally protected by law; Improve the quality of life of all citizens and free the potential of each person; and Build a united and democratic South Africa able to take its rightful place as a sovereign state in the family of nations.[10]

To these two nations, which have so recently overcome the great afflictions of their past, one can add the anguished bravado of a third nation that has not. This is the Iraqi constitution of 2005.

We the people of Iraq, who have just risen from our stumble, and who are looking with confidence to the future through a republican, federal, democratic, pluralistic system, have resolved with the determination of our men, women, the elderly and youth, to respect the rules of law, to establish justice and equality, to cast aside the politics of aggression, and to tend to the concerns of women and their rights, and to the elderly and their concerns, and to children and their affairs and to spread a culture of diversity and defusing terrorism.[11]

The triumph of most peoples in the past century was winning sovereignty over their countries away from the powers that had oppressed them, and gaining control of the resources that those powers were so shamelessly taking.[12] In this context – in our world as it is now – an attempt to attenuate peoples' sovereignty over resources with 'the common ownership of the earth' will not counter power.

Think of being a citizen inside a former colony such as Algeria or Indonesia or Zimbabwe, where the national identity hardened in bloody struggles to wrestle national territory and its resource wealth away from relentless empires that clothed their exploitation in the colours of morality. Westerners now come to you saying that you do not entirely own your country's resources, because the British and French, the Dutch and Japanese, and even the Americans partly own them too. However worthy are the derivations from this principle, the principle itself will be hard for many to hear. There just is not enough trust of those who are coming to say that they bear gifts.

A proposal such as Pogge's, which uses 'common ownership of the earth' to argue for a tax on resources that countries extract, may be especially hard to hear. Imagine living in South Sudan, one of the poorest countries in the world, and being informed that because of the oil, your country owes a debt to the Swiss.[13]

Demands like Pogge's would also be counterproductive because they would set peoples in resource-rich and resource-poor developing countries against each other. Many of the leaders of resource-rich countries today are strongmen who still wear the clothing of the anticolonial revolution. These strongmen would say to their peoples: 'The big powers want to take from us what we have won at such a price, and give it to strangers.' And they would be right.

Pogge's goal is 'global social justice'. Yet actual social justice (as opposed to a theory of social justice) requires that people have shared beliefs about the world and the moral problems that face them. It requires that people are willing to compromise and sometimes to sacrifice for the sake of a common good. Social justice needs trust, and trust across borders is today sadly quite low.

'The common ownership of the earth' resonated with Locke's readers in the seventeenth century, and with colonial Americans in the eighteenth century, because of its scriptural source and their shared Christian faith. In countries like India and China, common ownership has never had that kind of resonance – and in countries that have recently escaped empire (including these), it may today seem like a Western Trojan horse.

Some philosophers who favour a distributive perspective may well have become impatient at this point in the discussion. Take the worldwide distribution of natural resources itself, these philosophers will say. Isn't it just luck that some are born in countries rich with mineral bounties, like Botswana, while others are stuck with empty plains, as in Paraguay?[14] It is incontrovertible (they may say) that great wealth is gained from natural resources, and that peoples do not deserve the natural wealth they just happen to have. Those super-rich Norwegians and Qataris, for instance. Surely their natural windfalls can be taken and used to help individuals regardless of nation – to feed the poor, to cure disease, to fund education.

Justice (these philosophers say) demands the redistribution of resource wealth away from the lucky peoples in resource-rich countries towards the unlucky peoples in resource-poor countries. The baseline should be that each person in the world has a claim to an equal share of the world's resources. We should in the future see humans not as citizens of lucky or unlucky countries, but instead as cosmopolitans – as equal citizens of a common world. We should stop seeing natural resources as rightly controlled by nations (they conclude) and start seeing them as resources for all humanity, considered as a United Persons.

Again, the moral seriousness here is admirable; the causes that these thinkers favour are important. And the ideal of humans uniting across borders is undeniably attractive. The difficulty is not in finding good causes to support globally. That is easy – in a sense, there are too many. From the 'power' end of the spectrum, all the interesting questions are about finding the paths that will actually achieve these worthwhile ends. The real difficulty is finding cosmopolitan principles that it would be reasonable to press hard enough right now to achieve the ends that all agree are good.

Taking the broadest view, what the world has now is a decent consensus on principles for good governance within countries: principles such as popular sovereignty and human rights. There is also relatively firm agreement on what should happen in basic relations between countries, such as that territorial conquest is wrong and keeping treaties is right. These agreements are by no means univocal, but they are substantial. In coming to consensus, it has been quite useful that modernity has generated a small, globally shared vocabulary to describe human beings and what should happen to them. 'Human rights' and 'genocide' are in this shared vocabulary; 'capabilities' is making a bid for inclusion; 'responsibility to protect' may not make it.

What remain absent as yet are substantive shared principles and concepts for relations among individuals as such, considered not as citizens of nations but as 'citizens of the world'. Philosophers have imagined many cosmopolitan alternatives, yet in the absence of agreement, the question is how power could responsibly be used to realize any one of them.

At this transnational level, collective thinking today is still turbid – much like it was within Europe during the Middle Ages. After a long review of early European politics in his masterful *General History of Civilization in Europe*, the French politician François Guizot offers this summary:

> I have now run over all the great attempts at political organization which were made in Europe, down to the end of the fourteenth or beginning of the fifteenth century. All these failed. I have endeavoured to point out, in going along, the causes of these failures; to speak truly, they may all be summed up in one: society was not yet sufficiently advanced to adapt itself to unity; all was yet too local, too special, too narrow: too many differences prevailed both in things and in minds. There were no general interests, no general opinions capable of guiding, of bearing sway over particular interests and particular opinions. The most enlightened minds, the boldest thinkers, had as yet no just idea of administration or justice truly public. (1838: 311)

Regarding a cosmopolitan agenda, the world is now in a condition similar to what Guizot describes here. 'There were no general interests, no general opinions' is vivid enough today. Imagine, for example, that you are the cosmopolitan who has been chosen to present a case to Venezuela or Kuwait to submit itself to a global resource-redistribution regime. That will be challenging.

Given the divergences in interests and opinions, the issue becomes one of power. Picking up Guizot's passage again:

> The most enlightened minds, the boldest thinkers, had as yet no just idea of administration or justice truly public. It was evidently necessary that a very active, powerful

civilization should first mix, assimilate, grind together, as it were, all these incoherent elements; it was necessary that there should first be a strong centralization of interests, laws, manners, ideas; it was necessary, in a word, that there should be created a public authority and a public opinion. (1838: 311–12)[15]

The question for cosmopolitan philosophers is how much 'grinding together' they are proposing in order to impose their controversial principles. Redistributions must be enforced; entreaties will not suffice. All the important questions surround the agency that will implement the cosmopolitan ideal. What is the nature of this agency's coercive power? Will anyone suggest that it be backed by armed force? Yet, if not, how does a global redistributive agency require compliance? How, for instance, to make today's oil-enriched authoritarians give up their source of power?

At their least edifying, cosmopolitans use a passive voice to insist on aggressive reforms. Something – something even quite difficult – must be done, yet who is to do this difficult thing, and how, remains hazy. Occasionally, a gesture may be made to some hypothetical body, like a widely trusted and incorruptible global panel of experts, or a world citizenry willing to accept majority decisions for the sake of humanity as a whole. Yet what is meant to happen when some powerful group – say, the Russians or the Saudis – rejects the ideal is left unsaid. If some pattern is to be imposed across the planet, the power that does this cannot be passive.

While waiting for the 'grind together' proposals to become more complete, we might consider the virtues of a different principle for control over natural resources. This principle leaves control over resources at the national level (though possibly constrained by duties concerning the environment, future generations and so on). And instead of emphasizing the need to distribute the value of resources between states, it emphasizes the importance of citizen control over resources within each country. The principle here is that the resources of each country belong to the people of that country, and that citizens have the ultimate right to decide whether the nation's resources should be privatized through an auction, sold off to foreigners or simply left in the ground. This principle is 'popular resource sovereignty'. Popular resource sovereignty is the principle that peoples everywhere have actually insisted upon across the past century to counter the powers that have oppressed them, and it is the principle that can counter the powers that continue to hound them today.

In the big picture, the world's transition to popular sovereignty is going well. In 1973, democratic countries were outnumbered by almost three to one. Today, the democracies form a majority.[16] Progress is good – except, as the Ross quotation above suggests, in the authoritarian oil exporters, where the regimes survive on an external source of power. Almost no country where the government is highly dependent on oil revenues has ever transitioned to democracy.[17] The struggle of these countries to overcome their resource-enriched 'kings' – some of whom even today maintain their divine rights – continues.

Popular resource sovereignty is a counterpowerful principle for the world we are in now, where authoritarians and armed groups can gain excessive power by selling off resources – and use that power to threaten the people of their own country and sometimes those of other countries as well. The real problem of power in our world is that it operates under the principle of what Pogge first identified as the 'international resource privilege':

> A group that overpowers the guards and takes control of a warehouse may be able to give some of the merchandise to others, accepting money in exchange. But the fence who pays them becomes merely the possessor, not the owner, of the loot. Contrast this with a group that overpowers an elected government and takes control of a country. Such a group, too, can give away some of the country's natural resources, accepting money in exchange. In this case, however, the purchaser acquires not merely possession, but all the rights and liberties of ownership, which are supposed to be – and actually *are* – protected and enforced by all other states' courts and police forces. (2008: 119)

Having wrested control over their territories' resources from foreign empires and armies, peoples now need power to counter the usurpation of their resources by 'internal colonialists' and domestic militias as well. Popular resource sovereignty is the principle that can frame policies for abolishing the international resource privilege and achieve that goal.

One great advantage to this approach from the perspective of power is that popular sovereignty is already the world's ideal. This is a legacy of the great twentieth-century struggles for national self-determination. Major treaties declaring popular resource sovereignty have already been ratified by nearly all nations; national leaders and mass movements reflexively speak its language.[18]

Popular resource sovereignty can also be seen as a transitional principle towards a more cosmopolitan future. Unlike the 'grind together' model of the redistributive cosmopolitans, popular resource sovereignty can advance a 'grow together' model of increasing transnational integration. The great promise of popular sovereignty is that self-determining nations do grow together. Democracies are less likely to go to war with each other. They are also more likely to create and participate in international institutions and more likely to respect international treaties (Christiano, 2011). Even better, national democracy is the best school known to make individuals capable of connecting across borders too.

To whatever extent a cosmopolitan future will arrive, it will require individuals who are able to act together despite the features that distinguish them. For that to be possible, individuals in many of today's resource-rich countries will have to become more democratically capable than they now are: more knowledgeable about the safe use of political power, more accustomed to the give-and-take of life within a self-ruling group. The surest way we know for these individual capacities to develop is within the institutions of popular sovereignty.[19]

The most judicious cosmopolitans praise the value of individuals freely associating to determine their common future (e.g. Beitz, 1999: 92–104; Caney, 2005: 177–81). Moving power over resources away from authoritarians and militias and towards sovereign peoples will advance that weighty goal. Those who wish to see power spread still further, from peoples to persons, can see popular resource sovereignty as a stage along their way.

Enabling peoples to control their fates and to grow together will make humans better able to choose for themselves the principles that might someday constitute a United Persons. Peacefully promoting popular sovereignty will encourage the kinds of relations across borders that may eventually allow justice to emerge in some richer form. In the meantime, strengthening peoples will enhance humanity's ability to meet its current and future challenges. If we can now succeed in countering the dangerous power that natural resources now bring in our world as it is, then perhaps we can then leave it to our more democratic and more united descendants to decide for themselves what forms of justice they want to reach for, given the relations they have formed, and the conditions of the world that they will see much better than we now do.

References

Armstrong, C. 2014. 'Justice and Attachment to Natural Resources', *Journal of Political Philosophy* 22: 48–65.

Armstrong, C. 2015. 'Against Permanent Sovereignty over Natural Resources', *Politics, Philosophy & Economics* 14: 129–151.

Barry, B. 1981. 'Do Countries Have Moral Obligations? The Case of World Poverty', in Sterling McMurrin, ed., *The Tanner Lectures on Human Values*, vol. 2, 25–44. Cambridge: Cambridge University Press.

Barry, B. 1982. 'Humanity and Justice in Global Perspective', *Nomos XXIV*: 219–252.

Beitz, C. 1999/1979. *Political Theory and International Relations*, rev. edn. Princeton, NJ: Princeton University Press.

Blake, M. and Risse, M. 2009. 'Immigration and Original Ownership of the Earth', *Notre Dame Journal of Law, Ethics & Public Policy* 133: 134.

Caney, S. 2005. *Justice Beyond Borders: A Global Political Theory*. Oxford: Oxford University Press.

Casal, P. 2011. 'Global Taxes on Natural Resources', *Journal of Moral Philosophy* 8: 307–327.

Christiano, T. 2011. 'An Instrumental Argument for a Human Right to Democracy', *Philosophy & Public Affairs* 39: 142–176.

Diamond, L. 2008. *The Spirit of Democracy*. New York: Holt.

Guizot, F. M. 1838. *General History of Civilization in Europe*, 2nd edn. Oxford: DA Talboys.

Kolers, A. 2009. *Land, Conflict and Justice: A Political Theory of Territory*. Cambridge: Cambridge University Press.

Locke, J. 1988/1689. *Two Treatises of Government*, ed. Peter Laslett. Cambridge: Cambridge University Press.

Mazor, J. 2009. 'A Liberal Theory of Natural Resource Property Rights', PhD thesis, Harvard University.

Mazor, J. 2010. 'Liberal Justice, Future People and Natural Resource Conservation', *Philosophy & Public Affairs* 38: 380–408.

Miller, D. 2007. *National Responsibility and Global Justice*. Oxford: Oxford University Press.

Miller, D. 2012. 'Territorial Rights: Concept and Justification', *Political Studies* 60(2): 252–268.

Moore, M. 2012. 'Natural Resources, Territorial Right, and Global Distributive Justice', *Political Theory* 40: 84–107.

Nine, C. 2008. 'A Lockean Theory of Territory', *Political Studies* 56: 148–165.

Nine, C. 2012. *Global Justice and Territory*. Oxford: Oxford University Press.

Nine, C. 2013. 'Resource Rights', *Political Studies* 61: 232–249.

Pogge, T. 1994. 'An Egalitarian Law of Peoples', *Philosophy & Public Affairs* 23: 195–224.

Pogge, T. 2008. *World Poverty and Human Rights*, 2nd edn. Cambridge: Polity.

Pogge, T. 2011. 'Allowing the Poor to Share the Earth', *Journal of Moral Philosophy* 8: 335–352.

Rawls, J. 1999. *The Law of Peoples*. Cambridge, MA: Harvard University Press.

Risse, M. 2012. *On Global Justice*. Princeton, NJ: Princeton University Press.

Ross, M. 2012. *The Oil Curse*. Princeton, NJ: Princeton University Press.

Schrijver, N. 2008. *Sovereignty over Natural Resources*. Cambridge: Cambridge University Press.

Simmons, A. J. 2001. 'On the Territorial Rights of States', *Philosophical Issues* 11: 300–326.

Simmons, A. J. 'Territorial Rights: Justificatory Strategies', working paper. www.law.upenn.edu/live/files/1284-simmons–territorialrights-strategies-2pdf.

Steiner, H. 2004. *An Essay on Rights*. Oxford: Blackwell.

Steiner, H. 2011a. 'The Global Fund: A Reply to Casal', *Journal of Moral Philosophy* 8: 328–334.

Steiner, H. 2011b. 'Sharing Mother Nature's Gifts: A Reply to Quong and Miller', *Journal of Political Philosophy* 19(1): 110–123.

Stilz, A. 2009. 'Why Do States Have Territorial Rights?' *International Theory* 1: 185–213.

Stilz, A. 2011. 'Nations, States, and Territory', *Ethics* 121: 572–601.

Wenar, L. 2016. *Blood Oil*. Oxford: Oxford University Press.

Ypi, L. 2011. *Global Justice and Avant-Garde Political Agency*. Oxford: Oxford University Press.

CHAPTER ELEVEN

Fairness in Trade

Aaron James

When is trade between countries fair? The answer depends on how we resolve a consequential ambiguity in the language of 'fair trade'. The term has both interpersonal and institutional meanings, and rival conceptions of fairness give one or the other meaning explanatory priority.

The interpersonal meaning of 'fair trade' refers to *transactions* between market actors that reach across borders, nearly always as part of complicated supply chains. Thus, for example, we might take care not to deceive or coerce a buyer or seller, and perhaps pay a premium for certified 'fair trade' coffee or clothes or electronics in the hope of not being complicit in the developing country farmer's or factory worker's seemingly unfair wages.[1] The institutional meaning, by contrast, refers to the *international trading system*, and the unfairness, for example, of rich country farm subsidies that impoverish developing world farmers, or of World Trade Organization (WTO) prohibitions (e.g., on export subsidies and infant industry protection) that inhibit industrial development, to the general benefit of rich countries. Here the concern is not with any given market exchange, or chain of production via relations among transnational firms, but rather with the larger set of 'embedding' social relations that create and shape the flow of goods, services or capital, in view of their larger socioeconomic consequences for the wealth of nations.

Linguistically speaking, it is a curious fact that the language of 'fair trade' is used in such different ways. Philosophically speaking, the question arises of whether the two meanings are finally separable. Might a principled account of the one allow us to understand or explain the other?

According to one such explanation, fairness in international trade is primarily, or even simply, a matter of fairness in separate trades. Institutions count as fair according to whether they facilitate cross-border exchanges for fair, mutual personal gain. On a right-libertarian version, minimal states would protect people against wrongful force and fraud, but otherwise leave outcomes to the market, in the hope that voluntary exchange for mutual benefit will emerge the world over. A Marxist variant adds further institutions, of property and politics, in order to protect relatively disadvantaged workers from exploitation, by ensuring that labour agreements give workers their fair share of the firm's cooperative surplus. And on a distributional egalitarian version, still further institutions would help the mass of separate exchanges along, not only in advancing human welfare, but also in equalizing life prospects for people worldwide (this is one reading of Julius, 2013,

2014). The general approach shares the idea that interpersonal fairness, perhaps mediated by institutions, explains fairness generally.

An opposing approach – which I modestly call 'world-historical' – takes the institutional meaning as its point of departure.[2] Our task as theorists, on this approach, is not to formulate our own favoured ideal for global economic life, but rather to say what people are owed in the global economy as we know it, roughly as received from history, in the hope of intervening in major decisions about its overall shape and future direction. We thus begin from our best understanding of its organizing social practice, in view of its history and our best evidence about the available directions for its future in coming centuries (e.g., James, 2005b, 2006, 2012, 2014a; Risse, 2007, 2013; Risse and Kurjanska, 2008; Risse and Wollner, 2014). On one interpretation, for instance, the global economy is constituted by an international social practice, in which whole societies mutually rely on common markets, for the sake of augmenting their national incomes (James, 2012: ch. 2). Accordingly, it may be added, fairness is chiefly an *international* rather than interpersonal issue: claims of fairness against the resulting gains in national income, seen as the fruit of specifically international cooperation, are held by the societies that principally uphold the practice (although individuals may have separate claims to a fair share of their societies' fair share) (James, 2012: ch. 5).

On a straightforward reading, a 'transactions first' approach offers an ahistorical ideal of fair transactional arrangements, which makes no essential reference to the state practices and institutions that in fact historically explain the emergence of a global economy. Those systems may help fair trade along, but if they don't, or if they become a hindrance, we can simply call for their abandonment in the name of the favoured independent idea of fair trade (in favour of anarchy, minimal states or a global state, depending). The world-historical approach, by comparison, can see the global economic order as an emergent subsystem of the modern state system. Governments face the familiar question of removing barriers to international trade only when political authority is divided over different territorial jurisdictions, and the contemporary global economy reflects the historical success of government coordination around open border policies. This is a contingent achievement and, even now, we can perhaps realistically imagine governments closing borders down (as they did, more or less, during the interwar years, and as they might have – but didn't – in the more recent Great Recession). But the background state system itself, on this picture, is taken largely as given, not only as our inheritance from modernity, but also as our only available option for the foreseeable future. For, it may be argued, we are at best highly uncertain about how a completely radical departure, rather than deep reform, would actually work. (For different versions of this point, see de Bres, 2011; James, 2012: ch. 4; Risse, 2013: ch. 3.)

So, for the world-historical approach, trade relations are not so many market transactions in the first instance, and if there is a further question of transactional fairness, it is a separate question. In that case, if our hope was to illuminate one meaning of 'fair trade' by the other, it would seem that only the 'transactions first' version offers an explanatory proposal: institutions are fair insofar as they advance fair exchange. In treating the trading system as a relatively autonomous subject of evaluation, a world-historical approach offers nothing so direct or immediate in the opposite direction of explanation. Indeed, on one possible version, market choices are a 'morally free zone' (Gauthier, 1986: ch. 4; and for a general defence of morality in the market, see Satz, 2010).

It could be, of course, that the term 'fair trade' is simply ambiguous. And one might simply be, as many economists are, sceptical about whether fairness applies in market choices. But a world-historical approach can also take a less sceptical position, by simply providing a further account of how institutional fairness bears on personal obligation. It may be said, for example, that, although institutions come first, we inherit certain personal obligations in our market choices and political relations by virtue of being involved in the larger international practice of trade, as a matter of indirect associative obligation.

In this discussion, my aim is to develop some key features of this position. While trade is my focus, I mean to indirectly address the more general question of the relation between interpersonal morality and the morality of institutions.[3] The social contract tradition, especially in Hobbes and Locke (and perhaps also Kant), powerfully advanced the idea that interpersonal morality in a 'state of nature' is not only independent of political morality, but in some sense *primary*: it dictates the moral form and even bare permissibility of any society, before we are in a position to pose the question of justice in international relations. My own view is that this picture, although useful for some analytical purposes, is largely misleading. Indeed, its main rival is often simply not appreciated, and I suggest that examining the relation between interpersonal and institutional obligations of 'fair trade' can help show how political philosophy could instead be relatively autonomous from interpersonal morality. We see how its bounds could be set, not by possibilities of personal action and independent ideas of interpersonal right or duty, but by world-historical moment, which is to say, by the basic social forms we inherit from prior generations and the credible directions for their future, from a historically given point of departure. When the morality of personal action bears on larger questions of social justice, the bearing is mainly that of subservience to what each era of humanity can collectively make of itself in its most basic, historically given social practices.

I take this to be true of the state itself, however often the state has been taken in isolation. Every state has evolved within the modern state system, which divides presumptive rights of sovereignty to political groups across distinct territorial units worldwide. The shape of the just state – including its territorial demarcation – depends on what is justifiable within this larger social practice, a distinctive creation of the modern era (see James, forthcoming). But here I develop the world-historical approach by focusing on the trading system. It is more plainly a creation of recent times. And because it stands one step removed from ruling the lives of individuals, it usefully highlights a central reason for the autonomy of political philosophy: the limits of our personal powers, and our personal obligations, in the face of things world-historical.

1   Personal and Institutional Fairness

If the 'transactions first' approach suggests how the two meanings of 'fair trade' might be related, its primary challenge is to account for the appearance that they are distinct. For the two concepts have very different preoccupations. In an institutional argument against unfair rich world farm subsidies, whether or not I buy coffee or cotton or corn, at any price, is not immediately relevant, if only because my market choices, taken alone, make no difference to the consequences chiefly at issue. As a consumer, one usually has at best a very indirect and limited causal and/or evidentiary relation to the important outcomes of larger social structures, which only emerge because of the way large patterns of action are coordinated. What *is* plainly at issue is a larger choice of policy, which does determine whether the coffee farmer stays in business, what prospects he or she sees over a lifetime, and whether one has the option to consume his or her beans in the first place. The trading system thus initially appears to present a relatively autonomous site of fairness assessment. We can object to farm subsidies without trying to say whether I have any particular obligation to buy 'fair trade'.

I also would seem to have certain personal obligations. I presumably shouldn't deceive or coerce a buyer or seller, at the very least. And even in more diffuse relations, when one has very good reason to believe that certain goods are produced by slave labour, or other sufficiently outrageous processes of production, buying them can seem intrinsically objectionable; to profit from the gross injustice, even at the far end of a long supply chain, is not something one could possibly justify to the mistreated persons if they were to ask why this should be acceptable. Even so, this also can seem true in only a limited range of cases. Often, and indeed normally, a given individual's market choices will 'make no difference' at all (not even an imperceptible one) without assurances that enough others are choosing likewise. In the normal conditions of life in commercial society, one lacks any very good evidence about one's specific relation to sufficiently objectionable outcomes, in which case one's reasons to forbear will usually depend on whether one has sufficient assurances that enough others are making choices that coordinate in favourable directions.

One might say that one should therefore simply leave fairness out of one's market choices and take political action instead.[4] If structural change really can make a difference for fairness, should one should skip the 'fair trade' coffee and, instead, seek to influence policy – whether by taking to the streets in protest of the US farm bill or of the NAFTA-style investment provisions in new trade agreements; or by writing a blog post or letter to the editor; or by advising an international organization, if asked; or by joining or starting a nongovernmental organization (NGO)? Yet it is not clear why there should be a special problem for market choices. One will have no special assurances of 'making a difference' in politics, either; the influence of one's vote or one's presence at a protest will only matter in conjunction with the like conduct of many others, in which case any difference in assurance in comparison to market choices will be a matter of degree, perhaps depending on the political or the market context at issue.

In fact, 'fair trade' certification schemes often recognize the need for assurance by trying to provide it: one is invited to presume that enough others really are complying in their market choices such that one's participation, via the purchase of 'fair trade' products, at least has a chance of advancing a worthy social objective. Are we then obliged in fairness to buy 'fair trade'? Paying a premium for certified products seems reasonable enough when the cost to oneself is low, and when there are high chances that one's contribution would mitigate unfair disadvantages, or promote fair demands for economic development. If one is, in some very diffuse way, causally complicit in the farmer's or the factory worker's objectionably low pay and dangerous working conditions, then paying a premium would seem only fair, or at least would form part of one's responsibility in fairness. And yet it remains true, as suggested, that one will rarely have very good evidence about the outcomes of any scheme in particular, let alone evidence that one's own part in it makes very much of a difference, if any. The risk is not simply that of pointless or excessively costly personal sacrifice. Acting without assurances also has expected moral opportunity costs, to alternative moral aims that one might support instead. For any extra money spent for uncertain gains in the name of trade fairness is money not spent on other worthy causes, such as climate change mitigation or direct poverty relief.

This problem depends on a crucial assumption: that we are to consider only the expected influence of a given person's choice, taken by itself. But certification schemes can instead be seen to have a specifically institutional objective: not to help individuals make a personal difference to worthy outcomes, but to establish social practice that *itself* makes a difference, which individuals might then personally support. One's aim could be to materially support a 'fair trade' scheme, or simply to help to send a collective message, at once a market signal and a political demand. If enough of us join the cause, we might signal our view that 'sweatshops' and the transnational firms that do business with them should be raising wages and improving working conditions. If together we 'vote' with our pocketbooks, rewarding 'good firms' with our support while punishing the 'bad firms' by withholding it, then it is hoped that firms will respond, much as they respond to any market signal, but with the added tug of reasonable moral expectation, and perhaps even pangs of conscience.

Here again, assurances matter; much still depends on whether or to what extent such schemes can be supposed to translate into favourable outcomes. It matters whether or not they mainly worsen the plights of desperate workers, who are rising from poverty and would be even worse off if unemployed. But consumer-driven change also wouldn't have to be a panacea to have a worthwhile effect. It may be enough if they supplement, rather than substitute for, more traditional top-down regulation that benefits workers directly (Locke, 2013; see also James, 2012: ch. 10).

All of this suggests that market choices are not a 'morally free zone'. If we take appearances at face value, the question becomes how we should understand what we are each responsible for, in view of the nature and basis of such responsibilities in principle. I will tentatively assume that we have different responsibilities in different contexts, some of which apply to institutions, others to individuals. In that case, we can now more fully characterize one potential class of personal obligations: the personal obligations we have in relation to institutional fairness.

2   Obligations of Personal Fairness

In trade relations, in contrast with the domestic state, there is no legal order that lays claim to our personal obedience as persons. The rules of international trade – even when we include administrative or judicial rulings on their meaning – are addressed primarily to states, and to persons only in official capacities. So we can't be said to have the traditional duty to obey the sovereign's directives. Yet international rules and institutions do plausibly purport to exercise power in legitimate ways, and they can be said to ask for our acceptance, at least implicitly, on pain of public objection, within emerging forums for broadly democratic accountability. Even beyond the formalities of domestic electoral democracy, international 'governance' is now often subject to non-official influence and suasion. Various modes of 'transnational governance', from NGOs to social networks to public protests, not only direct the flow of information, ideas and expertise, but also serve to hold officials accountable for official decisions, as legitimated within a public political culture that can be said to embody a kind of 'global public reason' (Cohen, 2006–7).

Here, I will for the moment take as given the going basic political framework of the state system and the various international regimes. One question, in that case, is what obligations we might have in relation to these larger opportunities for governance, in virtue of the trading system's implicit claim to legitimacy. One answer comes in the following framework of obligations, which (while perhaps incomplete) at least covers a wide range of choice situations for market and political action. Each obligation can be either 'perfect' or 'imperfect', and admit of special justifications, in special circumstances.

First, we plausibly have basic *duties of acquiescence*: we each have a stringent duty to comply, or at least not to interfere, with established, sufficiently fair practices, to the extent our choices are relevant to them. Even if the citizen is not personally addressed with a directive of action (e.g., in an IMF ruling intended to direct state choices), we are obliged to at least not interfere with compliance when our conduct is relevant (e.g., one decides not to take to the streets in protest, or to refrain from calling for the IMF's outright abolition).

One can arguably have such an obligation even when it has not been assumed voluntarily; the social practice in question need only be of sufficiently great importance to others.[5] According to the duty, however, when the policies in question are not 'sufficiently fair', one is not necessarily obliged to acquiesce. So if WTO rules are grossly unfair (as, e.g., TRIPS rules arguably are; James, 2012: ch. 9), one might permissibly call for their abandonment or non-enforcement, perhaps by taking to the streets or writing an op-ed, even if no positive reform is being proposed. Unconventional forms of protest or expression may also be permissible when a group (e.g., poor farmers) is deprived of effective mechanisms for making demands for change.[6] (The public suicide committed by a Korean farmer in 2003 at the WTO meeting in Cancun was surely supererogatory; if it was nevertheless permissible, this would only be true given the importance of the issue in question.) Even with no positive reform on offer, the point of protest may simply be to urge that *something* major must give. The beneficiaries of unjust institutions cannot reasonably complain of such purely negative protests per se, especially when they are peacefully voiced, perhaps despite considerable disruption. Along with some limits on time, place and manner, it is only when the general point of an institution is threatened, and this would deny others of very important benefits, that beneficiaries might have grounds for objection (for further discussion of such limitations, see Scanlon, 2010).

Second, we plausibly have further *reform responsibilities*: when a new rule, policy or platform would credibly advance the cause of fairness, and one has evidence of a critical mass of effective support, one has a duty to do what can be expected to help in the adoption or maintenance of that cause, at a moderate or even significant expected cost to oneself. Advocacy or protest that can be expected to help lead to reform may be not only permissible, but also required. (One's duty of acquiescence not to interfere with 'sufficiently fair' established rules might be satisfied as long as this would not jeopardize what fairness has already been achieved.) One might thus vote for certain officials or parties, and support their political campaigns, when they credibly promise fair reforms and have sufficiently good chances of winning. But at the very least, one would have to make one's willingness to join the proposed cooperative equilibrium known to others, as well as accept an appropriate sacrifice as a signal of good faith, for instance, by making a (perhaps merely symbolic) point of buying 'fair trade' often enough. One may be required to make the political point even if, for lack of wide compliance with the reform policy at the moment (perhaps despite avowed support in principle), one has little assurance that one's particular sacrifice (e.g., the 'fair trade' premium paid) will make any further difference. (This may not be required when it comes at a high expected moral opportunity cost, as when one could instead, directly, assuredly relieve someone's condition of destitution. In that case, one could still rightly donate the premium to the impoverished man down the street.)

Third, in certain further cases, we plausibly have *bandwagon duties* to comply as a reform practice is catching on, before fully 'general' compliance has taken hold and even before a critical mass of effective support has been achieved, at least provided that there is decent evidence of support at some basic level. One's reform responsibilities might not yet apply, because support has not yet reached a critical level, but, with decent evidence of support at some basic level, one may have a (perhaps less stringent) duty to join cause at an increasing level of sacrifice to oneself, as the reform practice gains prominence. Assuming that 'fair trade' cooperatives can be expected to at least help prospects for otherwise unfairly treated workers in the developing world *if* they attract wide enough attention, one may be required to back them, even without assurances that sufficiently wide support has taken hold. Perhaps, for all one knows, the sacrifice in paying the premium may well be pointless, or come with moral opportunity costs. Even so, one can be obliged to take one's chances (that is, provided that one does indeed have decent evidence that the practice is catching on, or attracting support at or beyond some basic level).

Fourth, in still further cases, we plausibly have *duties of cause* to take up a worthy reform effort, in vanguard action, in the mere hope that compliance and basic support will catch on. While bandwagon duties may require joining the reform efforts of others only after support achieves a basic level, one may also have sufficient reason to find and initiate activities that offer a reasonable hope of attracting a critical mass of effective support. For such ventures, a significant expected cost to oneself would be called for even when one has no assurance that others will come on board. When they assuredly won't join the cause, one is presumably obliged to try something else. But when the matter is at least uncertain, and exploratory efforts are needed to find out what has a reasonable chance of success, one might be obliged to invest a significant part of one's income in the discovery process. This may be required even if much of the expenditure goes to waste (or at least pays only in information about what will or will not finally work).

3   Revolutionary Duties?

Later, I explain how emergent international trade practice might give rise to principled structural demands of its own. I also elaborate on how the personal responsibilities described above can be seen to arise because of our personal involvement in the market relations created by international trade practice. Such 'indirect associative obligations', I want to suggest, fully account for our personal responsibilities of fairness, quite aside from natural duty.

By stipulation, the obligations I have been discussing apply to opportunities to shape governance *within* the going basic political framework of the state system and the various international regimes. I take it that continuous structural reform, in domestic or international affairs, depends on the steady fulfilment of such obligations, by an engaged, politically active, networked and perhaps transnational populace. Yet, at least as far as we've seen so far, these obligations would not call for the fomentation or even support of revolutionary action. They show that a world-historical approach can be supplemented to account for a range of significant personal fairness obligations, and they do so precisely because, as stated, they are consistent with taking the basic existence of international trade practice for granted.

But is this unduly conservative? Consider what may be called the *revolutionary's objection*. In view of the independent force of interpersonal morality, it may be said, we surely owe things to the developing world coffee farmer, aside from any economic associations. We owe things to him or her qua fellow human, if only as a matter of natural duty. But, it may be objected, that alone precludes taking the international trading system as a starting point for moral reflection. It also potentially obliges us to try to bring about something completely different, something fundamentally fairer. One version of this objection goes so far as to propose revolution. In a Marxian version, for instance, workers of the world should unite against a capitalist global economy that exploits them, seizing any chance to usher in a more socialistic, egalitarian system of property, and perhaps the 'withering away' of the very state and state system itself. But the present objection can claim only that we must persistently ask the *question* of revolution, in which case a theory of justice must leave the possibility open, as, for instance, many (often non-Marxist) 'cosmopolitan' views do (see Pogge, 1992; Held, 1995; Beitz, 1999/1979; Moellendorf, 2002; Tan 2004; Caney, 2006; Gillian, 2009). Although revolution may ultimately be unnecessary, we owe it to each person of the world to at least be open to, and perhaps on the lookout for, that possibility.

Does interpersonal fairness really have this force? I suggest not. The demands of interpersonal morality in global economic life seem more modest, given the limitations of our personal powers.

Rawls's natural duty of justice is often invoked to explain why we might have reason to take action in the name of potentially radical, perhaps 'cosmopolitan' visions of a just global order. In Rawls's own formulation, however, the duty assumes an independent conception of justice for institutions (what he calls 'principles for social forms'), and is therefore fully consistent with taking such institutions to have autonomous application and justification, quite aside from interpersonal morality (Rawls, 1971: 110, 115; James, 2005a).[7] The duty's first part concerns institutions that exist, are just and apply to us (e.g., a domestic legal order). In that case, everything depends on the prior question of social interpretation and moral reasoning about what such institutions are like. The duty's second part adds that we can be asked to further 'just arrangements not yet established', at least at a 'reasonable' cost to ourselves. In that case, however, the duty will not ask one to act in support of revolutionary arrangements at an unreasonable level of sacrifice – whether because of high personal cost, or simply for lack of assurance that enough others will join the cause. Insofar as this is our usual situation as individuals, any reason we have to take up revolutionary actions will not then rise to the level of a normally conclusive moral obligation.

But *might* one be so called, in certain possible scenarios, in which case the duty would apply? If so, this is a properly controversial extension or interpretation of Rawls's stated duty. On an alternative conception, a moral principle has an essential regulatory function. A regulative moral principle, it may be said, is addressed to an agent as a normally conclusive expectation for action in some relevant circumstances (barring special or extenuating justifications), which the agent in question is asked to work into his or her plans, even before the moment of performance. If I'm required to aid the needy, I'm equally required to budget my finances accordingly, before I find myself in front of someone asking for assistance (Scanlon, 1998: 203, suggests this point in developing the regulative conception of a moral principle just described). By the same token, as long as one cannot be reasonably expected to plan for revolutionary actions, if only because the occasion for them is too unlikely for planning purposes, the natural duty of justice would not require them, even as a matter of principle. Working in the cause of revolution might be worthy and laudable, but it would not be *owed* to others, as a matter of natural duty or otherwise.

To be sure, on rare occasions, one may have a real chance of *domestic* political revolution, or at least major, sudden reform. Perhaps one lives under an odious regime, and on the days when the likelihood of a bloodbath is low (depending on what is afoot in Tahrir Square), one presumably can and really should march, despite risks of stray bullets and manhandling by police. But this is not to say that the average person is equally obliged to stand ready for action that might somehow overthrow the whole fabric of political life. Should one stand ready to support a *global* scale transformation that goes beyond a deep reform within the current general framework for human social cooperation? If so, one would want to know whether one should be prepared not only to call in sick or use vacation time from work, while arranging childcare, but also whether to amass the savings needed to weather an uncertain aftermath, and thereby forgo buying a house, or sending the kids to college or giving to charity. The matter seems too uncertain for proper personal planning, in a way that bears not simply on *how* applicable principles of personal action apply, but on what principles of conduct apply at all, even as a matter of basic expectation.

The framework of personal obligations outlined earlier is sensitive to such considerations of cost, risk and assurance. So their relevance does not, per se, undermine the positive obligations whose steady fulfilment is so crucial for steady, progressive reform. The present suggestion is that interpersonal morality does not seem to require something still more demanding.

The foregoing point, about the relevance of uncertainty to personal expectations for action, equally bears on what one can be required to do in cooperation with others, for the sake of ends achievable only through cooperation. As suggested earlier, one will need assurances about the conduct of others in order to go ahead with something one wants to call 'one's part' in a larger pattern of conduct. Otherwise, one risks pointless sacrifice, or excessive costs to oneself or – still more important – opportunity costs to moral ends one might have pursued instead. If I'm asking whether I am obliged to join a possible protest later today, instead of staying home and helping a poor neighbour down the street, or of doing fundraising or website maintenance for an NGO that builds water tanks in villages far away, I won't be obliged to show if there's a real risk that too few other protesters will gather, because the cause isn't especially salient at the moment. I won't have a bandwagon duty without a critical mass of engagement. And I won't have a duty of cause if I'm in the middle of promoting a good cause on some other front in the spare time I have away from work.

To be sure, by standing ready to seize any opportunities to support dramatic, even radical, changes, in the name of what one owes to each person of the world, one might make a special kind of social contribution. Perhaps, simply for keeping that frame of mind, I then see oft-ignored social possibilities and, at some point, have occasion to take a stand for them, perhaps inspiring others to do likewise. Perhaps I thus fulfil my duty of cause. At the same time, especially in global-sized affairs, truly revolutionary moments rarely, if ever, happen in a normal person's lifetime (on most versions of 'normality'), and one does not seem morally obligated to vigilantly stay on the lookout for such an exceedingly low probability happening. If some are called to man the watchtower, surely the duty of cause can be fulfilled in more modest ways.

This is not to deny or weaken one's reform responsibility to support appropriate institutional reforms through political action. As suggested, this may require one to buy 'fair trade' products as an expression of good faith. Even then, however, the issue of fairness wouldn't be one of personal market exchange between oneself and the coffee farmer, or any of the innumerable intermediaries on either side of our 'transaction'. The issue is still international rather than interpersonal fairness in trade, and so fully consistent with reform, rather than a complete replacement, of the international trading system.

Nor, then, will a complete replacement be morally required as long as we are sufficiently uncertain about what that might be like, except in the roughest of detail (a 'global state' or 'federation' like the EU or the US). Whether or not it is eligible as a real social possibility, as a future form of global-sized cooperation, would depend on millions or billions of people coming to understand, in sufficient detail, how a new world order might work in practice. Even if enough of them could come to understand, well enough, in the fullness of time, it would remain a further question when that time could possibly come, and whether there is any real chance, in the foreseeable future, that enough people would actually move together to a new but risky equilibrium, on a timeframe that bears on present action.

The risks in question here aren't simply a matter of predictable lack of concern for fairness, which we can idealize for purposes of 'ideal theory'. The basic problem of assurance can arise even among morally motivated people (James, 2012: ch. 4). Given the risks of unilateral action to moral goals that one might have advanced instead, what risks one can be reasonably asked to take, for exactly what sorts of action, depends on the public emergence of pretty good evidence that a better equilibrium may, or will indeed, take hold soon enough, along with the establishment of some common understanding of why a radically new order would be needed, because deep reform morally won't do. If speculation about total replacements, about the 'withering away' of the state system, could only be (admittedly fascinating and useful) speculation, we can still sensibly ask: why should it command our moral confidence? Would the proposed moral gains be large and likely enough to justify all the risks of venturing into wholly unknown, possibly dangerous territory, in which, morally speaking, the cure could well be worse than the disease?

While the force of such substantive concerns will of course vary across different policy contexts, my main point is that they have a general rationale in the limited nature of our personal powers.[8] At least when it comes to the very basic social forms that organize human social life, including the state system and basic system of trade, our predicament as persons is that we are mainly bound up in the social worlds we are born into. With rare exceptions, the normal plight of individual human agents is marked not only by the basic limits of their mental and physical capacities, but also by the risks of working with others – including the risks to morally important goals – that accompany any attempt at cooperation. Perhaps, over a decade or lifetime, one can hope to help to make larger things a little bit better as the opportunity arises. Occasionally, a few concerted souls of good will can indeed spur major change (though usually with the help of considerable talent, resources, expertise and fortuitously aligned events). As global politics gradually develops the mechanisms of informal democracy, we do have increasing opportunities for activism. And yet, because we are each generally limited in what we can personally expect to accomplish, our obligations for progressive action largely concern our role in collective action.

In a related vein, Rawls points to the limits of personal motivation, as a matter of normal social and psychological tendencies. The task of global political philosophy, he says, is to propose a 'realistic utopia', whose mere credible possibility would reconcile us to our social condition (1999: 12, 128). What is 'realistic' depends on 'conjecture and speculation' about credibly available futures, given our basic social institutions and our best current evidence about human nature. As for exactly how credible the chances must be, Rawls does not say; he does not say, for example, that a proposed vision must be likely, let alone highly likely. What is crucial is that the conjecture be credible enough to provide reasonable grounds for hope (even if not expectation) to those who might advance the proposed vision; they must be able to find it within themselves to persist in what may be costly and protracted efforts of social reform, without slipping into resignation and despair. As attractive as a revolutionary ideal might be to the theorist, then, if the ideal isn't 'realistic' enough to keep hope reasonable, it isn't 'social justice' in the relevant enabling sense. It won't count as a conception of justice that advances political philosophy's distinctive way of trying to shape, or enable the shaping of, history's direction.

In the case of trade fairness, the parallel point would be that a central task of a theory of fairness is to justify the more plausible complaints of WTO protesters, to bolster NGO reform work, and to enable public officials to move trade policy and law further towards fairness, in legislation, administrative rulings and treaty negotiations. In protesting grossly unfair farm subsidies, farmers aren't asking for a radically different global economic order, but for major reforms to the state-based global economy as we know it, which may dramatically improve the coffee or cotton farmer's existence. A central task of philosophy is to say why this sort of demand is justified, in a way that enables such efforts at reform, normatively and motivationally, whether or not global revolution is forthcoming, or even imaginable.

So, as a matter of substantive obligation, the revolutionary's objection seems unmotivated. Or at least interpersonal morality is not inconsistent with taking our given basic social practices as political philosophy's presumptive point of departure.

4 Normative Political Philosophy

In political philosophy, it matters where one starts, what one takes as given. And yet any question of social justice must take at least *some* things as simply given. We'll presumably need people on hand who have some chance of interacting (being roughly co-located in space and time, as Kant suggested). And we'll have to assume something like a common human condition, lest any presumed circumstances seem simply unrecognizable to us.

To such givens, a world-historical approach to trade fairness, or social justice generally, adds the bounds set by history for personal and collective action (Nagel, 2005; Beitz, 2009).[9] Within the era in question (suitably identified), we assume the basic social forms inherited from prior generations, and we ask what justice demands among the credibly available versions of their future, starting from a historically given point of departure, where 'credible availability' is shaped by the going (usually evolving) state of human knowledge.[10]

Other approaches take less for granted, perhaps much less. A *wholly* unbounded approach would simply ask what people the world over are owed if justice is to obtain. Beyond assuming people and goods or well-being to be distributed, not even the basic human condition is a given. Indeed, its ugly reality might itself be the unfortunate, undeserved cause of justice's never coming to be (as on some versions of luck egalitarianism). On a slightly more bounded version, justice must be feasible in the human condition (on some specification), but needn't be, or have ever been, available, by any historical path, from any actual historical condition. On a still more bounded version, justice must be available to real people at *some* point, though the moment of possibility may have been long lost to history, and now be forever unavailable in the future. And on still another, even more bounded, version, justice must be available in the future, for a given generation, though perhaps only as a matter of *metaphysical* possibility, quite aside from what may be the unfortunate state of human knowledge at a given era of history. Depending on the progress of human understanding, we may still never know enough to get very far in justice's direction. What all such versions share is the idea that justice, or fairness, global or otherwise, is not bounded to a given era of history, either in what social forms people happen to inherit or in what might then be credible for their future.

Suppose for the moment, for the sake of argument, that a properly central aim of political philosophy is to intervene in political argument in a given era of world history. A central task of political philosophy – not its *only* task, but an essential task, of *central* importance – is to say what we now ought to do, as a principled matter of what justice, or fairness, requires of us. Justice, or fairness, would then be 'normative for us' in just that sense: its principles say what specified real-world political agents normally have sufficient reason to do, absent extenuating circumstances, and despite a range of competing considerations and the inevitable risks and uncertainties of collective or personal action. In that case, it may be argued, a world-historical approach is natural, appropriate – and arguably necessary – if political philosophy is to rise to one of its most important occasions.

The approach would be necessary insofar as all relatively unbounded approaches leave their favoured ideals (in one or another sense) 'unavailable to us'. To the extent that this is true, by their own admission, they can't claim to have offered an answer to political philosophy's 'normative' question, at least not without some further argument about their favoured ideal's availability and practical significance. And, for this, it won't suffice to say merely that we have *some* reason to advance a favoured ideal, as practicality permits – if it ever permits. If the reason we have is merely a worthy ideal, and normally insufficient to outweigh competing values, it still won't count as *normative*, in the intended strong sense. For all that says, no principles of justice ever give rise to any normally sufficient reasons for action, despite a range of competing values.[11] Justice is 'fine for a perfect world', as conservatives sometimes put it, but not, alas, necessary for us.

Now let us suppose, again for the sake of argument, that political philosophy can rightly have other aims as well. We might simply seek to explain our own convictions about justice to ourselves, without regard to practicality (except insofar as that, too, reflects pure conviction) (Cohen, 2008). Then an unbounded theory might be necessary – at least for this particular objective. Yet the world-historical approach can simply admit this. Why not admit an unbounded theory for any purposes of sufficient theoretical interest? Why can't a thousand flowers bloom in political philosophy's garden? Surely we can welcome any clarification on offer. The world-historical theorist engaged in normative political philosophy would only insist that an unbounded theory does not serve *all* of political philosophy's central purposes. It won't help political philosophy rise to one of its most important occasions, as interesting and clarifying as it may otherwise be, if it largely neglects the strongly 'normative' demands of justice.

Such ecumenism about the aims of political philosophy invites the question: why not further enlarge the tent, by admitting different and perhaps less demanding conceptions of 'normativity'? Could we not have diverse and blooming flowers even within the world-historical approach? In theory, we could take the international trading system in some very general way for granted, without supposing that principles of fairness should be tailored very closely to the nature and aim of a going practice, with any degree of sensitivity to prevailing social understandings. In which case one might wonder: why then be sensitive to given practice, to any great degree, or at all?

My own account of fairness in the international trading system is highly practice-sensitive for at least one key reason: it seeks a high degree of credibility in the demands of fairness it purports to justify (James, 2012). Consistent with the world-historical approach, it begins with the question of how, if at all, the global economy as we know it might generate responsibilities of fairness in its own right. I answer by looking to the nature of the global economy's organizing social practice, an international practice of market reliance, whose aim is the augmentation of national incomes. My general method is to justify principles, by moral reasoning, for a social practice, identified and characterized by way of (perhaps 'constructive') social interpretation (James, 2005a, 2012, 2013b). And while a constructive interpretation of its understood aims and organization might pay relatively little deference to prevailing, even if 'implicit' social understandings – in Dworkin's terms, it might put 'fit' behind 'value' – my own 'catholic' methodology of interpretation hews closely to its given animating understandings (see James, 2013b, 2014b). It is partly for this reason that I take the understood aim of trade practice to be the augmentation of national incomes, and why I take trading societies, rather than individuals, to be the primary claimants to national income gains, seen as the fruit of specifically international cooperation. Other conceptions of 'the aim of trade' may be more attractive to us as theorists; but they rightly take a backseat to prevailing social understandings, for the sake of credible address.

But why, one may then ask, isn't the 'forward-looking' question of feasibility all that matters? Why should 'backward-looking' questions about the social nature of what we've inherited from history be relevant? And then why be so deferential to given social understandings, instead of offering a fresh and attractive alternative? If there are perhaps different possible approaches, all of which are to be compared on their overall merits, my general answer is that a 'catholic' approach serves the aims of normative political philosophy. It seeks to go beyond justifying conclusive demands of fairness simply by our own lights as theorists, so as to justify them in a way that makes them plain to those to whom the demands are addressed.[12]

To elaborate: as suggested earlier, a centrally important task of political philosophy is to address public life with principled conclusions about what ought to be done, at least under certain normal circumstances. As Rawls suggests, following Rousseau, any reasons people do have, especially in the form of normally conclusive principles that we morally expect them to follow in practice, have to be *available* to them from where they are – 'taking men as they are' – by some credible, perhaps constructive, stretch of their given reasoning and motivational capacities. When principles are not already accepted, but supposedly available upon reflection, the burden falls to us, as theorists, to make the force of those principles plain to those who might intelligently and in good faith consider the matter. The practice-based method of justification, especially on its 'catholic' variation, is a way for us to rise to this potentially difficult justificatory task.

How so? Because the method offers a way of proposing principles that are recognizable as normally conclusive requirements for action, rather than mere worthy and perhaps readily overridden values, on a basis that is available to the agents being addressed. We credibly address a practice under way, given its understood structure and purposes. Because its participants will have some understandings of its workings, or at least the basis for gaining a deeper understanding beyond what may be their superficial awareness of its elements, we can say that they are in a position to grasp and admit demands of fairness that arise and apply to them by virtue of the relationship they're already in. If they've understood the argument, they won't be in a position to slough off a particular demand as a mere worthy ideal, which is not applicable to them, or as 'fine for an ideal world' but otherwise 'impractical' or 'too utopian'. We'll have given them an argument that the principles are indeed normative for them: they not only, in fact, have certain normally conclusive reasons for action; they can see this for themselves, in part by way of understanding themselves.[13]

In that way, a world-historical, practice-based argument at least bids fair to fulfil the high aspiration of normative political philosophy. Other forms of argument arguably do not fare as well.[14] If a similarly plausible argument can be made with less or no practice-sensitivity, the argument has to be given,[15] and in a way that makes the force of proposed principles plain to those who do not already accept or appreciate them, while addressing honest doubts about whether it is 'too utopian' or otherwise insufficiently practically engaged.[16]

5 Principles

In view of the two meanings of 'fair trade', I tentatively suggested that we have at least two different kinds of responsibilities of fairness, some of which apply to institutions, others to individuals. I've also now suggested how principles of each kind might be motivated. In one way, though, this is of limited import. All can agree that different agents are subject to different 'principles of regulation', which amount to different institutional or personal 'responsibilities'. For all that says, however, is that such responsibilities may only differ as ways of implementing more *basic* or *fundamental* principles (Cohen, 2008). Despite all we have said so far, there may, after all, be no fundamental difference between institutional and interpersonal 'fair trade'.

This suggests what might be called an *identity theory*: that is, the relation between institutional and personal or interpersonal principles is simply identity. Not only do we all owe things to each other as persons – e.g., not to coerce or manipulate or deceive one another, etc. – any principles that express what is owed in the name of social justice, in social practices or otherwise, are also, at least ultimately, interpersonal, in a way that constrains the permissibility of any and all social practices and institutions (Julius, 2014; see also James, 2014b).

This view readily supports the revolutionary's objection. Asking what persons owe to each other, taken as so many individuals, can be said to provide an Archimedean platform for assessing what is given to us by history, as perhaps radically unjust. That may give us decisive reason to do something completely different. Since the world-historical approach forecloses doing something completely different from the start (at least without credible enough reasons to think this possible, given our historical inheritance), it can seem to simply ignore the question of fundamental justice at issue. It can seem instead to speak to a secondary, 'merely practical' concern of how much justice can be realistically achieved.

On a slightly weaker variation, the relation between institutional and personal or interpersonal principles is not identity but *interpersonal priority*.

Principles for interpersonal and institutional morality are fundamentally different, but the justifiable interpersonal principles (e.g., Lockean natural rights and duties) nevertheless constrain the possible scope, if any, of justifiable institutional principles. Then, much as above, we might owe it to each other person to abandon even the deep social forms we've inherited for something completely different (e.g., anarchy, or a global state).

The foregoing views naturally support the revolutionary's objection, but do not entail it. One could still deny revolutionary obligations for the substantive reasons given earlier: perhaps, as argued above, they do not seem plausible as a claim about what a person morally should do. If broader philosophical considerations about the nature of principles are supposed to lead us to revise this substantive judgment, it should be clear why they translate into substantively relevant concerns. What I have argued earlier suggests that this is at least an uphill climb.

Other views are still less friendly to the revolutionary's objection, and so more amenable to a world-historical approach. Consider an *interdependence theory*. The relation between institutional and personal or interpersonal principles is again not identity. Yet they do bear an important relation to one another, at least in any reasoning about their content: the justifiability of one kind of principle must be sensitive to the justifiability of the other, within a broader reflective equilibrium. In that case, what justice requires in social practices or institutions can be different, even as a matter of fundamental principles, from what interpersonal morality calls for. But – perhaps because justification is itself ultimately 'holistic' – the final acceptability of any separately motivated principles depends on the final acceptability of other separately motivated principles, provided that there is a suitable understanding of their relationship.

This implies no position on the status of revolutionary obligations by itself. It places no pressure on a world-historical approach on the grounds of what people are interpersonally owed. Our conception of what each owes to each can equally be tailored according to our considered view about the morality of historically given institutions. If the very question of institutional fairness is to be bound by world-historical possibility, then what we each personally owe to each other could be as well.

A still stronger position would add that the non-identity relation is one of *institutional priority*: the principles justified for institutions generally settle the scope of permissible personal action (Rawls, 1971, takes this view of justice; Sangiovanni, 2008, applies it more broadly). In that case, if institutional principles must be world-historically bounded, then any personal obligation of revolutionary action would be foreclosed. If the very question of institutional fairness is bound by world-historical possibility, then what we each personally owe to each other not only can, but *must be* so bound as well.

If my earlier reply to the revolutionary's objection is successful, it removes at least one reason for accepting either an identity or an interpersonal priority view. Had that objection carried the day, we'd have to reject a world-historical institutional priority theory, at least for global economic affairs. The world-historical theorist could still take recourse in an interdependence view, which affords greater room to accommodate putative interpersonal obligations. But then the approach also would not rise to our initial challenge of showing how one meaning of 'fair trade' (in this case, the institutional one) could explain the other (the interpersonal one). On that score, the 'transaction first' approach would still have an advantage.

As a matter of general morality, an interdependence view does strike me as correct. But an institutional priority view might still be correct in certain social settings; it might be correct about the relation between personal and institutional fairness in global economic affairs in particular. In the remainder of my discussion, I explain why a domain-sensitive, institutional priority theory might seem natural for reasons arising from trade relations themselves.

6 Personal Fairness in Practice

As I understand them, principles for international trade practice are for trading countries in the first instance, rather than for persons or firms. By choosing to mutually rely on common markets, countries incur an 'associative' political responsibility for making trade practice fairer (James, 2012: ch. 2). Whatever else we say about the possible grounds for such obligations in general (e.g., which, depending on the case, might include membership, receipt of benefits, acceptance of benefits, or explicit or tacit consent), one such ground seems sufficient: sovereign states officially choose to rely on common markets, and so are obliged by association.[17]

Natural persons, on the other hand, are mainly wrapped up in the consequent market relations, perhaps against their will, with little hope for escape (even if one quits the country, most other countries may have freed trade as well). Whatever qualms one may have about objectionable processes of production in the developing world, the interpenetration of different market sectors leaves little hope of 'keeping clean hands', no matter how conscientious one's choices about what to buy or eat. So even if one's society and its officials have international associative obligations in trade practice, persons in the market relations thus created may seem either not responsible or responsible only as a matter of natural duty.

Here my suggestion is that persons so involved, however involuntarily, can be indirectly associated in international trade practice. By virtue of our involvement in the market relations that practice creates, we become obliged (defeasibly) to act in ways that might make international trade practice fairer, at least as opportunity arises, as specified, for example, within the framework of personal obligations outlined earlier. This is true quite aside from natural duty, which may, but needn't, apply.

The 'involvement' in question does not come by means of a simple exchange in the market, but rather by social participation in a normal range of basic forms that, in a market-oriented, open society invariably place one within cross-border market relations. In a modern global economy, most routine market transactions are not only regulated by law and policy, but also constitutively embedded in larger social structures, including the state system and domestic and international institutions of property, trade, money and finance and the cross-border trade flows they create. In the absence of these background relations, which include an international market reliance practice, the global economy as we know it would not, and perhaps could not, be.[18] Accordingly, in being involved in the market relations thus created, one counts as being involved in those enabling and shaping relations themselves, such that one can be reasonably expected, as appropriate, to take responsibility for their direction.

One might say that being so involved leaves one *complicit* in the practice's continued unfairness. Taken by oneself, one will rarely be correctly blamed for an institutional failing, once involved, one can nevertheless become responsible for continuing unfairness, in the sense that it becomes one's problem: one thereby comes to share collective responsibility for making trade practice fairer, in personally available ways. This is especially plausible when one reaps significant benefits from the normal forms of social participation, as augmented by gains from trade. But even when one is unfairly burdened (e.g., by persistent trade-induced unemployment, without compensation), one may still incur responsibility, if only to not further one's own mistreatment (e.g., by voting for the party that undermines unemployment support, if there is a choice). And even if mere benefit and burden are insufficient by themselves, all that must be assumed for present purposes is that persons can be so obliged by way of being citizens of their respective political communities. Arguably, we are each responsible by association for the choices made by our separate societies, especially in democratic societies. In that case, at least presumptively, we each have associative obligations of fairness because our respective societies do.

Quite aside from natural duty, such obligations can be seen as 'associative' in much the way other relationship-based obligations are. The nature of a relationship shapes the content of obligations, along with setting a general condition of their application. Transactions among strangers, friends and marriage partners can have very different meanings, and come with quite different obligations, according to the kind of relationship in question. Likewise, the principles that say when that practice is getting fairer can be sensitive to what the practice is like, and thus differ markedly from the vision of fair exchange one might reach while abstracting away from trade's embedding relationship, as in an ahistorical, 'transactions first' vision of fair market exchange.

None of this is to say *how far* normal market transactions are to be assessed as fair or unfair, beyond market prices set by voluntary exchange. In theory, if embedding institutions could reliably produce whatever outcomes are needed for the whole set of relations to be acceptable to everyone, many or most or even all particular exchange relations could still fairly be a 'morally free zone': one could fairly follow a pared-back set of minimal market norms. How often this situation obtains depends on how optimistic one is about the prospects, even the long-run prospects, that markets will be sufficiently well governed, such that persons can be freed from responsibility.

According to republican counsels of wisdom, but for the vigilant efforts of citizens, this happens rarely, if ever, and then only temporarily. Fairness is gained or preserved only because citizens persistently hold rulers accountable for its demands, in political action, but perhaps also in market choices. One can always hope (even if not expect) to help set a good example, to send a message or offer a proposal about how we might jointly carry on, and maybe to help nudge enough others along in favourable directions (at least when people are watching, and perhaps otherwise as well, if one's more general market dispositions send signals as well). Buying certified bananas or coffee or clothes might then be a matter of bandwagon duty once a good trend is taking hold. And even when there's no sign of a critical mass of support, if one has a chance of starting a trend, one will have occasion to fulfil one's duty of cause.

Here I merely mention the possibility of such republican obligations. Their mere possibility shows that an institutional priority view can be quite similar in practical upshot to an identity or interpersonal priority thesis, at least for economic relations. This can be true despite a real, even fundamental, difference in underlying principle, and despite the limits of personal natural duty. Even at the personal level, fairness can be institutional: the principles upheld can be those generated by and for the international rather than the interpersonal practice of trade.

References

Beitz, C. 1999/1979. *Political Theory and International Relations*, rev. edn. Princeton, NJ: Princeton University Press.

Beitz, C. 2009. *The Idea of Human Rights*. Oxford: Oxford University Press.

Caney, S. 2006. *Justice Beyond Borders*. New York: Oxford University Press.

Cohen, G. A. 2008. *Rescuing Justice and Equality*. Cambridge, MA: Harvard University Press.

Cohen, J. 2006–7. *Power, Reason, and Politics*. Tanner Lectures.

de Bres, H. 2011. 'What's Special about the State?' *Utilitas* 23(2): 140–160.

Estlund, D. 2014. 'Utopophobia', *Philosophy & Public Affairs* 42(2): 113–134.

Gauthier, D. 1986. *Morals by Agreement*. Oxford: Oxford University Press.

Gilabert, P. and Lawford-Smith, H. 2012. 'Political Feasibility: A Conceptual Exploration', *Political Studies* 60: 809–825.

Gillian, B. 2009. *Global Justice: A Cosmopolitan Account*. New York: Oxford University Press.

Held, D. 1995. *Democracy and the Global Order: From the Modern State to Cosmopolitan Governance*. Palo Alto, CA: Stanford University Press.

James, A. 2005a. 'Constructing Justice for Existing Practice', *Philosophy & Public Affairs* 3(33): 281–316.

James, A. 2005b. 'Distributive Justice without Sovereign Rule: The Case of Trade', *Social Theory and Practice* 31(4): 533–559.

James, A. 2005c. 'Power in Social Organization as the Subject of Justice', *Pacific Philosophical Quarterly* 86: 25–49.

James, A. 2006. 'Equality in a Realistic Utopia', *Social Theory and Practice* 32(4): 699–724.

James, A. 2012. *Fairness in Practice: A Social Contract for a Global Economy*. Oxford: Oxford University Press.

James, A. 2013a. 'Political Constructivism', in John Mandle and David Reidy, eds., *A Companion to Rawls*, 251–264. Oxford: Wiley-Blackwell.

James, A. 2013b. 'Why Practices?' *Raisons Politiques* 51: 43–61.

James, A. 2014a. 'A Theory of Fairness in Trade', *Moral Philosophy and Politics* 1(2): 177–200.

James, A. 2014b. 'Replies to Critics', *Canadian Journal of Philosophy* 44(2): 286–304.

James, A. Forthcoming. 'Authority and Territory: A Practice Account', in Claire Finklestein and Sharon Lloyd, eds., *Sovereignty and the New Executive Authority*. Oxford: Oxford University Press.

Johnson, B. L. 2003. 'Ethical Obligations in a Tragedy of the Commons', *Environmental Values* 12: 271–287.

Julius, A. J. 2013. 'The Possibility of Exchange', *Politics, Philosophy & Economics* 12(4): 361–374.

Julius, A. J. 2014. 'Practice Independence', *Canadian Journal of Philosophy* 44(2): 239–254.

Korsgaard, C. 1996. *The Sources of Normativity*. Cambridge: Cambridge University Press.

Locke, R. M. 2013. *The Promise and Limits of Private Power: Promoting Labor Standards in a Global Economy*. Cambridge: Cambridge University Press.

Miller, D. 2010. 'Fair Trade: What Does It Mean and Why Does It Matter?' CSSJ Working Paper Series, SJ013. http://social-justice.politics.ox.ac.uk/materials/SJ013_Miller_Fairtrade.pdf.

Moellendorf, D. 2002. *Cosmopolitan Justice*. Boulder, CO: Westview Press.

Nagel, T. 2005. 'The Problem of Global Justice', *Philosophy & Public Affairs* 33: 113–147.

Pogge, T. 1992. 'Cosmopolitanism and Sovereignty', *Ethics* 103(1): 48–75.

Rawls, J. 1971. *A Theory of Justice*. Cambridge, MA: Harvard University Press.

Rawls, J. 1999. *The Law of Peoples*. Cambridge, MA: Harvard University Press.

Risse, M. 2007. 'Fairness in Trade I: Obligations from Trading and the Pauper-Labor Argument', *Politics, Philosophy & Economics* 6: 355–377.

Risse, M. 2013. *On Global Justice*. Princeton, NJ: Princeton University Press.

Risse, M. and Kurjanska, M. 2008. 'Fairness in Trade II: Export Subsidies and the Fair Trade Movement', *Politics, Philosophy & Economics* 7: 29–56.

Risse, M. and Wollner, G. 2014. 'Three Images of Trade: On the Place of Trade in a Theory of Global Justice', *Moral Philosophy and Politics* 1(2): 201–225.

Räikkä, J. 1998. 'The Feasibility Condition in Political Theory', *Journal of Political Philosophy* 6: 27–40.

Sangiovanni, A. 2008. 'Justice and the Priority of Politics to Morality', *Journal of Political Philosophy* 16(2): 137–164.

Satz, D. 2010. *Why Some Things Should Not Be For Sale*. New York: Oxford University Press.

Scanlon, T. M. 1998. *What We Owe To Each Other*. Cambridge, MA: Harvard University Press.

Scanlon, T. M. 2010. 'Individual Morality and the Morality of Institutions', public lecture, Harvard University. http://ethics.harvard.edu/public-lecture-tim-scanlon.

Shelby, T. 2007. 'Justice, Deviance, and the Dark Ghetto', *Philosophy & Public Affairs* 35: 126–160.

Sinnott-Armstrong, W. 2010. 'It's Not My Fault', in Stephen Gardiner, Simon Caney, Dale Jamieson and Henry Shue, eds., *Climate Ethics: Essential Readings*, 332–346. Oxford: Oxford University Press.

Tan, K.-C. 2004. *Justice without Borders*. Cambridge: Cambridge University Press.

CHAPTER TWELVE

The Ethical Aspects of International Financial Integration

Peter Dietsch

It is commonplace today to hear that we are experiencing an unprecedented wave of globalization in economic activities. Indicators of cross-border trade in goods and services have followed an upward trend, albeit with some corrections occurring in the wake of the financial crisis of 2008 (Donnan, 2013). Even more impressive has been the rise in cross-border financial flows in recent decades (see, e.g., Lane and Milesi-Ferretti, 2003). It is natural to conclude from these developments that the world is becoming more integrated financially.

Key factors that are frequently cited as causes of this trend are innovations in the IT sector – funds can be transferred halfway around the globe at the click of a mouse, and the information about geographically distant markets available to investors has become much more readily available and reliable – and, more importantly, the widespread abolition of capital controls that came with the demise of the Bretton Woods institutions in the 1970s.

What are the normative implications of international financial integration (IFI)? In other words, how does the increase in cross-border financial transactions impact important social objectives such as efficiency or growth, the distribution of income and wealth both nationally and internationally, and the ideal of democratic self-determination in socioeconomic matters? It is only when we understand this impact that we will be in a position to assess whether increasing IFI, all things considered, is desirable or not. Perhaps more plausibly, it might be the case that some aspects of IFI are to be welcomed, whereas others prove to be problematic. The challenge in this case would be to develop feasible reforms that allow us to reap the benefits of IFI while counteracting some of its negative side-effects.

This chapter aims to provide a conceptual framework within which to ask these questions. In a first step, I propose to render the rather vague notion of IFI more precise by identifying the institutional background against which this integration takes place. While section 2 sets out the promise of IFI in theory, I shall argue in sections 3 and 4 that, in a politically fragmented world IFI necessarily creates tensions that undermine its potential to deliver socioeconomic benefits. More specifically, IFI in a world of nation-states and different currencies creates two kinds of risk. The first type of risk arises from the volatility of cross-border financial *flows*, their influence on exchange rates as well as on the prospects for sustained economic growth. The second type of risk lies in the fact that certain kinds and levels of cross-border financial *holdings* can undermine processes of democratic self-determination within states. I will use the international investment position of a country to analyse both these risks. The final section of the chapter identifies two additional ethical dimensions of IFI that only become apparent once we look beyond the international investment position that informs my argument in the previous sections.

I should add a brief note on two things that I am *not* aiming to achieve. First, I do not intend to contribute to the sizeable empirical literature providing different measures of IFI (e.g., Quinn et al., 2011). While section 1 will provide a working definition of IFI and later sections will cite various statistics to fill in the empirical premises of my argument, this is not a paper about how we should measure IFI but about how to use such measures in policymaking. Second, as already implicit in the opening paragraph, I want to delineate IFI from questions of trade in goods and services, at least to the extent that this is possible. The ethical dimensions of trade, as, for example, the question of how the surplus from trade is distributed, are distinct from the issues raised by IFI that I will discuss here.[1]

1   Integration of What?

Let us start by putting a working definition of IFI on the table. IFI has two facets – namely, capital stocks and capital flows. Concerning the former, as Lane and Milesi-Ferretti point out, 'a summary volume-based measure' of IFI is the sum of foreign assets plus foreign liabilities of a country divided by its GDP (2003: 86).[2] As the authors show, between 1983 and 2001, this measure increased by over 250 per cent for their sample of 14 OECD countries. While relatively coarse, this measure nicely illustrates that IFI, at base, represents a match between people who want to borrow funds with people who are prepared to lend them, but who are situated in a different country.

As to capital *flows*, foreign exchange turnover can serve as a proxy for the level of integration between currency zones. The latest triennial central bank survey of foreign exchange market turnover of the Bank for International Settlements (BIS) shows that the *daily* averages, measured in US dollars, are up from $1527 billion in April 1998 to $5345 billion in April 2013 (BIS 2013: table 1). While foreign exchange market turnover shot up in reaction to the abolition of the capital controls of the Bretton Woods system in the 1970s, these figures illustrate the fact that even in the early 2000s – that is, in a decade of relative regulatory stability – the volume of transactions increased by 350 per cent. Foreign exchange market turnover is an imperfect measure for international *financial* integration, since it also reflects increases in trade, but for our purposes here it is sufficient to observe that most of the increase in international financial flows over the last two decades is unrelated to trade in goods and services.

I should flag an important difference in the way in which these two measures are constructed. While the summary measure of IFI in terms of stocks refers to countries, looking at foreign exchange markets implies that we are looking at currencies, which in some cases span several countries. However, this difference does not represent an obstacle to my using the two measures side by side here.

You may ask what is so special about the cross-border aspect of these financial holdings and transactions respectively that we qualify them as 'integration'? How are they different from a debtor–creditor relationship (in the case of stocks) or from a transfer of funds (in the case of flows) within one and the same country? To see the differences, imagine for a moment a counterfactual world with just one currency and one federal world government.[3] The fact that there is only one currency means that there is no exchange rate risk; and the existence of a world government entails that the distinction between domestic versus foreign assets and liabilities loses its meaning. The latter point explains the difference in treatment of the debts of Greece and California, say. The comparison between this thought experiment and our actual world, I will suggest, allows us to better understand the phenomenon of financial integration and to formulate the ethical questions it raises.

In the hypothetical world just described, there would be no point speaking of IFI, since markets would by construction be fully integrated. Most contemporary discussions of actual globalization explicitly or implicitly depict IFI and other aspects of globalization as signs of progress, as if we were moving towards a world of full integration and as if that were necessarily a good thing. This analysis is misleading, or at least incomplete.

Even though the facts that we live in a world dominated by states and a world with many currencies rather than a single one are contingent products of history rather than deliberate choices of institutional design, there are good rationales for organizing the world in this way. Giving *states* a certain level of autonomy over their socioeconomic affairs can be defended on the grounds that people should have a say in the decisions that affect them – a federal world government would not be able to achieve this goal.[4] As to the question of *currency*: having different currencies represents a way to give states an additional lever of macroeconomic policy – the euro crisis is the latest illustration of the potential damage that can arise from lacking this lever. In the economic literature, the value of having monetary policy as a lever for macroeconomic policy is captured by the idea of optimal currency areas (Mundell, 1961). A currency zone should only be as large as the homogeneity of its members' economies permits.

What can we learn from this for our assessment of IFI? First, if we had the chance to redesign the global economy from scratch today, it is an open question whether we would opt for more or less IFI compared to the status quo.

Second, and more importantly, if we take the organization of the world into different states and multiple currencies as legitimate constraints, this high-lights the fact that IFI, by construction, happens in a world that is fragmented along state and currency lines. These lines do not fade as integration proceeds, but they act as a constant break on the dynamics of integration. As we shall see later, this is crucial, since the likelihood that IFI will yield positive results diminishes in such a scenario.

2 The Promise of International Financial Integration

Before turning to the specific case of IFI in a fragmented world, it is important to spell out in detail the general case for IFI. For states to be willing to give up some of their political autonomy and macroeconomic flexibility along the lines sketched in the previous section, IFI must be worthwhile for them. This section will sketch the economic textbook argument in favour of IFI.

There are two basic components to this argument.[5] First, standard growth models predict that if you match consumption and savings preferences in a bigger pool of people, you will get a better match and thus more growth (Obstfeld and Rogoff, 1996: ch. 7). More specifically, opening the capital account between a country with a relative preference for saving and a country with a relative preference for consumption means that the funds from the capital-exporting country will find more profitable investments than they would have at home. Since high expected returns increase the rate of saving and since they generate more output per unit invested, world capital accumulation proceeds faster. In theory, this growth should benefit the less-developed country in particular, thus leading to convergence.

The second benefit from financial openness lies in the access to risk-sharing it provides. Even if the returns on investment in two countries are the same, provided their risk profile is different, being able to invest across national borders will have a diversifying and thus stabilizing effect. Expressed in the terminology that we will adopt more systematically in the next section, the international investment position of a country can help to hedge domestic economic risks. Moreover, and related to the point of the previous paragraph, this diversification means that investors will tend to go for higher yield but riskier investments even on their domestic market, again boosting output (Obstfeld and Rogoff, 1996: sec. 7.3.2).

These two arguments provide the theoretical foundation for the case for deregulating international financial markets that has been widely documented (e.g., Braithwaite and Drahos, 2000: ch. 8; Abdelal, 2007). As we shall see in the next section, this case is made under theoretical assumptions that do not hold in the real world.

An important qualifier has to be added at this point. It would be naive to infer from the fact that higher overall growth and better risk diversification support the case for IFI that all cross-border transactions that show up in our various measures of IFI in fact pursue these two objectives. There are some kinds of cross-border transactions that not only pursue different ends, but for which one might plausibly ask whether they should be regarded as forms of IFI in the sense put forward in this chapter in the first place.

I shall give but one example here. A non-negligible share of international financial transactions today is motivated by fiscal considerations. Different estimates put the worldwide private wealth hidden in tax havens at between $5.1 trillion (Zucman, 2013) and $21–31 trillion (Henry, 2012). At the same time, corporate tax avoidance strategies, by shifting multinational profits to low-tax jurisdictions, succeed in lowering the effective tax rates paid to a fraction of nominal rates in many cases. Some of the techniques used by multinationals, as for instance thin capitalization where the subsidiary in a high-tax jurisdiction takes a loan from the subsidiary in a low-tax jurisdiction in order to then deduct the interest payments from its tax liabilities, make a significant contribution to cross-border financial flows. All these fiscally moti-vated transactions boost our measures of IFI. As a result, the financial assets and liabilities of the offshore centres to which the wealth or profits in ques-tion are transferred are often a multiple of their GDP, and these centres on paper appear as the poster children of IFI.

It is important to debunk the idea that these kinds of transactions represent any positive form of IFI. They do not result in higher growth, but at best in a different distribution of existing growth. Rather than being a form of risk diversification, they merely represent a form of rent-seeking by avoiding to pay taxes that should be paid according to the basic provisions of interna-tional tax law, namely the residence principle for individuals and the source principle for corporations. In sum, characterizing this kind of fiscally moti-vated transaction as a form of IFI is a misnomer. On the contrary, given the fiscal free-riding that is involved in both tax evasion and tax avoidance,[6] if anything, this kind of transaction seems to be a symptom of *dis*integration – in this case disintegration of the fiscal solidarity of political communities.

My analysis of the ethics of IFI in this chapter does not apply to such arti-ficial forms of IFI. I concentrate on 'pure' forms of IFI – that is, those that actually have the potential to deliver on the double promise of higher growth and better risk diversification.

3 International Financial Integration in a Fragmented World

We have established two things so far. First, IFI is happening in a world that is fragmented along state as well as along currency lines. Second, in theory, economic growth and risk diversification represent the two principal eco-nomic benefits we expect IFI to deliver – this does not, of course, exclude the possibility that there are other non-economic benefits such as, for example, a more peaceful international order due to increased economic interconnectedness. This section argues that when putting these two elements together, we face a catch 22. In a fragmented world, so the argument runs, IFI entails countervailing risks that undermine the prospects of more growth and better risk diversification. In some cases, they might be important enough for there not to be any net benefits of IFI at all. At that point, IFI no longer seems desirable. We will now look at some of these risks created by IFI in a fragmented world, as well as at their distribution. Understanding these risks lies at the heart of the ethics of IFI.

A useful tool for our purposes here is the so-called International Investment Position (IIP) as well as the financial account transactions of a country.

> The IIP is a statistical statement that shows at a point in time the value of: financial assets of residents of an economy that are claims on nonresidents or are gold bullion held as reserve assets; and the liabilities of residents of an economy to nonresidents. The difference between the assets and liabilities is the net position in the IIP and represents either a net claim or a net liability to the rest of the world. (IMF, 2009: 7)

The IIP and the financial account are the parts of a country's balance of payments that focus on financial assets. But note that the income from these financial assets, such as dividends paid on government or corporate bonds, will be reported in a different part of the balance of payments, namely the primary account. Whereas the IIP shows *stocks* of assets and liabilities, the transactions in the financial account represent the *flows* during any given period that result in these stocks, thus reflecting the two facets of IFI identified in section 1. In table 1, you see a fictitious IIP used in the IMF's balance of payments manual (IMF, 2009: 14).[7]

For simplicity, my analysis in this section will focus on the categories of direct investment and portfolio investment.[8] Foreign direct investment (FDI) refers to transactions in which investors acquire a lasting management interest (usually defined as 10 per cent of voting stock or more) of a company in the destination country (see World Bank Indicators). For example, if a UK company makes a $10 billion FDI in Canada, this will show up as an asset in the UK IIP and as a liability in the Canadian IIP. Portfolio investment, by contrast, lacks the ambition to influence management decisions and tends to be more short term. When a Canadian resident buys $10,000 worth of German government bonds, this will show up as an asset in the Canadian IIP and as a liability in the German IIP.

Against this background, we are now in a position to analyse the risks that increased IFI in a fragmented world creates. I will group these risks into two categories.

Increased volatility and a higher likelihood of contagion from economic crises elsewhere

This first kind of risk is one that arises from the volatility of financial *flows*. The central insight here is by no means new. It is the same preoccupation

TABLE 1

International investment position:	Opening position	Transactions (fin. acc.)	Other changes in volume	Revaluation	Closing position
Assets (by functional category)					
Direct investment	78	8	0	1	87
Portfolio investment	190	18	0	2	210
Financial derivatives (other than reserves) and ESOs	7	3	0	0	10
Other investment	166	20	0	0	186
Reserve assets	833	8	0	12	853
Total assets	1,274	57	0	15	1,346
Liabilities (by functional category)					
Direct investment	210	11	0	2	223
Portfolio investment	300	14	0	5	319
Financial derivatives (other than reserves) and ESOs	0	0	0	0	0
Other investment	295	22	0	0	317
Total liabilities	805	47	0	7	859
Net IIP	469	10	0	8	487

Note: ESO = employee stock option.

that motivated James Tobin in the 1970s to put forward his proposal of a financial transaction tax (FTT) to 'throw some sand in the well-greased wheels' of finance (1978: 158).

Consider the following stylized account of an emerging market crisis. In search of better returns, investors from rich countries put some of their money into an emerging market.[9] Now suppose an economic shock occurs in the rich country, for example a credit crunch due to the past neglect of systemic risks in the housing market. Alternatively, suppose that the central bank of the rich country embarks on a countercyclical tightening of monetary policy,[10] while the emerging market monetary conditions stay the same. In both scenarios, some of the rich country investors are likely to pull back some of their investments. Those who leveraged their investment with debt will do so because their interest rates are rising, and even unleveraged investments will face a higher opportunity cost and thus have an incentive to repatriate funds. This, in turn, will tend to put pressure on the value of the currency of the emerging market economy. The authorities of the latter now face a dilemma between engaging in a costly propping-up of their currency by using their (limited) foreign currency reserves, on the one hand, and letting the exchange rate fall, on the other. In the latter case, anticipating a further fall in the exchange rate, more investors are likely to pull out their funds, thus leading to a downward spiral. In many cases, the increased competitiveness of the emerging economy's export industries due to the lower exchange rate turns out to be insufficient to compensate the disruption caused by the sudden outflow of capital.

In the categories of the IIP introduced above, short-term portfolio investment is more likely to contribute to these volatile capital flows than longer-term direct investment, simply because short-term investments are more liquid. Paul Tucker, a former deputy governor of the Bank of England, highlights the importance of the composition of a country's national balance sheet in terms of maturities when he asserts: 'With too much short-term debt, a country can be as vulnerable to runs as a bank that has funded itself from fickle sources' (2014).

Needless to say, the above stylized account simplifies things, and in fact every emerging market crisis is different.[11] However, we can discern one feature that is common to these crises, namely that financial openness increases the volatility of capital flows into and out of countries (e.g., Ostry et al., 2010). While the inflows do spur investment and growth, they can also lead to asset price bubbles. By contrast, when sudden capital outflows occur, they disrupt steady economic development and thus dent growth. For some of the countries in question, it is no longer clear to what extent IFI overall results in higher growth, or even whether it does so at all. Moreover, since most developing countries' social security system is insufficiently developed to compensate the losers from economic downturns, there is a further question of the distribution not only of the benefits of economic growth, but of the burdens of recession.

Several contributions to the literature have tried to identify the determinants of successful financial openness. What types of countries benefit from IFI and why? According to one hypothesis that has emerged, countries whose financial and institutional infrastructure has passed a certain threshold are more likely to benefit from IFI than others (e.g., Eichengreen et al., 2011; Kose et al., 2011). One obvious alternative is to argue that the determining factor is the relative size of the capital flow to the size of the economy in question, as well as perhaps its diversification. If this alternative hypothesis were correct, then even developed economies would face considerable risks from IFI if only the capital flows are big enough. It is beyond the scope of this chapter to further assess the relative plausibility of these two hypotheses.

In practice, several countries in recent economic history have judged that, on balance, the potential benefits from IFI set out in section 2 were not worth the risks set out in this section. For example, during the 1990s, Chile created the so-called *encaje*, 'a one-year, mandatory, non-interest paying deposit with the central bank' (Neely, 1999: 25). If you pulled out your investment before the year was over, you had to pay a 3 per cent penalty. In other words, the *encaje* worked as a tax on, and thus a disincentive for, short-term investments. I do not intend to enter the controversy over whether the *encaje* was an effective means to insulate Chile from the risks of IFI. The important point for me is that the case of Chile illustrates the fact that in a fragmented world, the risks of IFI might well outweigh its benefits. Even a staff paper by the IMF, an erstwhile staunch defender of the idea that IFI is always beneficial, recognized in 2010 that capital controls can offer a useful policy option for countries to protect themselves against the risks of IFI (Ostry et al., 2010).

A more detailed analysis of the risks that capital flows pose to economic growth and to risk diversification is needed. Notably, this analysis needs to include the category of financial derivatives in the IIP above, which I have bracketed here.[12] Nonetheless, the above discussion warrants the general conclusion that, in a fragmented world, we cannot take it for granted that the benefits of IFI will outweigh its risks.

I believe the following analogy with welfare economics is appropriate here. In 1954, Arrow and Debreu famously proved the first fundamental theorem of welfare economics, namely that a perfectly competitive market will always yield Pareto-optimal results. Intuitively, one ostensible conclusion from this proof is to think that, for economic policy, which necessarily operates inside the Pareto possibility frontier, *more* competition would always lead to *more* welfare. However, two years after Arrow and Debreu's paper was published, Lipsey and Lancaster (1956–7) added an important twist to their analysis. Their second-best theorem shows that it is *not* true that a relatively small violation of the idealizing assumptions of the model of perfect competition will necessarily take us closer to the Pareto frontier than a bigger violation. In other words, in the real world, it is an open question whether any particular market intervention will be welfare-enhancing or not.

Similarly, I claim, the knowledge that full financial integration in a hypo-thetical world of a federal world state with a single currency would be welfare-enhancing does *not* warrant the conclusion that more financial integration in a fragmented world will be welfare-enhancing, too.

Important foreign liabilities as a threat to democratic self-determination in economic matters

As opposed to the first kind of risk that arises from cross-border *flows*, the second kind is linked to foreign holdings or *stocks* of financial assets. Most countries' IIPs today include considerable liabilities towards foreigners.

From a normative perspective, it matters whether the liabilities are held by the private or by the public sector. When a lot of private firms are under foreign ownership, this might trigger protectionist reactions, but it is relatively hard to underpin these reactions with a rationale that stands up in the court of public reason. After all, private assets are not supposed to be subject to democratic control, independently of whether they are held domestically or by foreigners.

By contrast, when a substantial share of the *public* debt of a country is held by foreigners, things get more complicated.[13] Governments become depend-ent on international capital markets to (re-)finance their debt. As a conse-quence, they become sensitive to market reactions to their policies.[14] Think of a concrete, and not entirely hypothetical example. Suppose the French government is contemplating two alternative, but by no means mutually exclusive, policy options in order to reduce its annual budget deficit. One policy package is centred around labour market reform and based on the assumption that making labour markets more flexible will stimulate eco-nomic growth and thus lead to higher tax revenues. The second option includes raising taxes on capital gains and introducing a tax on the stock of capital, as proposed by Piketty (2014); advocates of this second reform path consider that the additional tax revenue generated in this way will outweigh the negative impact the reform might have on investment.

Financial markets would react very differently to these two options. If the French government seriously considered choosing the latter policy package over the former, this would most likely entail that it will have to pay a 'risk' premium the next time it has to refinance part of its debt. As a consequence, the government will have a strong incentive to adopt what is considered the more 'market-friendly' policy. In fact, these are the dynamics we have observed repeatedly in recent years in those member states of the Eurozone whose debt was considered unsustainably high by financial markets.[15] Note that it is not necessary to presuppose that market participants are *intentionally* applying pressure on democratic governments. It is sufficient to rely on investors' objective to maximize return on their investments.

One foreseeable objection to this line of argument states that it is not spe-cific to *foreign* holdings of public debt, but reflects a more general 'structural dependence of the state on capital' (Przeworski and Wallerstein, 1988),[16] both domestic and foreign. Two things can be said in response to this objection. First, the literature also contains the opposite case, supporting the idea that foreign holdings of public debt pose a specific kind of threat to democratic self-determination. Przeworski and Wallerstein, for instance, argue that the state is not structurally dependent on domestic capital, in the sense that a variety of redistributive policies is compatible with continued domestic private investment (1988: 24). By contrast, they point out that a dependence on an inflow of *foreign* capital is likely to indeed limit the capacity of the state to choose among such distributions (1988: 21). Second, even if one rejected the Przeworski-Wallerstein conclusion and accepted the parallel between domestic and foreign capital in principle, social norms about investing domestically can mitigate the dependence of the state on domestic capital in practice. Consider the variety in the composition of the public debt in different countries. While Japan, for example, has a public debt of 220 per cent of GDP, the lion share of this debt is held domestically even though higher returns would have been available abroad. Other countries, with a lower debt-to-GDP ratio, have a higher share of foreign creditors. Arguably, both social norms and institutional dispositions can reduce the dependence of the state on domestic capital in ways absent in the case of foreign capital.

In short, the risk stemming from IFI that we are talking about here is that IFI understood as a significant public debt exposure to foreign investors compromises democratic self-determination. This can be read as one instance of what Dani Rodrik (2011) has called the *political trilemma of the world economy*. Rodrik argues that there is a fundamental tension between global markets and national democracy, and that we can manage this tension in three ways. 'We can *restrict democracy* in the interest of minimizing international transaction costs, disregarding the economic and social whiplash that the global economy occasionally produces. We can *limit globalization*, in the hope of building democratic legitimacy at home. Or we can *globalize democracy*, at the cost of national sovereignty' (2011: 370). Rodrik provides a useful conceptual framework in which to think about the risk of IFI that concerns us here. He argues in favour of option two – limiting globalization through a regulation of the global economy that enhances national sovereignty[17] – but I will bracket the issue of possible solutions here. The focus of this chapter consists in outlining the ethical challenges presented by IFI.

The remainder of this section will discuss the following objection. Someone might agree with the assessment outlined above, and yet disagree that this is problematic from an ethical perspective. The objector could argue as follows. Consider an individual who takes on a debt burden equal to a multiple of his annual income. Suppose also that he made the relevant decisions freely and could have acted differently. Now, if some external economic shock results either in the individual earning less or the interest rate on his debt increasing, most theories of justice – including liberal egalitarian theories

(Dworkin, 1981) – will tend to hold the individual responsible for his actions. One consequence of these actions is that the individual has manoeuvred himself into a situation of dependence on his creditors. Other members of society are under no moral obligation to bail him out.

The same reasoning, so the objections runs, should apply to collectives, and thus to the public debt of countries. Provided they accumulated the debt in question knowingly, and could have acted differently, they have to assume responsibility for the consequences. They have no moral claim on their creditors to accept a haircut or on other states to bail them out, but they instead have to find a way out of the situation through structural reforms.

This objection is simplistic in at least three ways, which considerably weakens its force. I shall present three counterarguments in ascending order of importance.

First, the idea of a black-and-white criterion to attribute responsibility to individuals or collectives is implausible. Just as the argument presented by some in the wake of the financial crisis that individuals should have known better than getting out a subprime mortgage ignores information asymmetries, governments are not fully rational agents acting on perfect information either. True, governments should be better informed than the average economic agent, but they are not immune to herd behaviour. When conventional wisdom in economics sees no problem with growing public debts and other states are running budget deficits, too, then it seems very demanding to expect any particular government to refrain from running public deficits.[18]

Second, the interest rate paid to investors who buy government bonds, or any other security for that matter, reflects the perceived risk of the investment in question. For example, while the bond yields of most Eurozone countries were relatively close to those of German Bunds before the financial crisis, as of 2010 several countries started paying a hefty premium to refinance their debt. Now, the very reason the investor receives this risk premium is that she knows there is a chance she might lose part of her capital. This suggests that when the loan turns bad, some kind of burden-sharing between bondholders and the issuing government is anticipated in the investment structure itself.[19] Some will point out that even partial bail-outs create a problem of moral hazard. If countries know that they can get away with defaulting on their debt, they will behave even more recklessly in the future. Note, however, that this characterization of the situation is incomplete. Defaulting on a share of one's debt will lead to a higher risk premium in the future, and as long as the disincentive set by this risk premium is large enough, moral hazard will be contained.

The first two arguments do not challenge the analogy between individuals and collectives as such, but they push us to draw different conclusions from it. The third argument, which I consider to be the most important one in this context, questions the analogy itself. By treating collectives as one agent, the analogy papers over differences within the political communities in question. First of all, when a 'country' decides to run budget deficits and accumulate public debt, should we assign the responsibility for the relevant decisions to the government or to the citizens? It is not straightforward to argue that the latter answer is correct, particularly in the case of citizens who did not vote for the government in question. But even if we grant the idea that holding citizens accountable is possible, collectives throw up the additional question of the distribution of the benefits and burdens that flow from political decisions. Plausibly, those who benefit from a policy of higher public debt and those who will have to pick up the bill under the austerity programmes to correct for past profligacy are two only partially overlapping groups. This is of course an empirical claim. Take the specific example of Greece. I am not denying that the average Greek citizen benefited from higher public debt, but I suggest that her relative benefit might be smaller than the relative burden she has to bear under the ensuing policy of austerity.

The important point here is the following. Think back to the idea with which we started out this section. Countries with high levels of public debt will find themselves under pressure to adopt more market-friendly policies. Such policies tend to favour capital interests over labour. This gives us a *theoretical* basis for anticipating that the average citizen's interests will indeed take a backseat in highly indebted countries. In this section, I hope to have corroborated the claim that IFI creates a deep-seated tension between global financial markets and national democracy. Both normative work on IFI and empirical work in international economics have yet to address this issue in a satisfactory manner.

4   Looking Beyond the Balance of Payments

While the IIP used in the previous section provides a good tool to illustrate the two characteristic risks of IFI outlined, there are additional ethical aspects of IFI. To understand these, we have to look beyond the balance of payments. In this section, I shall discuss two issues that fall into this category. This list by no means has the ambition of being comprehensive.

The first set of issues is related to the growing importance of central banks not only in international finance, but also in macroeconomic policy generally. Monetary policy, in particular through its impact on the exchange rate, has repercussions well beyond the currency zone for which it is designed. Think of the example given in the first category of risks analysed in section 3: a contractionary monetary policy – or just the anticipation thereof – can lead to significant capital outflows from other countries, in particular from emerging markets, thus contributing to increased volatility. Reddy (2003) provides an excellent overview of the normative dimensions of monetary arrangements. Here, I will focus on one particular aspect of recent monetary policy that is particularly relevant in the context of IFI.

As highlighted by Perry Mehrling in his book *The New Lombard Street* (2010), the financial crisis in the wake of the Lehman bankruptcy in 2008 has triggered a sea change in the role that central banks play in our financial system. Virtually all the major currency central banks have seen their balance sheet explode as they reacted to the crisis by buying up securities.[20] In the first instance, they did so mainly to shore up financial stability, but as the crisis dragged on, their goal shifted towards giving commercial banks more flexibility for lending in order to stimulate growth. A certain share of a central bank's assets will be foreign assets, thus representing a form of IFI as analysed in this chapter. This adds a new twist to the story told concerning the second category of risks in section 3. When a central bank holds a significant stock of foreign assets, including foreign debt, its interests change and become closer to that of an investor.[21] This might be a partial explanation for the fact that the financial market pressure in the case of Greece, for instance, now increasingly comes from the European Central Bank (ECB) – that is, from a public institution, rather than from private investors.[22] This new role of central banks as 'dealers of last resort', as Mehrling (2010) puts it, is one that lies outside their traditional mandate. This development might well push us to reopen the debate about central bank independence. At the very least, it illustrates that, in today's financial system, the role played by central banks has to take centre stage in our assessment of IFI.

A second issue needs to be mentioned here, without which a paper on ethical aspects of IFI would be incomplete. Most, if not all, the arguments presented thus far suggest that the risks of IFI are fairly symmetrical, in the sense that all countries face them to a similar extent. The economic weight of countries such as the United States or currency unions such as the Eurozone means that they are *less* susceptible to economic contagion, but if we control for the size of the economy, one would expect the risks of IFI to be more or less evenly spread. The argument we will turn to now shows that this is not the case.

Recall from section 1 that financial integration by construction happens in a fragmented world, and that one of the lines of fragmentation is that of currencies. What we have not yet considered is the fact that some of these currencies enjoy a special status in the global financial order. They are global *reserve* currencies. Holding currency reserves serves a variety of purposes, but the central one in the context of this chapter is to protect countries against economic crises and against the kind of volatility described in the first part of section 3. As laid out forcefully by Stiglitz (2006: ch. 9), the increased frequency of economic crises in recent decades has led countries to build up larger and larger protective buffers in US dollars, euros, pounds sterling, Swiss francs and other currencies that are considered safe havens. Among other things, building up reserves allows developing countries to react to significant capital outflows by using these reserves to buy, and thus prop up, their own currency. As Stiglitz documents, several Asian countries learnt the lesson about the need for currency reserves the hard way in the crisis of 1997. Subsequently, '[i]n just the four years between 2001 and 2005, eight East Asian countries (Japan, China, South Korea, Singapore, Malaysia, Thailand, Indonesia, and the Philippines) more than doubled their total reserves (from roughly $1 trillion to $2.3 trillion)' (2006: 247).

From an ethical perspective, the current global reserve system is problematic for several reasons. First, it comes at a huge opportunity cost to developing countries. Instead of investing the money in question into projects in education, health or infrastructure that might offer double-digit returns, developing countries as a whole 'earn on average a real return of 1–2 percent or less on the $3 trillion plus of reserves' (Stiglitz, 2006: 249).

Second, it confers a huge advantage to the issuers of reserve currencies (e.g., Eichengreen, 2011). For one thing, it gives them access to cheap loans. As Stiglitz puts it, 'were it not for the demand for reserves, their costs of borrowing would likely be markedly higher' (2006: 250).[23] Moreover, the demand for currency reserves allows countries to run balance of payments deficits without seeing their currency depreciate (Reddy, 2003: 86). Using the framework introduced in section 3, reserves are an asset in a country's IIP and, thus, a financial claim it has on foreigners. One way to build up these reserves is by running a current account surplus. If you export more than you import, you will start accumulating the reserve currency your clients use to pay for the excess in exports. To illustrate these two effects, take the case of the United States as the issuer of the world's most important reserve currency. The US public debt would weigh more heavily on its economy if it could not rely on the almost insatiable demand for treasury bills from other countries and the relatively low interest rates they are prepared to accept. At the same time, if this demand for US securities did not prop up the exchange rate of the US dollar against other currencies, the US current account deficit would push the value of the dollar down.

Put all these factors together, and you get a fundamental bias at the heart of the global financial system, one that favours the already rich over the poor. Economists have been aware of this bias for a long time. Stiglitz builds on John Maynard Keynes's work and the latter's reform proposal to create what he called a system of 'special drawing rights', that is, a sort of cooperative mutual insurance system against financial crises. The IMF already disposes of a system of special drawing rights, but states still mostly build up foreign reserves instead in order to protect themselves against financial crises. The IMF's programme would need to be expanded and reformed to serve the role envisaged by Keynes.[24] Stiglitz highlights that a group of Asian countries already created a regional version of such a system in the reaction to the 1997 crisis and against, unsurprisingly, strong resistance from the United States (Stiglitz, 2006: 260ff.). Theorists of global justice, on the other hand, have not given the global reserve system the critical attention it deserves. Two notable exceptions are Reddy (2003) and James (2012: e.g., 184). Especially in light of the link between the volatility of financial markets discussed in the first part of section 3 above and the dynamics of the global reserve system – the more volatile the global financial system, the more reserves developing countries will rationally hold – it is high time that this omission be rectified.

5 Conclusion

My main objectives in this chapter have been to provide a conceptual framework for discussing the ethical aspects of IFI, on the one hand, and to use this framework to provide a survey of some of the most pressing issues in this context, on the other. The phenomenon of IFI is often referred to with a considerable lack of precision. Working to correct this weakness of current debates, I started out by characterizing the institutional background against which IFI takes place as one of fragmentation along country as well as currency lines.

We saw that this fragmentation means that the theoretical benefits of IFI – economic growth and access to risk-sharing – in practice have to be weighed against the risks stemming from increased market volatility as well as from the tension between global markets and national democracies. Assessing these risks requires an understanding of how IFI manifests itself in the balance of payments of countries. It would be misleading to think that we can arrive at a general endorsement or condemnation of IFI. More realistically, we might be able to identify an optimal level of IFI both in terms of capital flows and in terms of cross-border holdings of capital stock. Furthermore, the verdict will depend on a number of empirical premises that will vary from country to country. I merely hope to have provided the conceptual tools we need for this case-by-case analysis.

While section 3 argued that the balance of payments provides the ideal tool to analyse the twin risks of IFI, namely increased vulnerability to economic crises elsewhere and the threat to democratic self-determination, section 4 illustrated that the ethical issues raised by IFI reach well beyond the balance of payments. Whether it is the question of the increasing role of central banks in macroeconomic management, or the fundamental bias introduced to the financial system by the global reserve system, these issues need to be on the radar of any ethical analysis of IFI.

This chapter has focused on describing the ethical challenges posed by IFI rather than on identifying potential solutions. While I have mentioned some existing reform proposals in passing, much work remains to be done on this front.[25]

References

Abdelal, R. 2007. *Capital Rules – The Construction of Global Finance*. Cambridge, MA: Harvard University Press.

Arrow, K. J. and Debreu, G. 1954. 'Existence of an Equilibrium for a Competitive Economy', *Econometrica* 22(3): 265–290.

BIS (Bank of International Settlements). 2013. 'Triennial Central Bank Survey. Foreign Exchange Turnover in April 2013: Preliminary Global Results', September. http://www.bis.org/publ/rpfx13fx.pdf.

Braithwaite, J. and Drahos, P. 2000. *Global Business Regulation*. Cambridge: Cambridge University Press.

Caney, S. 2006. 'Cosmopolitan Justice and Institutional Design: An Egalitarian Liberal Conception of Global Governance', *Social Theory and Practice* 32(4): 725–756.

Dietsch, P. 2011. 'Rethinking Sovereignty in International Fiscal Policy', *Review of International Studies* 37: 2107–2120.

Dietsch, P. 2015. *Catching Capital – The Ethics of Tax Competition*. Oxford: Oxford University Press.

Dietsch, P. and Rixen, T. 2014. 'Tax Competition and Global Background Justice', *The Journal of Political Philosophy* 22(2): 150–177.

Donnan, S. 2013. 'Into Uncharted Waters', *Financial Times*, 25 October.

Dornbusch, R. 2001. 'A Primer on Emerging Market Crises', NBER Working Paper 8326. http://www.nber.org/papers/w8326.

Durden, T. 2015. 'Who Owns Greek Debt and When Is It Due?'. http://www.zerohedge.com/news/2015-02-03/who-owns-greek-debt-and-when-it-due.

Dworkin, R. 1981. 'What is Equality? Part 2: Equality of Resources', *Philosophy & Public Affairs* 10(4): 283–345.

Eichengreen, B. 2011. *The Rise and Fall of the Dollar and the Future of the International Monetary System*. Oxford: Oxford University Press.

Eichengreen, B., Gullapalli, R. and Panizza, U. 2011. 'Capital Account Liberalization, Financial Development and Industry Growth: A Synthetic View', *Journal of International Money and Finance* 30: 1090–1106.

Fontan, C. 2013. 'Frankenstein en Europe', *Politique européenne* 42(4): 22–45.

Henry, J. S. 2012. 'The Price of Offshore Revisited: New Estimates for "Missing" Global Private Wealth, Income, Inequality, and Lost Taxes'. Report for Tax Justice Network. www.taxjustice.net/cms/upload/pdf/Price_of_Offshore_Revisited_120722.pdf.

IMF. 2009. *Balance of Payments and International Investment Position Manual*, 6th edn (BPM6). Washington, DC: International Monetary Fund.

James, A. 2012. *Fairness in Practice*. Oxford: Oxford University Press.

Kalbaska, A. and Gatkowski, M. 2012. 'Eurozone Sovereign Contagion: Evidence from the CDS Market (2005–2010)', *Journal of Economic Behaviour & Organization* 83: 657–673.

Kose, M. A., Prasad, E. S. and Taylor, A. D. 2011. 'Thresholds in the Process of International Financial Integration', *Journal of International Money and Finance* 30: 147–179.

Lane, P. R. and Milesi-Ferretti, G. M. 2003. 'International Financial Integration', *IMF Staff Papers*, vol. 50, special issue.

Lipsey, R. G. and Lancaster, K. 1956–7. 'The General Theory of Second Best', *Review of Economic Studies* 24(1): 11–32.

Mehrling, P. 2010. *The New Lombard Street – How the Fed Became Dealer of Last Resort*. Princeton, NJ: Princeton University Press.

Mundell, R. A. 1961. 'A Theory of Optimum Currency Areas', *American Economic Review* 51(4): 657–665.

Neely, C. J. 1999. 'An Introduction to Capital Controls', *Federal Reserve Bank of St. Louis Review* 81(6): 13–30.

Obstfeld, M. and Rogoff, K. 1996. *Foundations of International Macroeconomics*. Cambridge, MA: MIT Press.

Ostry, J. D., Ghosh, A. R., Habermeier, K., Chamon, M., Qureshi, M. S. and Reinhardt, D. B. S. 2010. 'Capital Inflows: The Role of Controls', IMF Staff Position Note, SPN/10/04.

Piketty, T. 2014. *Capital in the Twenty-First Century*. Cambridge, MA: Belknap Press.

Przeworski, A. and Wallerstein, M. 1988. 'Structural Dependence of the State on Capital', *American Political Science Review* 82(1): 11–29.

Quinn, D., Schindler, M. and Toyoda, M. 2011. 'Assessing Measures of Financial Openness and Integration', *IMF Economic Review* 59: 488–522.

Reddy, S. 2003. 'Developing Just Monetary Arrangements', *Ethics & International Affairs* 17(1): 81–93.

Rodrik, D. 2011. *The Globalization Paradox – Democracy and the Future of the World Economy*. New York: W.W. Norton.

Ronzoni, M. 2009. 'The Global Order: A Case of Background Injustice? A Practice-Dependent Account', *Philosophy & Public Affairs* 37(3): 229–256.

Stiglitz, J. 2006. *Making Globalization Work*. New York: W.W. Norton.

Strange, S. 1994. *States and Markets*, 2nd edn. London: Pinter.

Streeck, W. 2014. *Buying Time: The Delayed Crisis of Democratic Capitalism*. London: Verso.

Tobin, J. 1978. 'A Proposal for International Monetary Reform', *Eastern Economic Journal* 4(3/4): 153–159.

Tucker, P. 2014. 'The World Needs Different Ways of Taming Capital Flows', *Financial Times*, 10 October.

World Bank Indicators. http://data.worldbank.org/indicator/BX.KLT.DINV.CD.WD.

Zucman, G. 2013. *La Richesse cachée des nations – Enquête sur les paradis fiscaux*. Paris: Seuil.

CHAPTER THIRTEEN

Political Theory for the Anthropocene

Dale W. Jamieson and Marcello Di Paola

> In thousands of years ... our wars and revolutions will count for little ... but the steam engine, and the procession of inventions of every kind that accompanied it, will perhaps be spoken of as we speak of the bronze or of the chipped stone of pre-historic times: it will serve to define an age.
>
> Henri Bergson (1907/2007)

Introduction

One of the central themes of classical philosophy is persistence and the puzzling nature of change. There is a similar fascination in the sciences with the oscillations between order and disorder. The impermanence of our everyday world is a trope of many religions. Politics too – 'the art of the possible' – is an ongoing negotiation (and often struggle) between stability and transformation, utopianism and realism, the ideal and the feasible.

Our lives and the contexts in which they unfold are but moments in the history of the universe. Our own little planet, peaceful as it may seem when photographed from space, is in fact a cauldron of unruly forces occupying a violent neighbourhood given to cataclysms. The earth is constantly remade by such phenomena as solar radiation, movements in tectonic plates, volcanic activity, meteorite strikes, shifts in orbit and changes in the earth's tilt on its axis. Life itself is among the forces that have changed the planet, from cyanobacteria producing the first molecules of oxygen to human beings now increasing the concentration of carbon dioxide in the atmosphere. How ironic that human beings, who have lived on the earth during only four-thousandth of one per cent of its history, are now the main drivers of planetary change.

This chapter explores the ways in which the Anthropocene, this new epoch in which no earthly place, form, entity, process or system escapes the reach of human activity, puts under pressure some traditional categories and concepts of liberal democratic theory. We begin by explaining the notion of the Anthropocene, and then show how it may affect traditional liberal notions of agency, responsibility, governance and legitimacy. We conclude by describing the challenge of designing new institutions appropriate to the Anthropocene.

1   The Anthropocene

According to current geological classifications, we live in the Holocene. This epoch, part of the Quaternary Period of the Cenozoic Era, began almost 12,000 years ago following the end of the last Ice Age. The Holocene has been characterized by relatively stable planetary conditions, especially in regard to climate. This has proven quite congenial to the reproduction and proliferation of *Homo Sapiens*. Human life as we know it – from the beginning of written history to the first cultivated fields, from unconnected settlements to our mega-cities and satellite-based monitoring of ourselves and earth systems – has unfolded during the Holocene.

In 1997, a distinguished group of scientists published an influential article in which they assessed the human impact on the earth (Vitousek et al., 1997). They calculated that between one-third and one-half of earth's land surface had been transformed by human action; that carbon dioxide in the atmosphere had increased by more than 30 per cent since the beginning of the industrial revolution; that more nitrogen had been fixed by humans than all other terrestrial organisms combined; that more than half of all accessible surface freshwater was appropriated by humanity; and that about one-quarter of earth's bird species had been driven to extinction. Their conclusion, even at the end of the last century, was that 'it is clear that we live on a human-dominated planet' (1997: 494).

In recognition of the human domination of nature, some scientists have proposed that we have entered a new geological epoch: the Anthropocene. This term was coined by the ecologist Eugene Stoermer in the 1980s, but came to widespread public attention in a short article that he co-authored with Nobel prize-winning chemist Paul Crutzen in 2000. Crutzen and Stoermer claimed that humanity had come to exert such pervasive influence on the earth as to have effectively become the main driver of its geological and biological evolution (for a more recent presentation of the concept of the Anthropocene, see Steffen et al., 2011).

While the word 'Anthropocene' is relatively new, the idea has been around since at least the nineteenth century as scientists, theologians and naturalists struggled to give voice to the dawning realization that humanity, with its sheer numbers and technological power, was remaking the planet. In 1864, the American polymath George Perkins Marsh was struck by the massive changes he had witnessed from the time he was a child in Vermont, living alongside Native Americans, to the deforestation and desertification he witnessed as a diplomat working in the Mediterranean region. He wrote:

> There are parts of Asia Minor, of Northern Africa, of Greece, and even of Alpine Europe, where the operation of causes set in action by man has brought the face of the earth to a desolation almost as complete as that of the moon; and though, within that brief space of time which we call 'the historical period', they are known to have been covered with luxuriant woods, verdant pastures, and fertile meadows... (2003/1864: 42–3)

In 1873 the Italian scientist and priest Antonio Stoppani seemed to glorify what he called the 'Anthropozoic era', when he wrote: 'We are only at the beginning of the new era; still, how deep is man's footprint on earth already!'[1]

Today, a proposal to declare the Anthropocene a new epoch in the earth's history is under formal review by the International Commission on Stratigraphy (ICS), the authoritative scientific body that makes decisions about geological taxonomies. The classificatory decision it faces is highly controversial. Geologists think in long temporal spans, and the only evidence they countenance for their classifications is what can be found in the earth's crust. In geological terms, the 12,000 years we call the Holocene are a fraction of a second: the preceding epoch – the Pleistocene – lasted more than two million years. It has been difficult to find anything as sweeping or significant that has appeared in the earth's crust during these last 12,000 years as, for instance, the iridium-rich sediment that marks the distinction between the Cretaceous and the Paleocene.

The scarcity of evidence fuels disagreement even among proponents of the Anthropocene about when exactly the transition from the Holocene is supposed to have occurred – and a concomitant race to find congenial stratigraphic support (Zalasiewicz et al., 2011). Most scholars, however, simply point to the industrial revolution that began in the nineteenth century as the beginning of the Anthropocene. It is also often noted that the biological and geological changes that have been most transformative have recently been subject to a 'Great Acceleration', which began around 1950 and is still ongoing (Hibbard et al., 2006). The Great Acceleration also coincides with what may be the closest thing to a significant change in the composition of the earth's crust: the increase in radionuclides such as plutonium-239, which has occurred as a result of nuclear testing (Zalasiewicz et al., 2016). A recent review by Waters et al. (2016) argues vigorously for a mid-twentieth century Anthropocene onset.

Whatever the stratigraphic evidence for the proposed transition from the Holocene to the Anthropocene, there is widespread agreement in the scientific community that a vast range of major, ongoing anthropogenic processes may be leaving durable marks (i.e., millions of years) on the planet. These processes include habitat disruption and massive and increasing rates of species extinction; ocean acidification and alterations of the hydrological cycle; increases in sedimentation rates and soil erosion on land; and an unusually high concentration of climate-changing greenhouse gases in the atmosphere, caused by our massive utilization of fossil energy sources. Because earth's geological and biological fabric is to a large extent a function of its climate, climate change in particular can be expected to remake our planet.

Climate change thus ushers us grandly into the Anthropocene. It tracks the very form of life that *Homo Sapiens* has come to live – one that is resource-intensive, globalized and production- and consumption-driven. It also reminds us that the Anthropocene is not the age of perfect human mastery of nature. Humanity is changing the climate as an inadvertent by-product of other activities, and this will have unforeseen consequences, many of which will be damaging to the very species that is bringing them about: more frequent, extreme weather events; more sweeping epidemics; food and water shortages; and vast and diverse ranges of second- and third-order problems (such as political instability and mass migrations), whose details will vary in different places, times and sociopolitical contexts.

Even if the ICS declines to declare the Anthropocene a geological epoch, it will still be an important concept for understanding the defining circumstances of our present condition: unprecedented numbers of humans, rapid technological change, global interconnectedness, massive exploitation of nature and consequent ecological degradation. Each of these circumstances and their various combinations have political dimensions and consequences, and contribute to the configuration of novel operating spaces for political theory.

The most obvious feature of the Anthropocene is the growing human population and its demand for energy, food, goods, services and information, along with the need to dispose of its waste products. At the beginning of the Holocene there were probably about six million people living as hunter-gatherers; today, there are more than seven billion people, expected to grow to nine billion within the next 30 years, and into eleven billion by 2100. Many of these people command resources that not even the nobility would have enjoyed a few centuries ago; and all of them have legitimate aspirations to decent standards of living.

Improved healthcare and increased food availability have allowed many people to live better and longer, while globalized markets and technology enable constant access to all kinds of goods and services. However, none of this is for free, and many cannot afford the price. The earth is home to almost one billion people living in extreme deprivation at or below $2 a day. Many more are malnourished, die young of easily curable diseases, have no access to important information flows or are socially and politically marginalized.[2] While it is true that never have so many had so much as in the Anthropocene, it is also true that never have so many had so little.

Technology is another important part of the story. The humanity that is transforming nature is organized in highly complex systems bound together by oil and gas pipelines, electrical wires, air travel, highways, train tracks, fibre optic cables and satellite connections. Technology enables the production levels that have allowed humanity to grow in size to today's unprecedented numbers. It enables shipping raw materials and goods across oceans and continents, and empowers people to move around in search of a better life, inspiration or simply a good time. It also enables 'action at a distance' that would once have seemed inconceivable, whether as the instantaneous transfer of wealth, resources or power; as a remote exchange of corporate or diplomatic information; or as a sexual encounter in virtual reality with someone on the other side of the planet. Technology has penetrated our lives deeply. If the screens of our computers or phones, for whatever reason, never switched on again, many of us would suddenly find ourselves with no money, no job, unreachable distant lovers and few, if any, friends. Technology is no longer something that we use: it is now an integral part of who we are.

The conjunction and effects of large population, high consumption and powerful technologies have unprecedented implications. In some respects we feel empowered: we can save a child in a faraway land by making a phone call and pledging a contribution; someone in Las Vegas controlling an unmanned drone can stalk and kill a group of terrorists on another continent; the swipe of a credit card can deliver all sorts of amenities to remote parts of the world; a few clicks at a computer allow us to instantly register our opinions about pretty much everything and share them globally.

Also, because of technology small acts can now reverberate far beyond their spatial and temporal locations in surprising and unwanted ways. By flipping a light switch I may tap into some distant source of energy and activate, reinforce and further promote the emission of greenhouse gases that will remain in the atmosphere for centuries. The accumulation of such apparently trivial, localized, individually innocuous acts can alter fundamental planetary systems in ways that have global consequences, which in turn are locally actualized. Together we change climate, drive species to extinction and acidify the oceans – thus harming and burdening humans and ecosystems in faraway places and times, and ultimately bringing trouble to the very places where we live, to ourselves and to the families that we love.[3]

The arguments over the demarcation of the Anthropocene fundamentally turn on whether some region in time can usefully be spoken of as qualitatively different from some previous region. Qualitative distinctions can supervene on quantitative differences rather than requiring irreducible differences of kind. It is against this background that Vitousek et al.'s study is a good marker: done a thousand years earlier, it would have produced radically different results. Life has always affected the earth, but the extent to which humanity today affects the planet (and thereby itself) is unprecedented. Whether or not this is of geological interest, it is of great cultural and political importance.

2 Political Theory as We Know It

Political theory analyses the conceptual foundations of political life and evaluates the principles and institutions that regulate it. It has descriptive, explanatory and normative dimensions. Modern and contemporary Western political theory, to which we make exclusive reference in this chapter, has been mostly liberal and democratic. Liberal democratic political theory typically (though by no means exclusively) focuses on questions of agency, responsibility, governance and legitimacy.[4]

Questions of agency have to do with the units of descriptive/explanatory analysis and evaluative/normative concern: what are the protagonists of political processes and institutional realities? Whose decisions and actions do (or should) we evaluate: those of states, individuals, corporations, organizations, institutions, or others? Questions of responsibility have to do with who should do what, and why it is them rather than others who should do it. Questions of governance have to do with the operational structures and architectures of political life. Questions of legitimacy have to do with who has the right to make what decisions, on what grounds, and with what authority. In the next four sections, we discuss how the Anthropocene bears on these questions.

3 Agency

The democratic revolutions of the modern period brought us the idea that governments should act in the interests of all those who are governed, rather than acting only in the interests of a governing elite. The basic strategy of democracy is to make the governed and the governors coextensive by having the governed themselves, or their representatives, do the governing.

The agency presupposition and non-agents

One of the functions of political theory is to define the political community. Democratic theory typically presupposes that the political community is constituted by agents who initiate and conduct political action, and who themselves, and their interests and welfare, are what matter politically. These agents (often dubbed 'citizens') are the members of the community who warrant participation and consideration. Call this the 'agency presupposition'.

The agency presupposition explains why, historically, excluding women, slaves, children and others from the political community has been regarded as consistent with democracy. At various times and places, the members of these groups have not been regarded as full agents, so they and their welfare and interests did not matter politically or were heavily discounted. In a system in which being governed implies participating in governance, those who are not agents may be constrained, but they are not governed.

At different times and places democratic communities have become uneasy about many of these exclusions. This contributed to the abolition of slavery and the expansion of the franchise to include non-property-owning males, women and others. Donaldson and Kymlicka (2011) have advocated citizenship for domesticated animals, and the philosopher Eric Wiland (2015) has argued that citizens of any age should have the right to vote. Parity arguments are often employed in these efforts at democratic inclusion. For example, Donaldson and Kymlicka write that 'animals also exhibit various forms of agency' (2011: 65), and Wiland compares children to illiterate adult voters. In both cases, the argument is that members of an excluded class are agents and thus already are, or should be, citizens, and thus have rights to democratic participation. In both cases, the agency presupposition remains central to the characterization of the political community.

The agency presupposition arose at a time in which democratic principles, norms and institutions were being developed to govern relations between agents who lived in close proximity to one another in space and time, and whose decisions and actions had relatively direct impacts on each other. Institutional agents were created to mediate the decisions and actions of citizens and to resolve conflicts between them. These mediating agents took different forms, and democratic polities became more or less representative (rather than direct) democracies. Still, the doctrine of popular sovereignty remained the foundation of democratic theory and practice, and the political community continued to be viewed as a community of self-governing agents.

Following the rise of the nation-state, the agency presupposition was not only maintained, but extended. International relations were theorized as a domain in which bounded political communities, themselves pictured as self-determining agents, confronted one another, each promoting its own interests. There was of course always something mythical about this picture. Nation-states, like other human communities throughout history, have always interacted with each other through cultural exchanges, trade, alliances, migrations and wars, reflecting and creating various forms of interdependency and restrictions on self-determination.

Around 1950, however, 'a structural shift' occurred 'in the organization of human affairs: from a world of discrete but interdependent national states to the world as a shared social space … such that distant events acquire very localized impacts and vice-versa' (Held and McGrew, 2007: 2–3). In this globalized world, the fates of nation-states and their peoples became not just effectively interdependent but also structurally interconnected, with social, political and economic activities, interactions and infrastructures stretching beyond political frontiers, leading to a deepening enmeshment of the local and the global (Held and McGrew, 2007: 2–3). Political decisions and actions taken locally (in selected powerful countries, many of which were democratic) now systematically had planetary implications, impacting for better or worse the welfare and interests of people in all corners of the world. In response to globalization, political theory has produced sophisticated perspectives on global justice and democracy, as well as discourses on global governance. 'Cosmopolitanism', in its many forms, has become ascendant (Held, 2010).

Meanwhile, globalized infrastructures of production and consumption, powered by technological advancements in key industries, have damaged ecosystems, spread pollution and altered the physiognomy of the planet. This has caused disruptions of the earth's fundamental systems, including those that govern climate, whose effects we are just beginning to experience. Because such systems configure the very context of human and nonhuman life on earth, their alteration inevitably impacts the lives of future as well as present people, along with the nonhuman world.

Political theory enters the Anthropocene confronting these vast changes in both nature and culture. Political agents (living humans) have gained unprecedented power over a vast universe of non-agents that comprises animate and inanimate nature as well as those living on the periphery of both space and time. We are now in an epoch in which the circle of affected non-agents has expanded beyond cultural, genetic and spatiotemporal boundaries to include virtually everything on the planet, now extended indefinitely in time. This establishes an enormous asymmetry of power. Those on the periphery, and nature, cannot initiate and conduct political action: they cannot reciprocate, they cannot participate, they cannot protest, they cannot retaliate. In the Anthropocene, political agents have their way with the world to an extent and on a scale that is historically unparalleled. While the great empires of the past colonized great areas of the planet, the empire of the present now colonizes the global future as well.

The agency presupposition and new agents

New kinds of agents have also emerged in the Anthropocene: global agents such as multinational corporations, the International Monetary Fund (IMF), the World Trade Organization (WTO), financial networks and rating agencies, transnational social movements, private military companies, cross-border criminal cartels, nongovernmental organizations (NGOs) and others. Since they are neither individual people nor governments, these new agents escape the traditional agency categories of liberal political theory, as well as those of international relations theory. Peculiar as they may seem in theory, these new agents can nonetheless be extremely effective in practice. Their decisions and actions can have very significant impacts on the lives of people the world over, on the relations of states, and on the fate of future generations and nonhuman nature. Because they incarnate very different sets of interests and pursue different goals in very different ways, it is inevitable that the agendas of these agents can be mutually antagonistic. This lack of harmonization complicates the already unstable relations among states.

These new global agents are also largely unaccountable for the ways in which they pursue their agendas, at least by traditional democratic forms of governance (Keohane, 2003). In traditional liberal political theory, agents are reciprocally accountable: individuals to each other and to governments, and governments to each other and to individuals. The new global agents of the Anthropocene are not very accountable to individuals, and in many cases they are not very accountable to governments either. Ironically, the new global agent that many hope could order this proliferating complexity and coordinate a shared plan for the future of the planet – the United Nations – is all too accountable to governments, and thus too heavily constrained by competing national interests to play these roles.

In addition to such global agents, we may be creating altogether new forms of agency that were previously unknown in nature: digital agents such as super-intelligent computers, self-directing drones, robots, distributed sensory systems, and so on. What is born as a digital support for human activities can quickly become a determining force in human affairs. Without painting overdramatic pictures of sapient machines gone bad, we can point to the apparently more mundane case of 'smart urban infrastructures' – a case that matters especially since life in the Anthropocene is largely life in cities. Continuous monitoring, ubiquitous computing, and the real-time manipulation of 'big data' are increasingly becoming embedded in urban infrastructures, enabling the city to sense the events and activities that take place within its provenance. Powered by a capacity to remember, correlate and anticipate, these distributed digital systems can reflexively monitor our environments and our behaviours and, in many cases, respond without human input – thus becoming active agents in the organization of daily life (Shepard, 2011: 20). While many liberal theorists would agree that in some cases paternalism may increase the welfare of citizens and thus be politically desirable, digital agents risk introducing inappropriate, radically invasive forms of paternalism that become 'normalized' because they are practically unnoticeable. Traditional liberal political theory may not be well equipped to address such paternalism, especially since its sources seem not to be human, and it is difficult even to imagine how digital agents can be held accountable and to whom and for what exactly.

The agency presupposition and planetary collective action problems

The collective action problems we face in the Anthropocene go far beyond those that exercised traditional democratic theory, such as the apparent irrationality of voting. Even if I am convinced that my vote matters in a national election, my country may still seem powerless to address climate change.

No single agent can solve the problems of the Anthropocene. Cooperation among political agents is necessary, but remains structurally elusive. Individuals have their daily preoccupations, politicians have their constituencies to protect, governments have national interests to promote, global agents have their own very different agendas, and digital agents are a vast, enveloping force whose contributions are crucial yet unstable. The fact that the required cooperation also extends across generations complicates matters further (Gardiner, 2011). This shifting and only partially coherent landscape of agency leaves us disoriented and sceptical about our capacity to manage our ecological entanglements. Indeed, the main obstacle to taking action on climate change may well be the deep sense of its inevitability and our inability to affect its course.

Many people see no real alternatives to the choices and actions that are taking us over the cliff. Of course I can stop using electricity, but that will throw me out of step with the world around me and do little to stop climate change. And yet the second I flip a light switch I am forced into a global network of eco-altering financial and economic interests, political agreements and avenues of cultural reinforcement whose solid yet ever-changing configuration is largely unknown to me, but which I am at no liberty to side-step and which I suddenly find myself sponsoring with my behaviour (Di Paola, 2015).

Even firms may have relatively little room for manoeuvre. As long as markets are structured in such a way that the cheapest forms of energy remain fossil-based, companies that want to do something about climate change must accept loss of competitiveness, which is just the opposite of what companies normally seek to do.

States are similarly constrained in the Anthropocene. As the global spills into the domestic, a globally changing climate may have pernicious local impacts on the territory and population of any given state. Each state can do something to alleviate the domestic, and even the global, pernicious ecological implications of the activities of its own population – through laws, education and other means. But a state can do very little against the domestic and global implications of the activities of populations other than its own, since these populations belong to other self-determining states. However, no self-determining state is immune from the pernicious consequences of global climate change (Di Paola, 2015).

What is true of climate change is true of other anthropogenic processes now under way that involve the disruption of the hydrological cycle, the nitrogen cycle and other fundamental earth systems. They enmesh us in vast collective action problems that have intra- as well as intergenerational dimensions and pose unprecedented threats: multiple, multiscalar, probabilistic, indirect, often invisible, spatiotemporally unbound, potentially catastrophic and apparently beyond anyone's control (Jamieson, 2014).

The irony is that after centuries of modernity and its contributions to human welfare and autonomy, we find ourselves at the portal of the Anthropocene with the widespread sense of a loss of agency. Together, we are remaking the planet and undermining the conditions of our own existence, though no individual or collective decision was ever made to do so. Natural and human systems are being transformed not as a result of any rational (or sensible) plan, but rather because of the unintended effects of systemic, interlocking forces and structures that have congealed and stratified in such a way that they seem to dominate our lives, our economies and our politics. Never has humanity been more powerful, yet never have 'things' seemed more in control.[5]

4 Responsibility

Questions of responsibility are closely related to agency, and just as central to liberal theory. Liberalism sees responsibility as central because among its core values is the idea that political agents are morally autonomous. Autonomous agents should be free to make choices and take actions, but they should also feel and be held responsible for these choices and actions, particularly for their impacts on other autonomous agents. The circumstances of the Anthropocene problematize this picture.

Climate change, like other problems of the Anthropocene, has been brought about by humans and will have negative impacts on humans (as well as non-human nature). Yet it may be surprising how difficult it can be to move from this (often denied yet relatively uncontroversial) general claim to more specific claims about who is responsible for what.

One reason is causal fragmentation: collective action problems are not only impossible to solve in isolation, but also impossible to cause in isolation. Agents of all kinds – individuals, governments, corporations and global agents of other kinds – are implicated in the rise in global temperatures. What makes this fragmentation especially problematic in the case of climate change is that it is global and intergenerational.

Another reason why it is difficult to assign responsibilities is the complexity of the causal mechanisms at work. Climate change will kill people, but increasing the atmospheric concentration of a trace gas like carbon dioxide does not directly cause people to drop dead. Vast, complex, multiscalar physical and social systems mediate between the perturbation of the carbon cycle and the deaths, making causal knowledge or attribution extremely difficult or even practically impossible. What is true of deaths is true of other damages as well: to property, species, ecosystems, and so forth.

Responsibility and causation

It is widely held that causal responsibility is necessary for moral and legal responsibility: for how can I be morally or legally responsible for something I did not bring about?[6] This view is closely related to Mill's Harm Principle, according to which autonomous agents can do whatever they want as long as they do not harm others: choices and actions that do impose harm on others are, other things being equal, morally wrong.[7] While philosophers and political theorists argue about the scope of the Harm Principle and the details of its exact specification, it surely is the mark of a liberal state that it largely keeps its nose out of its citizens' harmless behaviour. It does the same with the harmless operations of firms and of other states. Traditionally, liberal political theory and practice want a harm for there to be a victim, a victim for there to be a wrong, and a wrong for holding an agent morally and legally responsible.[8]

In the case of climate change and some other problems characteristic of the Anthropocene, this sequence is upset. No one in particular seems to be harming anyone in particular: hence, no one seems to be morally or legally responsible for the deaths and damages that occur. Here is one way of reconstructing the problem: all agents are parts of the cause of climate change as they all contribute to it. To be part of a cause, however, is not to be the cause of any specific part of its effect, or any one of its many effects. The emissions produced by my car, for instance, will accumulate with those of the other billion cars in the world, travel across space–time, disperse into the workings and feedbacks of various physical and chemical systems at different scales, and at no point ever cause any specific flood, drought or hurricane. This in turn means that my emissions will not cause any of the harms that these phenomena will bring to people (or property or ecosystems).[9] The nonlinear, multilevel causal roller-coaster that goes from emissions to climate change and from climate change back to deaths and damages ensures that specific instances of the latter cannot be imputed singularly to any agent in particular.

In addition, because of the enlarged spatiotemporal reach and complexity of the causal mechanisms at work, both before and after anyone dies or anything is damaged it will be impossible to say exactly who or what are the victims of climate change. Before, because we will not know their identities in advance: looking ahead we will see no more than probabilities distributed across populations (Heinzerling, 2015). After, because we will never be sure that the culprit is climate change and not something else, as climate change will only kill and damage in indirect ways, sending hitmen like floods, droughts, food scarcity, respiratory deficiencies, epidemics and armed conflicts. No obituary will ever say of anyone that she or he was killed by climate change.

In short, when it comes to climate change, no particular agent harms any particular victim by emitting greenhouse gases. If we stick to harm-causation as a condition of moral and legal responsibility, then no such responsibility can be assigned to any particular agent for climate change and related damages, suffering and deaths. In a traditional liberal framework, this means that no moral or legal wrongs are committed.

In various societies at various times, people have been held morally responsible for the acts they have performed and not just for what these acts have brought about. Indeed, many people today are morally appalled by such apparently harmless acts as consensual gay sex or flag burning, while being completely unmoved by deaths caused in war or by environmental pollution. Contemporary psychologists Jonathan Haidt and Daniel Gilbert have argued that our everyday moral conceptions, even those of many liberals, are in fact only loosely associated with harm causation. According to Haidt (2012), at the foundation of morality as experienced by most people are considerations of fairness and reciprocity, in-group loyalty, authority and respect, and purity and sanctity, in addition to considerations about the causation of harm. The problem is that climate change does not really excite any of these further considerations any more than it provides a clear example of harm-causation. In an article in the *Los Angeles Times* in 2006, Gilbert wrote:

> When people feel insulted or disgusted, they generally do something about it, such as whacking each other over the head, or voting. Moral emotions are the brain's call to action. Although all human societies have moral rules about food and sex, none has a moral rule about atmospheric chemistry. And so we are outraged about every breach of protocol except Kyoto. Yes, global warming is bad, but it doesn't make us feel nauseated or angry or disgraced, and thus we don't feel compelled to rail against it.[10]

By and large, individuals do not feel greatly moved by the climate problem, nor by the fate of the spatiotemporally distant people, natural entities and systems that will suffer its worst consequences. Coupled with the difficulty in applying the Harm Principle, this results in almost no one feeling morally responsible, and in no individual, organization or institution being held morally and legally responsible – which in turn leads to widespread disengagement and thus inaction.

Responsibility and the private/public distinction

Liberal political theory and practice will have to navigate some uneasy waters in order to counter such disengagement. The individual behaviours that contribute to climate change and other systemic global problems of the Anthropocene are not only apparently harmless, but also generally regarded as private: driving cars, eating this or that, investing here or there, having children, and so on. Yet today, these apparently private behaviours have public consequences, however indirect, across spatial, temporal, genetic and cultural boundaries. Public and private behaviour is thus blurred in the Anthropocene in novel ways, generating new problems for liberal political theory and practice.[11]

At the heart of liberalism is a distinction between what is private and what is public. This distinction has its origins in two important junctures in modern history: the emergence of the sovereign nation-state, which helped configure the notion of a distinctively public realm; and the reactions to the claims of monarchs and parliaments to unrestrained legislative power, which developed into a 'countervailing effort to stake out distinctively private spheres free from the encroaching power of the state' (Horwitz, 1982: 1423).

One of the main theoretical functions of the public/private distinction is to help justify political respect for individual autonomy and diversity. Historically, this was mostly meant to guarantee religious toleration, later extended to toleration of cultures more generally, and recently extended to a broad range of 'comprehensive doctrines' (see Rawls, 2005/1993). Respect for individual autonomy and diversity of beliefs and behaviours is one basic value of liberalism, but a commitment to it is also a source of political instability. The liberal philosophical grandmaster, John Rawls, considered 'the fact of reasonable pluralism' to be the single greatest cause of instability in liberal political communities.

Rawls's guiding assumption was that the leading threat to stability would come from diverse and discordant behaviours, largely tracking diversity and discordance in beliefs. But the behaviours that drive the problems of the Anthropocene are largely uniform and not belief-driven at all. Whatever our 'comprehensive doctrine', we all cook and take showers; and even back-to-nature environmental activists have children. These widely shared behaviours, unrelated to particular beliefs, contribute to problems such as climate change. It is agreement in these relatively belief-independent behaviours, not diversity and discordance in beliefs leading to diverse and discordant behaviours, that is at the root of the problems of the Anthropocene, and traditional liberal theory has little to say about this novelty.

Liberals have not just traditionally postulated a clear-cut theoretical distinction between the private and the public, but have also been very concerned with ensuring that the distinction was respected in practice. In many cases – including the paradigmatic case of religious toleration – this has meant ensuring that the differences in the (harmless) private behaviours that individuals engage in were respected, both by governments and by other individuals. The response of governments to private behaviours that have pernicious public consequences, on the other hand, has been to regulate them coercively. In the Anthropocene, even taking a long hot shower is a type of action that has pernicious public consequences. Yet, from a liberal perspective, the desirability of top-down regulation of such apparently private behaviours as those concerning personal hygiene, diet, housing, investment, mobility and reproduction is most unwelcome, given the encroachments on individual liberty that it would entail.

The uneasy realization is that, insofar as one of the central tasks of a politics in the Anthropocene is to restore stability to earth's natural systems, the most effective way of doing so may involve disrupting patterns of everyday life in ways that liberals would find unacceptable. Sometimes, it seems, the Anthropocene forces us to choose between liberalism and environmental stability. Even worse, there is no guarantee that sacrificing environmental stability would not itself lead to the erosion of liberal ideals.

Responsibility and the sea of agency

As we have seen, the private/public distinction is blurred when agents acting in pursuit of their own private interests have significant impacts on other agents or non-agents. The problem is magnified in the Anthropocene by the plurality of agents operating at different levels of social organization, often with unclear causal powers and even less clear permissions and mandates. In this sea of agency it is difficult to assign responsibilities because responsibilities are enmeshed across units and levels of agency: the responsibilities of one agent (or set of agents) may only be activated by the fulfilment of responsibilities of other agents (or set of agents) operating at other levels of social organization. There is often no clear way to decide which agents are relevant in a particular case, which should act first, and what exactly are the duties of particular agents even when it is clear that they have them.

This problem seems especially acute with multinational corporations, which, as noted in section 3, are one of the largest and least tamed and understood creatures swimming in this sea. Liberal political theory has traditionally had much more to say about the relations between individuals and governments and their respective responsibilities than about the relations of corporations to both individuals and governments and their wider responsibilities to society and nature. The planetary influence exercised by multinational corporations today counsels a reconsideration of priorities.

In a landmark paper, Richard Heede (2014) showed that just 90 firms were responsible for 63 per cent of all carbon and methane emissions occurring between 1854 and 2010 (see also Frumhoff et al., 2015). Of these firms, 83 are industrial producers of oil, natural gas and coal, and 7 are cement manufacturers. And 50 of them are investor-owned, 31 are primarily state-owned and 9 are entirely government-run. They are headquartered in 43 countries: 54 in industrialized countries and 36 in developing countries. They extract resources everywhere in the world, and the energy and materials they produce are embodied in products that virtually everyone in the world consumes. These firms are all still operative today (with the exception of five, previously headquartered in the old Soviet Union) and their names are quite familiar. They include Chevron, Exxon Mobil, Shell, Saudi Aramco, BP, Gazprom and Statoil. More than half of these firms' emissions have occurred since 1988, and their emissions continue to rise each year. While these firms have different organizational cultures and behave in different ways, in many cases they fund misinformation campaigns and put pressure on governments to allow them to continue business as usual – that is, when they are not run or co-run by governments themselves, possibilities that liberal political theory seldom considers, since it tends to conceptualize business in contrast to government. Many of these firms are committed to using their power and market share to aggressively oppose or inhibit moving into a non-carbon future, thus devoting themselves to the unprecedented enterprise of trying to prevent humanity from adapting to potentially catastrophic environmental change.[12]

Multinational corporations often act in these ways, yet they also have the potential to act effectively to reduce greenhouse gas emissions. They have the financing and competence required to change their own practices, and they operate at a scale that can make a difference. Yet individual companies will not act aggressively on their own if others do not. Government action can 'level the playing field' and change incentives. But corporations that benefit from the existing system resist change, and governments themselves face the same collective action problems as corporations and individuals. NGOs and civil society can change corporate incentives by stigmatizing particular investments and behaviours and rewarding others, yet they too face important strategic challenges when it comes to proactive mobilization, such as poor networking, lack of funding or solid organizational structures, and internal competition. In the Anthropocene, we have multiple agents operating at different levels of social organization, with structurally enmeshed dynamics, facing problems at various levels and across levels. The result is that it is often just not clear who is responsible for doing what. Everyone, even the worst actors, can claim 'plausible deniability'.

This unsettled sea of agency is expressive of the systematicity of the forces that generate the problems of the Anthropocene. The manipulation of the carbon cycle is intrinsic to the global economy in the same way that driving a car or flipping a light switch are intrinsic to our daily lives. Coal is mined in Australia, shipped to China where it powers the manufacturing of cars, computers and other products that are then exported to Europe and the United States. We drive to work, switch on our computers and write papers about the Anthropocene. Others engage in their version of the same activities, with the same results for the planet: tons of carbon dioxide added to the atmosphere every day. Who is responsible? Australia, China, the United States or Europe, the multinationals involved, the WTO that oversees global trade, the financial networks that fund it through investment, the digital agents that monitor trans-continental shipments, me, everyone else, or no one at all? There are no clear answers to these questions.

Moreover, these processes are dynamic. As the global economy changes and morphs, Australia may be replaced as the energy provider, China as the manufacturing site, and the United States and Europe (and their citizens) as the consumers of finished products. Agency in the Anthropocene is an unsettled sea, but deep beneath the waves runs a constant current of fossil fuels. As long as the global economy is carbon-based, the problems of the Anthropocene will persist regardless of which countries, companies and individuals are occupying which roles. In this sea of agency, each wave contributes, but can be perfectly replaced by other waves.

Everything influences everything else in the Anthropocene, but responsibilities are elusive. The Anthropocene challenges liberal political theory by disabling the application of the Harm Principle and blurring the private/ public distinction, most notably when it comes to the operations of new global agents such as multinational corporations. In this world, cooperation among all political agents old and new is required, and yet the systematicity of the forces that generate its defining problems enmeshes responsibilities in such a way as to efface them. In the Anthropocene, it seems, there are no causes, only effects.

5 Governance

The Anthropocene is difficult to govern. There is a plethora of agents operating at different levels of social organization, with different goals, no clear responsibilities and no cop on the beat.

Global policy gridlock

At the global level, there is a disquieting gridlock in international cooperation (Hale et al., 2013) as the world order attempts to adjust to shifting power distributions following the emergence of new giants such as China, Brazil and India. When tackling the problems of the Anthropocene, the cooperation of these once second-line countries is no longer just desirable, but absolutely essential. As their cooperation becomes more valuable, the price for obtaining it rises accordingly. This complicates negotiations, causing gridlock, which seems only destined to worsen because this logic applies not only to presently emerging world powers, but also to those that have already emerged and those that will emerge in the future. Global governance in the Anthropocene is cooperation-hungry, and this increases the price of obtaining cooperation from every country. Worse still, as we have already noted, effective governance in the Anthropocene cannot be as state-centric as it has been in the past, yet attempts at governance continue largely to conform to the old paradigm.

In the Anthropocene, a multitude of agents must cooperate on complex issues that are still only beginning to be understood and are open to multiple ways of framing, each of which finds different resources relevant to their solution and counts different responses as successes and failures (Hulme 2009). For example, if climate change is a geopolitical problem, then new agreements and institutions are needed. If the problem is market failure, then we need effective carbon taxes or a functional cap and trade system. If the problem primarily reflects a technological failure, then we need a programme for clean energy or perhaps geo-engineering. If climate change is just the latest way for the global rich to exploit the global poor, then we need to renew the struggle for global justice. The phenomenon of multiple frames, each of which is plausible, is characteristic of what are called 'wicked problems', which are notoriously difficult for political systems to address successfully (Jamieson and Di Paola, 2014: 105).

Whatever framing is adopted, climate change remains a multidimensional problem that concerns ecology, demography, development, production, consumption, resource use, trade rules, health, security, urban planning, mobility, migration, and more. Each of these domains is owned by this or that international organization, this or that department of the United Nations, this or that ministry in this or that country. There is a great deal of operational interconnectedness among these agents, but little integration. No action can be taken without involving each organization or institution claiming jurisdiction over a given domain, but because no domain can be effectively managed without dealing with other domains as well, operating at different levels of social and geographical organization, each organization and institution sees its jurisdiction fade into that of others. Jurisdictions stratify, but responsibilities dilute.

Scepticism about global institutions is likely to increase. Global institutions are not just failing to inspire and push for progress on many urgent and important planetary issues, but they are failing even to ensure a solid and authoritative framework for sustaining themselves (Hale et al., 2013). Bilateralism is again the norm and the condition for the outcomes of multi-lateral negotiations to have any real force; functioning regional forums for cooperation are still but a distant aspiration, as recently shown by the poor performance of the European Union in matters as crucial as public debt management, migration and foreign policy. And yet there is little to go back to: the ability of individual states to respond to the problems of the Anthropocene is hampered by many of the same forces that hobble global or other supranational institutions, and by other problems which are distinctively their own.

Domestic policy gridlocks

It was Confucius who said: 'The Ancients who wanted to manifest their bright virtue to all in the world, first governed well their own states' (*The Great Learning*, 4).[13] It is unclear whether the Moderns can match the Ancients in this regard. In the Anthropocene, the global spills into the domestic, but the domestic also spills into the global.

Political dysfunction in one country can cripple efforts at global governance. Political divisions in the United States, for instance, have adversely affected attempts at global climate governance for almost 30 years (Jamieson, 2014: 22–60). Domestic policy gridlock, though most striking in the United States, is generally in evidence around the world, including in important European countries such as Italy, France, Spain and the United Kingdom.

One way of thinking about this dysfunction is through the concept of 'veto players' (Tsebelis, 2002). A veto player in a political system is an agent who can prevent a departure from the status quo. Veto players are specified by constitutions (e.g., the President, the Congress, the Courts in the United States), but can also emerge from a political system (e.g., political parties that are members of a government coalition in Western Europe), or from civil society (e.g., powerful industries, unions or other interest groups).

Veto players can protect minority interests, prevent destabilizing change and preserve important values and policies through periods in which they are unpopular. Veto players prevent a system from being excessively fluid and flexible. This is attractive when the status quo is desirable or an exogenous shock is beneficial; however, when the status quo is undesirable or an exogenous shock disturbs a desirable status quo, fluidity and flexibility are needed in order to respond quickly and decisively. This is arguably the situation in the rapidly changing world of the Anthropocene, with many important challenges such as migration, resource depletion, financial, cybernetic, and military insecurity, global health threats and climate change, all of which demand nimble political responses to which veto players would have to acquiesce.

Every political system has some number of veto players, with specific ideological distances among them, and each veto player displays some particular level of internal cohesion. Some veto players are relatively unified agents (e.g., the President of the United States), while other are relatively fragmented (e.g., the Democratic Party in Italy). These and other characteristics of veto players affect the set of possible outcomes that can replace the status quo. Significant departures from the status quo are extremely difficult when the set of possible outcomes is small – that is, when veto players are many, when they have significant ideological distances among them, and when they are internally cohesive. Veto players are also agenda setters, and the more of them there are, the less power each has to set the agenda. At the limit, where change from the status quo is impossible, it does not make any difference who controls the agenda (Tsebelis, 2002).

The presence of many veto players leads to domestic policy gridlock. Democracies seem particularly vulnerable to such danger, and the more veto players in a democracy the greater the degree of vulnerability. An especially high concentration of veto players explains why a powerful, rich, technologically leading country like the United States is uncannily slow to address consequential public issues like the politics of distribution, racial equality, immigration, the proper balance between liberty and national security, and of course climate change. The US Constitution separates powers in the federal government, reserves a broad range of powers to states and 'the people' and includes a bill of rights that in some instances effectively gives veto powers to individuals. In addition, practices have developed through time that also inhibit action, such as requiring supermajorities for certain kinds of political decisions.

The number and influence of veto players are associated with a wide range of political outcomes that go beyond blocking departures from the status quo. For example, political scientists Stepan and Linz (2011) have observed a positive correlation between the number of veto players in a national political system and the nation's economic inequality. They have also observed that the less representative the upper body of a national legislature, the greater the gap between the rich and the poor. Their data show that the United States has the most veto players among 23 countries surveyed, the least representative upper house, and the greatest degree of inequality.

These problems may be extreme in the United States, but they occur elsewhere as well, albeit in different forms. The European Union is also a complex constellation of veto players including the Council of Ministers, appointed by the member countries; the European Parliament, elected by the peoples of Europe; and the European Commission, appointed by the member countries and approved by the European Parliament. The Parliament in turn comprises an even more complex party system reflecting various ideologies and nationalities (see Tsebelis, 2002: 1). European Parliament parties ultimately refer to their national bases, which in national parliamentary systems function as veto players themselves. In most EU countries, vetoes are exercised by the parties that are members of a ruling coalition; in some – notably Italy, Spain and Greece – the parties themselves have strong, direct, historical ties to industry, unions or religious associations. Political consensus in such countries is often elusive even on relatively minor policy issues.

All this reinforces the scepticism generated by the global policy gridlock that we described in the previous section, and also breeds more general worries regarding the ability of systems of governance at every level to negotiate the pressing challenges of the Anthropocene. For every possible policy change, there is always a 'do-nothing' alternative (sometimes more respectably presented as a 'wait and see' alternative) that is invariably attractive to many people – even some who claim to want action – as well as to various institutions and organizations at every level.

Among the reasons to resist change are those based on a rational choice calculus of transition costs and uncertainty about both the process of transition and the final pay-off structure. Veto players give voice to such considerations, as well as other considerations that we have already noted. They also may give voice to less rational tendencies, however, which are inevitably present in society and are crystallized in votes and market choices. Among these may be heightened attention to sunk costs, avoidance of cognitive dissonance through various forms of rationalization (after all, if something potentially catastrophic like climate change tracks the very ways in which we live, the nagging thought is there that there must be something fundamentally wrong about these ways), search for refuge in 'what has always worked', fear of regretting the changes made, and even the desire to maintain and transmit a sense of control by not acceding to the demands of new circumstances (Samuelson and Zeckhauser, 1988).

At the dawn of this new epoch, our global, regional and national institutions are failing to act resolutely (and perhaps, seen with the eyes of future generations, even sensibly) to address the problems of the Anthropocene. These problems are processed differently by different countries and different political agents with different objectives, prompting different and differently motivated responses, often in contradiction with one another. But the result is undisputable: the challenges of the Anthropocene have thus far largely been met by inaction, squabbling and denial. The imperatives of change are often hard to accept.

6 Legitimacy

In light of these failures, it is not surprising that there is a crisis of legitimacy for liberal democracies the world over. In the United States, confidence in government has never been lower. Only 9 per cent of Americans say that the Republican Congress is doing a good job. Republicans give the Republican Congress even lower approval ratings than do Democrats. Many voters consider never having served in public office to be a better qualification for election than experience. In a recent poll, the majority of likely Republican voters indicated that they simply did not care about presidential candidates' policy positions.[14] Such lack of interest seems to be transcontinental: the EU parliamentary elections of 2014 registered the lowest voter turnout since 1979, when European elections were first held.[15]

Meanwhile populist movements are on the rise in the United States, as they are in the United Kingdom, France, Italy, Scotland, Greece, Spain, the Netherlands, Austria and other European countries. These movements oppose incumbent power structures that they portray as detached from citizens' everyday realities and needs; are critical of current policy trends for reasons that often cut across traditional ideological divides; and advocate change by popular demand, circumventing entrenched veto players and institutional agents and procedures.

What is often characteristic of these movements is a yearning for a mythologized past in which politicians came 'from the people', citizens' opinions and expertise were integral to the mechanisms of governance, bureaucrats did not rule, and work was rewarded rather than rent-seeking and speculation. These mantras are often coupled with a romance of the nation (and sometimes even the ethnic) state. In most European countries, these movements are strenuously anti-EU. They are fed by systems of governance with long and opaque chains of delegation, which to some extent occur precisely because of the complexity of the problems of the Anthropocene. They are fired by vivid, visceral and even uncivil expressions of disagreement that seem to ricochet permanently around the world on the internet, which in turn seems to intensify anger and impatience.

In some respects these movements are not political at all. When they come close to power they typically fracture. On the one hand, the very act of assuming the reins of power is seen as a betrayal of the impulse that gave rise to them; on the other, they are often co-opted into the traditional power structures against which they were born protesting. Either way, even the raw populist voice of the people seems quickly silenced by the status quo.

Nonetheless, these signals of popular disappointment express substantive challenges to the legitimacy of liberal democratic institutions in the Anthropocene. These challenges are of two basic kinds: first, liberal democratic systems of governance at various levels seem incapable of making effective policy in many important and urgent domains; second, their actions seem distorted by unequal access and influence. The 'dignity of legislation' (Waldron, 1995) is devalued by arcane procedures, delegated to courts and administrative agencies, and corrupted by partisan interests (Lepore, 2015). At the same time, citizens register a loss of jurisdiction over political life and even express difficulty in or indifference to developing informed views about key issues.

Traditionally, the sources of liberal democratic legitimacy are consent (in the spirit of Hobbes and, with differences, Locke), beneficial consequences (in the utilitarian legacy of Bentham and Mill), and public reason (in the Kantian and Rawlsian tradition). The circumstances of the Anthropocene threaten to block all those sources in one way or another.

The sea of agency, the multilevel complexities and governance gridlocks, and the systemic global spill-over into the domestic mean that much of what goes on in any given democratic country in the Anthropocene is, in fact, never consented to by its citizens. The route from individual vote to domestic policy is constantly and vertiginously perturbed by the incursions of various global or other agents and by their demands and vetoes.[16]

As for beneficial consequences, the two most basic functions of the liberal state are to provide security and to solve coordination problems, thus providing benefits that cannot be provided by private actors acting independently. The failure to address the emerging problems of the Anthropocene, such as climate change, combined with the erosion of the sense of security in many parts of the world, is a profound challenge faced by liberal states and the institutions for supranational governance that they have constructed (e.g., the EU, WTO, UN). If the state and these other institutions prove unable to provide the fundamental public goods of security and coordination at both domestic and global levels, this legitimacy is compromised.

Public reason theorists maintain that 'political power is legitimate only when it is exercised in accordance with a constitution (written or unwritten), the essentials of which all citizens, as reasonable and rational, can endorse in the light of their common human reason' (Rawls, 2001: 4). It is unclear that reasonable and rational individuals of such Kantian disposition could endorse the systematic dumping on future generations of the costs of climate change and other environmental problems of the Anthropocene – a dumping in which all contemporary liberal democracies are implicated. It is arguable that by Rawlsian lights no present democracy is fulfilling its intergenerational obligations of justice.[17]

There have always been tensions and trade-offs between these three sources of legitimacy, but typically there was also synergy. In the past, the governed could be expected to consent to policies that had beneficial consequences and were justifiable by the lights of public reason, primarily because these policies were meant and understood to bring benefits to them and had to be justifiable to them alone. In other words, the agency presupposition applied and the fate of non-agents was of little or no political concern. In the

Anthropocene, the correlation between consent and the other two sources threatens to break down.

A phenomenon like climate change creates the potential for ubiquitous tensions and trade-offs between the present and the future, and more generally between agents and non-agents – those who are governed, and those who are affected. The latter will suffer most from climate change, but a democracy responsive to the claims of future generations (or those living beyond its borders, or nonhuman nature) may often have to forgo opportunities for bringing beneficial consequences to those who empower it with their votes, favouring instead the interests of those who do not vote because they do not yet exist (or live in different countries or are not human). Even if those benefits to non-agents were great and conferring them was justified by the lights of public reason, such non-agent-oriented policies might not be consented to, particularly in democracies that are already being accused of not being responsive enough to their citizens. Many believe that ignoring or heavily discounting the welfare and interests of non-agents is morally wrong, but if consent is important, that may be a wrong that democracies cannot avoid committing.

It is difficult to see how these tensions and trade-offs can be addressed from within a perspective that is founded on the agency presupposition and makes government responsive to those who are governed but not to those who are affected beyond borders in space, time, citizenship or genetic make-up. A basic presupposition of liberal democracy appears to be threatened by the very actions that would have to be taken to express concern for all those affected by the actions of its citizens.

Widespread disappointment with the performance of liberal democracies and the supranational governance institutions that they have created has already translated in many countries into populist attempts to penetrate incumbent power structures. While these attempts are often politically inchoate, occupying the space between keeping it real and getting it done, they are unequivocal messengers of strong legitimacy challenges. These challenges address concerns of both justice and efficacy, and can be theoretically reconstructed as responses to blockages of traditional sources of liberal democratic legitimacy that are variously connected with the new circumstances of the Anthropocene.

Liberal political theory has always recognized the right to resist and even overthrow illegitimate political power. This right has been used to justify historical events that liberals typically applaud, including the English Civil War, the French Revolution and the American Revolution. Despite their blemishes, these revolutions forwarded liberal values and helped to entrench them in institutions. Unable to find consistent responses to challenges to their own legitimacy in the Anthropocene, liberal democracies may be in danger of warranting revolutions against themselves and the very institutions that should realize their values.

7   Concluding Remarks

We began this chapter by explaining the notion of the Anthropocene. We went on to show how it puts pressure on traditional liberal notions of agency, responsibility, governance and legitimacy. We claimed that innovation in both theory and practice is required if liberal democratic politics is to secure the survival of its core values in this new epoch. It is extremely difficult even to sketch the nature of the required innovations, and we will not try to do so here. Instead, we will close with a summary of the main challenges ahead and mention some possible responses.

The existing democratic deficit in liberal states will generally have to be reduced; yet, in the case of climate change and other problems of the Anthropocene, states will have to muster both the internal coherence and strength to better resist populism, and the external coherence and strength to be more cooperative partners within the framework of supranational institutions. This seems to suggest, perhaps paradoxically, that political institutions for the Anthropocene will have to be more democratic in some respects and less democratic in others. Responding to such a challenge requires imagination that itself can scarcely be imagined. But this should not be surprising. The Anthropocene is being shaped in real time by the very problems that characterize it, along with our clumsy attempts to address them. It is one of the features of the change that is now under way that we and our new institutions will have to coevolve with it.

Governance in the Anthropocene is cooperation-hungry at multiple levels. Never has there been less of a role for 'rugged individualists', whether as individual people or countries. Noticing this, some advocate world government and others global federalism. While there are powerful considerations for and against both views, it is difficult to see how either could move from inchoate dream to concrete reality. Governance in the Anthropocene is also cooperation-hungry intergenerationally, and it is especially unclear what such models of governance would mean in this domain and how they might be implemented (but see Thompson 2010; and Gosseries and González-Ricoy, forthcoming).

What does seem clear is that institutions of governance will have to work at multiple scales in both space and time, incorporating the interests of the global with those of the local, and those of the future with those of the present. Currently, we heavily discount the interests of the future and the far. Besides being morally dubious, this practice may also lead to unworkable outcomes in the Anthropocene, as the traditional instruments of collective decision-making increasingly seem inapplicable (Jamieson, 2014). In any case, it is difficult to see how to adequately take into account the interests of the future and the far without unjustly subordinating the interests of the near and the present, especially given the centrality of the agency presupposition in liberal democratic theory. Democratic governments are supposed to be responsive to all those who are governed, but those beyond its borders in space, time or citizenship are not governed but only affected.

If a 'social geology' existed, it would describe the Anthropocene as comprising a relatively small but highly complex sea of agency, agitated by creatures that are both private and public, individual and collective, human and non-human, local and global, and whose choices and actions are systemically interconnected at various levels by technologically enabled networks. This sea beats on the shores of much vaster continents inhabited by non-agents who are beyond the borders in space, time and common genetic make-up. They are not citizens of the Anthropocene. They live in the darkest shadows of liberal democratic politics. Their fate is entirely in the hands of ostensibly autonomous agents whose causal powers are unclear, responsibilities enmeshed, who share no common agenda or vision for the future.

A political theory for the Anthropocene must navigate the complexities of this unprecedented social geology. It will have to coevolve with it while at the same time continuing to indicate normatively acceptable directions for much-less-than-ideal politics. To preserve liberal democratic values in the Anthropocene, such theory may need to call into question some of liberal democracy's own basic constructions.

The task is daunting, but it is also almost unbelievably stimulating. As we move deeper into the Anthropocene, perhaps the best we can hope for is that we are entering a period of intense experimentation in both political theory and practice. Non-agents may find refuge in our politics through the introduction of institutions for the future, innovative global redistributive programmes, science courts, green courts, enlarged suffrage to children and advocates for animals and the rest of nature, and novel possibilities for participation. These ideas are being theorized and to some extent implemented. It remains to be seen if and how they will work, who will win and lose, who will be made responsible for what, and who will decide about all this and on what grounds. While we must begin to act now, we will not know the answers to many of these questions for a very long time.

References

Bergson, H. 1907/2007. *Creative Evolution*, ed. K. Ansell-Pearson, M. Kolkman and M. Vaughan. London: Palgrave Macmillan.

Crutzen, P. and Stoermer, E. 2000. 'The "Anthropocene"', *Global Change Newsletter* 41: 17–18.

Di Paola, M. 2015. 'Virtues for the Anthropocene', *Environmental Values* 24: 183–207.

Donaldson, S. and Kymlicka, W. 2011. *Zoopolis: A Political Theory of Animal Rights*. Oxford: Oxford University Press.

Driver, Julia. 2007. 'Attribution of Causation and Moral Responsibility', in W. Sinnott-Armstrong, ed., *Moral Psychology*, vol. II, 423–439. Cambridge, MA: MIT Press.

Frumhoff, P., Heede, R. and Oreskes, N. 2015. 'The Climate Responsibilities of Industrial Carbon Producers', *Climatic Change* 132(2): 157–171.

Gardiner, S. 2011. *A Perfect Moral Storm: The Ethical Tragedy of Climate Change*. Oxford: Oxford University Press.

Gosseries, A. 2001. 'What Do We Owe the Next Generation?', *Loyola of Los Angeles Law Review* 35: 293–354.

Gosseries, A. 2014. 'Nations, Generations, and Climate Justice', *Global Policy* 5(1): 96–102.

Gosseries, A. and González-Ricoy, I., eds. Forthcoming. *Institutions for Future Generations*. Oxford: Oxford University Press.

Gosseries, A. and Meyer, L., eds. 2009. *Intergenerational Justice*. Oxford: Oxford University Press.

Haidt, J. 2012. *The Righteous Mind: Why Good People are Divided by Politics and Religion*. New York: Pantheon Books.

Hale, T., Held, D. and Young, K. 2013. *Gridlock. Why Global Cooperation is Failing When We Need It Most*. Cambridge: Polity.

Heede, R. 2014. 'Tracing Anthropogenic Carbon Dioxide and Methane Emissions to Fossil Fuel and Cement Producers 1854–2010', *Climatic Change* 122: 229–241.

Heinzerling, L. 2015. 'Statistical Lives in Environmental Law', in G. Cohen, N. Daniels and E. Nyal, eds., *Identified versus Statistical Lives: An Interdisciplinary Perspective*, 174–181. Oxford: Oxford University Press.

Held, D. 2010. *Cosmopolitanism: Ideals and Realities*. Cambridge: Polity.

Held, D. and McGrew, A. 2007. *Globalization/Anti-Globalization: Beyond the Great Divide*. Cambridge: Polity.

Hibbard, K. A., Crutzen, P. J., Lambin, E. F., et al. 2006. 'Decadal Interactions of Humans and the Environment', in R. Costanza, L. Graumlich and W. Steffen, eds., *Integrated History and Future of People on Earth*, 341–375. Boston, MA: MIT Press.

Horwitz, M. 1982. 'The History of the Public/Private Distinction', *University of Pennsylvania Law Review* 130: 1423–1428.

Hulme, M. 2009. *Why We Disagree About Climate Change*. Cambridge: Cambridge University Press.

Jamieson, D. 2014. *Reason in a Dark Time: Why the Struggle Against Climate Change Failed, and What It Means for Our Future*. New York: Oxford University Press.

Jamieson, D. and Di Paola, M. 2014. 'Climate Change and Global Justice: New Problem, Old Paradigm?', *Global Policy* 5(1): 105–111.

Keohane, R. 2003. 'Global Governance and Democratic Accountability', in D. Held and M. Koenig-Archibugi, eds., *Taming Globalization: Frontiers of Governance*, 130–159. Cambridge: Polity.

Lepore, J. 2015. 'Richer and Poorer. Accounting for Inequality', *The New Yorker*, 16 March. http://www.newyorker.com/magazine/2015/03/16/richer-and-poorer.

Marsh, G. P. 2003/1864. *Man and Nature*. Washington: University of Washington Press.

Rawls, J. 2005/1993. *Political Liberalism*, 3rd edn. New York: Columbia University Press.

Rawls, J. 2001. *The Law of Peoples*. Cambridge, MA: Harvard University Press.

Shepard, M., ed. 2011. *Sentient City: Ubiquitous Computing, Architecture, and the Future of Urban Space*. Boston, MA: MIT Press.

Samuelson, W. and Zeckhauser, R. 1988. 'Status Quo Bias in Decision Making', *Journal of Risk and Uncertainty* 1: 7–59.

Steffen, W., Grinewald, J., Crutzen, P. and McNeill, J. 2011. 'The Anthropocene: Conceptual and Historical Perspectives', *Philosophical Transactions of the Royal Society A* 369: 842–867.

Stepan, A. and Linz, J. 2011. 'Comparative Perspectives on Inequality and the Quality of Democracy in the United States', *Perspectives on Politics* 9: 841–856.

Sternberg, E. 2010. *My Brain Made Me Do It: the Rise of Neuroscience and the Threat to Moral Responsibility*. New York: Prometheus Books.

Thompson, D. 2010. 'Representing Future Generations: Political Presentism and Democratic Trusteeship', *Critical Review of International and Political Philosophy* 13(1): 17–37

Tsebelis, G. 2002. *Veto Players: How Political Institutions Work*. Princeton, NJ: Princeton University Press.

Vitousek, P., Mooney, H., Lubchenco, J. and Melillo, J. 1997. 'Human Domination of Earth's Ecosystems', *Science* 277(5325): 494–499.

Waldron, J. 1995. 'The Dignity of Legislation', *Maryland Law Review* 54(2): 633–665.

Waters, C., Zalasiewicz, J., Summerhayes, C., et al. 2016. 'The Anthropocene Is Functionally and Stratigraphically Distinct from the Holocene', *Science* 351(6269): 137–138.

Wiland, E. 2015. "One Citizen, One Vote", *What's Wrong?* http://whatswrongcvsp.com/2015/08/12/one-citizen-one-vote/#more-257.

Zalasiewicz, J., Williams, M., Fortey, R., et al. 2011. 'Stratigraphy of the Anthropocene', *Philosophical Transactions: Mathematical, Physical and Engineering Sciences* 369(1938): 1036–1055.

Zalasiewicz, J., Waters, C. N., Williams, M., et al. 2016. 'When Did the Anthropocene Begin? A Mid-Twentieth Century Boundary Level Is Stratigraphically Optimal', *Quaternary International*. http://www.sciencedirect.com/science/article/pii/S1040618214009136.

CHAPTER FOURTEEN

Generations and Global Justice

Axel Gosseries and Danielle Zwarthoed

Introduction: Comparing or Combining?

Approaching issues of global justice through the prism of generations can be done in two ways. One consists in a *comparative* perspective. It aims at understanding how, and to what extent, issues of intergenerational justice differ from issues of global justice. Perceiving commonalities and differences serves several purposes. We can ascertain the consistency of our views across the two domains or deepen our understanding of the nature of the issues of justice at stake, whenever features are more salient in one realm than in the other (for the comparative perspective, see Gosseries, 2014a, 2015). The other perspective is *combinatory*. Instead of contrasting the anatomy of the issues at stake, it identifies issues of global justice in which the generational dimension plays a significant role. The goal is to find out whether demands of global justice have intergenerational implications and, conversely, whether intergenerational justice entails global demands.

To illustrate how the two perspectives differ, consider the case of migration. A *comparative* approach will look at whether someone can migrate from one period of history to another (time), as one would from one territory to another (space). If we find out that 'temporal borders' are closed for those belonging to a given generation, what – if anything – follows for theories of intergenerational justice (Gosseries, 2015: 157–68)? Conversely, how different would the demands of global justice be if migration were not an option?[1] Also, does anything significant follow from the fact that, while persons are inexorably stuck within their temporal borders, the material and immaterial goods they produce can travel beyond the temporal borders of their existence? These are the questions that a comparative approach would address. In contrast, a combinatory perspective looks at migration issues in which generational and global dimensions intersect (see section 3 below).

Consider a second example, from a comparative perspective. Imagine a 'reciprocity-based' (commutative) view according to which justice requires the *absence* of net transfers between individuals, be it domestically, globally or intergenerationally (Gosseries, 2009). According to this view, if A transfers x units to B, B should return x units to A at some point. In the intergenerational realm, we may want to adapt this principle, allowing for an *indirect* reciprocity view. The demands of *indirect* reciprocity are satisfied if generation G_x gives back at least as much as what it received from generation G_{x-1}, either to the same generation or to another one. Hence, if a generation inherits 10 units of z from the previous one, the demands of reciprocity are met if this generation returns at least 10 units of equivalent value to the next generation. Interestingly, this may be compatible with returning *more* than 10 units of z to the next genera-tion. That generation may thus in turn be able to reciprocate this extra transfer to its followers without violating the prohibition on net transfers. If G_x inherits 10 units of z from G_{x-1} and transfers 12 equivalent units to G_{x+1}, this will not force G_{x+1} to end up being a net beneficiary as it can also transfer 12 units of z in turn to G_{x+2}.

However, the reciprocity view seems more problematic when it is applied to the global realm. Were the Republic of Chad to benefit from transfers from the UK, the demands of indirect reciprocity would be met if and only if Chad returned the equivalent to the United Kingdom or to any other country at some point. For anyone holding the view that justice requires significant redistribution from wealthy to deprived countries, such as from the United Kingdom to Chad, the principle of reciprocity cannot serve as a complete theory of global justice. This questions, in turn, the validity of a principle of reciprocity as the core of a theory of *intergenerational* justice. For instance, we could imagine a generation as deprived as Chad (because of, say, a natural disaster) for which giving back what it received from another generation would be unreasonably demanding (Gosseries, 2009).

The upshot is that, while we may insist on the need for each generation to transfer 'at least as much' to the next one, indirect reciprocity might actually turn out not to be the appropriate principle to justify it.[2] This illustrates how a comparative perspective helps in emphasizing a problem that may not be as visible from a strictly intergenerational angle. A similar type of comparison can be pursued for other principles of justice, such as Rawls's institutional sufficientarianism as applied to both the global and the intergenerational realms (Gaspart and Gosseries, 2007; Gosseries, 2014a).

This chapter mainly adopts the combinatory perspective. Section 1 looks at the compatibility of global and intergenerational demands; section 2 focuses on one specific dimension of this interaction, that is, historical injustice; section 3 looks at replacement migration issues from the angle of global and intergenerational justice.

Before moving ahead, a word is in order on what we mean by 'generation'. Demographers distinguish 'age groups' from 'birth cohorts'. An age group is a set of people sharing the same age, whatever the period of history in which they live. For example, people who are in their forties in the 1430s or in the 1970s belong to the same age group. In contrast, a birth cohort is a set of individuals sharing the same date of birth. For instance, all those born during the decade of the 1990s can be said to belong to the same birth cohort. We approach the issues below from the perspective of justice between birth cohorts only, except for the migration issues discussed in section 3, which will also involve justice between age groups.

Moreover, there is another distinction between overlapping and non-overlapping generations. The former coexist during at least part of their lives, while the latter don't. Importantly enough, the 'birth cohort/age group' and the 'overlapping/non-overlapping' distinctions are not reducible to one another. We may tend to look at issues of justice between age groups when they coexist, but it is not meaningless to worry about fairness between those who are 30 today and those who will be 30 in 20 years. Conversely, although philosophers have focused a lot on the challenges raised by justice towards future, unborn generations, most of the issues of justice between generations also arise between overlapping birth cohorts.

1 Duties to the Future vs. Duties to Today's Global Poor

A crucial issue for the combinatory perspective is the extent to which the demands of global and intergenerational justice are compatible (see Glotzbach and Baumgärtner, 2012). Were they to conflict in some cases, should they be mutually adjusted, and/or should priority be given to one dimension over the other? Some debates between greens and the anti-poverty movement – as in the climate change context – tend to be framed as translating tensions between intergenerational and global demands of justice. Consider the following quote as a way of illustration:

> Even though an obligation to the future can be established, it is possible to imagine situations where the legitimate claims of present and future conflict, and where a choice must be made between them. Such a conflict is a very real one as concerns the environment in certain developing countries, inasmuch as certain urgent needs can only be satisfied at the expense of long-term ecological interests. (Visser 't Hooft, 1999: 84; see also: Anand and Sen, 2000: 2038; Sen, 2014)

To understand the nature of this tension, consider Barry's twofold conjecture, which could be labelled as 'compatibilism – moderate and radical':

> I do not believe that there will turn out to be any inconsistency between the requirements of [intra-generational and intergenerational justice]. ... I predict that whatever redistribution among contemporaries is required by justice will also be able to observe the constraints that the interests of future generations be protected. (1991: 268–9)

One could refer to Barry's first sentence as 'moderate compatibilism' and to the second one as 'radical compatibilism'. For *moderate* compatibilists, it is possible to simultaneously achieve *at least one* just distribution within generations (*intragenerational* justice) and *at least one* just distribution between generations (*intergenerational* justice).[3] The intersection between globally fair and intergenerationally fair distributions would thus always contain at least one option. This is how we interpret the meaning of 'there will turn out to be'. *Radical* compatibilism goes one step further. It claims that *any* globally fair distribution will meet the demands of intergenerational justice. Global and intergenerational justice would never conflict. If radical compatibilism were true, one could define the demands of global justice without having to worry about whether the demands of intergenerational justice could also be met.

Why is radical compatibilism implausible?

One counterexample would suffice to show that *radical* compatibilism is implausible. Consider a hypothetical 'last generation' case in which we are sure that no further generation will follow. Imagine that this last generation inherited from the previous one x units of non-renewable resources and y units of renewable ones. It would be perfectly permissible for it to distribute all the x units of non-renewable resources at the global scale. No injustice would follow from consuming it all. However, under any plausible view of justice, once the 'last generation' assumption is relaxed, such a distribution becomes intergenerationally unfair. Intergenerational justice requires leaving some of these x units of non-renewable resources – or a substitute thereof – to the next generations. And how much remains available for a globally just distribution depends on the intergenerational theory we adopt. For example, one theory may only require that we transfer 'enough' per capita to the next generation, or it may require that we transfer 'as much as what we inherited' per capita. This means that what we owe our contemporaries cannot be defined independently of what we owe the next generation(s).

As a result, the claim according to which 'whatever redistribution among contemporaries' required by global justice is compatible with intergenerational justice is *too strong*. The same holds for claims according to which whatever redistribution between generations would be compatible with global justice. A given generation within a country is unable to define what it owes its country's next generation without knowing about its duties of global justice. What could be saved for future people could also be consumed by one's contemporaries. This is, for instance, what the version of 'basic needs sufficientarianism' advocated by the Brundtland report captures (see WCED, 1987; Gosseries, 2008). It says that development is sustainable if and only if it neither jeopardizes the ability of the current generation to cover the needs of its members (the intragenerational, potentially global dimension), nor threatens the ability of the next generation to cover the needs of its members. Whenever an extension of the potential beneficiaries of justice is *not* associated with a proportional extension of the amount of resources available, radical compatibilism is implausible.[4]

Why is moderate compatibilism plausible?

Rejecting radical compatibilism does not entail rejecting *moderate* compatibilism. Rejecting the latter would require one to come up with a case in which the demands of *none* of the plausible views of intergenerational justice would meet those of at least one plausible view of global justice. Such a case is hard to come up with. As a first illustration, consider a cosmopolitan and 'chrono-politan' 'basic needs sufficientarian' view.[5] It requires that the basic needs of all persons be met, regardless of their country of residence or the birth cohort to which they belong. Imagine that we live in a very destitute world. Further assume that we have already lowered our consumption to a minimum. We realize that it is impossible to meet the demands of sufficientarianism unless we lower our procreation rates drastically. This would be very demanding. But this does not entail that global sufficientarianism is *incompatible* with intergenerational sufficientarianism. What this entails is that meeting the demands of both global and intergenerational justice would be hard, not that these demands are incompatible.

As a second illustration, suppose that we adopt 'leximin' as a principle of just distribution between individuals, whatever their country or generation. Under this principle, justice would require that the advantages be distributed so as to maximize the prospects of the least well-off. If there is a tie, or if the situation of the very least well-off cannot be improved further, one should maximize the prospects of the second least well-off, and so on (see Van Parijs, 2003: 209). Imagine, then, that we realize that the least well-off across countries *and* generations actually belong to the *present* generation. Leximin would require that we do not transfer *too much* to the next generation(s), out of a concern for today's least well-off (Gaspart and Gosseries, 2007). Does this mean that the demands of intergenerational justice conflict with the demands of global justice? Not really. And we could even read this concern for the present least well-off as *deriving* exclusively from the theory of *intergenerational* justice itself.

To understand why, let us distinguish between a narrow and a broad sense of intergenerational justice. Narrow intergenerational justice is concerned with distributive issues between generations as *wholes*. Broad intergenerational justice ultimately cares about *individuals* across generations, *whichever generation they belong to*, not about generations as black boxes (Barry, 1999: 112).[6] Hence, when intergenerational leximin insists on caring for today's least well-off, this should not be understood as a concession of intergenerational justice to global justice. Instead, it should be read as a requirement of *intergenerational* justice itself, in this *broad* sense, whenever today's least well-off are expected to be the least well-off intergenerationally. Narrow intergenerational justice may in fact just be a short cut to broad intergenerational justice, assuming that a just distribution between generations *as groups* will generally contribute to broad intergenerational justice. In other words, global and intergenerational justice are to be combined into a single intergenerational approach, broadly understood. We could then do without claims such as 'maldistribution in the future is intragenerational injustice in the future' (Barry, 1999: 112), and simply claim that maldistribution in the future, within a generation, is a problem of broad intergenerational justice.[7] We can thus reasonably expect the intragenerational and the intergenerational concerns to be compatible, since they could be read as two parts of a *single* theory. This is also why we can assume both the plausibility of moderate compatibilism and the need for mutual adjustment along the temporal and the geographical axis. Under such a broad reading of intergenerational justice, global justice extends the intragenerational axis for each generation to all the contemporaries of this planet.

The message here is thus threefold. First, radical compatibilism is implausible. Second, there is a real tension between demands of today's poor and demands of the future. Third, this tension is perfectly taken into account by a theory of intergenerational justice broadly understood. We should not choose between global and intergenerational justice, especially if we understand the nature of the latter broadly enough.

2 Inherited Duties vs. Duties to Today's Global Poor

Consider climate justice again. Claims focusing on historical emissions of CO_2 illustrate a different way in which the global and the intergenerational realms intersect (Gosseries, 2004). The issue is not whether global and intergenerational distributive justice should be mutually adjusted. The issue is, rather, whether global duties are affected by what *past* generations did or failed to do. While the previous section tackled the question of whether global duties are affected by our duties to future generations, this section addresses the issue of whether, and how, global duties are affected by the duties we inherited from past generations.

Consider as well the claims for reparation that today's Armenians are addressing at today's Turks for the 1915 genocide, or the possible claims of today's Congolese to today's Belgians for the harms done during the colonial period. Historical injustice problems in their simplest form typically involve four groups: past wrongdoers, past victims, the descendants of wrongdoers and the descendants of victims. Since we are focusing on the intersection with global justice, let us address historical injustices as an issue of justice between nations/countries rather than between individuals. Let us also assume that none of the past wrongdoers are still alive today and that none of the current descendants were adults when the wrong took place. We thus find ourselves in a non-overlapping generation context, which will be crucial. Finally, we shall consider two types of historical claims: *harm-based claims* as in our examples above (claims arising from past (wrongful) harms) and *contract-based claims* (claims arising from a contract or a promise made in the past). Our discussion will thus also be relevant to issues such as the third world debt cancellation debate.[8]

Historical injustice raises two issues in a non-overlapping generations context. The first one has to do with *the plausibility of claims for rectification in a cross-generational context*. Such claims hold members of one generation accountable for the consequences of the actions of their ancestors. The second issue is *the moral strength of rectificatory duties relative to distributive duties*. Let us begin with the former issue. Holding descendants of a group responsible for fixing the consequences of their ancestors' action is hard to defend philosophically. It presupposes that one be held responsible for the consequences of actions or abstentions against which one were unable to do anything – given the assumption of non-overlap. It somehow denies the 'separateness of generations' in the moral sense of this term. This idea of 'separateness of generations' may be derived from the idea of 'separateness of persons'.[9] It involves a moral claim about the need to treat individuals – including those from different generations – as distinct moral entities. One implication is that it is not enough to claim that a given policy maximizes well-being in a society. The distribution of the costs and benefits across people also matters. Another implication is that when a wrong has been committed, one cannot just assign responsibility to whoever is related in one way or another to that wrongdoer – for instance, through the mere fact of being a co-national.

Insisting on the separateness of persons or generations does not entail the rejection of all forms of collective responsibility. In our view, some groups of contemporaries, such as the current citizens of a democratic state, may be an appropriate site of collective responsibility, while groups composed of individuals who have not coexisted are not. The reason is that individual or collective responsibility can make sense if those held responsible could have changed something to the situation for which they are being held responsible. The daughter of a wrongdoer who wronged someone before her birth need not be considered a wrongdoer. One could of course suggest that the mere fact of benefiting from past injustice could constitute an alternative ground for collective responsibility. We will address this possibility below.

Our guess is that many people want to stick to a rectificatory approach, even in a cross-generational context, because they implicitly assume that such a view is more robust than a distributive one. This leads us to our second question: are rectificatory claims morally more robust than distributive ones? In typical cases, claims for reparation, or rectificatory claims, are voiced by a group that is less well-off than the group from which rectification is expected. In such cases, the demands of rectificatory justice and those of global distributive justice might roughly converge. Both require transfers from the wealthy to the poor, even though the importance of the transfers and their justification may differ.

However, in many cases, a divergence may occur. In such cases, the tension between cross-generational *rectificatory* claims and global *distributive* justice can be either direct or indirect. The tension is *direct* in a poor-descendants-of-wrongdoers/debtors case in which the descendants of the victim/lender are wealthier than those of the wrongdoer/borrower. Here, expecting the descendants of wrongdoers/debtors to compensate the descendants of their victims would be anti-redistributive. The third world debt cancellation debate is a case in point. The tension is *indirect* when rectificatory justice requires the descendants of wrongdoers/debtors to compensate the descendants of the victim/lender at the cost of not devoting this energy/money to a third group that would deserve priority if global distributive concerns alone were at play. Here, even if the descendants of the victims are poorer than the descendants of the wrongdoers, there are other groups that are even poorer. Distributive justice would require the descendants of wrongdoers to give priority to these other groups. The Irish Potato Famine (1845–52) is a possible illustration of this *indirect* tension. Suppose, even if it is not an uncontroversial claim, that the British government's insufficient response to the famine was responsible for the magnitude of the disaster. Whilst rectificatory justice may require the contemporary UK government to transfer significant resources to the Irish, distributive justice might require the British to focus first on poorer countries such as Chad, Niger or Afghanistan.

We must choose between a distributive and a rectificatory approach not only in divergence cases, but also in convergence cases. In the latter cases, while both approaches advocate transfers in the same direction, they might advocate transfers of different magnitude. Some might think it better to ground global justice on rectificatory claims, since the claim that a wealthy country should compensate for the harms it caused in the first place seems less controversial than the claim that a wealthy country should assist deprived foreigners, whatever the origin of their deprivation.[10] This may have to do with an asymmetric treatment of negative and positive rights. However, we should not overlook the fact that a complete formulation of rectificatory claims requires a distributive view. If A wrongly deprives B of a given good, what grounds the rectificatory claim is the fact that this good legitimately belonged to B in the first place. Depriving B of it against B's will entails a departure from a baseline situation. However, why would the situation in the wrong's absence serve as a baseline if we were not implicitly assuming that this baseline is fair? And in order to establish the fairness of such a baseline, we need a distributive view. This is why the strength of a rectificatory claim cannot be *stronger* or *less controversial* than that of a distributive one. The former is parasitic on the latter. This means that rectificatory claims cannot be firmer than distributive ones, even in contexts that are not cross-generational. And if we add the further complication associated with the separateness of generations, we can understand why addressing issues of historical injustice in non-overlapping generation contexts should be done as much as possible through the angle of intragenerational distributive justice rather than cross-generational rectificatory justice.

One could nevertheless be tempted to endorse the worry expressed about a rectificatory view in a cross-generational context, while resisting a move towards a purely distributive approach. One way out consists in advocating an intermediary 'free-riding-based' or 'beneficiary-pays' approach.[11] This view does not expect the descendants of wrongdoers to *fully* compensate the descendants of their ancestors' victims for the harm they suffered. Rather, it expects them to compensate the descendants of their ancestors' victims up to the degree to which the descendants of wrongdoers *benefited* from their ancestors' actions. Moreover, the beneficiary-pays approach does not necessarily need to reject separateness of generations. It could be dealt with through a 'package-deal-acceptance' approach: 'If you accept your inheritance package, you should also accept the need to compensate those who wrongly suffered from actions that led to accumulating what you ended up inheriting.' In practice, the 'package-deal-acceptance' approach may imply that, insofar as the Belgians born after 1960 accepted all the wealth the preceding Belgian generation bequeathed to them, including the profits generated by the exploitation of Congolese resources, they should also accept the need to fund, up to that level, any reparations due by the Belgians to the Congolese.

However, it is not clear why we should assume the existence of such an *actual* package deal or even rely on a *hypothetical* one of the type 'it would have been reasonable for you to accept a package deal such that...'. There are further worries. First, whenever *no benefit* is left, relying on this approach leaves the descendants of victims with no transfers at all. In our example, if we found out that the profits made possible under colonial rule have all been consumed or wasted, then, according to the beneficiary-pays approach, today's Belgians would not owe anything to today's Congolese. In such cases, the beneficiary-pays approach is unable to capture the intuition that we owe something to the victims' descendants (see Caney, 2006: 473–4). Second, and more importantly, the approach treats the benefits from past wrongs *separately* from all the other inherited benefits that may also contribute to a very unequal wealth distribution between countries. Imagine that a rich country is not richer because of past wrongs (colonialization, slavery, segregation...), but, rather, because of a long history of soil fertility accumulation due to favourable climatic conditions and wise farming in the past. Rectificatory and beneficiary-pays approaches alone could not explain why this country should assist others. Why treat differently advantages due to past *harmful actions* that took place before our birth from advantages due to past *non-harmful actions* or to past *natural events* that took place before our birth? From a distributive perspective, such a separate treatment is hard to account for without the implicit idea that some sense of responsibility for the past remains encapsulated in this 'beneficiary-pays' or 'free-riding' view. However, responsibility for the past is problematic because of the separateness of generations in non-overlapping generations contexts.[12]

Now, if we reject both a rectificatory and a beneficiary-pays view, we may simply fall back into a plain intragenerational and distributive view, such as a global egalitarian one. Recall that the main virtue of this view is that it does not assume that current people *should* be held responsible for what their ancestors did or did not *do* and thus takes the 'separateness of generations' seriously. What follows in practice? Consider again historical emissions of greenhouse gases. Residents of wealthy countries may still owe very significant distributive transfers to the victims of climate change, not because their ancestors emitted more in the past than theirs did, but simply because the victims are poorer and/or more affected by climate change. This view neither disputes the very existence nor questions the significance of pre-1990 greenhouse gas emissions. It simply takes a distributive path to address the problem, treating past emissions *as if* they were natural ones, and redistributing the means to address the climatic challenge on general distributive grounds, as if we were dealing with a natural disaster. Of course, space remains for rectificatory claims when the wrongdoer/debtor is still alive – in an overlapping generations context.

Now, if we take the separateness of generations seriously, and if we opt for an intragenerational distributive view approach to global historical injustices, we might face at least two challenges. First, we have to revisit our understanding of the grounds of some of our firmest moral intuitions in cross-generational cases. Consider the horrors of the Armenian genocide. We may hold the view that Turkish authorities have a very special duty to seek and tell the truth about the genocide, and that this duty is stronger than the general duty that any other country's authorities may have to seek and tell the truth on the matter. We may also claim that today's Turkish authorities should *apologize* for what happened, on top of admitting the truth. And we may go one step further, demanding a non-merely symbolic rectification: financial compensation, territorial access, etc.

Would taking the separateness of generations render these three genocide-related claims groundless? Several avenues are available to avoid such a conclusion. One says that the general 'seek-and-tell-the-truth' duty falls on *any* nation in relation to past genocides. While Turkey's duty in this respect would not be special in this case, it could nevertheless remain strong. However, one way of rendering this duty special for Turkey without deriving it from inherited responsibility could consist in pointing at Turkey's *very privileged access to sources of information on the genocide*. As to apologies, it is admittedly harder to justify them if we understand them in the ordinary sense, in a framework that takes the separateness of generations seriously. And with respect to financial transfers, one could of course invoke that Armenia's GDP per capita is much lower than Turkey's GDP per capita. However, this would still not explain why Turkey's distributive duties towards Armenia would be special compared to those of, for example, Belgium to Armenia or Turkey to Congo.

Incentives are the second challenge to a distributive approach to historical injustice. Consider a debt contracted by a poor country. Future generations cannot be consulted when we contract a long-term loan. They will have to pay for it though. One way of going distributive in country-to-country loans would consist in claiming that reimbursement is only due by the next generation to the extent that such reimbursement would contribute to equalizing wealth between the two countries at stake. The difficulty would be that rich countries would not lend to poor countries any more, even if the latter were democratic or intended to use the loan to the benefit of their people. It seems that going straightforwardly distributive in such a cross-generational case would be disastrous. Second-best rules would have to be designed to capture the distributive intuition and take the separateness of generations seriously, while not leading to strong disincentives to lend to poor countries. The same incentive-based approach might be adopted to address wrong-based historical injustice claims, such as the Armenian genocide. One might hold the current Turkish generation liable to compensation towards the Armenians, under the view that, while current people are not responsible for the actions of their ancestors a century ago, not holding them responsible would send the signal that such crimes could go unpunished. Of course, this incentive not to wrong would only be effective if we assumed that people care enough about the burdens that their actions will impose on their descendants a century later, which is far from obvious.

There is an important tension between rectificatory and distributive accounts to global justice. The rectificatory approach, which may sound plausible at first sight in cross-generational contexts, underestimates the philosophical challenge of the separateness of generations and overestimates its independence from a distributive approach. The distributive approach overcomes the separateness of generations challenge, but might require more indirect justifications of our moral intuitions in some very important cases of historical injustices, such as past genocides or past loans to third world countries. In contrast, in the historical emissions of CO_2 case, its implications sound much more straightforward. Admittedly, further work is needed to fully work out the implications of an intragenerational distributive approach to historical injustice claims.

3   Population Ageing and Replacement Migration

The challenges that Europe is facing include population ageing (Eurostat, 2015) and migration issues (UNHCR, 2015). Actually, migration could be part of the response to population ageing. According to the European Commission (2015):

> The EU is … facing a series of long-term economic and demographic challenges. Its population is ageing, while its economy is increasingly dependent on highly skilled jobs. Furthermore, without migration the EU's working age population will decline by 17.5

million in the next decade. Migration will increasingly be an important way to enhance the sustainability of our welfare system and to ensure sustainable growth of the EU economy.

Ageing – that is, 'the transformation of the age structure to relatively greater proportions in the older age group' (UN, 2001: 7), results from a combination of lowering fertility – even below replacement – and increasing longevity. As ageing raises difficulties (to which we return below), it should be mitigated. Current social and economic trends suggest that fertility is unlikely to return to replacement levels – that is, approximately 2.1 children per woman in developed countries (Espenshade et al., 2003) – in the near future (e.g. Lutz et al., 2006).[13] As to reducing longevity, it is arguably not a desirable option.

In such a context, it seems that migration, and in particular *replacement migration*, should be part of the answer to population ageing (UN, 2001: 99; European Commission, 2007: 28; Docquier and Marchiori, 2012: 244). Technically, replacement migration is more than migration aimed at bridging the gap between actual fertility rates and replacement fertility. To constitute a response to ageing, replacement migration should also be able to deal with the increase in longevity and its effects on the age structure of the population. It should be understood as 'the international migration that would be needed to offset declines in the size of population and declines in the population of working age, as well as to offset the overall ageing of a population' (UN, 2001: 7).

Replacement migration is thus supposed to address simultaneously below-replacement fertility *and* increased longevity. However, two difficulties should be considered. First, as the average age of migrants is not radically lower than the average age of natives in the host country, and as the size of the host population is relatively large, we would need very high inflows of migrants to have a significant impact on the average population age. According to the UN, the EU would need 80 million migrants to keep its working-age population constant until 2050 and an extra 74 million if it aimed at maintaining a potential support ratio of three active people to one retired (UN, 2001: 22–3). The 'potential support' ratio is calculated by the number of people of working age (15–64) to every individual aged 65 or more. Second, in the long run, it is unclear whether replacement migration can be a sustainable solution in a steady state in which, over a very long period, fertility rates would remain below replacement.

Note that, while the word 'ageing' may suggest that it mostly raises problems of justice between 'age groups', it is actually not the case. Population ageing modifies the relative size of the successive cohorts through one of its drivers, namely, fertility. Variations in cohort sizes could generate distributive problems between cohorts for any *demo-sensitive* (i.e., per capita) view of intergenerational justice (Gosseries, 2009: 137–44). Ageing thus concerns both justice between age groups and justice between birth cohorts. Moreover, our focus on replacement migration as a response to ageing shows that migration raises issues of global justice as well as of intergenerational justice, and that ageing raises issues of intergenerational justice as well as of global justice. This is key for a combinatory approach. We will illustrate how issues of justice between birth cohorts, justice between age groups and global justice intersect through three dilemmas.

Before we discuss these three dilemmas, the following assumptions should be made explicit. Insofar as ageing is concerned, we shall focus on specific difficulties, leaving open the question of whether population ageing is good news *all things considered*. For instance, we do not overlook the fact that the increase in longevity results in part from the reduction of child mortality, or that low fertility results in part from increased gender equality. As to migration, there are strong justice-based arguments supporting open borders (Carens, 1987; 1992; 2013: 225–54; Moellendorf, 2002: 61–7; Cole, 2011; Kukathas, 2014; Oberman, 2016). Here, we will assume that we live in a world in which countries do control access to their territory to some degree and that there might be reasonable *pro tanto* arguments in favour of it. We will thus suspend as well our all-things-considered judgment on whether justice requires open borders or not.

Identity transmission

The first dilemma says that, while ageing may involve economic inequalities between birth cohorts, addressing population ageing by increasing immigration may affect the preservation of the country's culture and might trigger other problems of justice between birth cohorts. While this dilemma could be tackled from a strictly domestic intergenerational justice perspective, it has a global dimension because it is triggered by migration.

The dilemma's first horn suggests that the present generation should address ageing as a matter of intergenerational justice. The challenge is to characterize the nature of the intergenerational obligation at stake. Consider a narrow reciprocity-based, or commutative, view of intergenerational justice. Other things being equal, below replacement fertility mechanically increases the contribution rate per capita of the working age population. And this can translate into inequalities in contribution rates over complete lives, that is, between birth cohorts rather than merely between age groups. This problem is exacerbated by the increase in longevity, insofar as such an increase translates into a more than proportional increase of the dependency stages of our life cycle compared to the activity stages.

The difficulty is to identify exactly how increases in contribution rates expected from certain birth cohorts should be judged in terms of intergenerational justice. The analysis might be relatively straightforward if we expect an *equivalence* in contributions and benefits between cohorts *and* if we understand the *nature* of these contributions and benefits in a relatively narrow way

– for instance, in terms of public transfers related to education and retirement pensions. Ageing would generate inequalities if justice required a per capita equivalence between the educational and retirement contributions of a currently active cohort and the educational and retirement benefits that it will itself have benefited from by the end of its life. Things become more complex if we question either (i) the idea of contributions/benefits equivalence as a requirement of justice and/or (ii) the narrow interpretation of such contributions/benefits. Regarding (i), we have already suggested that reciprocity-based views, and the idea of contributions/benefits equivalence they support, are problematic (see our introduction above). Insisting on potential contribution rates only, in the context of the ageing debate, belongs to the same reciprocity logic. Regarding (ii), it would be better (and more difficult) to interpret the notions of contribution and benefits in a sufficiently broad manner, so as to capture not only public, monetary, transfers, but also private transfers and transfers of natural capital and of technology.

Whether ageing leads to potential injustices between birth cohorts is thus less obvious than expected once we adopt a distributive *and* an all-things-considered approach. Two additional points suggest that ageing may not be so problematic for intergenerational justice. First, if distributive justice between cohorts is demo-sensitive, insofar as the availability of natural resources is limited, population decline means that it should be easier to leave their fair per capita share to the next generations. Second, if longevity keeps growing, this is also one respect in which the next generation will be better off, regardless of whether it will have to support a higher contribution rate.

Establishing the first horn is thus far from straightforward. Consider the dilemma's second horn: one may worry that replacement migration could threaten the preservation of a distinctive national culture, through bringing in people from a very different cultural background. One can answer this worry in various ways that echo different understandings of it. First, while a distributive theory of justice between birth cohorts may require the present cohort to transfer a certain set of goods to the next generation(s), including cultural goods, that are *equivalent* in value to those we inherited,[14] it does not follow that we *should* transfer the *same* cultural values or artefacts as those we inherited. Significant immigration may admittedly lead us to transfer to the next generation cultural values that *differ* from those we acquired through education and socialization. However, it does not follow that immigration would threaten our ability to embody *a* set of cultural values and practices in our lives and to transmit them.

Second, one may worry more specifically about the fact that increasing cultural diversity in a country may jeopardize solidarity and weaken distributive justice. Welcoming people from different cultures could threaten the ability of our institutions to operate under democratic rules. If it were true, this would be a serious worry, as maintaining just and democratic institutions is a key element of our intergenerational obligations (Rawls, 1999: 252). Among possible connections between cultural diversity and solidarity (Van Parijs, 2004), one hinges on trust. Sharing the same culture facilitates trust, and the latter would facilitate support for social justice, people being more willing to make the sacrifices that distributive justice and democratic participation require when they believe the beneficiaries will reciprocate such sacrifices (Miller, 1995: 91–8; 2004: 26). However, evidence from Canada shows that, even if ethnicity affects interpersonal trust, it does not have a significant impact on support for the welfare state (Soroka et al., 2004). Moreover, trust may be more strongly affected by factors other than cultural diversity, such as institutional design (see Miller, 2004: 29; Seekings, 2004; Pevnick, 2009: 153). Instead of renouncing immigration, states could, rather, work on their institutions.

A related worry arises from the mere fact that immigrants may endorse a non-democratic culture – as opposed to a merely different one. This could challenge the maintenance of just and democratic institutions over time. Again, it is worth reminding ourselves that democratic values are not foreign to non-Western cultures (Sen, 2007: 51–5). Moreover, Canadian evidence shows that immigrants coming from illiberal and non-democratic countries tend to accept their host country's democratic values (Kymlicka, 1998: 19; for historical uses of this argument against immigration, see also Carens, 1987: 87; 1992: 28; 2013: 176).

The first dilemma would thus only arise if some very specific normative assumptions (i.e., a narrow view of intergenerational bequests) as well as empirical ones (regarding the effects of immigration on trust and democratic values) turned out to be true.

Admission age

The second dilemma focuses more specifically on the age criterion. It can be looked at from the perspective of justice both between birth cohorts and between age groups. The dilemma is the following: replacement migration can only help in addressing ageing if the average age of migrants is lower than the average age of the host country. However, the very use of age limits itself potentially raises an issue of justice between generations of potential immigrants.[15]

Age is used in the Australian, Canadian and British 'point systems' for economic immigration. The use of age in selective immigration policies is not only justified by the need to rejuvenate the population, but also by the expected contributions of certain age groups to the economy. The net fiscal impact (future tax receipts minus government expenditures) of a migrant changes according to the migrants' age and education (Storesletten, 2000:

302). The Canadian government explicitly justifies giving priority to young immigrants as follows:

> Younger immigrants generally integrate more rapidly into the labour market, and they usually spend a greater number of years contributing to Canada's economy. By contrast, immigrants aged 45 or older experience unemployment rates almost double those aged 25 to 34 years. (Canada Gazette, 2012: Regulatory Impact, Analysis Statement, Description (a))

In order to examine the issue more closely, we need an account of both what is special about age limits (compared with, e.g., gender or racial criteria) and whether there is anything specific about age limits in immigration policy. Here is a sketch of a possible framework.[16] Let us begin with the intuition according to which age is a reliable proxy for variables that are relevant to the selection, but more costly, embarrassing or difficult to directly observe than age. This assumption is reasonable when we look at extreme ages. A newborn usually does not have the cognitive skills of a 25-year-old and an 80-plusser is generally physically less fit than someone in his forties. In the case of replacement migration, we could make two claims here. Insofar as what we are trying to do is merely to prevent the reduction in size of a population, age criteria seem irrelevant. However, if the main goal is to ensure that the working age population remains significant enough, it seems relevant to rely on an age criterion if the latter is used as a proxy for migrants' ability to work and for the level and the duration of their contributions. This could of course be challenged. In the specific case of asylum-seekers, it is neither the case that age is always an easily observable feature, nor the case that age is a very reliable proxy of their vulnerability. But let us assume here that age can be a reasonable proxy to predict someone's ability to work.

Now, the mere fact of being a good proxy does not suffice. As a matter of fact, race is a very reliable proxy in a racist society as is gender in a sexist society. It does not follow that they are morally acceptable proxies. The same applies to age. However, there is something special about the latter. We find many age criteria prima facie acceptable because our age changes. Not only does it entail that we will be negatively affected during only part of our life. It may even be that if certain conditions are met, none of us will have suffered from any differential treatment *over our complete lives* as a result of it. Consider age limits for voting. Not only can age be a relevant proxy for political competence. It is also such that, even if we are all subject to pre-18 exclusion from the right to vote, it does not necessarily follow that any of us will have ended up by the end of our life to have had less access to power than other citizens from different birth cohorts. This is what can be referred to as the 'complete-life neutrality' of the age criterion. Age-based differential treatment does not necessarily lead to differential treatment over complete life.

There are two main difficulties with the 'complete-life neutrality' claim. First, the practical conditions required to ensure that age-based differential treatment does *not* lead to any differential treatment over complete lives are often not met. It is the case with migration. The randomness of events that put people on the roads to seek asylum or better economic prospects is such that complete-life neutrality cannot be assumed. In a situation in which the non-safety of a country just came about, it is simply not true that someone above the age limits would have qualified for asylum if she had applied a few years ago. And telling post-2008 Portuguese emigrants that they should have left Portugal before the crisis, when they were younger, would simply add insult to injury. This shows that, in the case of immigration, the age criterion is not neutral over complete lives.

The second difficulty with the complete-life neutrality claim is that, even if an age criterion is neutral over complete lives, it requires some positive justification, as age limits entail a reduction of people's freedom. Under certain conditions, age-based compulsory retirement can equalize access to the job market between various successive birth cohorts. However, in the case of immigration, it is hard to see how the age criterion can increase equality between successive generations of potential immigrants. The only possible justification thus seems to be one that would rely on the need to address the ageing problem and possible benefits for immigrants in turn. Our guess is that, while several age criteria may be reasonably justifiable, such as age criteria for potential organ recipients (aimed at equalizing longevities between potential recipients), age-based compulsory retirement or minimum age for a set of activities, privileging younger people *in immigration policy* is likely to be much more problematic to justify. One might seek to justify a preference for younger migrants in the case of asylum-seekers by drawing a parallel with the organ donation case. We would privilege younger asylum-seekers assuming that, among all those whose life is under threat, older people have already had a chance to live longer. But this would only make sense if it were true that asylum slots in host countries are as scarce as organs to be grafted are, *quod non*. So, we are left with a true dilemma. The use of age criteria seems problematic in the immigration case. And without it, immigration cannot be as effective to address ageing.

Youth drain, brain drain

The third dilemma points at a tension between combatting ageing in the developed world and increasing global inequalities and/or worsening the situation of poorer countries by draining them of their working age population. In our world, countries of origin often count among the global worst-off. The problem is twofold. Are we trying to fix an intergenerational problem in destination countries at the cost of creating an intergenerational problem in sending countries (*youth drain*)? Are we not increasing global inequalities and worsening the situation of the least well-off in countries of origin (*brain drain*)?

Consider brain drain facts first. The presence of an educated, skilled population is generally seen as beneficial in various ways for the sending society's economy. Many have argued that their departure produces negative externalities on those who remain (e.g., Bhagwati and Hamada, 1974).[17] However, recent evidence suggests a more balanced view: brain drain may prove beneficial for countries of origin under certain conditions (Docquier and Rapoport, 2012: 683). It has positive effects in terms of growth and human capital formation, because of workers' remittances,[18] but also because potential migration prospects incentivize inhabitants of poor countries to invest more in education (Beine et al., 2001, 2008; Docquier and Rapoport, 2012: 699). The net effect of brain drain tends to be positive for sending countries where the emigration rate is lower than 15–20 per cent and/or lower than 5 per cent of the population with a higher education degree. Conversely, it tends to be negative when these conditions are not met (Docquier, 2007; Beine et al., 2008). Moreover, there are other channels through which a brain drain may be beneficial for sending countries. For example, educated diasporas may facilitate technology diffusion and foreign investments and induce improvements of the quality of governance and political institutions in their country of origin (Docquier and Rapoport, 2012: 709–12). It is thus crucial to always consider the net effect of replacement migration on sending countries, as there is a significant range of cases in which it can be positive.

Besides brain drain, there might be a *youth drain* problem. One could see youth drain as a win–win phenomenon: low-fertility countries would gain youth, while high-fertility ones would avoid overcrowding. However, high-fertility countries also face a young-age dependency burden, since children need the provision of education and healthcare. Emigration does not help here, since it concerns working age adults who could contribute to alleviate the costs associated with raising children. Moreover, fertility is declining, even in high-fertility countries (UN, 2014), which means that replacement migration cannot be a permanent solution to ageing in the North (Docquier and Marchiori, 2012: 253–6).

These are the stylized facts. What about the normative perspective? Issues at stake can be approached from at least two perspectives, a *distributive* one and a *commutative* (reciprocity-based) one. The *distributive* approach looks at the effects of a replacement migration policy on the global distribution of advantages (see Brock, 2009: 190–219). For example, a basic needs sufficientarian distributive principle of global justice would imply that replacement migration is compatible with (or even required by) justice if it contributes to securing basic needs for all, especially in sending countries. The empirical literature on brain drain suggests that replacement migration may have positive impacts on some needs (such as education) and negative ones on others (health, for instance, because of occupational shortages). Sufficientarians might thus have to handle trade-offs between different basic needs.

Another distributive principle is leximin (see section 1 for a definition). Here, we should look at whether replacement migration, compared to alternative arrangements, maximizes the lifetime social and economic prospects of the global worst-off. It could, provided that the conditions specified above for net positive effects on sending countries are met. Note that we must also look at the effect of replacement migration on the sending country's *future* generations. A Rawlsian perspective on intergenerational justice in less advantaged societies would state that these societies should accumulate enough capital to secure the material basis of just institutions, and that once this is reached, further generational savings are no longer mandatory (Rawls, 1999: 256–8). A cross-generational leximin would even prohibit further generational savings, as they involve an opportunity cost for today's worst off (Gaspart and Gosseries, 2007). Here again, the positive effects of emigration on the accumulation of human capital or technology transfers, for instance, might count in favour of reasonable levels of replacement migration. But in order to provide a definitive answer, we need a complete assessment of the various effects of emigration on the capacity of sending countries to save for the future.

Let us now consider the commutative approach. It looks at whether destination countries relying on replacement migration owe something to the countries of origin, not in virtue of these countries' economic situation, but in virtue of these countries' contributions to the migration scheme. In sending countries, families, taxpayers and others bear significant material and non-material costs to bring future migrants into existence, to care for and to educate them. The moral intuition at stake is captured by the fairness principle, which states that, when agents participate in a mutually advantageous cooperative venture, those who have contributed their share have a right to a similar contribution on the part of those who have benefited from the joint effort (Rawls, 1999: 96).[19] The commutative approach thus amounts to a prohibition of violations of reciprocity such as *free-riding* and *exploitation*.

For free-riding or exploitation to occur, specific conditions should be met (see Gosseries, 2004; Olsaretti, 2013). It must of course be the case that the potential free-rider would be a net beneficiary of the cooperative scheme at stake – here the replacement migration scheme. Let us thus suppose, for the sake of argument, that replacement migration is beneficial for ageing destination countries. One problem is that a replacement migration scheme may not be a cooperative venture in the sense required for the fairness principle to apply. First, one could deny that the participation of sending countries is truly voluntary – if not, replacement migration is not a cooperative venture, but rather something more akin to a 'theft'. A contribution would be voluntary in the *strong* sense if the purpose of sending countries' efforts was *to benefit ageing destination countries*. But most care and education systems do not primarily aim at supplying foreign countries with young workers – the Philippines, where more nurses than are needed are purposively trained so that some can find work abroad, might be an exception. However, the voluntariness condition may be understood in a weaker sense, whereby it suffices that the care and education systems are aimed at raising the young – whoever the ultimate beneficiary will be.[20] This understanding seems closer to our intuitive grasp of free-riding situations.

Second, free-riding situations generally occur when the joint product of the cooperative venture is a public or a socialized good – otherwise, we should rather talk about deprivation (Gosseries, 2009: 131). Are international working age migrants a public good? Public goods are non-excludable and often non-rivalrous. Migrants are not a public good in the way clean air is. The product of their labour does not spontaneously benefit their society. It is socially beneficial because of the way institutions are structured. Migrants, like children, are thus 'socialized goods' (Olsaretti, 2013: 252) rather than 'public goods'. The product of immigrants' labour benefits host countries, not only as a result of the welfare system (as in the case of native children), but also as a result of how the crossing of borders is organized (this is where migrants are different from domestic children). In our world, host countries enjoy a complete discretion to admit or exclude immigrants, while sending countries are not allowed to prevent their people from emigrating. This situation can be seen as the result of the asymmetric treatment of exit and entry by international law.[21] A country that would seek to control emigration as strictly as immigration might incur sanctions. This can also be seen as the result of an asymmetry of power between immigration and emigration countries. Countries of immigration enjoy greater control in the sense that they have the capacity to sanction illegal immigrants by denying them a status (and the advantages attached to it). Countries of emigration tend not to have this capacity. Ageing countries are thus able to purposely set up a social security system and open their borders to additional workers and taxpayers, while sending countries are unable to prevent the redirection of the product of their efforts to foreign citizens.

If a replacement migration scheme only results in sending countries subsidizing a share of the education and childcare of ageing countries' future working age population, without otherwise affecting sending countries' inhabitants, replacement migration amounts to free-riding. This might be so because, as suggested by the empirical literature, some beneficial effects of emigration may offset its negative effects. What if replacement migration policies *worsen* the situation of sending countries in net terms? In that case, the diagnosis of exploitation applies (Gosseries, 2009: 131). If indeed replacement migration involves a situation of free-riding or exploitation, commutative justice approaches require ageing countries to compensate sending countries' citizens for the efforts provided in terms of care and education.[22] In the case of exploitation, an additional compensation is due for the deprivation they incur. Perhaps a general prohibition on exploitation might require limiting the replacement migration scheme or changing the global socioeconomic conditions that produced this situation of exploitation. Our third dilemma thus turns out to be a real one too.

4 Conclusion

Having contrasted a comparative and a combinatory perspective, we first presented a framework under which prima facie tensions between global and intergenerational demands may be addressed. We defended the plausibility of moderate compatibilism and insisted on the fact that global and intergenerational justice may actually be conceived as two dimensions of a single theory of trans-generational justice. We then insisted on the need to take the separateness of generations seriously and on the importance of properly articulating rectificatory and distributive views. We defended an approach to historical injustice that relies centrally on a global, intragenerational distributive approach whenever alleged duty-holders were not contemporaries of the wrong committed or of the contract signed. The full implications of such a non-rectificatory perspective would still require further exploration. Finally, combining the intergenerational and the global dimensions in the assessment of replacement migration has raised three dilemmas. If the first dilemma, the potential trade-off between alleviating the economic burden of ageing and preserving a national culture, is less serious than expected, the two others certainly require further reflection on the compatibility of counter-ageing policies with our other obligations of justice between countries, cohorts and age groups.[23]

References

Anand, S. and Sen, A. 2000. 'Human Development and Economic Sustainability', *World Development* 28(12): 2029–2049.

Barry, B. 1991. 'The Ethics of Resource Depletion', in *Liberty and Justice: Essays in Political Theory 2*, 259–273. Oxford: Clarendon Press.

Barry, B. 1999. 'Sustainability and Intergenerational Justice', in A. Dobson, ed., *Fairness and Futurity: Essays on Environmental Sustainability and Social Justice*, 93–117. Oxford: Oxford University Press.

Beine, M., Docquier, F. and Rapoport, H. 2001. 'Brain Drain and Economic Growth: Theory and Evidence', *Journal of Development Economics* 64(1): 275–289.

Beine, M., Docquier, F. and Rapoport, H. 2008. 'Brain Drain and Human Capital Formation in Developing Countries: Winners and Losers', *The Economic Journal* 118(528): 631–652.

Bhagwati, J. and Hamada, K. 1974. 'The Brain Drain, International Integration of Markets for Professionals and Unemployment', *Journal of Development Economics* 1(1): 19–42.

Brock, G. 2009. *Global Justice: A Cosmopolitan Account*. Oxford: Oxford University Press.

Canada Gazette. 2012. *Regulations Amending the Immigration and Refugee Protection Regulations*. http://www.gazette.gc.ca/rp-pr/p2/2012/2012-12-19/html/sor-dors274-eng.html#b.

Caney, S. 2006. 'Environmental Degradation, Reparations, and the Moral Significance of History', *Journal of Social Philosophy* 37(3): 464–482.

Carens, J. 1987. 'Aliens and Citizens: The Case for Open Borders', *The Review of Politics* 49(2): 251–273.

Carens, J. 1992. 'Migration and Morality: A Liberal Egalitarian Perspective', in B. Barry and R. E. Goodin, eds., *Free Movement: Ethical Issues in the Transnational Migration of People and of Money*, 25–47. Philadelphia: University of Pennsylvania Press.

Carens, J. 2013. *The Ethics of Immigration*. New York: Oxford University Press.

Cavallero, E. 2006. 'An Immigration-Pressure Model of Global Distributive Justice', *Politics, Philosophy and Economics* 5(1): 97–127.

Cole, P. 2011. 'Open Borders: An Ethical Defence', in *Debating the Ethics of Immigration: Is There a Right to Exclude?* New York: Oxford University Press.

Docquier, F. 2007. 'Fuite des cerveaux et inégalités entre pays', *Revue d'économie du développement* 15(2): 49–88.

Docquier, F. and Marchiori, L. 2012. 'The Impact of MENA-to-EU Migration in the Context of Demographic Change', *Journal of Pension Economics and Finance* 11(02): 243–284.

Docquier, F. and Rapoport, H. 2012. 'Globalization, Brain Drain, and Development', *Journal of Economic Literature* 50(3): 681–730.

Espenshade, T. J., Guzman, J. C. and Westoff, C. F. 2003. 'The Surprising Global Variation in Replacement Fertility', *Population Research and Policy Review* 22(5–6): 575–583.

European Commission. 2007. *Europe's Demographic Future: Facts and Figures*. Green Paper. Brussels: European Commission.

European Commission. 2015. 'Communication on the European Agenda on Migration'. http://ec.europa.eu/dgs/home-affairs/what-we-do/policies/european-agenda-migration/background-information/docs/communication_on_the_european_agenda_on_migration_en.pdf.

Eurostat EC. 2015. *Population Structure and Ageing. Statistics Explained*. http://ec.europa.eu/eurostat/statistics-explained/index.php/Population_structure_and_ageing.

Gaspart, F. and Gosseries, A. 2007. 'Are Generational Savings Unjust?' *Politics, Philosophy & Economics* 6(2): 193–217.

Glotzbach, S. and Baumgärtner, S. 2012. 'The Relationship Between Intragenerational and Intergenerational Ecological Justice', *Environmental Values* 21(3): 331–355.

Goodin, R. 1992. 'If People Were Money', in B. Barry and R. Goodin, eds., *Free Movement: Ethical Issues in the Transnational Migration of People and of Money*, 6–22. Philadelphia: University of Pennsylvania Press.

Gosseries, A. 2004. 'Historical Emissions and Free-Riding', *Ethical Perspectives* 11(1): 36–60.

Gosseries, A. 2007. 'Should They Honor the Promises of Their Parents' Leaders?' *Ethics & International Affairs* 21: 99–125.

Gosseries, A. 2008. 'Theories of Intergenerational Justice: A Synopsis', *Surveys and Perspectives Integrating Environment and Society* 1: 39–49.

Gosseries, A. 2009. 'Three Models of Intergenerational Reciprocity', in A. Gosseries and L. H. Meyer, eds., *Intergenerational Justice*, 119–146. Oxford: Oxford University Press.

Gosseries, A. 2014a. 'Nations, Generations and Climate Justice', *Global Policy* 5(1): 96–102.

Gosseries, A. 2014b. 'What Makes Age Discrimination Special? A Philosophical Look at the ECJ Case Law', *Netherlands Journal of Legal Philosophy* 43(1): 59–80.

Gosseries, A. 2015. 'Les Générations, le fleuve et l'océan', *Philosophiques* 42(1): 153–176.

Kukathas, C. 2014. 'The Case for Open Immigration', in A. I. Cohen and C. H. Wellman, eds., *Contemporary Debates in Applied Ethics*, 2nd edn, 376–388. Maldon, MA: Blackwell.

Kymlicka, W. 1998. *Finding Our Way: Rethinking Ethnocultural Relations in Canada*. Toronto: Oxford University Press.

Lutz, W., Skirbekk, V. and Testa, M. R. 2006. 'The Low-Fertility Trap Hypothesis: Forces that May Lead to Further Postponement and Fewer Births in Europe', *Vienna Yearbook of Population Research* 4: 167–192.

Miller, D. 1995. *On Nationality*. Oxford: Clarendon Press.

Miller, D. 2004. 'Social Justice in Multicultural Societies', in P. Van Parijs, ed., *Cultural Diversity versus Economic Solidarity. Proceedings of the Seventh Francqui Colloquium*, 13–31. Brussels: De Boeck, pp.

Moellendorf, D. 2002. *Cosmopolitan Justice*. Boulder, CO: Westview Press.

Oberman, K. 2011. 'Immigration, Global Poverty and the Right to Stay', *Political Studies* 59(2): 253–268.

Oberman, K. 2016. 'Immigration as a Human Right', in S. Fine and L. Ypi, eds., *Migration in Political Theory: The Ethics of Movement and Membership*. Oxford: Oxford University Press.

Olsaretti, S. 2013. 'Children as Public Goods?' *Philosophy & Public Affairs* 41(3): 226–258.

Parfit, D. 1984. *Reasons and Persons*. Oxford: Clarendon Press.

Pevnick, R. 2009. 'Social Trust and the Ethics of Immigration Policy', *Journal of Political Philosophy* 17(2): 146–167.

Pogge, T. 2013. *World Poverty and Human Rights: Cosmopolitan Responsibilities and Reforms*. Cambridge: Polity.

Rawls, J. 1999. *A Theory of Justice*. Oxford: Oxford University Press.

Rawls, J. 2003. *The Law of Peoples; with 'The Idea of Public Reason Revisited'*. Cambridge, MA: Harvard University Press.

Seekings, J. 2004. 'Institutional Design, Cultural Diversity and Economic Solidarity: A Comparison of South Africa, Brazil and Nigeria', in P. Van Parijs, ed., *Cultural Diversity versus Economic Solidarity. Proceedings of the Seventh Francqui Colloquium*, 101–138. Brussels: De Boeck.

Sen, A. 2007. *Identity and Violence: The Illusion of Destiny*. Delhi: Penguin Books India.

Sen, A. 2014. 'Global Warming Is Just One of Many Environmental Threats That Demand Our Attention', *The New Republic*. http://www.newrepublic.com/article/118969/environmentalists-obsess-about-global-warming-ignore-poor-countries.

Soroka, S., Johnston, R. and Banting, K. 2004. 'Ethnicity, Trust and the Welfare State', in P. Van Parijs, ed., *Cultural Diversity versus Economic Solidarity. Proceedings of the Seventh Francqui Colloquium*, 33–57. Brussels: De Boeck.

Storesletten, K. 2000. 'Sustaining Fiscal Policy Through Immigration', *Journal of Political Economy* 108(2): 300–323.

Testa, M. R. 2012. *Family Sizes in Europe: Evidence from the 2011 Eurobarometer Survey*. European Demographic Research Papers, Wittgenstein Centre, Vienna Institute of Demography of the Austrian Academy of Sciences. http://www.oeaw.ac.at/vid/download/edrp_2_2012.pdf.

UNHCR (United Nations High Commissioner for Refugees). 2015. Statement by UNHCR António Guterres on refugee crisis in Europe. http://www.unhcr.org/55e9459f6.html.

UN (United Nations). 2001. Population Division. *Replacement Migration: Is It a Solution to Declining and Ageing Populations?* http://www.un.org/esa/population/publications/ReplMigED/Cover.pdf.

UN (United Nations). 2014. Population Division. *World Fertility Report 2013: Fertility at the Extremes.* http://www.un.org/en/development/desa/population/publications/pdf/fertility/worldFertilityReport2013.pdf.

Van Parijs, P. 2003. 'The Difference Principle', in S. Freeman, ed., *The Cambridge Companion to Rawls*, 200–240. Cambridge: Cambridge University Press.

Van Parijs, P., ed. 2004. *Cultural Diversity versus Economic Solidarity. Proceedings of the Seventh Francqui Colloquium*. Brussels: De Boeck.

Visser 't Hooft, H. P. 1999. *Justice to Future Generations and the Environment*. Berlin: Springer Science & Business Media.

WCED (UN World Commission on Environment and Development). 1987. *Our Common Future: The Brundtland Report*. Melbourne: World Commission on Environment and Development.

Ypi, L. 2008. 'Justice in Migration: A Closed Borders Utopia?' *Journal of Political Philosophy* 16(4): 391–418.

Notes

Chapter 1   The Point and Ground of Human Rights: A Kantian Constructivist View

1   A more positive variant of this is the idea that human rights are claims to resources required to realize fundamental forms of well-being; this is forcefully argued by Talbott, 2005, 2010.

2   I discuss the difference between my approach and that of Philip Pettit in Forst, 2013, 2015.

3   Even Allen Buchanan, who stresses the status egalitarian function of human rights, partakes in this, as he mainly refers to the quality of being protected by law in this regard, less so to the right to be a political authority; see his discussion of the 'status egalitarian function', where democratic rights are missing (2013: 28–30).

4   Beitz argues similarly with respect to rights of gender equality (2009: 195).

5   I think that Buchanan's constructive justificatory arguments for human rights are to be interpreted in that way; they aim to provide the best philosophical justification for a system of human rights at the centre of national and international legal practice, which is different from Beitz's approach.

6   In her book on global justice, Lea Ypi (2012) rightly stresses the importance of political agency in theorizing emancipatory forms of politics, yet leaves the criteria for such progress (as dialectical learning processes facilitated by avant-garde political agents) undetermined (though in the discussion of first-order normative principles, Kantian moral equality is usually the reference point – 2012: 54f., 60).

7   Thanks to Mahmoud Bassiouni for drawing my attention to this collection and for instructive conversations about it.

8   Permission to reproduce the picture was kindly granted by the photographer.

9   This aspect of Kant's approach is stressed by O'Neill (1989) and Habermas's discourse ethics in their respective interpretations.

10 For the opposite argument that a Kantian notion of dignity rests on metaphysical foundations comparable to a Catholic one, see Rosen, 2012. For a general discussion of the notion of dignity in the context of human rights, see McCrudden, 2013.

11 I cannot go into this here, but based on such statements it is often argued that for Kant only rationally autonomous beings have to be treated with dignity, and thus human beings who are not yet, or no longer, possessing their rational capacities have no such claim to respect. This is a mistake, however. First, this interpretation does not sufficiently distinguish between the dignity of rational agents as

acting subjects and the dignity of human beings as objects of actions; and, with regard to the latter, Kant always speaks of human beings as representatives of humanity without any further qualification. Second, and more importantly, this view reads an empirical capacity into a noumenal, non-empirical characteristic of persons, which is contrary to Kant's approach. He affirms that his notion of persons as autonomous ends in themselves is 'not borrowed from experience' (1997: 4:431), thus is a general moral ascription to human beings who do not have to take a rationality test to qualify as ends in themselves.

12 The notion of rank is stressed by Waldron, 2012; see also the discussion in Kateb, 2011.

13 Flikschuh (2015) rightly stresses the relational and strictly reciprocal character of any rights claims within Kant's scheme, but finds the innate right incompatible with the 'non-foundationalist' and constructivist character of Kant's general approach. That view, however, cannot explain the moral character of Kant's concept of right asking for strict justificatory reciprocity that Flikschuh discusses (2015: 662).

14 Andrea Sangiovanni argues that there cannot be a Kantian theory of human rights despite the innate right as an appropriate ground, because 'it is constitutive of a human right (in my sense) that its violation licenses unilateral action by third parties' which is 'straightforwardly denied by Kant's account of the moral obligation to exit the state of nature' (2015: 675). This argument is a good example of the hold of the internationalist-interventionist imagination over current human rights thinking. For having a justifiable claim to human rights is one thing, whereas the question of the legitimate institutions or agents to intervene in a state is another. And here a lot is to be said for Kant's scepticism about unilateral interference; yet that is a point that is irrelevant to the question of which rights persons have within a state.

15 This unites the very different approaches by Talbott, 2010; Griffin, 2008; Buchanan 2013.

16 In the case of persons who are not yet or no longer capable of exercising the full capacity of justification, justifications of representatives or by justified authorities in light of what could be justified to such persons are required.

17 The following overlaps with a section of my 'Human Rights in Context: A Comment on Sangiovanni' (Forst, forthcoming).

18 Pace Andrea Sangiovanni and also Seyla Benhabib, I do not see how we can move directly from the general concept to more particular political conceptions in either the interpretivist way Sangiovanni (forthcoming) thinks correct or the discourse-theoretical view that Benhabib proposes with her notion of 'democratic iterations' (2011: 126–31).

19 This is the worry of Buchanan (2013: 14–23).

20 Many thanks to Nate Adams and Tobias Albrecht for their help in preparing this text and to Pietro Maffettone, David Held and Sarah Dancy for important suggestions to improve it.

Chapter 3   Global Distributive Justice: The Cosmopolitan View

1 I'm grateful to Pietro Maffettone for many useful comments, which helped improve this chapter considerably.

Chapter 4   Global Political Justice

1   By 'power', I mean the capacity of an agent to bring about its goals. By 'political power', I mean power exercised within and through political institutions, which are sites for the organized contestation and collaborative pursuit of multiple agents' varied goals.
2   By 'domination', I mean arbitrary or institutionally uncontrolled power (see Pettit, 2012).
3   It is important to note, however, that the distinctions between these two types of global justice theories are far from clean, and that theoretical problems of these two kinds are deeply intertwined in some areas of debate – for instance in arguments about the character and normative significance of the 'global basic structure' (Ronzoni, 2009).
4   The justificatory structures for internationalist and cosmopolitan models of global democracy are thereby parallel, albeit with the input of different assumptions at endogenous and exogenous levels; for further discussion, see Macdonald, 2003.
5   Accounts of this kind depend in part on values exogenous to the democratic ideal, in order to specify *which interests* warrant special democratic empowerment within transnational political institutions.
6   It is important to note that the authors I cite here invoke varying conceptions of the 'political' and the nature of 'political' institutions, some of which differ from the conception I am invoking here (as described in note 1). As such, not all would use the label 'political', as I do, to describe the international institutions that are subjects of legitimacy assessments.

Chapter 5   The Legitimacy of International Law

1   This characterization of ruling or governing takes practical authority to be its essential feature. Some contend instead that coercion constitutes its essential feature, so that ruling or governing consists of enacting, applying and enforcing the law, but not necessarily commanding or ordering conduct; i.e., asserting that subjects have a duty to obey the law as such. I discuss the relation between legitimate authority and coercion later in this section. For an overview of different conceptions of political legitimacy, see Peter, 2014.
2   Three points warrant mention, lest the reader take the argument in the text to show the legitimacy or illegitimacy of international law to be practically irrelevant. First, to claim that on some occasions an agent ought to act as an illegitimate authority would have her act is not to say that she should always, or even often, do so. Second, it is quite common to appeal to legal obligation both in private deliberation and public justification or criticism. It is worth considering, therefore, when such arguments succeed and when they do not – i.e., when law is legitimate and when it is not – even if in some cases where such appeals carry no weight there are independent moral and/or prudential reasons to do that which the law would have one do. Finally, it may be that some of the moral value of conformity to law can be realized only if the law is legitimate; for instance, if obedience to legitimate law is not merely a means to treating others justly, but constitutes respect for others' equal claim to determine what justice requires. I

develop these last two points in slightly greater detail in the final section of this chapter.

3 These two categories correspond closely to the categories of output and input legitimacy employed by many international relations or IR-influenced scholars; see Bodansky, 2013: 330.

4 Note that the claim here concerns whose *judgment regarding what justice requires* ought to control. As I discuss below, an agent's consent to perform some act cannot render permissible what it would otherwise be unjust for him to do.

5 See also Pogge, 2002, for an argument that partiality is permissible only within the confines of impartial rules structuring interactions between states, not in the making of the rules that are to govern those interactions.

6 See Bodansky, 2013, for a brief overview of empirical studies regarding factors contributing to international law's *de facto* legitimacy.

7 This conclusion holds for Christiano as well.

Chapter 6   Legitimacy and Global Governance

1 We would like to thank Eva Maria Nag and David Lefkowitz for their extensive written comments on this chapter.

Chapter 7   Just War and Global Justice

1 In his piece, to which I am indebted and which has partly inspired my work on this subject, Nardin suggests that designing a general framework for thinking about just war and global justice is an important challenge for political theory, and hypothesizes (drawing on Kant) that focusing on the justifiability of coercion might help us address it. As a first step in building such a framework, Nardin then discusses the ethics of humanitarian intervention. This discussion, though, suggests that Nardin himself has not fully appreciated the implications of his original insight. He argues that humanitarian intervention is grounded in concerns of justice, rather than beneficence. From this, he extrapolates a general duty of justice to protect people from violence. But, he continues, 'if states have a duty to intervene when people are being massacred, they might also have a duty to act [coercively] when people are dying of starvation or disease' (2006: 464). Nardin then concludes that 'a coercive (tax-based) scheme of global poverty relief might be justified' (2006: 465). The problem with this argument is that it does not show any so-far unappreciated connection between global justice and just war theory. If one's preferred theory of justice says that the current global distribution of entitlements is unjust, then *it follows* that coercion may be rightfully employed to enforce the correct scheme. The idea that people might be taxed for the sake of justice is one most theorists of justice already accept. The more interesting point, which I try to develop in this chapter, is not that justice-based entitlements may be rightfully enforced, but that *war itself* (which involves not only the use of coercion, but of *lethal* coercion) can be seen as a species of enforcement of *entitlements*. This, in turn, opens up the possibility for mutual testing between theories of the just war (specifically *jus ad bellum*) and theories of global justice – a possibility Nardin himself does not consider.

2 On reflective equilibrium, see Rawls, 1999a: 18, 43–4.

3 For an overview of that tradition, see Orend, 2008; Lazar, 2013.

4 The extent to which principles of *jus post bellum* should contribute to the all-things-considered justification of a war (as opposed to the justification of what occurs after a war) is a matter of debate.

5 See Coates, 1997; Caney, 2005: ch. 6; Orend, 2008. What I have offered is only one prominent formulation of the further *ad bellum* conditions. Other formulations are also available in the literature.

6 As Seth Lazar has pointed out to me, the inclusion of humanitarian interventions under 'wars that respond to aggression' is unusual. I am aware of this, but I think considerations of parsimony – at least in the present context – justify the inclusion of humanitarian wars within this broader category.

7 Cf. Walzer's (1977: 58) treatment of what he calls 'the domestic analogy'. For a discussion and critique of the extent to which war can be seen as an act of collective self-defence analogous to individual self-defence, see Rodin, 2002.

8 Other cosmopolitan treatments of just war can be found in Caney, 2005; Moellendorf, 2002.

9 There may be circumstances in which certain in-principle enforceable entitlements are not 'effectively enforceable' due to the lack of well-functioning enforcement mechanisms. In such circumstances, the said entitlements would still count as rightfully enforceable, despite not being *de facto* enforceable.

10 Indeed, on Rawls's account, principles of justice place moral demands (duties) on states, or state-like institutions; what he calls the 'basic structure' of society.

11 One exception is Nagel (2005) – although the role that enforcement plays, in his view, is not entirely clear. That is, it is not clear whether Nagel thinks of enforcement as instrumental to justice, as a ground of justice or (as I suggest here) as something that can be rightfully done in relation to duties of justice.

12 This conclusion somewhat echoes a view set out by Rodin (2002: ch. 8), who first exposes the deficiencies of the 'domestic analogy' between war and individual self-defence, and then goes on to suggest that war is best understood as a form of punishment or law enforcement. For Rodin, though, war so conceived could only be legitimate in the presence of a global sovereign that has the right to lay down international law and enforce it. The view I am sketching here differs from Rodin's in two respects. First, I am establishing a connection between war and *justice* enforcement rather than war and *law* enforcement. Second, and relatedly, on the general schema I offer, the moral permissibility of war does not depend on the existence of a global state.

13 See also note 1 for further clarification of the relationship between this piece and Nardin's.

14 For this distinction see Sangiovanni, 2007: 5–6.

15 For a sustained critique of this approach, see Rodin, 2002; Luban, 1980.

16 In Nagel's (2005) case, unlike *arguably* in the case of Rawls (1999b), duties of assistance do not count as duties of justice but as duties of charity/humanity. Interpreters of Rawls disagree about whether his 'duty of assistance' is a duty of justice or one of charity. Pogge (2004), in particular, has suggested that it is best understood as a duty of charity, while advocates of Rawls have insisted that it should be considered a duty of justice. (For an overview, see Brock, 2009: ch. 2.) In *this* chapter, I assume the latter interpretation, which also seems to apply in the case of Blake

(2001). David Miller (2007: ch. 9) offers a qualified version of the duty of assistance, according to which a state in need is entitled to assistance, *so long as it is not responsible for its neediness*, and there are other states which could offer assistance at reasonable costs. (For a discussion of the demandingness of Rawls's duty of assistance, see Maffettone, 2013.)

17 Again, from this it does not follow that they would be all-things-considered justified in doing so; this conclusion could only hold if the other just war criteria were met in the case at hand – and they probably would not (consider, e.g., 'last resort' and 'likelihood of success').

18 Though, of course, I am not excluding that some might want to just bite the bullet, and radically expand our understanding of what counts as a just cause for war; or altogether reject the integrated approach sketched here.

19 In the case of relational cosmopolitans, the expression 'burdened' by unfavourable conditions can be given more or less expansive readings. On one reading, being burdened means being affected by absolute deprivation. On the other, being burdened means being comparatively disadvantaged, even when one is not deprived in absolute terms. While, for relational cosmopolitans, both types of 'burdened conditions' raise concerns of justice (provided the right social relations are in place), only the former, involving absolute deprivation preventing individuals from leading minimally decent lives, might rightfully invite war as a response.

20 The inspiration for this type of view can be most readily traced to Kant's (1999/1797) political writings. For contemporary versions of this view, see Christiano, 2008; Rawls, 1999b. It is a matter of controversy whether Rawls's preferred version of international public reason is genuinely liberal, insofar as it recognizes the legitimacy of hierarchically organized societies. For a critique of Rawls, see Tan, 1998.

21 Recall that I have explicitly focused on wars as international phenomena (while also acknowledging, of course, the existence of domestic wars, such as civil wars).

22 I am grateful to the participants at the CSSJ seminar (Oxford, May 2011), the workshop on Just War and Global Justice (IAS, Jerusalem, July 2011), the SCAS Fellows' Seminar (Uppsala, Sweden, October 2011), the Harvard University Political Theory Colloquium (March 2012), and the Political Philosophy Seminar Series, Pavia University (April 2012) for discussion. Special thanks go to James Brandt, Emanuela Ceva, Cécile Fabre, Benjamin Hertzberg, Seth Lazar (twice), Alex Leveringhaus, Christian List, Kasper Lippert-Rasmussen, Pietro Maffettone, Andrea Tivig and Lea Ypi for their written comments on an earlier version of this piece. Finally, I thank the editors of this volume for their comments, assistance and support.

Chapter 8 The Associativist Account of Killing in War

1 Suppose each of the five also has valuable relationships with their children, which will obviously be terminated when they die. Should A take these into account? I think not – the reasons relationships give are agent-relative, and can only be transferred to another when that other is both authorized by the relevant agent and accepts that authorization, as I discuss in the next section.

2 For an extensive discussion of the nature and grounds of the duties that arise between comrades-in-arms, see Lazar, 2013.

3 Thanks to David Rodin for suggesting this example.

4 This is a substantially revised version of a paper that appeared in the *Journal of Practical Ethics* 1(1): 3–48. Thanks to that journal for permission to use material from the earlier paper, and to Pietro Maffettone and Anne Gelling for their help with the revisions. My greatest debts are to Henry Shue, Jeff McMahan and David Rodin, as well as other colleagues in the Oxford war workshop: Cécile Fabre, Per Ilsaas, Zahler Bryan and Janina Dill. I presented versions of the chapter at Oxford's Uehiro Centre, its Centre for Ethics, Law and Armed Conflict, and the Nuffield political theory workshop, as well as to audiences in Dartmouth, Washington University St Louis, Chicago, Toronto, Stanford and Melbourne. Thanks to all those who participated in those events and to their organizers. Particular thanks to Michael Bratman, Kimberley Brownlee, Josh Cohen, Julia Driver, Tom Hurka, John Filling, David Miller, Julian Savulescu, Andrew Sepielli, Nic Southwood, Adam Swift, Laura Valentini, Juri Viehoff and Lea Ypi. And thanks to Lachlan Umbers for research assistance. Research on this project was supported by an Australian Research Council Discovery Early Career Researcher Award, DE130100811.

Chapter 9 Territorial Rights

1 Some authors label this power 'meta-jurisdiction' – see, e.g., Buchanan, 2003.

2 See, e.g., Kuper, 2004; Keane, 2003: esp. ch. 3. Thomas Pogge (2002a) has argued for dispersing sovereignty upwards and downwards in a multilayered political order, but since his proposals envisage the different units nesting inside one another, this is less of a radical departure from the principle of territorial authority.

3 The concept of an ethnogeography is developed in Kolers, 2009.

4 Simmons (2001: 309–11) argues that while act-utilitarian approaches to territory will lead to instability, as the relative efficiency with which different prospective rights-holders are able to use land shifts, rule-utilitarian approaches will be unjustifiably conservative.

5 The following discussion draws in part on Miller, 2011.

6 Kant referred to this as a *foedus pacificum* and made it clear that its primary purpose was to prevent states from settling their disputes by force (*foedus* is sometimes translated as 'federation', but given the connotations that this word has now acquired, we think 'league' – according to the *OED*, 'a military, political or commercial covenant or compact made between parties for their mutual protection and assistance against a common enemy' – better captures the spirit of Kant's proposal).

7 It may therefore be preferable to classify Stilz's theory as a hybrid between Kantianism and the self-determination approach that we discuss below.

8 In this section we are concerned with individualistic theories of territory inspired by Locke; that is, theories that build territorial rights on the foundation of individual property rights. There are also 'quasi-Lockean' theories that begin with the appropriation and improvement of land by groups or institutions: see, e.g., Nine, 2008; Meisels, 2009, ch. 7, which weaves a Lockean thread into a liberal nationalist theory of territory.

9 For an attempt to defend Locke on this point, see Simmons, 2001: 314–15.

10 This issue needs much fuller discussion than we are able to give it here: see further Miller, 2016.

Chapter 10   Natural Resources

1   This chapter will attempt to isolate the debate over resource rights from the larger debate over rights over territory. For a more careful distinction of these two, see Nine, 2013. For a survey of the larger debate, see Simmons, working paper.

2   Ross's definition of an oil state is in terms of its oil production per capita.

3   *Declaration of Independence*, 1776, paragraph 2.

4   Risse also deploys the common ownership premise within arguments relating to immigration, future generations and climate change.

5   Although Pogge offers his proposal for a Global Resource Dividend as fulfilling a modern Lockean proviso, it is not clear that he endorses the Lockean approach, all things considered.

6   *United Nations Convention on the Law of the Sea* 1982, Article 136; *Outer Space Treaty* 1967, Article 1.

7   See www.skyshares.org.

8   The noble exceptions include Peter Singer, Michael Walzer, Charles Beitz, Henry Shue, Onora O'Neill, James Nickel and Thomas Pogge.

9   *Constitution of the Republic of Namibia* 1990, Preamble.

10 *Constitution of the Republic of South Africa* 1996, Preamble.

11 *Constitution of the Republic of Iraq* 2005, Preamble.

12 Third World countries were the prime movers in getting Article 1(2) into the human rights covenants as well as in pushing other declarations of permanent sovereignty over natural resources. See Schrijver, 2008: Part I.

13 'Nations (or persons) may appropriate or use resources, but humankind at large still retains a kind of minority stake which … confers no control but a share of the material benefits' (Pogge, 1994: 200).

14 Paraguay currently produces a little iron and not much else. As in many poor countries, however, natural riches may yet be discovered. As noted in the discussion of Miller on Steiner, a country's resource revenues are a function not only of natural endowment but also of the investment put into exploration and extraction.

15 Guizot's centralizing force was the nation-state, which became progressively more powerful over the succeeding centuries.

16 Here, extending Larry Diamond's series to 2014, see Diamond, 2008: 372. According to *The Economist Democracy Index* (2014) almost half of countries are democracies.

17 As Ross notes, some countries like Indonesia and Ecuador have transitioned to democracy as their oil rents per capita have declined (2012: 74–5, 238). And, for example, Nigeria has transitioned to democracy while its government is still highly dependent on oil.

18 For more detail on popular resource sovereignty and policies aimed at promoting it, see Wenar, 2016. Some material in this chapter is adapted from that book.

19 For a rich account of popular sovereignty in the creation of cosmopolitan agency, see Ypi, 2011: ch. 6.

Chapter 11   Fairness in Trade

1   For discussion of several such transactional objections, along with more institutional forms of unfairness, see Miller, 2010.

2 This is an opposed, but not logically contrary, position. An institutional view needn't be 'world-historical'. I say why it should be below. The position is 'historical', or sensitive to what has come before. Because most countries of the world participate in the trading system, the view is 'world-historical'.

3 As the question is often posed: is justice the first virtue of social institutions, with principles for institutions different in kind from, and perhaps prior to, principles for personal action, as for John Rawls (1971)? Or are any such principles fundamentally one and the same, as for G. A. Cohen (2008)?

4 For relevant arguments that we lack obligations to unilaterally reduce our emissions, while being required to take political action, see Johnson, 2003; Sinnott-Armstrong, 2010.

5 T. M. Scanlon (2010) makes this point in reply to Robert Nozick's famous objections to the Hart/Rawls principle of 'fair play'.

6 In domestic society, the analogous actions may include unconventional civil disobedience, perhaps including forgoing work or 'necessary' crime, as defended by Shelby, 2007.

7 Rawls for the duty itself, and James on its potential practice-sensitivity.

8 I discuss this further, in responding to G. A. Cohen's critique of Rawls, in James, 2005c.

9 This historical orientation is suggested (for socioeconomic justice) by Nagel, and (for human rights) by Beitz.

10 Note that a 'credible' possible future needn't be *likely* to come about. It can thus be 'aspirational' or even 'utopian' in the sense that Estlund (2014) defends as a proper subject of inquiry. I return to the question of what considerations might shape an appropriate evidentiary threshold. On feasibility and related debates about 'ideal theory', see also Räikkä, 1998; Gilabert and Lawford-Smith, 2012, and the references cited therein.

11 Because the common appeal to 'promoting' a value often brackets the relative force of different competing values, I regard it as a fudge, or at best a placeholder for further views of the kind I am considering.

12 I take this to be a – and perhaps *the* – central ambition of Rawls's theory of justice, especially in his *A Theory of Justice*. The point of the original position is to make evident the demands of justice to those who otherwise do not appreciate them, and so fashion a publicly recognized basis for mutual justification from what people share in common. For a development of this aspiration to 'moral geometry', seen as akin to mathematical demonstration, see James, 2013a.

13 This can be true quite aside form the individual agent's particular aims or loyalties. Korsgaard (1996) reads Kant as developing a similar but more general argument for 'categorical' demands as against the moral sceptic, on the basis of a person's own rational self-understanding. One might add that people in a social practice are appropriately subject to criticism and held accountable to a degree they might not be for principles that are not normative for them in some such strong sense. For further discussion of Rawls's appeal to the Kantian idea of 'autonomy', see James, 2013a, forthcoming.

14 Here the suggested argument is that (i) practice-based justification suffices to meet certain theoretical desiderata, which themselves limit appraisal to existing practices, and (ii) other forms of justification don't meet these requirements. For all that says, genuine principles could still be justified with different theoretical

objectives, which require less or nothing by way of 'credible address'. A practice theorist can simply grant such principles, or accept them and argue that they are of peripheral rather than central importance for political philosophy (given some appropriate characterization of 'centrality', which practice-sensitive principles satisfy).

15 And note that it won't do to argue that any practice-sensitive argument must depend on or be derived from principles less sensitive to practice – or at least not within certain larger, context-sensitive moral theories (e.g., contractualism or intuitionism). The case for such a dependency relation or derivation would have to be made for the context at issue. Even when it can be made, this may only show that certain principles are *over-determined* by both practice-sensitive and relatively practice-insensitive arguments (see James, 2013b, 2014b).

16 In 'ideal theory', what and how much we idealize, by abstracting away from untoward or irrelevant realities, are in part dictated by the demands of credible address. This may mean leaving much of social life in place, even beyond the general and fixed realities of human nature and society. That does imply an inevitable compromise to critical depth. In trade practice, principles less sensitive to the economist's understanding of its point, justified in relatively abstract terms, may well have deeper critical purchase, affording a platform for a more fundamental challenge to the global economy's very basic forms or bare existence. But the trade-off needn't be unacceptable. Plenty of room may be left for deep critique, by rejecting its basic aims as illegitimate, or by abstracting from a practice's actual institutional realization. In short, if there are two key theoretical desiderata, credibility of address *and* critical depth, ideal theory argument can to some degree compromise each in order to optimize for both.

17 To be sure, once having chosen integration, they cannot readily turn back. Yet, because they have chosen the practice, they at least cannot claim to have been denied an adequate opportunity to avoid any obligations to comply with its terms in good faith and work towards making the practice fairer. And to the extent that they are afforded great discretion in how they interpret market reliance expectations, in a way that recognizes their own fairness concerns, they can't reasonably say they lack an adequate opportunity to avoid unwanted burdens. It is fair for them to be asked to do the work of making trade practice fairer.

18 In Hobbes's version of the point, the sovereign upholds the industry of its subjects, which would not emerge in a state of nature, for lack of stable property and security assurances. For a more recent illustration, from the international scene, consider the interwar years, in which lack of assurances against 'beggar-my-neighbour' policies brought what was a flourishing global economy more or less to a halt.

Chapter 12   The Ethical Aspects of International Financial Integration

1 See the chapter by Aaron James in this volume for a discussion of the ethical aspects of trade.

2 The countries they analyse are the United States, the United Kingdom, Austria, Belgium, Germany, Italy, the Netherlands, Norway, Sweden, Switzerland, Canada, Japan, Finland and Spain.

3 Perhaps surprisingly, the use of such counterfactuals is popular not only among political philosophers, but also among economists. Both Lane and Milesi-Ferretti (2003: 92) and Rodrik (2011: 370–71) reflect on the implications of a fully globalized world economy with no cross-border transaction costs.

4 On the desirability of political self-determination from a global justice perspective, see Caney, 2006.

5 I thank François Claveau for helping me to sharpen my argument on these two points.

6 For a detailed account of tax evasion and tax avoidance as free-riding, see Dietsch and Rixen, 2014: sec. II.A. For a comprehensive normative evaluation of the tax competition between states that makes tax evasion and avoidance possible, see Dietsch, 2015. Among other things, chapter 3 of the latter addresses the misguided claim that tax competition is good for growth.

7 The IMF document does not specify the units, because their purpose is mainly to show interrelationships between items, but suppose they represent millions of dollars.

8 Section 4 will also comment on the role of reserve assets.

9 Cf. the theoretical argument for IFI in the previous section.

10 In one of the latest episodes of this type, the fact that the Federal Reserve started *talking* about an end to its quantitative easing programme in mid-2013 was sufficient to trigger substantial capital outflows from emerging markets.

11 For a good overview of the dynamics of emerging market crises, see Dornbusch, 2001.

12 For a study analysing the risks of contagion posed by the market for credit default swaps, see Kalbaska and Gatkowski, 2012.

13 Statistics are available from the Joint External Debt Hub (www.jedh.org) compiled by the Bank for International Settlements, the International Monetary Fund, the Organization for Economic Cooperation and Development and the World Bank.

14 For insightful contributions to the literature of states versus markets, see Strange, 1994; Streeck, 2014.

15 I deliberately do not enter into a detailed discussion of the Eurozone in this chapter, because the fact that Eurozone countries no longer have an independent monetary policy makes them a special case. Consider the fact that Spain had a lower public debt to GDP ratio than the UK at the onset of the financial crises, but the UK never got sucked into the sovereign debt crisis to the same extent.

16 Przeworski and Wallerstein's classic article provides an excellent summary of the structural dependence of the state on capital hypothesis in the domestic context, which they end up rejecting.

17 Ronzoni (2009) and Dietsch (2011) also advocate a strengthening of national sovereignty as a response to economic globalization. For an example of how such a policy could be implemented in the fiscal context, see Dietsch and Rixen, 2014.

18 Nothing I have said here precludes the possibility that governments sometimes strategically drive up public debt in order to get re-elected.

19 Note that the rationale for today's sizeable risk management industry would be seriously undermined if there were no real risk of default.

20 The programmes of quantitative easing pursued by central banks in particular have contributed to this trend. The European Central Bank was the last to engage in such a programme in January 2015, while the Bank of Japan already had comparable programmes well before the crisis of 2008.

21 I thank Clément Fontan for drawing my attention to this point. One prominent example is the ECB's – or, ultimately, Eurozone governments' collective – holdings of debt from crisis-hit countries of the Eurozone such as Greece. See Fontan, 2013.

22 The fact that only a small portion – probably less than 25 per cent – of Greek debt is negotiable, that is, traded on financial markets, is one of the neglected aspects of the Greek situation. See, for instance, Durden, 2015.

23 Stiglitz points out that '[i]f the interest rate America has to pay is just one percentage point lower than it would otherwise be on these $3 trillion of loans from poor countries, what America receives from the developing countries via the global reserve system is more than it gives to the developing countries in aid' (2006: 250).

24 In an unpublished paper, Aaron James presents a normative case for such expansion and reform.

25 A previous version of this paper was presented at the conference *The Ethics of Economic Institutions* at Utrecht Universiteit in January 2015. Thank you to participants there, as well as to Vincent Arel-Bundock, François Claveau, Clément Fontan, and to the two editors of this volume, David Held and Pietro Maffettone, for their comments. I also thank François Papale and Thibault Calmus for their research assistance.

Chapter 13   Political Theory for the Anthropocene

1 See relevant excerpts at http://www.geologicnow.com/2_Turpin+Federighi.php. A full text of Stoppani's 1873 *Corso di geologia* is available at http://catalog .hathitrust.org/Record/001518767.

2 See http://www.worldbank.org/en/topic/poverty/overview.

3 US President Barack Obama underscored the urgent and close-to-home nature of climate-related risks in his speech at the GLACIER conference in Alaska on 31 August 2015. https://www.youtube.com/watch?v=jjcAZNRfm1g.

4 Justice and rights are other important domains of interest for liberal democratic political theory. We shall largely ignore these here, but see Jamieson and Di Paola, 2014.

5 Another source of this sense of loss of agency is the growing feeling that science (especially neuroscience) is providing explanations of human behaviour and decision-making that exclude traditional notions of agency and autonomy. See, e.g., Sternberg, 2010.

6 For a defence of this claim and discussion of some difficult cases, see Driver, 2007.

7 The canonical statement of the Harm Principle is the following: 'The only purpose for which power can be rightfully exercised over any member of a civilized community, against his will, is to prevent harm to others' (J. S. Mill, *On Liberty*, ch. 1, sec. 9; available in many editions including at http://www.econlib.org/library/Mill/ mlLbty1.html).

8 Of course, we sometimes hold agents morally and legally responsible for the good things they bring about as well. Here, we are only concerned with the dark side.

9 Walter Sinnott-Armstrong makes this point in an online dialogue with Avram Hiller. http://www.philostv.com/avram-hiller-and-walter-sinnott-armstrong/.

10 http://articles.latimes.com/2006/jul/02/opinion/op-gilbert2.

11 Others (feminist and communitarian thinkers in particular) have criticized the sharp liberal distinction between the private and the public on normative grounds. Our point, however, is that a conceptual blurring of the distinction is intrinsic to the Anthropocene.

12 For an investigation of the behaviour of one powerful firm, see http://insideclimatenews.org/news/15092015/Exxons-own-research-confirmed-fossil-fuels-role-in-global-warming.

13 See http://www.acmuller.net/con-dao/greatlearning.html.

14 See http://www.bloomberg.com/politics/articles/2015-08-29/ben-carson-edging-close-to-front-runner-trump-in-latest-iowa-poll.

15 See http://www.euractiv.com/sections/eu-elections-2014/its-official-last-eu-election-had-lowest-ever-turnout-307773.

16 The case of Italy, which since 2011 has been run by non-elected governments congenial to the EU and other global agents, and which has nonetheless been engaged in significant constitutional reforms, is most emblematic of this fracture between democratic consent and domestic policy-making.

17 For discussions, see Gosseries, 2001, 2014; and essays in Gosseries and Meyer, 2009. See also Gardiner, 2011.

Chapter 14   Generations and Global Justice

1 On whether there should be a right to international freedom of movement, see Carens, 1987; Rawls, 2003: 9; Ypi, 2008. On access to wealthy territories as a substitute for redistributive cash transfers by wealthy countries, see Goodin, 1992; Oberman, 2011: 256–7. On migrations as an indicator of global inequalities, see Cavallero, 2006.

2 On reciprocity, including on the distinction between open and closed contexts, see Gosseries, 2009.

3 Given this chapter's focus, we use 'intragenerational' and 'global' interchangeably.

4 Could an extension of resources not be achieved at *no cost* to the present generation, through technological improvements and increases in human capital? Such increases involve opportunity costs for the present generation. Technology progress requires investments. Increasing access to education means less resource left for other demands of distributive justice, such as elderly care.

5 By 'chronopolitan', we mean the temporal equivalent of cosmopolitan, under its various meanings. For present purposes, it claims that demands of justice hold towards all, whatever one's period of existence.

6 We could refer to this broad sense as 'transgenerational' or 'cross-generational' justice, in a way that differs from the one used elsewhere for historical injustice issues; see Gosseries, 2004: 46.

7 This should also help us understanding why social science studies on 'intergenerational mobility', while being, strictly speaking, studies on 'cross-generational mobility', are relevant to those concerned about intergenerational justice.

8 On the third world debt cancellation debate from a cross-generational perspective, see Gosseries, 2007.

9 On separateness of persons, see Parfit, 1984: 329–41, esp. 337–8.

10 See Pogge, 2013: 10–12, 40–4. Our views open two lines of criticism against Pogge's negative duties account of global justice. One against the implicit view that global rectificatory claims are less controversial than global distributive ones. The other against the use of the rectificatory approach in cross-generational contexts.

11 On 'beneficiary-pays' in cross-generational contexts, see Gosseries, 2004; Caney, 2006: 471–4.

12 It has also been argued that in an overlapping generation case, in which the generation of wrongdoers is still present and in which its descendants already derived benefits from such past wrongs, it is likely that one would turn to the wrongdoing generation alone, which suggests that the obligations are driven by the wrong rather than by the benefits (Caney, 2006: 472–3).

13 European parents do not have as many children as they would like, the difference between the mean ideal family size and the mean actual family size being 0.3 children (Testa, 2012). Even if fertility reached its highest plausible point (e.g., 2.36 children per woman in France in 2040–50), the potential support ratio (see below) would still almost be halved in comparison with 1995 rates. In France, it would evolve from 4.36 in 1995 to 2.52 in 2050, and even to 1.95 in the low-fertility hypothesis (UN, 2001: 9).

14 Equivalence in value should be assessed through the currency of our theory of justice (e.g., resources, capabilities, etc.) as opposed to mere market value.

15 On the use of the age criterion in the immigration context, see Carens, 2013: 135–8; 183–5; ECJ cases *Parliament v. Council*, 27 June 2006, C-540/03, and *Noorzia*, 17 July 2014, C-388/13.

16 For further developments, see Gosseries, 2014b.

17 Brain drain would not only decrease the proportion of educated people; it can also increase the technological gap between sending and host societies, increase unemployment and generate occupational shortages in the sending society (Docquier and Rapoport, 2012: 698).

18 On whether educated people remit more, the evidence is mixed (Docquier and Rapoport, 2012: 701–3).

19 Note that Rawls only applies this principle to relationships between individuals within a state.

20 On weak vs. strong voluntariness, see Olsaretti, 2013: esp. 247.

21 'Everyone has the right to leave any country, including his own' (International Declaration of Human Rights, article 13.2).

22 On the calculation of fair compensations, see Gosseries, 2004.

23 For invaluable discussions, references and comments on earlier drafts, we are very grateful to Arshak Balayan, Frédéric Docquier, Bruno Schoumaker and to the two editors of this volume. Any remaining errors are our own.

Index

Abizadeh, A. 41
accountability 6, 106
  agency and 261–2
  broad 133
  global governance and 89, 106
  horizontal 89
  institutionalized relationship 89–90
  legitimacy and 139
  normative ideal of 89
  piecemeal 90
  reciprocal 261–2
'action at a distance' 2, 257–8
affected interests principle 113
agency
  agency presupposition 259–60, 275
  in the Anthropocene 259–63, 267–9, 270
  and consent 107–8
  digital agents 262
  interactions between agents 113, 115
  international 46–7, 48
  loss of 263, 315
  moral duties of agents 110, 113
  new forms of 261–2
  non-agents, discounting of 261, 276
  nonstate institutions 48
  reciprocal accountability 261–2
  and responsibility 264, 267–9
  in the transnational world 46
Allied occupation of Germany 189
animals, citizenship and 259, 260
Anthropocene epoch 254–78
  agency and 259–63
  challenges to liberal political theory 262, 264, 266–7, 269, 274–5, 277
  collective action problems 262–3
  concept and features of 255–8
  crisis of legitimacy 274–6
  demarcation 256, 258

  experimentation 278
  governance and 270–3
  responsibility and 264–9
  social geology of 278
Arab Spring 25–6
Archibugi, D. 79, 84
Armenian genocide 286, 290
Armstrong, C. 184, 203
Arrow, K. J. 244
assistance, duties of 150–1, 152
associational justice 60–1, 62, 63, 64, 66
  non-voluntariness condition 63–4
  social justice duties 60–1
associations
  association-specific positions, powers and goods 67
  collective control by members 60, 65, 66
  common good association 62, 63
  and duties of justice 59–60, 65
  non-voluntary 61, 65
  protective 183
  strength of 60, 65
  voluntary 60, 113
associative duties 14, 60, 61, 62, 160–77
  civilians 171
  evil relationships and 175–6
  gravity 162, 163–70, 174
  grounding 161–3, 174
  institutionalist argument 171–2
  and killing in war 160–77
  non-voluntary 61
  operationalizing 170–4
  to protect 161–2, 164, 166–7, 170, 171, 172, 173, 174–7
  restriction of 174–7
  special relationships and 160, 161–2, 172, 174, 175–6
  stringency 162, 167–8

319